Hellenic Studies 13

# THE *LIFE AND MIRACLES OF THEKLA*

# A LITERARY STUDY

# THE *LIFE AND MIRACLES OF THEKLA*

## A LITERARY STUDY

## Scott Fitzgerald Johnson

CENTER FOR HELLENIC STUDIES
Trustees for Harvard University
Washington, DC
Distributed by Harvard University Press
Cambridge, Massachusetts, and London, England
2006

The *Life and Miracles of Thekla*: a literary study
   by Scott Fitzgerald Johnson
Copyright © 2006 Center for Hellenic Studies, Trustees for Harvard University
All Rights Reserved.
Published by Center for Hellenic Studies, Trustees for Harvard University,
   Washington, DC
Distributed by Harvard University Press, Cambridge, Massachusetts, and
   London, England
Volume Editor: Jennifer Reilly
Production Editor: Ivy Livingston
Cover Design and Illustration: Joni Godlove

LIBRARY OF CONGRESS CATALOGING-IN-PUBLICATION DATA

Johnson, Scott Fitzgerald.
The *Life and Miracles of Thekla* : a literary study / by Scott Fitzgerald Johnson.
      p. cm. — (Hellenic studies series ; v. 13)
   Includes bibliographical references and index.
   ISBN 0-674-01961-X
1. Praxeis tes Hagias Apostolou kai Martyros tou Christou Theklas, kai
   thaumata. 2. Thecla, Saint—Legends—History and criticism. 3 Christian
   women saints—Legends—History and criticism. 4. Miracles—History
   of doctrines. 5. Christian hagiography. I. Center for Hellenic Studies
   (Washington, D.C.) II. Title. III. Series: Hellenic studies ; 13.
   BR1720.T33J64 2005
   270.1′092—dc22
                                                2005020626

*To my parents and grandparents*

# Contents

# Preface

THE APPEARANCE OF SCOTT JOHNSON'S *THE LIFE AND MIRACLES OF THEKLA, A LITERARY STUDY* in the series "Hellenic Studies" marks an important new direction for the publications program of the Center for Hellenic Studies. The field of study represented by this book is Late Antiquity, a vital era of transition from the Classical to the Byzantine and the Modern Greek eras. The world of Late Antiquity, with its vibrant mix of Christian and Classical traditions, shines forth in these pages as a highly experimental and creative phase of Greek civilization writ large. Withstanding the negative prejudices of earlier generations of Classicists, the study of Late Antiquity has by now become one of the most dynamic areas of research and teaching in the field of Classics and in other fields that transcend the ancient world. A case in point is the present book, a literary and historical gold mine that exemplifies the precious contributions of Late Antique studies to Hellenic Studies in general.

Gregory Nagy
Washington, DC
August 2005

# Acknowledgments

W HILE A NUMBER OF SCHOLARS have had a defining role in this book coming to fruition, certainly the most influential of all is my Oxford supervisor, Professor Averil Cameron. Her gentle yet directed guidance has been invaluable to me along the road of learning how to do scholarship. Although it goes without saying that any errors of fact or interpretation in this book are my own, I have relied heavily on her knowledge, advice, and support. I will always be grateful for the kindness she has shown me.

Also notable among my scholarly benefactors are the following individuals: Dr. Sebastian Brock, who shared with me his love for Syriac; Professor Peter Brown, who graciously invited me to Princeton for a crucial sojourn in 2002; Professor Elizabeth Jeffreys, who deftly guided me through the intricacies of Byzantine literature; Professor Fergus Millar, who first encouraged me to come to Oxford; and Dr. Charles Weiss, who has played alternately the indispensable roles of sounding-board and confidant for several years now.

Special thanks are due to my two D.Phil. examiners, Dr. Jaś Elsner and Professor Charlotte Roueché. I am exceedingly grateful for the close attention that they paid to my work and for the wise counsel they gave me in moving towards publication. This study is much improved because of their input. I feel privileged to have had such accomplished and genial scholars examining my thesis.

The Harvard Society of Fellows has provided a supremely tranquil environment in which to turn my Oxford thesis into a publishable study. I am chiefly grateful to Professor Gregory Nagy, Professor Walter Gilbert, and Ms. Diana Morse for their warm welcome to Cambridge. My colleagues in the Society have played a special role in crystallizing ideas that found their way into this book. I would like to thank especially Avner Ben-Zaken, Elisabeth Camp, Michael Gordin, Eric Nelson, and Bence Ölveczky for taking the time to discuss these ideas at length.

I would also like to thank the publications team at the Center for Hellenic Studies: Joni Godlove, Zoie Lafis, Ivy Livingston, Leonard Muellner, Jennifer Reilly, and Jill Robbins have been patient, warm, and professional throughout the entire pre-publication process. I am grateful to them and to the editors of the Hellenic Studies Series for welcoming me into their fold.

Many more colleagues and friends at Oxford, Harvard, and elsewhere, assisted or encouraged the progress of this book. I would like to render my thanks to the following people: Jonathan Barnes, Hilary and Jeff Becker, Ann Blair, François Bovon, Ewen Bowie, Catherine Burris, William Childs, Chip and Sarah Coakley, Tom Curtis, Stephen Davis, Alan Dearn, Bruce Denson, Robert Drews, Mark Edwards, Laurence Emmett, Bill and Susan Frazee, Robert and Courtney Frazee, William and Priscilla Frazee, Kathy Gaca, John Gager, Martin Gamache, James George, David Gwynn, Jim Hankins, Michael Jeffreys, Christopher Jones, Jeremy Kath, Jonathan Kirkpatrick, Derek Krueger, Michael Maas, Marlia Mango, Matthew McClellan, Tom McGinn, David Michelson, Teresa Morgan, Ryan Olson, J. T. Paasch, Yannis Papadoyannakis, Matthew Polk, Simon Price, Claudia Rapp, Dan Schwartz, Ben Scott, Christos Simelidis, Greg Smith, John Stroup, Alice-Mary Talbot, Jack Tannous, David Taylor, Iain Taylor, Günder Varinlioglu, William Weaver, Mary Whitby, and Susan Ford Wiltshire.

Essential to the completion of this long project has been the steady support of my family. In particular, I cannot even begin to repay with thanks the enormous debt that I owe to my parents and grandparents. They encouraged my studies from the very beginning, and, in response to their love and their unwavering commitment, I dedicate this book to them.

Finally, my wife Carol has been an inspiration to me ever since we first met. Her open zeal for life, language, and people daily provides the context in which my work can become meaningful. Above all things in this world the bond that we share is to me the most solid—this book simply would not have been possible without her.

Scott Johnson
Cambridge, Massachusetts
June 2005

# Abbreviations

| | |
|---|---|
| *ABD* | *Anchor Bible Dictionary*, 6 vols. (New York, 1992) |
| *ABzF* | *Acta Byzantina Fennica* |
| ACW | Ancient Christian Writers: The Works of the Fathers in Translation (New York) |
| *AJP* | *American Journal of Philology* |
| *AnBoll* | *Analecta Bollandiana* |
| ANRW | J. Vogt et al., eds. *Aufstieg und Niedergang der römischen Welt* (Berlin and New York, 1972–) |
| *ATh* | *Acts of Paul and Thekla* (for critical text, see LB below) |
| BDAG | W. Bauer, F. W. Danker, W. F. Arndt, F. W. Gingrich, eds. *A Greek-English Lexicon of the New Testament and Other Early Christian Literature*, 3rd ed. (Chicago, 2000) |
| *BHG* | F. Halkin, *Bibliotheca Hagiographica Graeca*, 3rd ed. (Brussels, 1969) |
| *CAG* | M. Berthelot and C. E. Ruelle, eds., *Collection des anciens alchemistes grecs*, 3 vols. (Paris, 1888; reprinted, Osnabrück, 1967) |
| CCSA | Corpus Christianorum Series Apocryphorum (Turnhout) |
| CCSL | Corpus Christianorum Series Latina (Turnhout) |
| CFHB | Corpus Fontium Historiae Byzantinae (Berlin, Paris, Vienna, Washington, DC) |
| *CPG* | M. Geerard et al., eds. *Clavis Patrum Graecorum*, 5 vols. (Turnhout, 1974–2003) |
| *CR* | *Classical Review* |
| *DOP* | *Dumbarton Oaks Papers* |
| *FGrHist* | F. Jacoby et al., eds. *Fragmente der griechischen Historiker* (Leiden, 1954–) |

| | |
|---|---|
| GCS | Die griechischen christlichen Schriftsteller der ersten Jahrhunderte, neue Folge (Leipzig and Berlin) |
| *GRBS* | *Greek, Roman, and Byzantine Studies* |
| *HTR* | *Harvard Theological Review* |
| *IG* | *Inscriptiones Graecae* (Berlin, 1897–) |
| *JBL* | *Journal of Biblical Literature* |
| *JECS* | *Journal of Early Christian Studies* |
| *JESHO* | *Journal of the Economic and Social History of the Orient* |
| *JJS* | *Journal of Jewish Studies* |
| *JRS* | *Journal of Roman Studies* |
| Lampe | G. W. H. Lampe, ed. *A Patristic Greek Lexicon* (Oxford, 1961) |
| LB | Lipsius and Bonnet 1891, esp. vol. 1, pp. 235–272 |
| LCL | Loeb Classical Library (London and Cambridge, MA) |
| *LM* | *Life and Miracles of Saint Thekla* (for critical text, see Dagron 1978 in References) |
| LSJ | H. G. Liddell, R. Scott, and H. S. Jones, eds. *A Greek-English Lexicon*, 9th ed. with supplement (Oxford, 1968) |
| NPNF | Nicene and Post-Nicene Fathers (Edinburgh) |
| *NTS* | *New Testament Studies* |
| *OCD* | *Oxford Classical Dictionary*, 3rd ed. (Oxford, 1996) |

| | |
|---|---|
| OCT | Oxford Classical Texts (Oxford) |
| ODB | A. Kazhdan et al., eds. *Oxford Dictionary of Byzantium*, 3 vols. (Oxford, 1991) |
| ODCC | *Oxford Dictionary of the Christian Church*, 3rd ed. (Oxford, 1997) |
| OLD | *Oxford Latin Dictionary* (Oxford, reprint 1997) |
| PG | J. P. Migne, ed. Patrologiae cursus completus: Series Graeca (Paris) |
| PLRE | A. H. M. Jones et al., eds. *Prosopography of the Later Roman Empire*, 3 vols. (Cambridge, 1971–1992) |
| PO | *Patrologia Orientalis* |
| RE | A. F. von Pauly et al., eds. *Paulys Real-Encyclopädie der klassischen Altertumswissenschaft*, 49 vols. (Stuttgart, 1894–1980) |
| RIL | *Rendiconti dell' Instituto Lombardo, Classe di Lettere, Scienze morali e storiche* |
| SC | Sources Chrétiennes (Paris) |
| Suda | Adler, A., ed. *Suidae Lexicon*, 5 vols. (Leipzig, 1935) |
| TAPA | *Transactions of the American Philological Association* |
| TU | Texte und Untersuchungen zur Geschichte der altchristlichen Literatur (Leipzig) |
| YClS | *Yale Classical Studies* |

# A Note on Terminology and Transliteration

B Y WAY OF EXPLANATION rather than apology, I should clarify what I mean by the term "literary" in the title of this book. I do not mean to claim that the *Life and Miracles* is high literature on the level of Homer, the tragedians, or the ideal Greek Romances. However, I would suggest that the difference between the *Life and Miracles* and the canon of classical literature is one of degree rather than kind. In other words, from a literary critic's point of view the same tools of close analysis commonly employed to interpret high Greek literature should also be applied to the *Life and Miracles*. In addition, I think it a reasonable claim that Late Antiquity has not yet seen very much of this type of scholarship—no doubt due to the period's relative youth as a field of study in its own right. On this basis I am prepared to admit that this study is, like the *Life and Miracles* itself, something of an experiment. If this book can therefore stimulate more interest in late antique texts as worthy of close analysis and contextualization, then it has achieved its primary goal.

It will be immediately clear from the Table of Contents that this study is something of a double-headed Byzantine eagle. I attempt in it to do both literary analysis and literary history, two scholarly practices that do not normally appear side by side. Yet, if the literary analysis in this book has anything important to contribute, that contribution directly concerns the reception of literary form in late antiquity, that is, a literary historical question which has been unduly neglected by classicists. The continuity of classical forms of literature—in this case marginal forms—and their adoption by Jewish and Christian writers of the Roman and post-classical periods is, I contend, one of the most important interpretive clues to the fascinating hinge period that we now reverentially call Late Antiquity. Literary theorists have made it abundantly clear that content and form belong together, so I have tried in this study to highlight the diachronic resonance of paraphrase (μετάφρασις) and collection (συλλογή) while at the same time being more or less New Critical in my treatment of the *Life and Miracles* on its own terms.

In transliterating ancient names from Greek I have generally tried to adhere to the spelling that I consider to be the most widely used: thus Severus of Antioch and not Severos or Sebêros. However, in transliterating names from the *Life and Miracles of Thekla*, I have strayed from this practice and sought to adhere more closely to the literal Greek: thus, Thekla, Seleukeia, Tryphaina, Aulerios, etc. Exceptions include Paul, Onesiphorus, Alexander, Basil, and a few others. When a historical character in the *Miracles* is better known by a Latin name, such as Satornilos (Saturninus) in *Mir.* 13, I have made note of it. My hope is that the Hellenic aesthetic of the *Life and Miracles* will be more prominent through this method of transliteration and that my choices in presentation will encourage readers to consider the literary nature of that work's composition.

# Outline of the *Life and Miracles of Thekla*

(chapter numbers based on the critical text, Dagron 1978:168–412)

## *Life*

Preface

1–13 at Iconium

14 outside Iconium

15–24 at Antioch

25–26 at Myra

27–28 from Myra to Iconium, then Seleukeia

29 disappearance into the ground; spiritual activities

## *Miracles*

Preface

1–4 Thekla fights against *daimones*

5–11 various miracles of defending, helping, and healing locals

12 two miracles concerning the author; healing, excommunication, and reinstatement

13–25 various miracles of healing and protecting individuals

26–30 protection of various towns and churches

31 appearance to the author, encouraging him to write

32–35 miracles of vengeance

36–41 various healings, including the author and three of the local literati

42–46 various healings of locals

Epilogue

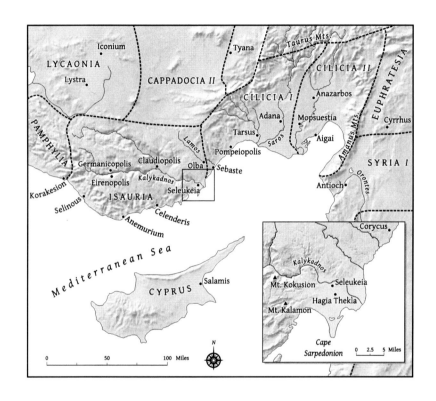

Map of Seleukeia and Environs
(© The Alpine Mapping Guild/Martin Gamache)

Et sic proficiscens de Anthiocia faciens iter per mansiones aliquot peruени ad prouinciam, quae Cilicia appellatur, quae habet ciuitatem metropolim Tharso, ubi quidem Tharso et eundo Ierusolimam iam fueram. Sed quoniam de Tharso tertia mansione, id est in Hisauria, est martyrium sanctae Teclae, gratum fuit satis ut etiam illuc accedere, presertim cum tam in proximo esset. Nam proficiscens de Tharso perueni ad quandam ciuitatem supra mare adhuc Ciliciae, que appellatur Ponpeiopolim. Et inde iam ingressa fines Hisauriae mansi in ciuitate, quae appellatur Corico, ac tertia die perueni ad ciuitatem, quae appellatur Seleucia Hisauriae. Vbi cum peruenissem, fui ad episcopum uere sanctum ex monacho, uidi etiam ibi ecclesiam ualde pulchram in eadem ciuitate. Et quoniam inde ad sanctam Teclam, qui locus est ultra ciuitatem in colle sed plano, habebat de ciuitate forsitan mille quingentos passus, malui ergo perexire illuc, ut statiua, quam factura eram, ibi facerem. Ibi autem ad sanctam ecclesiam nichil aliud est nisi monasteria sine numero uirorum ac mulierum. Nam inueni ibi aliquam amicissimam michi, et cui omnes in oriente testimonium ferebant uitae ipsius, sancta diaconissa nomine Marthana, quam ego aput Ierusolimam noueram, ubi illa gratia orationis ascenderat; haec autem monasteria aputactitum seu uirginum regebat. Quae me cum uidisset, quod gaudium illius uel meum esse potuerit, nunquid uel scribere possum? Sed ut redeam ad rem, monasteria ergo plurima sunt ibi per ipsum collem et in medio murus ingens, qui includet ecclesiam, in qua est martyrium, quod martyrium satis pulchrum est. Propterea autem murus missus est ad custodiendam ecclesiam propter Hisauros, quia satis mali sunt et frequenter latrunculantur, ne forte conentur aliquid facere circa monasterium, quod ibi est deputatum. Ibi ergo cum uenissem in nomine Dei, facta oratione ad martyrium nec non etiam et lectione actu sanctae Teclae, gratias Christo Deo nostro egi infinitas, qui mihi dignatus est indignae et non merenti in omnibus desideria complere. Ac sic ergo facto ibi biduo, uisis etiam sanctis monachis uel aputactites, tam uiris quam feminis, qui ibi erant, et facta oratione et communione, reuersa sum Tharso ad iter meum.[1]

---

[1] Ed. CLCLT5, *Itinerarium Egeriae seu Peregrinatio ad loca sancta* (CPL 2325, 22.1—23.6); corrected according to Maraval 2002:226–230.

Then, leaving Antioch, we went on by several staging-posts and reached the province called Cilicia; Tarsus is its capital city, and I have already been there on my way out to Jerusalem. But in Isauria, only three staging-posts on from Tarsus, is the martyrium of holy Thekla, and, since it was so close, we were very glad to be able to make the extra journey there. Leaving Tarsus, but still in Cilicia, I reached Pompeiopolis, a city by the sea, and from there I crossed into Isauria, and spent the night in a city called Corycus. On the third day I arrived at a city called Seleukeia of Isauria, and, when I got there, I called on the bishop, a very godly man who had been a monk, and saw a very beautiful church in the city. Holy Thekla's is on a small hill about a mile and a half from the city, so, as I had to stay somewhere, it was best to go straight on and spend the night there. Round the holy church there is a tremendous number of cells for men and women. And that was where I found one of my dearest friends, a holy deaconess called Marthana. I had come to know her in Jerusalem when she was up there on pilgrimage. She was the superior of some cells of apotactites or virgins, and I simply cannot tell you how pleased we were to see each other again. But I must get back to the point. There are a great many cells on that hill, and in the middle a great wall round the martyrium itself, which is very beautiful. The wall was built to protect the church against the Isaurians, who are hostile, and always committing robberies, to prevent them trying to damage the monastery which had been established there. In God's name I arrived at the martyrium, and we had a prayer there, and read the whole Acts of holy Thekla; and I gave heartfelt thanks to God for his mercy in letting me fulfill all my desires so completely, despite all my unworthiness. For two days I stayed there, visiting all the holy monks and apotactites, the men as well as the women, after praying and receiving Communion, I went back to Tarsus to rejoin my route.[2]

[2] Trans. Wilkinson 1999:140–141.

# Introduction

T HE EXTENDED EPIGRAPH printed on the previous pages comprises the pilgrim Egeria's journal account of her journey to the shrine of Saint Thekla near Seleukeia (modern Silifke in southeastern Turkey). Her visit occurred in May of AD 384 on the way back to Constantinople from visiting Jerusalem and the Holy Land. Egeria's journey was not unusual for her time and situation in life. A number of wealthy pilgrims from the West are known to have made such journeys from the fourth century onwards.[1] However, one unusual aspect of her account is this very visit to Thekla's shrine in Seleukeia: she is the only pilgrim to have made such a journey and recorded it. The absence of any account besides Egeria's is remarkable given that she describes such an impressive amount of activity at Thekla's shrine.

Egeria offers a number of details suggesting that the cult of Thekla was very popular indeed. There were "a tremendous number of [monastic or pilgrimage] cells for men and women" around the church, a "great wall" around the "very beautiful martyrium," and a deaconess Marthana, also a pilgrim to Jerusalem, who was "the superior of some cells of apotactites or virgins."[2] Given the scarcity of accounts like hers of Christian pilgrimage sites in the fourth century, the amount of information is highly significant. Perhaps the most significant detail, however, is the description of her own worship at the shrine: "In God's name I arrived at the martyrium, and we had a prayer there, and read the whole Acts of holy Thekla." For Egeria, her devotion to Thekla involved a story so well known that she only has to name it as the "Acts". Egeria's account of reading this story in the martyrium is told briefly and without special

---

[1] The first of these whose account survives is the Bordeaux Pilgrim in 333. Egeria's is the second earliest detailed account from the period. For Egeria, see Maraval 2002, Wilkinson 1999, and Sivan 1988a, 1988b; and for the Bordeaux Pilgrim, see Elsner 2000. On pilgrimage to healing shrines in Byzantium, see Maraval 1985 and Talbot 2002a, 2002b.

[2] The term "apotactites" is taken directly from Egeria's Latin (*aputactites*), which is itself a direct borrowing of the Greek word ἀποτακτικαί and thus means "hermits"; in this case it is clear that the hermits are female since they are equated with "virgins" and under the direction of a female superior, Marthana.

pleading—she is grateful to God that she has the opportunity to do this—and it seems an entirely appropriate act of worship in the setting.

What is this story and why is Egeria reading it at the shrine in Seleukeia? The "Acts" which Egeria names is probably the famous late second-century apocryphon called the *Acts of Paul and Thekla* (hereafter *ATh*), which details Thekla's adventures with the apostle Paul and, in particular, her miraculous escape from two attempted martyrdoms.[3] At the beginning of that story, two hundred years earlier in its composition than Egeria's visit, Thekla is described as a well born young woman from Iconium who is engaged to be married to a young man named Thamyris. One day, while sitting by the window, she hears the Apostle Paul's voice wafting her way from the neighboring house. Paul is preaching "about abstinence and the resurrection." Thekla is immediately struck with a desire to be near Paul and to "attend to his words." On this basis she refuses to talk at all with her fiancé Thamyris, who subsequently figures out what has happened and drags Paul before the governor. The governor throws Paul into prison, where Thekla secretly goes and visits him at night, only to be discovered the next morning and accused of impropriety. This time both of them are dragged before the governor, with the result that Paul is expelled from the city and Thekla is condemned to be burnt on the pyre, to her furious mother's delight. Once the fires are lit around her, however, God sends a miraculous torrent of rain which extinguishes the fire and allows Thekla to escape to Paul, who is mourning her death outside the city. From there they proceed to the city of Antioch (perhaps not the Syrian one) only to be accosted at the gates by a town councilor named Alexander. Alexander attempts to rape Thekla, and she tears his ceremonial cloak in the process. For this she is dragged again before a governor's tribunal and she is condemned to be fed to wild beasts in the arena of Antioch. In the meantime, however, she is entrusted to a local dignitary, Queen Tryphaina, who admires her faith and asks her to pray for her dead daughter Falconilla. On the appointed day, Thekla is thrown to the wild beasts and in an act of desperation casts herself into a pool, baptizing herself in the process. Despite this apparent suicide, she miraculously survives unscathed. The governor ultimately releases her because Queen Tryphaina has fainted watching Thekla's trials, and he and Alexander fear retribution from the emperor. Thekla leaves Antioch, having thus survived her second martyrdom, and she finds Paul in the city of Myra.

---

[3] The precise date of the *ATh*'s composition is unresolved but must be between the composition of the *Acts of Peter* (c. 180), to which it alludes, and Tertullian's condemnation of the text c. 200. See Hennecke and Schneemelcher 1992:2.214–216 for all the ancient attestations to the work.

Paul approves her trials and sends her out to preach the Gospel. She then returns to her home city of Iconium and, finding her former fiancé dead, calls on her mother to believe in Christ. Without any further elaboration the story abruptly ends with the notice that Thekla spent the remainder of her life in Seleukeia.

This romantic epic is most likely the very story Egeria read aloud two hundred years later at the site of Thekla's last resting place. Where did Egeria get this text? The story is said by ancient authorities, notably Tertullian, to have been composed in Asia Minor, which seems likely given the geographical compass of its narrative.[4] But the evidence of Tertullian shows that the text, and perhaps even a Latin translation of it,[5] was available in the western Mediterranean from a very early date: he condemns it as "falsely written" (*perperam scripta*) in his *On Baptism* of c. 200.[6] Therefore, it is very possible that Egeria knew the account in Latin before her pilgrimage, but she could easily have learned about Thekla in Jerusalem or in Antioch.[7]

Egeria's detour to the shrine of Thekla in Seleukeia thus opens a new window on the importance of the *ATh* as a foundational text for Thekla's cult in early Christianity. Without the entry in her pilgrimage account we would have very little idea, beyond Tertullian's brief aspersions, that the *ATh* was so important before the fifth century. Furthermore, certain circumstantial details involving Thekla in the fourth century make more sense in this context. For instance, the writer Methodius has the personified Arete crown Thekla the

---

[4] Ramsay 1893:375–428.

[5] Tertullian knew Greek, of course, and could have read the *ATh* in its original language: see Barnes 1971:67–69. Tertullian is known to have written (now lost) works in Greek on the baptism of heretics, on shows and games, and on the veiling of virgins. Barnes argues for a Greek-speaking audience in Carthage for these works.

[6] *On Baptism* 17 (ed. Refoulé and Drouzy 2002:90–91): "Quodsi quae Acta Pauli quae perperam scripta sunt—exemplum Theclae!—ad licentiam mulierum docendi tinguendique defendunt, sciant in Asia presbyterum qui eam scripturam construxit quasi titulo Pauli de suo cumulans convictum atque confessum id se amore Pauli fecisse loco decessisse. Quam enim fidei proximum videtur ut is docendi et tinguendi daret feminae potestatem qui nec discere quidem constanter mulieri permisit? 'Taceant,' inquit, 'et domi viros suos consultant!'" (cf. 1 Corinthians 14:35). Tertullian is primarily correcting here a misreading of the *ATh*: Thekla does indeed baptize herself in an act of desperation, but this does not give Christian women the license to do it as a matter of course. However, Tertullian goes further and casts aspersions on the origins of this work. In his opinion, the priest in Asia Minor who authored it went too far and has rightly yielded his seat (*loco decessisse*). Note also that the authenticity of this passage has been doubted on the basis of textual problems in the manuscript record (MacKay 1986; see also Davis 2000).

[7] Dagron posits a library at fourth-century Seleukeia where Egeria consulted the text. This is possible but it lacks any literary or archaeological evidence (cf. Dagron 1978:33).

supreme virgin in his *Symposium*, written around 300.[8] Likewise, Gregory of Nazianzus retreated to Thekla's shrine at Seleukeia following the death of his father in 374, just ten years earlier than Egeria's visit.[9] And Gregory elsewhere points fleetingly to Thekla as a model for imitation by Christian women and lists her among the apostle martyrs.[10] Alongside Egeria's pilgrimage account, Methodius' and Gregory's approving nods to Thekla bespeak a crucial role for the *ATh*—much more crucial, in fact, than allowed by Tertullian's (and subsequently Jerome's) dismissive appraisal of the text.[11] Surely one of the most dramatic witnesses to Thekla's reputation in the fourth century is the secret, spiritual naming of Saint Macrina as "Thekla" in Gregory of Nyssa's *Life of Macrina* (c. 380): Macrina's mother is visited in a dream three times by a divine being who instructs her to name her child Thekla. As Gregory says, it was not meant to be his elder sister's public name but rather a secret name that predicted the type of (ascetic) life that she would come to lead.[12]

After the fourth century, evidence of the importance of the *ATh* begins piling up in earnest. Stephen Davis has recently drawn attention to the significant material remains of her cult in Egypt—notably, pilgrim flasks (*ampullae*)—terracotta tokens which often depict Thekla in a posture of prayer (*orans*) and framed by two lions.[13] This image is, of course, a visual reference to the arena scene in Antioch, demonstrating a familiarity with the traditional legend

---

[8] *Symposium* 283–284, ed. Bonwetsch 1917:131; trans. Musurillo 1958:151. On the *Symposium*, see Brown 1988:183–188, Cameron 1991:177–178, and now Clark 2004:172–173.

[9] *On His Own Life* 548–549 (PG 37.1067).

[10] *Oration* 4.69, *Against Julian* (PG 35.589). On Thekla's reputation in the fourth century, see Davis 2001:4–5. However, there are many more references to Thekla in the works of the Cappadocian Fathers than Davis cites. A more complete list can be found at Maraval 1971:146n2, though the latter was published before Dagron 1974 and still mistakenly names Basil of Seleukeia as the author of the *Life and Miracles of Thekla* (see below).

[11] Jerome *De Viris Illustribus* (*On Imminent Men*) 7 (cf. *Epistle* 107.12). Origen also knew the *ATh*, though he (like Tertullian and Jerome) only refers to its generic name, the *Acts of Paul* (Πράξεις Παύλου; *Acta Pauli*), a larger text about Paul of which the *ATh* takes up the middle third. Unlike Tertullian and Jerome, however, Origen makes no mention of Thekla specifically: see Davis 2001:85–86. I have left to the side Athanasius of Alexandria's (potential) use of the *ATh* because, while Stephen Davis has done a fine job of analyzing the treatise *On Virginity* (2001:87–103), the Athanasian authorship of that work is not conclusive: see the review in Johnson 2004a. Nevertheless, the conclusion of his analysis—that Thekla was "already actively embraced by [the *On Virginity*'s] audience" (89)—confirms the argument of this Introduction thus far. Likewise the pseudonymous treatise *On Virginity* which is included among the works of Basil of Caesarea (Amand and Moons 1953).

[12] Gregory of Nyssa *Life of Macrina* 2.21–34, ed. Maraval 1971:144–149.

[13] Davis 2001:113–126, 195–200 with Figures 7–12. Some of these flasks are very elaborate, including several of the different beasts mentioned in the *ATh* narrative of her martyrdom at Antioch (lions, bulls, and a bear).

among this Egyptian concentration of Thekla devotees, perhaps women, who bought and carried the *ampullae*.[14] Similarly, pilgrimage to Thekla's shrine in Seleukeia continued after Egeria, as evidenced by the fifth-century writer Theodoret of Cyrrhus, who says that two holy women of his own time, Marana and Cyra, made a pilgrimage there from Beroea (in Roman Syria).[15] Finally, in the late 470s the emperor Zeno, himself of Isaurian origins, is thought to have constructed at least one major church on the site. Evagrius Scholasticus, writing in the late sixth century, says that the emperor dedicated a "huge sanctuary (μέγιστον τέμενος) of outstanding beauty and magnificence" at Thekla's shrine near Seleukeia, out of gratitude for a vision of the martyr and his subsequent victory over the usurper Basiliscus.[16] The excavations of the hilltop site suggests that this "huge sanctuary" may have included up to three churches, bringing the potential number of churches at the shrine to as many as five in the late fifth century.[17]

In the midst of all this activity arises the crowning jewel of Thekla devotion in late antiquity. This is the anonymous *Life and Miracles of Thekla* and the subject of the present study. The *Life and Miracles* (hereafter *LM*) is a literary work in Greek, about 10 times as long as the *ATh*, completed around AD 470 (just under three hundred years after that foundational text).[18] Manuscript

---

[14] Davis proposes in addition that the very popular cult of Saint Menas in Egypt appropriated part of the *ATh* for its own foundational legend (2001:135). This combination of Thekla and Menas in Egypt is exemplified by many of the pilgrim flasks which portray Thekla on one side and Menas on the other (Davis 2001:117–120 with Figures 7–12). Menas is said himself to have been martyred (by a governor) in Asia Minor, which provides a parallel narrative for the transmission of Thekla's legend to Egypt (Davis 2001:121–122).

[15] *On the Syrian Monks* 29.

[16] Evagrius Scholasticus 3.8, trans. Michael Whitby 2000:142. Evagrius also says that Zeno adorned the sanctuary with "very many imperial dedications [marble? mosaics? inscriptions?], which are preserved even in our time," suggesting that the shrine had not fallen into disrepair in the late sixth century, a hundred years after Zeno's dedication. After Evagrius I have been able to find no references in Byzantium to contemporary devotion at the cult site. However, as in Egypt, Thekla's cult traveled widely, and there is a Byzantine convent dedicated to Mar Takla at Maalula, fifty kilometers northeast of Damascus. Likewise, there was a shrine to Saint Tecla in Rome from around the seventh century, founded perhaps by duothelete Byzantine exiles in the wake of the Arab conquest of Syria (Cooper 1995). Interestingly, Thekla's name is found today in the Roman Catholic prayers for the dying (*Commendatio animae*): see Hennig 1964.

[17] For the archaeology of the hilltop site, called Hagia Thekla in some sources (modern Meriamlik), see now Hill 1996:209–234 with Figures 42–45 and Plates 98–99. Earlier studies of the site include Herzfeld and Guyer 1930:1–89, Hild et al. 1984:228–241 with Figures 19–22, and Hild and Hellenkemper 1990:441–443 with Plates 383–390.

[18] On the closing date of the *LM*, see Dagron 1978:17–19, where the limiting factors are the mention of Porphyrios, bishop of Seleukeia from c. 468, and the absence of any mention of Zeno's embellishment of the site c. 476. Dagron convincingly posits multiple

copyists in the middle ages ascribed the *LM* to the fifth-century bishop Basil of Seleukeia, but the text's modern editor, Gilbert Dagron, has rightly denied this ascription on the basis of evidence in the text itself.[19] (Apparently, the Byzantine copyists of the text were not very close readers because the anonymous author actually attacks Basil in *Miracle* 12, making it very unlikely, assuming *Mir.* 12 was not interpolated by a copyist, that Basil wrote the work.)[20]

The *Life and Miracles* takes a very similar view of Thekla devotion to Egeria's account in one important respect. It assumes that the traditional legend about her, embodied in the *ATh*, is the foundation of contemporary devotion. The anonymous author achieves this by beginning his work with a literary paraphrase of the *ATh*, a paraphrase which makes up the first half of his text, the *Life*. The *Life* is written in a much higher register of Greek than the *ATh* and it erases syntactical difficulties in the original for its educated contemporary audience. It also smoothes out ethical difficulties as well, mitigating in particular a dominant emphasis on sexual renunciation in the earlier text.[21] The author of the *LM* softens this emphasis considerably while at the same time keeping details that were objectionable to Tertullian, such as Thekla's right to baptize herself and to teach.[22] His appropriation of the text is complete—after all, he chooses to write a literary paraphrase of it—but it is idiosyncratic and does not correspond exactly to anyone else's picture of Thekla: neither that of Tertullian, Methodius, Egeria, or Gregory of Nazianzus.

---

redactions of the *Miracles* half (the *Life* having been written previously): 1) a first version with its conclusion at the awkward *Mir.* 44, completed after 444 but before 448; 2) a second version which included *Mir.* 12 as an addition, written between 448 and 468; and 3) a final version that attaches to the false conclusion of *Mir.* 44 two further miracles and an epilogue, written (as just mentioned) between 468 and Zeno's building project c. 476. As Dagron notes, this redaction-history aligns neatly with the careers of four bishops of Seleukeia between 430 and 470—Dexianos, John, Basil, Porphyrios (1978:19).

[19] Dagron 1974, 1978:13–15.

[20] Throughout this study I use simply "author" or "writer" to stand in for the author's name. I consider "Pseudo-Basil" unacceptable because it perpetuates a positive association between the *LM* and the bishop which, for the sake of reading the *LM* correctly, ought to be discontinued.

[21] This was the subject of an unpublished paper presented at the Byzantine Studies Conference in 2002 (Johnson 2002a). The argument of that paper appears again, in a more nuanced form, in Chapter One below (esp. pp. 23–26, 38–40).

[22] The author of the *LM* cannot be expected to know Tertullian's *On Baptism*, since there is no indication that he read Latin or knows of any Latin authors. However, he was doubtless familiar with Gregory of Nazianzus' approval of Thekla in the late fourth century and even at one point seems to quote from one of Gregory's Trinitarian sermons during the *Life* (see pp. 32–35 below).

The *LM*'s singular vision of Thekla emerges most prominently at the very end of the *Life*. Thekla has come to Seleukeia, as in the *ATh*, and lives out the rest of her life there, "evangelizing, catechizing, baptizing, and enlisting many for Christ." However, instead of dying at the end of her career, as the *ATh* reports, the *Life* says emphatically that she does not die:

> After she had brought everyone to faith, especially through the miracles (διὰ τῶν θαυμάτων μάλιστα), did she die (ἐκοιμήθη)? Absolutely not! (οὐδαμῶς) Just as the most widespread and more sure tradition (ὁ πολὺς καὶ ἀληθέστερος λόγος) attests, she sunk down while alive (ἔδυ δὲ ζῶσα) and went under the earth (ὑπεισῆλθε τὴν γῆν)—the decision of God being that this earth would separate for her and be cleft from below (ὑπορραγῆναι), on the very spot where is fixed the divine and holy and liturgical table (ἱερά καὶ λειτουργικὴ τράπεζα), established in a circular peristyle, shining in silver. This is where she dispenses fountains of healings (πηγὰς ἰαμάτων) for every suffering and every sickness, her virginal grace pouring out healings (ἰάματα) there, as if from some rushing stream, upon those who ask and pray for them.
>
> *Life* 28.5–14

Thekla's death is rewritten into a "living" disappearance, after which she continues to work "the miracles" (τὰ θαύματα) which she worked beforehand "to bring everyone to faith." This is the author's vision for the *LM*: while Thekla's apostolic career culminates in her arrival at Seleukeia, as in the *ATh*, her arrival and subsequent living disappearance into the ground of Seleukeia ushers in a new, boundless era during which "she dispenses fountains of healings" for the local inhabitants and the pilgrims at her shrine.

The working of these wonders post-disappearance in Seleukeia is the subject of the second half of the work, the *Miracles*. The author narrates forty-six of these miracles, most of which happen around the city of Seleukeia. It is somewhat misleading, however, for the author to have announced at the end of the *Life* that these miracles are healings. Many of them are, to be sure, but the slim majority (26 miracles) contain no mention of sickness or healing at all. They are displays of Thekla's miraculous power in other modes, such as vindicating innocent victims of crimes or defending local cities from the pillaging of ubiquitous Isaurian brigands. The implicit argument of the *Miracles* is that Thekla is firmly in control of the region which she has claimed by disappearing into the very earth of the place. In that sense the *Miracles* could easily be labeled a "patriographical" work: it rewrites and updates what has become by the fifth century a foundational legend, not just for Thekla, but for the city of Seleukeia.

The healing miracles, however, are the aspect of the *LM* that has received by far the most attention by scholars. Patricia Cox Miller has said, for instance, that Thekla is "the most spectacular instance of the Christian appropriation of [the classical healing god] Asclepius" in late antiquity.[23] When at least three fourths of the *LM* is not about healing at all, are scholars right to highlight that element? Are they not ignoring the primary import of the text as described above?

One must be careful at this point. The reason the healing miracles are so dominant in the scholarship is because they are, from a cultural or anthropological standpoint, some of the most interesting stories in the *LM*. In particular, they show close parallels with modes of non-Christian healing in the centuries prior to them. Asclepius' typical method of curing the sick in the ancient world required them to sleep in the god's temple at night (a practice called "incubation").[24] At night in the temple if you were successful you would receive a dream from the god, in which he either cures your illness immediately or gives you a prescription to carry out when you wake up. The former (and more ancient) mode of healing appears in the *Miracles* and, in fact, it proves to be the mode used in the most important miracle of the entire collection: in *Mir.* 12 the author himself is healed by the martyr. She appears to him sleeping in the church of her shrine and she fights off a swarm of wasps which is attacking him. In the morning he wakes to find that his hand has been healed of a very serious inflammation. The story is clearly symbolic or analogical, not quite as visceral as some of the healings done by Asclepius, but in its general outlines it retains the shape of a traditional, Asclepian incubation story. Thekla directly interacts with the illness in a nighttime dream occurring in the shrine. This type of miracle is thus significant for those who study the patterns of cultural exchange between Greco-Roman beliefs and practices and those of early Christianity.[25]

Let us return to the objection posed above, namely, that the majority of the *LM* is not about healing at all.[26] Perhaps what is needed is a way of reading

---

[23] Cox Miller 1994:117.

[24] For a brief account of ancient incubation see Edelstein and Edelstein 1998:2.145–158.

[25] The practice of Christian incubation has continued into modern times at pilgrimage centers such as Lourdes and Santiago: see Gessler 1946.

[26] The numerous Byzantine miracle collections beginning in the late sixth century are often solely devoted to healing miracles, such as that of Artemios (Crisafulli and Nesbitt 1997) and that of Cosmas and Damian (Deubner 1980 [1907]; Csepregi 2002). The Byzantine collections thus appear distinct from the *LM* in their literary aims and their lack of depen-

the *LM* that takes account of the compelling nature of the healing stories while at the same time appreciating the whole of what the author is trying to accomplish. This is the reading which I attempt in the chapters below, arguing that the healing stories in the *Miracles* are written with a clear vision that Thekla's holy character is based on her apostolic status and her protection and care for the city of Seleukeia and its environs. In other words, the author is writing about healing for the purpose of confirming the image of Thekla that appears at the very end of the *Life*. Her living descent into the ground is about claiming the city for herself: as Paul could claim Tarsus (or Rome) and John could claim Ephesus (or Patmos).

The *Miracles* follows up and confirms this argument at every turn. First, in the preface to the *Miracles*, the author claims that the miracle collection is a dossier of proof, not that she is an authentic healer (which is obvious), but that her apostolic legend—which he has just presented to the reader in elaborate detail and literary Greek—is true, historical, and trustworthy (*Mir.* preface 16–18). Second, the first four miracles describe Thekla's triumphs over local pagan deities: Sarpedon, Athena, Aphrodite, and Zeus all fall before her conquering might, and she claims their territory and temples for herself, establishing a real, physical control over the region. Finally, the miracles of vengeance and protection, which comprise the majority of the *Miracles* as a whole, sit very comfortably alongside the healing stories that I have noted are so compelling in their own right. The author does not make any theoretical distinction, for example, between the restitution to Aulerios' children of their stolen inheritance (*Mir.* 35) and the healing of Pausikakos' blindness (*Mir.* 23). Thus, the image of Thekla as the guardian and tutelary spirit of Seleukeia is the matrix within which the healing miracles should be read. In claiming the *LM* as a product of late antique Christian devotion, which is of course right and proper, it is nevertheless important to interpret the healing aspect of Thekla within the internal argument of the work as a unity. I offer below a close reading of the text which can explain how the details fit together with the overarching literary argument that I have just been describing.

What has been left out of previous studies on the *LM* is the role of the *Life* in the organization of the whole. The *Life* has been ignored, I suggest, because of its apparently innocuous form. What does a literary paraphrase in Attic Greek have to do with the cult of Thekla in fifth-century Seleukeia?

---

dence on classical models. These collections deserve a study in their own right, but I am doubtful as to whether the *LM* ought to be read as part of their tradition. For an overview of the Byzantine collections, see Festugière 1971, Maraval 1985:17–18, Efthymiadis 1999, and Talbot 2002b, all of whom include the *Miracles of Thekla*. See also Appendix 3 below.

I argue in Chapter One that the literary paraphrase serves, in fact, a very defined purpose in the author's depiction of the cult. Its purpose is to bring the apostolic past into the late antique present, reiterating and claiming her foundation myth (with a few very significant changes) for the enterprise of publishing her famous miracles more widely. By connecting the contemporary cult to her apostolic narrative, the author of the *LM* is wisely cashing in on the cultural capital that the *ATh* had accrued over three centuries. He is speaking directly to educated devotees like Egeria a century earlier, who know and approve of Thekla prior to reading the text: he is expanding their expectations of who Thekla was and what she has become. Any cultural capital he accrues to himself is dependent on those expectations.

Still, why would one choose to attempt this audacious endeavor through a literary paraphrase, the most boring schoolroom exercise of all? As I show in Chapter Two, the literary paraphrase plays an important didactic role among educated Jews and Christians of the ancient world. True, it was a rhetorical exercise common to Roman schoolrooms, but Jewish and Christian biblical exegetes, in particular, adopted it as a standard mode of biblical interpretation and exposition: retelling the story is a way of explaining the story. Moreover, the paraphrase as a literary genre implies a certain given status of the text being paraphrased. Early Christian copyists and interpreters of biblical texts often manipulated important, especially canonical, texts for the very reason that they are important texts: the process of changing the text thus both reveals and confirms the authoritative status of the source text. But the *ATh* is not canonical and is even condemned by some authorities in the early church—surely it does not fall into this group? Indeed it does, since, as we have seen, late antique Christians devoted to Thekla took the *ATh* as a foundational text for her contemporary status: this appears true for Egeria as much as for the author of the *LM*. Therefore, the changes made to that foundational charter by the *LM* take on the role of exegesis, confirming its status and explaining its contemporary significance. To take up again the example cited above, by emphatically denying that Thekla dies at the end of the *Life* the author is reinterpreting the contemporary significance of the *ATh*: Thekla's apostolic history should be (and is) claimed by the citizens of Seleukeia as their own apostolic imprimatur. In other words, on the basis of the *LM* Seleukeia is adopted into to the pantheon of apostolic landscapes. The city is not mentioned in the Acts of the Apostles or in Paul's letters, but it has an apostolic role nonetheless.[27] The

---

[27] The irony is that it is Seleukeia and not Iconium which has a pilgrimage shrine to Thekla, since Iconium has a prominent role in the New Testament (Acts 13:51–14:6; 16:2; 1 Timothy 3:11). The trend in late antiquity, however, seems to be that the traditional site of the apostle-martyr's death

paraphrase achieves, among other things, this status for the city and makes possible its expanded preeminence as the site of the *Miracles*.

If it is true that prior studies of the *LM* have tended to ignore these literary characteristics of the *Life*, it is fair to say also that the *Miracles* has consistently captured scholars' imaginations. For instance, in his introduction to the text, Gilbert Dagron devotes most of his attention to the various groups of people (on the ground, as it were) whom the *Miracles* appears to describe more or less realistically. It is indicative of the attractiveness of the *Miracles* for this type of research that the longest and most comprehensive chapter in Dagron's introduction is entitled "La société des miracles" (1978:109–139); by contrast, the chapter on "Langue, style, structure" is the shortest (152–162). To be fair, in its attention to detail Dagron's interpretation of the work is more akin to my approach than not: the two studies are both attempting to take the *LM* seriously as an example of late antique writing. Still, I am much less confident than Dagron that the details of the *LM* can be easily mapped onto real people on the ground, not least because the miracle stories are so stylized and literary.

The literary character of the *Miracles* is particularly notable for its "paratactic" structure: by paratactic I mean that the miracle stories are strung together endlessly without any overarching narrative or chronological development.[28] Topical clusters emerge, such as the miracles dealing with the local grammarians and orators (*Mir.* 37–41), but Thekla's character does not develop "realistically" through time in the way one sees in the *ATh/Life*. (Her miraculous activities might also be called "episodic", but without any of the character development that term suggests.) The paratactic structure, therefore, is primarily a method of organizing the stories and not an account that mimics reality, so I am wary of any attempts to get beyond it.[29]

A reader might say in opposition that the paratactic structure is a naive way of writing down the actual miracles happening on site and that, conse-

---

is more venerated than his or her birthplace (e.g. Paul in Rome, even though Tarsus held a claim on him; cf. *Mir.* 26.40–46). It is convenient, of course, when the site of martyrdom (like Rome) already plays a role in the New Testament: this is the very status the *Life* achieves for Seleukeia.

[28] For a more complete definition of parataxis/paratactic, see pp. 114–116 below.

[29] Of course, narrative saint's Lives from late antiquity also exhibit a paratactic structure: the sixth-century *Life of Theodore of Sykeon* (Festugière 1970) or that of Nicholas of Sion (Ševčenko and Ševčenko 1984) could be cited as evidence of this style. Nevertheless, the *Miracles of Thekla* does not follow Thekla's life chronologically, as in these later Lives, but presents a static picture based on the narrative paraphrase presented in the *Life*. For this reason, and because the later Lives are so clearly modeled on Gospel narrative, I would only group all of these texts together if their unique literary uses of the paratactic style could remain autonomous.

quently, we do have an accurate record (within limits) of what the society of fifth-century Seleukeia looked like. In such an argument, it would matter less that Thekla's character develops; more significant than Thekla herself are the named people, locals and pilgrims, in the individual miracle stories. This is certainly a possibility, but when the paratactic structure of the *Miracles* is examined in earnest there begin to emerge certain stylized similarities among both the locals and pilgrims. I highlight these similarities in my analysis of the *Miracles* in Chapter Three, and I propose a different model for reading the miracle collection as a whole. In my reading the goal is not to get beyond the author's static characterization of Thekla but rather to see the individual stories as directly supporting that characterization, as well as reinforcing the author's own opinions as they appear in the accounts.

The author's vision of Thekla's miracle-working or "thaumaturgical" activity (from the Greek θαῦμα, "miracle, wonder") is an intimately personal one: the miracles that she performs for the author himself punctuate the collection and give it the overarching structure that it lacks in other ways. This personal investment in the character of Thekla comes to a head in the epilogue, where he invokes her as the one who will ensure that his collection gets a fair hearing and a positive reception (*Mir.* epilogue 9–15). When read as a personal literary endeavor, therefore, the consistency of his portrayal of Thekla, who has become his literary patron, is clearly more important than the historical accuracy of his reporting. In other words, the literary nature of the work is prominent when the author places so much emphasis on his own authorship and the future success of the work.[30]

Therefore, I would argue that parataxis as a literary mode is only naive on the surface. When considered as a literary form, it has a long history stretching back at least to Herodotus and it was taken up with vigor in the Hellenistic and Roman periods by writers in many different genres. In other words, paratactic writing has a distinguished pedigree extending throughout classical and late antique literature and has plenty of exponents in the *LM*'s own era. I examine this pedigree in detail in Chapter Four. A reader conscious of classical literary history would never readily dismiss this style as naive.

In addition, the author of the *LM* writes in complicated Greek that is miles away from the simplistic healing narratives one finds, for example, in the inscriptions at Asclepius' healing shrine in Epidaurus. I also examine these texts in Chapter Four and suggest that the literary history of the paratactic

---

[30] This argument concerning the author's role in the *Miracles* is similar to one put forward recently by Derek Krueger (2004:79–92). I distinguish my analysis of the *Miracles* from Krueger's in Chapters Three and Four below (esp. pp. 164–165 and 218–220).

style provides a much more welcoming context for the *Miracles* than any healing literature from the ancient world. This, of course, reinforces my argument that the *LM* is not primarily about healing at all but about a specific image of the apostolic Thekla as the tutelary spirit of late antique Seleukeia.

To sum up, something suspiciously literary is going in both halves of the *LM* which is linked to the author's emphatic denial that Thekla ever died. His favorite Greek word for Thekla's contemporary activities is ἐπιφοιτάω, which means "to haunt."[31] There is therefore a penumbra of Thekla's presence in late antiquity which covers the whole region of what is today southeastern Turkey. Tarsus is Paul's, of course, but to the west of Tarsus and extending north to Iconium, Thekla is preeminent. In the *LM* she continues to claim this area as her own and defends it against outsiders and local brigands.

Most of all, Thekla shows a unique interest in seeing the publication of her own miraculous activities come to pass. While the author of the *LM* is directly encouraged by Thekla on a number of occasions, only in *Mir.* 31 does she appear before him while he is awake—he has a vision (ὄψις) instead of a dream (ὄναρ). In this critical scene she helps him physically to write down the miracles that she has just been working. What is more, this epiphany is claimed as a miracle in its own right: even when helping him to write the *Miracles* she is working a miracle. The sense conveyed by *Mir.* 31 is that her thaumaturgical activities directly intersect with his collection in a very tangible way. She takes from his hand the notebook (τέτρας) that he used for transcribing the miracles and recites back to him what he had written, all the while smiling and indicating "by her gaze" (βλέμματι) that she is pleased with it. The author thus lets us into his process of composition, and even there Thekla is present.

Juxtaposed with this vision, however, is the fact that Thekla's miracles remain innumerable, despite the correspondence indicated in *Mir.* 31. As the author says towards the end of the *LM*:

> The collection (συλλογή) exceeds my ability, and I will not reach the end of its writing (συγγραφή), nor is my life long enough to be sufficient for so great and so infinite a font of miracles (ἀπείρῳ πλήθει θαυμάτων).
>
> *Mir.* 44.16–19

The collection represented by the *Miracles* is necessarily indefinite, as similarly claimed by the writer of the Gospel of John:

---

[31] See Dagron 1978 "index grec," s.v. "ἐπιφοιτῶ."

> But there are also many other things that Jesus did; if every one of
> them were written down, I suppose that the world itself could not
> contain the books that would be written.[32]
>
> 21:25

The Gospel of John like the *Miracles* is only proportionally related to the whole
of what was really accomplished by the divine protagonist. In this sense the *LM*
is as much about the future as it is about the apostolic past or the late antique
present: not only is the archive open to reception and interpretation, it is also
always possible for other stories to be added to the archive. What is to come,
after the dissemination of his work, is therefore at the center of the author's
literary conception. A reader of this study might even go so far as to say that
the invocation of Thekla in the *LM*'s epilogue, to promulgate and to ensure
the positive reception of the *LM*, is also being fulfilled by the present study:
Thekla's haunting presence is at work among those who continue to find her
life and miracles worth reading.

---

[32] Trans. NRSV.

# Chapter 1

## Paraphrase in Practice: The *Life of Thekla* and Literary Inheritance in Late Antiquity

### The Ever-Present Past in the *Life and Miracles*

THE FORM OF THE LITERARY PARAPHRASE says a great deal about what the author of the *Life of Thekla* is attempting to do in literary historical terms: by choosing to write a saint's Life through the lens of a second-century apocryphon, the author associates his work with a much earlier period in Christian history—the apostolic period. The literary paraphrase, called μετάφρασις in Greek, is clearly a backward looking form, but it also consolidates the past and reinterprets it for contemporary cultural and literary concerns. In Chapter Two I present a brief literary history that situates the *Life* amidst a wealth of paraphrasing activity in ancient Jewish and Christian literature.

Of primary importance, however, is to have a clear idea of how the author of the *Life* himself describes and employs the paraphrase form. This is the subject of the present chapter: a running literary and rhetorical analysis of the *Life* which focuses on the changes that it makes to the original source text, the *Acts of Paul and Thekla* (ATh). What I consider significant in my analysis below are the contemporary connotations of these changes and how they contribute to the construction of an authorial voice. These are elements of the *Life* that most need to be explained for the sake of broader issues current in late antique studies. (Some of the most important of these issues are, to my mind, the reception of the earliest Christian literature in late antiquity, the keen competition between literary (specifically, biographical) forms at this time, and the perennial interpretive question of how do cult and text relate in the Christian cultures of late antiquity.)

Gilbert Dagron, in his *Vie et Miracles de Sainte Thècle* (1978) calls the *Life* "une honnête travail de professionnel et un document de premier ordre pour une histoire du goût littéraire" (23). Dagron's study, however, lacks the analytical apparatus necessary to explain what he means by "honnête travail" and "goût littéraire." The meaning of "literary taste" for eastern late antiquity has yet to be adequately defined by scholars and requires a literary history that could place the *LM* in some kind of context. How popular were paraphrases of apocryphal Acta at this time? How did they contribute to the mix of biographical writing in late antiquity? I attempt to provide answers to these questions in Chapter Two below.

As for "honnête travail," this requires a close reading of the *ATh* and *Life* together so as to track changes made to the former by the latter. Dagron did not perform this analysis but concentrated on the *Miracles* in the aim of revealing a cross-section of Seleukeian society in the fifth century.[1] However, the significance of the *LM* is broader than social history, and it could reasonably be argued that much of the detail from the *Miracles* is invented for the sake of the overarching goals of the author. The analysis in this chapter will, therefore, examine the author's programmatic statements and how he tries to work them out, or how he fails to do so. I offer some conclusions on how the author is trying to arrange the narrative material within his chosen form and how this arrangement reveals his attitudes towards the apostolic past.

On the topic of "the past," it should be reiterated that the *Life* speaks to perennial themes in late antique, medieval, and Byzantine history.[2] In collecting, redacting, and arranging, the author is imposing an order on his material that reveals certain lurking ideas about the past, and about its relationship to the present. This is true for the *Miracles* as much as for the *Life*. But for the latter—our present concern—the processes of reception and re-publication are especially vivid because the textual products have survived: both the source text and its literary paraphrase are extant and complete. Thus, the later text can be "mapped" in order to bring to light the ideals and assumptions of the Christian writer who worked with them.[3]

For the author of the *Life*, it is clear that his interest in the apostolic past centers around the *ATh*, which offers him direct access to the living world of his spiritual patron, Thekla. The survival of this one text, on a papyrus or in

---

[1] Dagron admits he is offering "une analyse qui ne se voulait pas encyclopédique" (1978:7).

[2] Eastern late antiquity still lags behind the medieval West in terms of scholarship on memory and attitudes to the past (but compare Averil Cameron 1999). The present chapter has been aided by the following studies on the textual past in the Middle Ages: Stock 1990, Yates 1966, Carruthers 1998, Spiegel 1997, Coleman 1992, and Rita Copeland 1991.

[3] I take this concept of mapping from Kirsti Copeland 2000, but it is made to perform more sophisticated tasks by Jonathan Smith 1978.

whatever form he held it, is a piece of living history. As Edward Shils wrote in his famous study of *Tradition*:

> Documents have primarily a heuristic value. But it is also their sheer pastness which confers value on them: a person who holds them has brought the past into his presence. They embody some quality which is inherent in their pastness—both in their own physical identity with what they were in the past and because they carry a record of a past event.[4]

The sense of "pastness" in the present, as Shils describes it, is keenly felt by the author of the *Life* because he believes Thekla can be shown to live and work even in his own day. Thus her legend takes on additional "past in presence" since it belongs to an active saint and patron.

As will be shown below, Thekla's death in the *ATh* is written out of the *Life* so as to confirm her "haunting" presence at Seleukeia. In this way the legend continues, and the author of the *Life* feels confident enough to add another substantial volume to a Christian saga that tracks her movements and epiphanies from a historic, apostolic beginning to his present day. These contemporary traces of her bodily presence in Seleukeia—the *Miracles*—are themselves pieces of the past, and the author has written them to conform to the history of Thekla that he presents in her *Life*. Thus, despite his claims that the *Miracles* were written only to confirm the "truth" of her past legend (*Mir.* preface 1–21), the rewritten *Life* forms a unified whole with the *Miracles*, and the work appears designed from the start to serve as a historical monument for later readers.[5]

This first chapter of my study is organized around four central sections, dealing the with four main narrative sections of the *Life*: 1) Preface (*Life* preface), 2) Iconium (1–14), 3) Antioch (15–25), and 4) Myra, Iconium (again), and Seleukeia (26–28).[6] In terms of analysis, the paraphrastic nature of the *Life* seems more suited to a running commentary than to a thematic study. Chapter One begins, therefore, where the *Life* begins, with the preface (προθεωρία): this is a programmatic passage which lacks its complement in the *ATh*. In this section the author explains his reasons for writing the *Life* and offers some

---

[4] Shils 1981:77.

[5] "The past was very real to the men and women of late antiquity: as they saw it, it had not so much to be remade as reasserted" (Averil Cameron 1999:2).

[6] In his edition of the text Dagron explains that, unlike the *Miracles* which were already numbered in the manuscripts, the *Life* requires numbered chapters to facilitate reading (1978:171n1). These numbers are used for the sake of reference below. See the Table of Contents for an overview of how the sections of these four chapters fit together.

general reflections on the impetus to historiography, which he claims as his own divine vocation (*Life* preface). The Iconium section which follows narrates Thekla's conversion, trial, and first (attempted) martyrdom on the pyre (1-14). It closes with Thekla's reunion with Paul outside the city and their setting off together for Antioch (14). The next section details Thekla's capture at the gates of Antioch, her subsequent trial, her alliance with Queen Tryphaina, and her second (attempted) martyrdom with various wild beasts in the arena (15–25). This section closes with her leaving Tryphaina's house in search for Paul at Myra (25). The final section begins in Myra with Thekla's lengthy address to Paul (26). From this point her character begins to take on features essential to the way she is portrayed in the *Miracles*. Paul sends her to Iconium, which she passes through only briefly on her way to Seleukeia. The *Life* ends with a description of Seleukeia and of Thekla's ministry there prior to her fateful disappearance into the ground (27-28).

## Preface (*Life* preface)

The preface to the *Life* offers a look at certain assumptions held by its author concerning his literary project and his relationship to Thekla. While substantially shorter than that of the *Miracles*, the preface to the *Life* reveals in particular his awareness of his place in the history of writing on Thekla. For instance, he admits in the second sentence to making use of a previous work: "Receiving the narrative from another, more ancient history, I follow that account step by step" (ἐξ ἑτέρας μὲν καὶ παλαιοτέρας ἱστορίας ἐκληφθεῖσα, κατ' ἴχνος δὲ αὐτῆς ἐκείνης συντεθεῖσα; *Life* preface 3-4). That he is here referring to the *ATh* is borne out by the narrative of the *Life*: he follows closely a text very similar to the ones that have survived.[7]

Moreover, that he is referring to an actual text and not to the legend in general is suggested by his seriousness on the question of alteration. He

---

[7] There is currently no complete critical text for the *Acts of Paul*, of which the *ATh* comprises the middle third. The Lipsius-Bonnet text (LB) is used below, though with reference to the "critical translations" of Hennecke and Schneemelcher 1992:2.213–270 and Elliott 1999:350–389, which cite many passages not available in LB. "Lipsius-Bonnet based their edition [of the *ATh*] on eleven Greek manuscripts, but over forty are now known to be extant" (Elliott 1999: 353). There are also numerous versions in almost all the ancient Christian languages; the Syriac version, the earliest and the one with which I am most familiar, does not show any significant variations from the Greek *ATh* (Wright 1990 [1871]:2.116–145), though it is clear that other translations do (most of which are probably later than the sixth century): see Elliott 1999:350-363. Willy Rordorf's new critical edition of the *Acts of Paul* for the CCSA is eagerly anticipated. Unless otherwise noted, the translations from the *ATh* are Elliott's; the translations from the *LM* are mine.

recommends that his readers pay attention to the changes that has made to the received text and ask themselves whether these changes are in the spirit of that tradition:

> I would request those living now, and likewise those who may come upon this work in the future, to take note that when I say something extraordinary [i.e. beyond the original]—and I shall—it is not outside the aims of the ancient accounts (οὐκ ἔξω τοῦ σκοποῦ τῶν πάλαι συγγραφέντων).
>
> *Life* preface 12–15

He admits only to changes in "composition and style" (συνθήκη καὶ λέξις), and he places under these headings the insertion of invented speeches (δημηγορίαι).[8] The speeches, he says, provide Thekla with "an old-fashioned beauty" (ἀρχαιότροπον κάλλος), though he claims not to have attempted to adhere rigorously to Attic style. "Truth" (ἀλήθεια), "clarity" (σαφήνεια), and the "order of the acts" (ἡ ἐν τοῖς πράγμασι τάξις)—by which he may mean the order as presented in the *ATh*—are his three expressed stylistic goals.

Towards the end of the preface he mentions Herodotus and Thucydides, which appears to be a conscious attempt to place the *Life* in the tradition of classical Greek historiography:

> Herodotus the Halicarnassian and Thucydides the Athenian, and anyone else after them who wrote ancient or contemporary history (τῶν ἱστορίας παλαιὰς ἢ νέας συγγεγραφότων)—each of these says that he came to his labor (οἰκεῖον πόνον) of writing with an individual purpose and passion (οἰκείᾳ γνώμῃ καὶ προθυμίᾳ).
>
> *Life* preface 29–32

The novelty of this rhetoric lies not in a Christian writer appropriating the Greco-Roman historiographical tradition but rather in his specific appropriation of the rhetoric of history for rewriting the *ATh*, a text taken by most scholars of Christian apocrypha to be the paradigm "Christian Romance".[9]

Clearly more important than the Greek Romance in this case are the personae of ancient historiography, including the persona of Luke, whom he

---

[8] For the place of speeches in ancient historiography, see *OCD* 1434 s.v. "speech presentation"; for the much debated subject of speeches in Thucydides, see Hornblower 1987:45–72 and Woodman 1988:11–15.

[9] Whether the *ATh* is called a Christian Romance (Hägg 1983:154–165; Burrus 1987:49–60) or a Christian anti-Romance (Aubin 1998), it is always read in terms of the ancient genre of the Greek Romance.

also mentions at the end of the preface. The author of the *Life* considers Luke to be the historian behind the Luke-Acts pair and reminds his readers that Luke dedicated his works to a certain Theophilus:

> Just as, therefore, the admirable Luke (ὁ θαυμάσιος Λουκᾶς) clearly did among the divine Gospels and in his narrative concerning the apostles [i.e. Acts] (τῷ περὶ τῶν ἀποστόλων συντάγματι), when he placed Theophilus at the front (προτάξας τὸν Θεόφιλον), to whom he dedicated all the toil of his divine composition.
>
> *Life* preface 43–47

The overall effect of this final section of the preface is to cast the entire *LM* in a historiographical light.[10]

Finally, here in the *Life*'s preface, the author alludes to an important, overarching theme that influences the execution of his narrative:

> Not that these things would become forgotten or obscure after a long time (οὐχ ὡς ἂν μὴ ἐξίτηλα, μηδὲ ἄδηλα τῷ μακρῷ χρόνῳ γένηται), for the deeds of the saints (τὰ τῶν ἁγίων ἔργα) are guarded by God and always remain steadfast, solid, and immortal, for the sake of his own eternal renown (εἴς τε οἰκεῖον ἀεὶ κλέος), and for a help to men who still roam about on earth.
>
> *Life* preface 36–39

Through this quotation from the opening of Herodotus' *Histories*—ὡς μήτε τὰ γενόμενα ἐξ ἀνθρώπων τῷ χρόνῳ ἐξίτηλα (Herodotus 1.1)—the author reveals a motif that remains pertinent for the rest of the work, "divine memory." This motif works itself out, as will be shown, in the introductions and conclusions of various scenes where the author claims the necessity of "making mention" of a given story he remembers or has collected (e.g. μνημονεύω; *Mir.* 11.1–2).[11] When he "remembers" a story—the whole of the *Life*, perhaps, or an individual

---

[10] Between his appeal to the ancient historians and this mention of Luke comes a brief reflection on the "individual" impetus to historiography, during which he names his own patron "Achaios" (*Life* preface 34). The emulation here of Luke is thus made even more explicit. However, in terms of organization, the mention of Achaios serves as a link between the pre-Christian and Christian historiography, a chronological order which the author appropriates for his own project. It could be further noted that the dedicatee is quite possibly an invention of the author—as of course could be the case for Luke also (cf. Bovon 2002:22–23)—the name "Achaios" may thus be harkening back to a pristine time of truer faith or perhaps to a time of purer Greek. In either case the point is that our author's rhetoric of historiography (and perhaps also his anonymity) seems to be directly modeled on Luke.

[11] See the opening sentences of *Mir.* 17, 20, 25, 26, 42, and 43; similar openings, such as κἀκεῖνο δέ μοι ῥητέον, can be found at *Mir.* 23, 24, 45, and 44.

miracle—the assumption is that he is fulfilling a divine vocation, helping to preserve the storehouse of Christian memory which is ensured by God to be "steadfast, solid, and immortal" in the face of time's forgetfulness.

The author of the *Life* thus offers a uniquely altered vision of the historiographical process. To start, the traditional historians' values—autopsy, accurate sources, and the importance of preservation—clearly still resonate with this author. However, the institution of Christian historiography, as inaugurated by Luke, has affected him to the degree that he sees the history of the apostolic times as having been miraculously preserved by God. His argument at the end of the preface is, therefore, that the deeds of the apostles are substantively different from the deeds recorded in Herodotus and Thucydides.[12]

## Thekla in Iconium (*Life* 1–14)

### Thekla the Apostle

Following the programmatic preface to the *Life*, Thekla is introduced in the narrative of the *Life* as "present" (πάρεισι) at the same time as Jesus' "rising" (ἄνοδον) into heaven. Reminiscent of the opening chapter of the canonical Acts, the author here places the reader in the archaic Christian past, a time of nostalgic value as much (or more) for a fifth-century historian as for a first or second. Moreover, he is here reestablishing the basic fact about Thekla, that she was the first female martyr:

> Again, at this time, Thekla too was present (πάρεισι): not that she came after numerous martyrs, nor indeed after numerous female ones, but that she is immediately in second place (δευτέρα εὐθύς) after the apostles and the martyr Stephen, whom the word of truth knows as first (πρῶτον οἶδεν ὁ λόγος τῆς ἀληθείας). But she was first among all the women (πρώτη δὲ πασῶν γυναικῶν), so that Stephen was reckoned the leader among the men fighting on behalf of and through Christ, and Thekla the leader among the women, having fought in similar contests.
>
> *Life* 1.11–18

There is no mention of Stephen in the original *ATh*, which, in turn, indicates that the tradition of Thekla as the first Christian female martyr had probably

---

[12] This is a argument that he continues in the preface to the *Miracles*, where he compares the oracles found in Herodotus to the posthumous healing work of Thekla at Seleukeia: *Mir.* preface 73–77.

grown up since the late second century, the date of the *ATh*. In other words, if Thekla had achieved by the second century the same protomartyr status that she held in late antiquity, then Stephen would likely have been mentioned in the *ATh*. His conspicuous absence perhaps demonstrates that the *ATh* was, in the early period of Christian literature, read as just one of many martyr acts, yet by the fifth century it had become one of the most authoritative of these—authoritative enough to establish Thekla's primacy among the female saints.[13]

This primacy is due mostly to her association with Paul, whose historical character was becoming more and more popular in the late fourth and fifth centuries. Indeed, after associating Thekla with Stephen, the author of the *Life* continues his scene-setting by introducing Paul into the narrative.

> The divine Paul, being a Jew from birth, a persecutor, and a zealot for the patriarchal Law, as he himself says somewhere, was nevertheless deemed worthy of divine baptism and preaching (ἀξιωθεὶς δὲ τοῦ θείου βαπτίσματος καὶ κηρύγματος), and of being an apostle—precisely how is what we have learned from the blessed Luke—and he himself ended up on his apostolic course.[14]
>
> *Life* 1.19–23

The references here to Paul's own letters as well as to, once again, the canonical Acts of the Apostles are indicative of one of the motivations for paraphrase which will be further examined in the next chapter—that is, certain casual, suggestive details in the scriptures could provide a tantalizing window on a world accessible only to the imagination. It was standard practice for ancient writers to attempt to invent or reconstruct history on the basis of a few tidbits of information.[15] In the *Life*, of course, the windows are already offered by its *Vorlage*, the *ATh*, but not just by that: the apostolic world of the New Testament was still very much a part of imaginative Christian writing, especially in Asia Minor—evidenced, for example, by the late fourth-century *Visio Pauli*,

---

[13] For the term protomartyr, see Bowersock 1995:75–76. Refer to the discussion in the Conclusion of this study for Thekla's cultic status in comparison with the Virgin Mary.

[14] The phrase ἀξιωθεὶς δὲ τοῦ θείου βαπτίσματος καὶ κηρύγματος is loosely repeated by Thekla as she prepares to baptize herself in Antioch: διὰ Παύλου. . .σφραγῖδος καὶ χάριτος ἠξίωσας (*Life* 20.10–11). This correspondence emphasizes the unity of thought between the two, as well as Thekla's inheritance of teaching from Paul, two themes which will come to the fore later in the *Life*.

[15] On historical forgery, or *Schwindelliteratur*, in antiquity, see Speyer 1971. See also Shils 1981:54–62: "The desire to know the past, to locate the present self in a setting of temporal depth, or to account for one's origin, is served by the memory of the individual, his elders, and by the historiographic discovery of what has been forgotten or never known. It is also served by imagination, which supplements or takes the place of memory when the latter fails" (52).

written most likely in Tarsus, Seleukeia's neighboring capital.[16] In addition, the religious landscape, including ancient cult sites like Thekla's at Seleukeia, could also provide windows on the past, opportunities for reconstruction and reinvention.[17]

## Paul teaches; Thekla responds

The initial, brief summary of Paul's ministry serves as an introduction in the *Life* for one of the most famous scenes from the *ATh*, that of Thekla's conversion to chastity by hearing the preaching of Paul from a neighboring window. This is, of course, not the first scene in the *ATh*: Paul's journey to Iconium, his arrival, and the famous "encratic beatitudes" all come before Thekla is even mentioned. In the original text Paul is described as having fled Antioch along with two sycophants Demas and Hermogenes, to whom Paul witnessed along the way (cf. Acts 13:48–14:1). A resident of Iconium, Onesiphorus, and his family prepared a place for Paul to stay in the town, "Titus" having informed them what Paul looked like. Then follows a description of Paul's appearance— "small in size, bald-headed, bandy legged, of noble mien, with eyebrows meeting, rather hook-nosed, full of grace" (*ATh* 3). Paul's proto-ascetic speech, the "encratic beatitudes," is then reported, echoing Matthew 5:

> Blessed are the merciful, for they shall obtain mercy and shall not see the bitter day of judgment; blessed are the bodies of the virgins (παρθένων), for they shall be well pleasing to God and shall not lose the reward of their chastity (ἀγνείας). For the word of the Father shall become to them a work of salvation in the day of his Son, and they shall have rest for ever and ever.
>
> *ATh* 6

The *Life* includes this speech after the narrative introduction of Thekla and her place at the window, but, as we shall see, it is significantly changed. For now it is enough to point out that the opening of the story has been substantially reworked to achieve certain goals. What is gained by the original telling, and lost in the *Life*, is Thekla's subsequent, dramatic appearance at the window; however, what is gained in the paraphrase is a heightened awareness of Thekla as protagonist.

---

[16] On the *Visio Pauli*, see Hennecke and Schneemelcher 1992:2.712–748, Elliott 1999:616–644, Dinzelbacher 1991, and Kirsti Copeland 2000.

[17] On the visual imagination in pilgrimage contexts, see Frank 2000, Elsner 1997, and, more theoretically, Schama 1995.

The opening description in the *Life* therefore reads as a conscious, artful attempt at drawing together multiple traditions concerning Paul and Thekla, including the canonical Acts. The *Life*'s description of Thekla at the window, while coming much earlier than it does in the *ATh*, nevertheless gains a certain dramatic element, as the pair draw near to one another unwittingly. Thekla is described as a well born young virgin, who "was often the object of thought and rivalry among many of the fortunate young men" of Iconium. When she settles on a fiancé, Thamyris—a liaison negotiated by her mother Theocleia—she is satisfied and seats herself, still "in the darkness of error," by that fateful window. As Paul's words begin to waft her way from the neighboring house, she is transfixed:

> She was struck from the start, as if hearing some strange and foreign voice (ξένης καὶ ἀήθους φωνῆς)—Christ wanted it this way, in order to assure the capture of such a beautiful prey. And understanding certain words of the divine lesson (θείας ἀκροάσεως), she was immediately vexed in her soul by the words, and she remained fixed (προσπήγνυται) at the window by the words of Paul as if by some adamantine nails.
>
> *Life* 1.51–56

Paul's opening speech in the *Life* comes immediately after this quotation, but its content is completely different from the *ATh*: the famous "encratic beatitudes" have been rewritten by the author of the *Life*. Their heavy emphasis on virginity as a way to salvation is replaced by a series of musings on the coincident beauty of marriage and celibacy. This is perhaps a reflection of the effect of the closing of the canon of Pauline writings, not yet completely formed in the middle of the second century, but taken as fact in the fifth. Texts urging chastity, such as 1 Corinthians 7, were now in the same corpus as later, more lenient teaching, like Ephesians 5:22–33, which paints a comparatively positive picture of the married life.[18] Of course, few late antique writers (like second-century writers before them) were ever very careful to balance their picture of Pauline sexual ethics, but the author of the *LM* takes some pains to de-asceticize the *ATh*'s portrait of Thekla—not completely erasing the ascetic but toning it down significantly, perhaps to be in line with the fuller Pauline

---

[18] The author of the *ATh* alludes to 1 Corinthians 7:29 and Romans 8:17 in Paul's speech, though most of the allusions are understandably to Matthew. On the nuances of the sexual ethics urged in 1 Corinthians 7, which the author of the *ATh* has clearly not picked up on, see Brown 1988:53–54: "If anything, it is striking how little weight Paul placed on the fact that he was, apparently, unmarried or had left a wife."

corpus, perhaps also in response to the anti-encratic movement of the late fourth and early fifth centuries.

Paul's speech in the *Life* begins with a meditation on "that blessed one" (μακαριστὸς ἐκεῖνος), the Christian who "views God eternally and unhindered" (*Life* 2.11–12).[19] He does not once give into the "the most shameful of pleasures" but lives a "spotless" and "blessed" life. Yet no less "blessed," says the author, are those who live in holy marriage, according to the commands of God, but they must limit their relations to the production of children (2.17–22). Even still, those who live as virgins from baptism are the best of all (2.22–27). The latter are "zealous for the life of angels on earth" (τὸν τῶν ἀγγέλων ἐπὶ γῆς βίον) and they do not "defile the garment of Christ (τὸ ἔνδυμα τοῦ Χριστοῦ) through shameful works and deeds" (2.27–32). At this point the author closes Paul's speech with a general admonition for all categories of Christians to be zealous for the poor and to maintain "the chief of the virtues"—that is, "faith in Christ"—and to receive in turn "the whole body of piety (εὐσεβείας)." Emphasized at the end are the rewards of "rest" (λήξεως) and "crowns and prizes" (στεφάνων καὶ ἄθλων) in heaven and the threat of "Hades" to those who fail to gain the crowns (2.34–43).

The language is almost completely biblical, and mostly Pauline, and is thus on its own unremarkable. However, when compared with its source text, this passage's adherence to Pauline themes—particularly to the characteristic mingling of personal and corporate "body" imagery—is very striking.[20] There is an agreement between the texts that eternal life, the angelic state, and a virginal calling on earth are equivalent, a common theory in late antique Christian, especially Syriac, thought.[21] Otherwise, the mention of the married life as commendable reveals the *Life*'s attempt at rendering a more complete picture of Pauline teaching. This revised speech of Paul, once programmatic for the sexual ethics of the *ATh*—and indeed for the whole legend—is in fact now also strikingly programmatic for the *LM* but for a completely different reason: the wider picture of New Testament history and thought has become the backdrop for Thekla's story. Much more emphasis is placed here on the

---

[19] The theme of divine vision ("perfect," "unhindered," "omnipresent," "omniscient," etc.) is a favored one in the *Life*. It recurs in the *Miracles* as an example of the implicit definition of Thekla's post-disappearance, spiritual state (e.g. *Mir.* 22.7).

[20] Hardly noticed in New Testament scholarship is the ease with which the *ATh* places Jesus' Sermon on the Mount from Matthew 5 in the mouth of Paul. This wholesale reworking of the beatitudes deconstructs authoritative personae and their teaching within a century or so of their being written down. Nevertheless, this deconstruction corresponds well to the picture of early Christian textuality presented in Chapter Two below.

[21] See Brown 1988:95–102 with references.

documents received from the period—Acts of the Apostles, of course, but Paul's letters as well—and the felt need for precision on the topic of Pauline sexual ethics seems indicative of an awareness of the boundaries (and depth) of the apostolic inheritance.

Following Paul's speech the *Life* resumes its description of Thekla at the window. However, the *ATh*, as mentioned above, introduces Thekla here for the first time, a delay which adds drama to the scene (lost in the *Life*):

> And while Paul was speaking in the midst of the church in the house of Onesiphorus, a certain virgin (πάρθενος) named Thekla—the daughter of Theocleia—betrothed to a man named Thamyris, was sitting (καθεσθεῖσα) at the window close by the house and listened (ἤκουεν) day and night to the discourse of virginity, as proclaimed by Paul.

> *ATh* 7

In the *Life* a contrast is made between those who are able to see Paul by being with him at Onesiphorus' house and Thekla, who can only hear and imagine him:

> Some were present and listening (ἀκρωμένων), but she, not being present, and not seeing Paul, nevertheless grasped (ἐδράττετο) Paul's words, and was held fast (ἀπρίξ) at the window, as if it were [an instrument] supplying to her the beloved sound, and as if it were making her in no way inferior to those watching and standing around Paul.[22]

> *Life* 3.14–19

This brief *ekphrasis* on the famous window where she heard the teaching of Paul for the first time also serves as a lesson on imagination and, further, could be read as a foreshadowing of Thekla's omnipresence at Seleukeia as displayed in the *Miracles*. While "held fast" in one place, her spiritual self is present with Paul already through the sound, which is relayed somehow through the physical window itself.

Because of the strangeness of Thekla's "adamantine" position at the window and her "passionate excitement for the stranger" (*Life* 3.26), Thekla's mother Theocleia summons her fiancé Thamyris to speak with her. In the *ATh* Theocleia explains to him without emotion:

> I have a story (διήγημα) to tell you, Thamyris. For three days and three nights Thekla has not risen from the window either to eat or to

---

[22] "À la fenêtre comme à l'instrument" (Dagron 1978:181).

drink; but looking earnestly as if on some pleasant sight (εὐφρασίαν), she is devoted to a foreigner (ἀνδρὶ ξένῳ) teaching deceitful and artful discourse (ἀπατηλοὺς καὶ ποικίλους λόγους) ... He says one must fear only one God and live in chastity (ζῆν ἀγνῶς).

*ATh* 8–9

The scene as it is told in the *ATh* is thus wooden and unimaginative.[23] By contrast, the author of the *Life* takes this opportunity to demonstrate his abilities at narrative expansion by inventing a long speech for the mother:

Your Thekla has left behind what we hoped and prayed for her, and she shows contempt for me her mother, and for you her suitor, and she does not wish to know anything about the affairs of this house; but she loves (ἐρᾷ) some stranger (ξένου), a charlatan (ἀπατεῶνος) and a vagabond (πλάνου), who has descended on the house just next door—to the detriment of ours! ... Therefore, hurry up, Thamyris, and make haste to strip from her hands that which has already turned her attention to that other man [i.e. the window], and call her back again to us, and preserve the time-honored prosperity of the family, yours and mine.

*Life* 3.46–56

Theocleia has been given a personality and here conveys something more of the imaginable horror a respected matron could feel at her daughter succumbing to an itinerant preacher. Her new character takes on added importance in the narrative of the *Life*, and, consequently, her later condemnation of Thekla before the judge at Iconium is somewhat more emotionally charged.

Thamyris' much lengthened address to Thekla in the *Life* offers a heightened sense of dramatic romance not deployed in the *ATh*. The latter text reads:

And Thamyris greeted her with a kiss, but at the same time being afraid of her overpowering emotion said, "Thekla, my betrothed, why do you sit (κάθησαι) thus? And what sort of feeling holds you distracted? Come back to your Thamyris and be ashamed (αἰσχύνθητι)."

*ATh* 10

---

[23] Theocleia's description of Thekla in the *ATh*, though stilted, does have echoes in the *Life*: cf. *ATh* 9, "Moreover, my daughter, clinging to the window like a spider (ὡς ἀράχνη ἐπὶ τῆς θυρίδος δεδεμένη), lays hold of what is said by him with a strange eagerness and fearful emotion (ἐπιθυμίᾳ καινῇ καὶ πάθει δεινῷ)."

In its attempts to improve upon the *ATh*, the *Life* brings to the fore here a conflict between two young lovers, characteristic of earlier novelistic works like the Jewish novella *Joseph and Aseneth*.[24] Thamyris' attempt to play on her aristocratic sensibilities is a new addition in the *Life*. Likewise, the romantic link between the Thekla and "the stranger" is newly felt by Thamyris as he reports what other, respectable Iconians are saying about her repudiation of his love and her own family loyalties:

> That man sings (προσᾴδει), seated at a window, but this girl has been captured by his songs (ᾄσμασιν) and is riveted to a window. Her mother is despised while counseling and questioning her every hour, and her fiancé is despised—her soon-to-be husband—who admonishes and implores her. She is entirely for that man [Paul], for his words and for his deceptive charms (δολερῶν ἰύγγων).
>
> *Life* 4.27–32

The author of the *Life* reveals in his heightening of the scene how such meager elements of the legend, like the window, have become romanticized in the cultural context of Thekla's received character. These small details of the original story have been transformed into a literary iconography, and the *Life*'s author's attempt at bringing into relief the romance between Paul and Thekla, through Thamyris' invented speech, shows a late antique, literary iconographer at work. The love triangle between Thamyris, Thekla, and Paul is also part of this literary iconography, and the techniques used here are clearly borrowed from other, earlier novelistic texts (including other apocryphal acts) that play on the social sympathies of the characters. The values of an itinerant preacher are contrasted with social order among the wealthy in a provincial town: while certainly a topos of apocryphal acts generally, this element seems to have had special resonance in the late fourth and fifth centuries.[25]

## Demas and Hermogenes accuse Paul

In both the *ATh* and the *Life*, Thamyris, leaving Thekla's house, seeks out Paul. On his way to the apostle he runs into Demas and Hermogenes, Paul's shady companions from Pisidian Antioch. These traitors are only too willing to help Thamyris against Paul, in both accounts.[26] However, the liberties the *Life* takes

---

[24] For *Joseph and Aseneth*, see Wills 2002:121–162.

[25] E.g. here and in the fourth-century Latin translation of the *Acts of Peter*: see Christine Thomas 2003:61–64.

[26] A Hermogenes is mentioned as having deserted Paul in 2 Timothy 1:15—this one is called "the coppersmith" at *ATh* 1.

with its source are for the sake of bringing out the psychology of the two and serve as an interesting attempt at portraying anti-apostolic jealousy.[27] The two respond to Thamyris' questioning with similar sentiments to those found in Thamyris' speech to Thekla:

> This stranger, whence he comes and who he is, we do not know well; only that he is a deceiver and a wanderer (ἀπατέων καὶ πλάνος), and while veering away from the common arrangement of life and good order he has corrupted everything . . . This man tries to throw out, to overturn and to destroy, with all his strength, the path designed by nature itself for the race of men: namely, that of marriage and having children.
>
> *Life* 5.22–28

Demas and Hermogenes rhetorically paint the blackest picture of Paul they can but are implicated from the beginning as much by saying they do not know where Paul comes from as by the substance of their accusations. The theme of Paul's rejecting or altering Nature recurs at a later point in the *Life* when Paul is arraigned before the judge at Iconium (*Life* 6): clearly the author of the *Life* is trying to correct something like the "encratic" image of Paul that condemns marriage and requires virginity for salvation.

Demas and Hermogenes report what Paul has been so disturbingly teaching: "There is for you no resurrection unless you remain chaste and do not pollute the flesh" (*ATh* 12). According to the original text this is truly an accurate summary of the "encratic beatitudes" speech from *ATh* 5–6 (quoted above). However, in the *Life* this accusation is not at all in concert with Paul's rewritten speech at the house of Onesiphorus. The duplicity of Demas and Hermogenes is thus brought to the fore in the *Life*, since what they report about Paul is much more rigorous and perverts the balanced picture of chastity and marriage offered in his earlier speech. The reader recognizes this duplicity from the description of the two as well as from their reporting on Paul to Thamyris. The careful reader, however, would also note that there is here in the *Life* an implicit rejection of the picture of Paul as presented in its source text. The condemnation of Paul by Demas and Hermogenes becomes a condemnation of the *ATh* since the accusation they make against the apostle is what he actually did teach in the "encratic beatitudes."

---

[27] The treachery of Demas and Hermogenes in the *ATh* perhaps owes something to Luke's portrayal of Simon Magus in the sense that both authors set up apostolic rivals whose powers are shown to be fruitless (Acts 8:9–24). On Simon Magus, see Edwards 1997.

However, the picture of Demas and Hermogenes, and consequently of Paul, in the *Life* is even more sophisticated than this. The two sycophants have turned Paul's preaching on resurrection into a reductionistic philosophy, which serves as a caricature of pagan critics unwilling to come to grips with the import of Paul's sexual ethics in a broader frame of Christian thought. Their take on Paul's teaching on resurrection is explored in the following passage:

> He is trying to proclaim and to introduce a certain resurrection for those long dead and for the bodies decomposing in the earth, a novel practice also never heard from anyone before. The true and authentic resurrection in human nature itself is preserved and accomplished daily: the succession of children born from us (with the image of those parents who conceived and bore them being renewed afresh on their children) is and tends to be some way of being raised again, so that those who were alive long ago appear among the living again and are seen among the men around them.
>
> *Life* 5.31–41

Even if it is taken into account that these two wrongful accusers are supposed to be offering a perversion of Paul's teaching, their summary here of Paul's teaching on resurrection is exceptionally superficial. They are portrayed as legitimately reductionistic with regard to Paul's teaching on the resurrection. Therefore, the force of Thamyris' questioning them is to bring these characters into relief. Already sufficiently evil in the *ATh*, they are highlighted (and somewhat caricatured) in the *Life* and shown to be much less knowledgeable about Paul's teaching, which the author of the *Life* has taken pains elsewhere to represent more accurately.

Paul is dragged before the court

Following this encounter in the *ATh*, Thamyris takes the two to his home for dinner, during which they offer their host the idea of bringing Paul before the governor Castellius (14). Rising in the morning, Thamyris goes to the house of Onesiphorus "with rulers and officers and a great crowd with batons (ἀρχόντων καὶ δημοσίων καὶ ὄχλου ἱκανοὺς μετὰ ξύλων)" to apprehend Paul.[28]

---

[28] These groups are altered in the *Life* to read, "some other citizens and town councilors and men willing to undertake anything (μετὰ δημοτῶν τινων καὶ ἀγοραίων καὶ πάντα τολμᾶν εἰθισμένων ἀνθρώπων)." For the meanings of the multivalent titles δημοτῶν and ἀγοραίων, see Dagron 1978:189n1; he translates the phrase, "des hommes du peuple et du marché, gens habitués à tout oser."

The crowd cries out, "Away with the sorcerer (τὸν μάγον) for he has corrupted (διέφθειρεν) all our wives!" (15), and then the scene moves immediately without any further elaboration to the tribunal and Thamyris' opening accusation.

This transition between Thamyris' banquet with Demas and Hermogenes and the trial of Paul provides evidence in the *Life* of the author's stated intention of altering the style/diction (λέξις) of the work (preface 18), as in the following example from Thamyris' speech before the governor:

> Everything was full of uproar, disorder, and wailing, as if enemies had suddenly fallen on the town and they were plundering everything.[29] Together with this mob Thamyris made a great stride (ἔθει μακρὰ βιβάς), one might say poetically (ποιητικῶς), to the tribunal (τὸ δικαστήριον), and led Paul before the court (παρὰ τῇ δίκῃ) with his own hand, as if having wrenched some tyrant from the acropolis (ὡς ἄν ἐξ ἀκροπόλεως τύραννόν τινα καθῃρηκώς). Coming into the judgment circle (εἴσω δὲ τῆς δικαστικῆς κιγκλίδος) and standing before the bema (ἐπὶ τοῦ βήματος), he began with the following words.

*Life* 6.20–27

The poetic rhetoric is thicker here, appearing again as part of the author's heightened emphasis on what he considers to be crucial scenes. His allusion, "Thamyris made a great stride," is to Homer's descriptions of Ajax's striding, e.g. *Iliad* 7.213 and 15.686 (both also, ἔθει μακρὰ βιβάς; cf. *Odyssey* 9.450).[30]

Thamyris' formal accusation before the judge (δικαστής) is written in similar terms to those used by Demas and Hermogenes, repeating their feigned ignorance of who Paul is and where he comes from, "For he is a stranger and unknown to any of us" (6.37–38). He also reiterates the theme that Paul's teaching is contrary to the natural order, adding a litany of human activities and institutions that would have been impossible without marriage and children:

[29] This is perhaps a reference to contemporary brigandage in fifth-century Isauria, on which see Chapter Three below.

[30] These three allusions to Homer are cited by Dagron 1978:191n3, but there are several more uses of μακρὰ βιβάς (or μακρὰ βιβάσθων or μακρὰ βιβᾶσα) in the Homeric epics: *Iliad* 13.809 (Ajax), 15.307 (Hector), 15.676 (Ajax), 16.534 (Glaukos), and *Odyssey* 11.539 (Ajax). The use of "long-striding" at *Odyssey* 9.450 is blind Polyphemus' description of the ram Odysseus escapes underneath. The formulaic descriptions of Ajax are probably what the author had in mind for Thamyris. Instances of Homeric language in the *LM* seem stale and forced; these allusions always serve the purpose of poetic diction and never appear to be thematically related to the narrative. Homer is explicitly named at several points in the *LM*: *Life* 27.58; *Mir.* 16.14–15, 27.19, 35.14–15, 38.15, 44.33. In addition, Plato is alluded to a few times (*Mir.* 14.31–32, 26.16, 39.4–5), as is Euripides (*Mir.* 13.7–8, 33.62–63). For these and other references, see Dagron 1978:157.

... families, cities, fields, and villages ... empire, rule, laws, rulers, justice, soldiers, and generals ... temples, sacred precincts, sacrifices, initiations, mysteries, prayers, and entreaties. All of these things ... are accomplished and performed through men, and man is the orchard of marriage (ἄνθρωπος δὲ γεώργιόν ἐστι γάμου).[31]

*Life* 6.42–51

This passage contrasts with Thamyris' speech in the *ATh*, which is much more succinct: "O proconsul, this man—we do not know where he comes from—makes virgins averse to marriage. Let him say before you why he teaches thus" (16). Thamyris' small role in such a defining scene in the *ATh* offers the author of the *Life* an opportunity for expansion, in order to display the values of pagan Iconian society, vis-à-vis Paul's Christian testimony that follows.

Paul's defense before the governor becomes a completely different speech in the *Life*. Unlike in the *ATh*, Paul here does attempt to counter the specific accusations against him. Of course, in the *ATh* those accusations, particularly that he drives women to virginity, were true according to his reported preaching. Moreover, consistent with the *Life*'s attempt to approximate Paul's broader sexual ethics in the sermon at Onesiphorus' house, Paul's speech in the Iconian court shows the *Life*'s ability to draw on multiple sources of Pauline teaching.

In the *Life* Paul opens by countering the charges against him. He claims that he is not the "creator and inventor" (δημιουργὸς οὔτε εὑρετής) of his teachings but, rather, God is truly their creator and their teacher (*Life* 7.5–8). Paul then launches into a theological diatribe that bears no resemblance at all to the source text. Thus Paul begins in the *ATh*:

The living God, the God of vengeance, the jealous God, the God who has need of nothing, who seeks the salvation of men, has sent me that I may rescue them from corruption (φθορᾶς) and uncleanliness (ἀκαθαρσίας) and from all pleasure (ἡδονῆς), and from death, that they may sin no more.[32]

*ATh* 17

---

[31] Thamyris is made to use Pauline language here: at 1 Corinthians 3:9, Paul says that Christians are the γεώργιον θεοῦ. Educated Christian readers of the fifth century would certainly have recognized the irony of this allusion.

[32] Although there appears to be no direct quote in this speech of any single Pauline text, the language is innocuously Pauline: e.g. "uncleanliness" (ἀκαθαρσία) is found with the same sense (i.e. moral impurity; synonymous with πορνεία) at 2 Corinthians 2:12, Galatians 5:19, Colossians 3:5, Ephesians 5:3, and passim.

A comparison with the same speech from the *Life* is instructive as to how far theological language had come since the mid second century. The formulae used by Paul in the *Life* are clearly post-Nicene:

> Therefore on account of these and many other evil acts of irreverence, God took pity, as I have said, and had compassion for this nature (οἰκτιζόμενος τὴν φύσιν ταύτην), so that, while being its molder and creator (πλάστης καὶ δημιουργός), he discharged us apostles through his only begotten Child (Παιδός) to go out and visit the entire earth, and to cleanse it from the evils I described and others I omitted, but also to introduce faith, knowledge of God, piety (εὐσέβειαν), and most of all that which characterizes and betokens (τεκμηριοῖ) the Father, Son, and Holy Spirit, the holy and worshipped Trinity (ἡ ἁγία καὶ προσκυνητὴ Τριάς), the uncreated (ἄκτιστος) and same-substance (ὁμοούσιος) divinity, the eternal (ἀΐδιος) and unchanging (ἀναλλοίωτος), the inseparable (ἀχώριστος) and incomprehensible (ἀπερίγραφος), transcending time (ὑπέρχρονος) and the visible world (ὑπέρκοσμιος), sharing the same honor (ὁμότιμος) and the same throne (ὁμόθρονος) and the same glory (ὁμόδοξος), impalpable (ἀναφής), unfathomable (ἀπερίληπτος), upon which all things depend and to which all things run, and from which nothing has been separated (κεχωρισμένον).
>
> *Life* 7.38–50

Still central to the speech are the divine epithets—e.g. "unchanging, undivided, and incomprehensible"—but instead of being divine self-descriptions from Exodus (e.g. "living," "jealous," etc.), they have become technical terms from late antique Trinitarian theology. The language of the speech has thus ceased to be strictly Pauline, or even Biblical, and is now made up of theological terminology.

Not surprisingly, the terminology seems to be mainly Constantinopolitan in its creedal significance (AD 381); even though some of these terms were used in the Christological debates of the fifth century, their valence here is clearly Cappadocian.[33] In fact, there is a significant lexical correspondence between this passage and parts of Gregory of Nazianzus' three sermons "On Peace" (*Orations* 6, 21, and 23; PG 35). One passage from these orations is particularly similar to Paul's speech quoted above:

---

[33] See the Conclusion to this study below (pp. 222–223).

Ἕν γὰρ οὐχ ὑποστάσει, ἀλλὰ θεότητι· μονὰς ἐν Τριάδι προσκυνου-
μένη, καὶ Τριὰς εἰς μονάδα ἀνακεφαλαιουμένη, πᾶσα προσκυνητή,
βασιλικὴ πᾶσα, ὁμόθρονος, ὁμόδοξος, ὑπερκόσμιος, ὑπέρχρονος,
ἄκτιστος, ἀόρατος, ἀναφής, ἀπερίληπτος, πρὸς μὲν ἑαυτὴν ὅπως
ἔχει τάξεως, αὐτῇ μόνῃ γινωσκομένη, σεπτὴ δ' ἡμῖν ὁμοίως καὶ
λατρευτὴ, καὶ μόνη τοῖς Ἁγίοις τῶν ἁγίων ἐμβατεύουσα.

*Oration 6; PG 35.749*

Not one in substance, but in divinity. One worshipped singly in
Three; Three recapitulated in One. All worshipped, all kingly,
sharing the same throne, the same glory, heavenly, transcending
time, uncreated, invisible, impalpable, unfathomable, unto itself in
order/rank, being known to itself alone, but it is likewise sacred and
worshiped by us, and alone enters the Holy of Holies.

This selection from Gregory's first sermon "On Peace" (*Oration* 6) contains eight
of the same terms as epithets of the Trinity as in Paul's speech: προσκυνητή,
ἄκτιστος, ὑπέρχρονος, ὁμόθρονος, ὁμόδοξος, ἀναφής, ἀπερίληπτος. Further,
two pairs of these terms are in the same order in which they are used by Paul
in the *Life*: ὁμόθρονος/ὁμόδοξος and ἀναφής/ἀπερίληπτος. While this alone
is not incontrovertible proof of quotation, there is sufficient agreement, in
this selection and throughout Cappadocian writings, to show that the author
of the *Life* was actively gathering post-Nicene Trinitarian formulae.[34] The
epithets appear elsewhere in Gregory's corpus, as well as occasionally in the
other Cappadocians, and the accumulation of agreements is suggestive of
conscious borrowing.[35]

More significant perhaps than the potential allusions in Paul's speech is
the fact that the author of the *Life* did not find it aesthetically displeasing to put

---

[34] The term "inseparable" (ἀχώριστος) from the *Life* passage, while not used by Gregory in *Oration*
6, does appear twice in *Oration* 21 in similar contexts (i.e. the union of the Trinity; PG 35.1160.30
and 1164.10); this term was employed by both Theodore of Mopsuestia and Nestorius in the
fifth century in reference to the union of Christ's natures (see Lampe s.v. "ἀχώριστος"), but this
sense would clearly be out of place in the passage quoted above. Dagron 1978 does not list any
verbal parallels with the Cappadocians at this point or anywhere else in the LM.

[35] E.g. the terms ὁμόθρονος and ὁμόδοξος appear together in Gregory of Nyssa's *Against
Eunomius* (3.3.36); ὁμόθρονος appears with ὁμότιμος and ὁμοούσιος (and σύνθρονον) in
Basil of Caesarea's *Against Eunomius* (PG 29.760.27). It should be noted that all of these terms,
though coined in the late fourth century, were part of creedal formulae that would have been
widely known and acknowledged by the mid fifth century. The *Life's* partiality for Gregory of
Nazianzus may have had something to do reciprocally with Gregory's partiality for Thekla (for
the latter, see Dagron 1978:55–56). For the appeal to the Cappadocians as a commonplace in
later Greek writing, see Averil Cameron 1990.

into the mouth of the apostle technical language from fourth and fifth century theology. His nostalgia for apostolic times and literature thus only extended so far, and he consciously removed the strictly Pauline language from the original speech to introduce specialized language of his own time, which would have been familiar from theological texts as well as from sermons.

This speech is helpful for showing that there were limits to the author's reconstruction of Paul: (near) contemporary theology and ecclesiastical issues also played an important role in his composition. Nevertheless, for the sake of consistency in the area of sexual ethics (obviously a concern for Thekla devotees), Paul does attempt to redress the accusation that he preaches only virginity, against Nature, and to the detriment of humanity. As noted above, there is no way for Paul to refute this charge in the original *ATh* since his beatitudes speech at Onesiphorus' house is certainly "encratic" in this sense, but that speech is rewritten in the *Life*, and, on that basis, the author has Paul acknowledge the divine character of both virginity and marriage:

> And this marriage is a remedy (φάρμακον) and an aid from God given to the whole race of men, being likewise an antidote (ἀλεξιφάρμακον) to fornication and a kind of spring (πηγή) and flowing and succession of our common race, instituted by the creator (δημιουργοῦ) of all himself for the salvation, preservation, and lasting life of men, succeeding one another and renewing in their turn ever-decaying nature.[36]
>
> *Life* 7.65–69

The *Life* is clearly struggling to combine several strands of Pauline teaching here while also attempting to answer seriously Thamyris' charge that virginity destroys the human race. The paraphrase genre allowed for this thoroughgoing revision, so that the author could bring a source text fully into a different thought world while maintaining the pretense of simply copying the original.

## Paul and Thekla's liaison in prison

Thekla returns to the story when Paul is thrown in prison awaiting the judge's decision on his punishment. In the *ATh*, Thekla goes to the jail, bribing her way through two gates with her bracelets and a silver mirror. Then, while sitting by Paul's feet she listens to "the deeds of God" and kisses his chains (*ATh* 18). The *Life* at this point emphasizes the rashness of her endeavor, attempting to

---

[36] The word "spring" (πηγή) is used for Thekla's post-disappearance healing shrine (*Life* 27.12).

heighten the dramatic tension of the moment: "she conceived and carried out a deed very rash for a young girl, very courageous for an older woman, and even very zealous for a Christian initiate" (*Life* 8.15–17). Thekla's clinging to Paul is certainly conceived of in romantic terms—she has left her fiancé for another man—but, as this quotation shows, there is already an element of the supernatural in Thekla's behavior. She does not behave as any normal woman, even as a Christian woman, would.

In fact, Thekla's movement or passage in the *Life* from the outside world into the prison is conceived of in terms of a late antique pilgrimage: she passes through certain necessary gates of access where she relinquishes her material possessions as bribes, which she does gladly; by these "inventions of female vulgarity," she "purchased the right of seeing (ἰδεῖν) Paul and marveling (θεάσασθαι) at him" (8.20). As Georgia Frank has recently written in her study of visual pilgrimage in late antiquity, "Pilgrims to holy places valued the sense of sight as a primary mode for religious understanding, even when their devotions at the holy places became increasingly tactile."[37] In the *Life*, Thekla's visual access to Paul is certainly emphasized over their tactile contact, even though the tactile (and auditory) element appears primary in its second-century source.

The first meeting of Paul and Thekla, therefore, takes place in the prison. In the *ATh*, this encounter is brief, since Thamyris, while looking for Thekla, discovers that she has gone to the other man—"chained to him in affection"—and then drags both of them before the tribunal. These scenes are imprecise in their detail: the author of the *ATh* was hurrying on to Thekla's first martyrdom. The *Life* takes the opportunity to elaborate the hastily written scenes by inserting a long speech of Paul to Thekla in the prison. Paul confesses to her his frustration that his words were not well received by the Iconians. Now that he has seen her devotion, however, his mind is put to rest and he rejoices:

> I was afraid of leaving this city without fruit and profit, failing to save a life or lead anyone to Christ. But behold, you yourself have appeared to me, materializing from I don't know where, and you have destroyed this fear.
>
> *Life* 9.5–9

Thekla is already playing the patroness/protectrix role that she takes up at the end of the *Life* and retains throughout the *Miracles*. In this speech Paul

---

[37] Frank 2000:104.

rehearses all that Thekla has given up "for piety and faith" (τῆς εὐσεβείας καὶ πίστεως; *Life* 9.12–13). Her renunciation, Paul says, was despised by the Devil (διάβολος), whom Thekla "will make a fool and will utterly destroy in an instant" (*Life* 9.22–23). Paul warns her of coming trials and how "the tyrant" will try to take his revenge on her. However, Paul predicts Thekla's future triumph, which he compares to that of Job (*Life* 9.37–38).

Paul concludes his exhortations with the assurance that she will be reckoned an apostle for her struggles and victory:

> For you will rule, I know well, over every weapon of war set against you, and you will conquer the tyrant in every situation; not by yourself alone but through many others. For you will teach many others and you will lead them to your bridegroom, like Peter, like John, like each of we apostles, among whom you yourself will certainly be counted, I know this well.
>
> *Life* 9.75–80

Taken as a whole, this additional speech serves to fill out a rough patch in the original text, but it also serves to promote a certain received version of what Thekla achieved, emphasizing her historic place among the martyrs of the early Church. Several elements are put in place to presage the spiritually-present Thekla who haunts Seleukeia in the *Miracles*: the comfort Thekla brings to Paul, the allusion to pilgrimage, and Paul's prediction of her reception into the company of the apostles—such as Peter, John, and himself who have already achieved success in their ministry. That the latter is an anachronistic assumption from the point of view of Paul in prison at Iconium (c. 50s AD?) is clearly not a paramount consideration for the author of the *Life*, since he (like the author of the *ATh*) is reconstructing the character of Paul from received tradition.

Following Paul's address to Thekla in the prison, the *Life* enters into a long description of the hunt for Thekla. This description includes a dramatic account of her mother's maidservants discovering that Thekla was missing while performing their morning chores. This section is an expansion of one sentence in the *ATh*: "And when Thekla was sought for by her family, and Thamyris was hunting through the streets as if she had been lost" (*ATh* 19). In the *Life* the scene of the maidservants' discovery, and the mourning and wailing which ensued, is interrupted by a view of Thekla sitting serenely at Paul's feet (*Life* 10.26–27). Thamyris, having discovered the truth, bursts onto the scene thinking that Paul has seduced Thekla in the prison. The love-triangle suggested by the vague narrative in the *ATh* has become in the *Life* an explicit case of misidentification.

A second appearance in court

Following their discovery, Thamyris grabs Paul and takes him before Kestillios the proconsul (named here for the first time in the *Life*): "with the townsfolk and citizens he had with him, he dragged Paul before the court" (10.48–51). This mob scene resembles the last, except that the more serious charges of "enslavement" and "seduction" are now at the fore of Thamyris' case against Paul (10.57). Kestillios, however, being sympathetic to Christianity for unexplained reasons, only "whipped Paul a little and expelled him from the city" (10.59).

The *ATh* account is more compressed but essentially the same except for three small differences. First, Paul is called "sorcerer" (μάγος) by the crowd, which is apparently the main charge against him. Second, mention is made of Thekla sitting "at the place where Paul sat while in prison" (*ATh* 20); Paul's cell is thus likened to the window where she heard Paul's words wafting from Onesiphorus' house. Third, "the governor," before ejecting Paul from the city, "gladly heard Paul speak about the holy works of Christ" (τοῖς ὁσίοις ἔργοις τοῦ Χριστοῦ; ibid.).

In the *Life* there is no mention of Paul preaching again to the governor; rather, simply "he was taken with the man, and there had entered into him some desire for what Paul said about piety (εὐσεβείας)" (*Life* 10.53–54). Εὐσέβεια ("piety," "devotion") is the author's normal description of Paul's teaching, to which Thekla clings: its generalized meaning probably helped him de-asceticize Thekla's character, while still keeping her personally devoted to Paul's counter-cultural stance.[38] By the end of the *Life* the word has taken on a programmatic significance for Thekla's ministry in Seleukeia.

Thekla's association with Paul has by this point been more directly affirmed than in the ambivalent *ATh*. This has been accomplished through an exaggerated personal devotion to the apostle, Paul's invented prophecy about her triumph as a martyr, and their romantic misidentification in the prison. However, Paul's authoritative role now recedes into the background as Thekla is brought forward for her own trial before Kestillios in Iconium.

The most striking element of Thekla's first trial scene in the *ATh* is her own mother Theocleia's demand that she be burnt for deserting Thamyris. She

---

[38] Other occurrences of εὐσέβεια include, *Life* 1.26, 36; 2.38; 3.4; 7.44; 8.21; 9.12, 59; 12.47; 18.18; 26.43, 51; 27.19, 21; cf. *Mir.* epilogue 38.

cries, "Burn the wicked one; burn her who will not marry in the midst of the theater, that all women who have been taught by this man may be afraid" (*ATh* 21). This outburst is removed in the *Life*, even though an invented speech by the proconsul clearly focuses on her refusal to marry.

His speech is an interesting amalgam of Thamyris' accusation against Paul and Paul's own defense, signaling Kestillios' vacillation between these two positions. Kestillios, on one hand, argues with Thamyris that marriage "fills the whole earth with men and other living things" (*Life* 11.20), and he also argues, playing on her aristocratic lineage, that marriage "guards the preserves the surnames (ἐπωνυμίας) of the families unmixed and distributes their inheritances to whom it is befitting when it is befitting" (11.30–32). However, he argues from an ethical point of view with Paul that marriage "through a lawful union, always prevents illicit relations and pleasures" (11.27–28). His arguments on procreation also have the ring of Paul's teaching on resurrection: "Each of us leaves this life without exception, but through marriage each replaces himself with another being similar to himself" (*Life* 11.37–38).

Compare Paul's earlier statement before Kestillios that "[marriage] was instituted by the creator (δημιουργοῦ) of everything for the salvation, preservation, and lasting life of men, succeeding one another and renewing in their turn ever-decaying nature" (*Life* 7.68–71). It seems the author of the *Life* is trying to show in these speeches that Paul's teaching is actually affecting the proconsul's thoughts on marriage, rather than simply stating that the "governor gladly heard from Paul about the works of Christ," as *ATh* 20 does.

Of course, the irony in all of this is that Thekla still chooses renunciation, even though the author has gone so far to resuscitate marriage. Thus, despite the proconsul's (Pauline) defense of marriage,[39] Thekla remains unmoved by his speech. In fact, she is so confident and resolved that the author likens her to the predator rather than to the prey: "Not compromising or bending to anything at all, she looked like some lion-cub (λεόντειος) amidst a herd of gazelles" (*Life* 11.9–11).[40]

Following this characterization, however, the author compares Thekla to Christ the lamb: "she stood there—if I may say so—like a silent lamb before her shearer, not seeking to utter anything, but dreaming of what and when she might suffer for Christ's sake" (12.7–10). There is thus a lack of confidence

---

[39] The proconsul goes so far as to suggest he officiate in Thekla and Thamyris' wedding (*Life* 11.57–59).

[40] This characterization anticipates her friendship with the lioness in the arena at Antioch (*Life* 18–19).

about how to portray the young martyr, as a conqueror or as a martyr, an ambivalence which is present in the Gospels' descriptions of Jesus himself.[41] Intriguingly, the author of the *Life* has signaled here his reluctance to liken her to Jesus—" if I may say so"—even though he is making use of a messianic interpretation of Isaiah 53:7 (see Acts 8:32).

Before he finally decides to burn her at the stake, the judge is once more described as divided in mind over his decision. Ultimately, he decides that Thekla should die because of Thamyris' "power" and "just anger" and because Kestillios "was influenced by opinions about Christians which at that time were around and being discussed" (12.27–29). This suggests the author of the *Life* was aware of secular criticisms of Christian sexual ethics in previous generations, perhaps even with specific relation to the legend of Thekla. Thus, the knowing statement that Kestillios consented to punishing Thekla because he was "just like other pagans of his day," so to speak, adds more weight to the hypothesis that the author is intentionally trying to write asceticism out of the original legend. This is because the argument that Christians renounce marriage as a matter of course is being implicitly condemned (in line with its explicit condemnation earlier). The character of Kestillios is therefore affected to some degree by the full Christian teaching on marriage and is sympathetic to it, but the combined weight of his prior assumptions and Thamyris' anger is simply too great to prevent the execution.

Thekla on the pyre

Following the judge's final condemnation of Thekla in the *ATh*, she casts about the tribunal, looking for Paul, "as a lamb in the wilderness looks for a shepherd." Instead of Paul, however, Christ appears to her, "in the likeness of Paul." In response she says her first words of the original story, "As if I were unable to endure, Paul has come to look after me." Next the Christ-Paul disappears into heaven while she is "gazing earnestly at him."

This scene is included in the *Life* but it happens once she is already on the pyre, a change which serves to increase her sense of abandonment. In the *Life*, Christ still appears to her in the form of Paul, but there is no intimation, as there is in the *ATh*, that Paul should have been present. Christ is thus not filling-in where Paul failed, "for she truly thought him to be Paul, and not Christ" (12.41–42), an aside which alleviates some of her disorientation in the original. Her first words, explicitly "to herself" in the *Life*, are typically expanded:

---

[41] Compare, for example, the application of Zechariah 13:7 to Jesus in Matthew 26:31 with the application of Psalm 118:26 to him in Luke 19:37–40.

Behold, Paul watches over me and protects me, lest bending, lacking conviction, and shrinking at the fire I betray the beautiful and blessed confession (ὁμολογίας). But rather, may it not be that I give up the Christ evangelized to me by you yourself, Paul, nor the piety (εὐσεβείαν), and disgrace your teaching (διδασκαλίαν). Only stay a little while, teacher (ὦ διδάσκαλε), and call Christ to my aid, so that by the breeze (τῇ αὔρᾳ) of the Spirit he may scatter and sprinkle this fire and he may strengthen the weakness of my nature (ἀσθένειαν τῆς φύσεως) through its help.

*Life* 12.43–51

The phrase "weakness of human nature" (ἡ ἀνθρωπίνης τῆς φύσεως ἀσθένεια) is originally Platonic (*Laws* 854a), but it finds its peculiar Christian expression in 2 Corinthians 13:4, where Paul says that "Christ was crucified out of weakness" (ἐσταυρώθη ἐξ ἀσθενείας). As Origen later pointed out, this concept is a conscious reversal of Plato's understanding of the broader import of human spiritual weakness (*Against Celsus* 3.42.11).

That the author of the *Life* had this Christian play on classical ἀσθένεια in mind is confirmed by the description of Thekla's actions immediately following: "and after these words, first tracing (ἐκτυπώσασα) the form (τὸν τύπον) of the cross on herself, and then even more, rendering (ἀπεικάσασα) her whole self in the form (τὸν τύπον) of the cross through the extending of both her hands . . ." (12.51–54). Her purpose, therefore, in word and gesture, is an imitation of Christ's crucifixion. This characterization was signaled earlier by the author's somewhat hesitant quotation of Isaiah 53:7.

It is important at this point to compare the visualization of her martyrdom in the *ATh*. The well known scene is succinctly described:

And the boys and girls brought wood and straw in order that Thekla might be burned. And when she came in naked the governor wept and admired the power that was in her. And the executioners arranged the wood and told her to go up on the pile. And having made the sign of the cross (ἡ τὸν τύπον τοῦ σταυροῦ ποιησαμένη) she went up on the pile. And they lit the fire. And though a great fire was blazing it did not touch her. For God, having compassion upon her, made an underground rumbling, and a cloud full of water and hail overshadowed the theater from above, and all its contents were poured out so that many were in danger of death. And the fire was put out and Thekla saved.

*ATh* 22

It is immediately clear that the author of the *Life* chose to interpret "the sign of the cross" from the *ATh* in a much more theologically rich manner, which calls upon Paul's (and perhaps Origen's) own anti-Platonic formulation of ἀσθένεια. Thus, in the *Life* the author has first exonerated Paul by removing the denigrating insinuation that the apostle had left Thekla to die. Second, the author has actually made Paul present in the language of Thekla's self-typology of "weakness" in martyrdom. The formulation is even more complex, however, since Christ, whose crucifixion is being imitated, is emphatically present in the theater with Thekla, watching her gesture the motions of a Pauline theology of his own execution!

In the *Life*, the fire is shamed by the cross and backs away from Thekla. The pyre thus becomes "a bridal-chamber (θάλαμος) rather than a furnace for the virgin" and it shields Thekla's nakedness from the crowd (12.58–59). The author says that the Babylonian furnace from Daniel 3 was "a similar philanthropy of fire" to Thekla's "bed-chamber" (κοιτωνίσκος): in both cases God "tamed" (ἡμερώσαντος) the blaze (12.62–65). The rest of the natural wonders—rain and hail—are described similarly to the *ATh*, except that the *Life* states openly that the downpour "drowned many of the Iconians," a claim the *ATh* does not make. In the latter "many were in danger of death," but God's wrath for Thekla's mistreatment has no place in the events.

### Reunion outside Iconium

In neither the *ATh* nor the *Life* is there a description of Thekla's escape from Iconium. The scene simply shifts to Paul and Onesiphorus outside the city, waiting by a prepared tomb to find out what ultimately happened to her. When she arrives at the tomb, Thekla comes upon Paul praying for her safety.

In the *ATh*, a child tells Thekla that Paul has been praying for her and fasting "for six days already." This strange statement does not fit the fast pace of the narrative thus far—there has been no indication that more than a day has passed—and it is understandably expunged from the *Life*. In the latter the reader does not immediately come upon the words of Paul, as in the *ATh*; rather, it is reported that Thekla only sees him praying for her, then she proceeds to utter her own prayer of thanksgiving.

This is a typical device in the *Life*: to substitute a summary for the actual text (here, the prayer of Paul), then to modify an existing speech, or to add an invented one, to try to offer a different perspective on the scene. Thekla's revised prayer is interesting for its theological language, similar in this way to Paul's final speech before the judge:

God, King and Blessed Creator (δημιουργέ) of everything, and Father (Πατήρ) of your great and only begotten Child (Παιδός), I give you thanks . . . for having seen this Paul, my savior (σωτῆρα) and teacher (διδάσκαλον), who preached to me the might of your kingdom and the greatness of your authority, as well as the unchanging (ἀπαράλλακτον), equal-in-power (ἰσοδύναμον), equal-in-state (ἰσοστάσιον) nature of divinity (θεότητος) within the Trinity (ἐν Τριάδι), the mystery of your only begotten Child's incarnation (ἐνανθρωπήσεως) . . .

*Life* 13.27–37

Thekla's student/teacher relationship with Paul is again pushed to the fore, much more so than in the *ATh*. And her reiteration of the late antique technical terminology—mimicking Paul's revised defense at Iconium—emphasizes their unity in thought and action. Post-Nicene Trinitarian language once again describes (anachronistically) the substance of their faith.

Paul's excitement at hearing Thekla's thanksgiving is heightened in the *Life*: he "springs up" from kneeling on the ground "as if from some machine" (καθάπερ ἔκ τινος μηχανῆς). He then gives thanks for Thekla's rescue from the fire, saying, "A martyr has been born, also a disciple (μαθήτρια), and a little later, an evangelist (εὐαγγελίστρια)" (13.53–55). Paul's anticipation of Thekla's fame as a preacher/teacher does not occur in the *ATh* and thus serves as another example of the predictive imprimatur given to Thekla by this author through Paul. He also seems to be attempting to iron out any ambivalence on the point of Thekla's teaching authority which (it might be argued) is present in the *ATh* itself, though it obviously appears more prominently in later tradition, such as in the aspersions cast on the *ATh* by Tertullian and Jerome (see the Introduction above).

Thus, just following this scene in the original, Thekla asks to become Paul's apostolic companion but is rebuffed:

And Thekla said to Paul, "I will cut my hair off and I shall follow (ἀκολουθήσω) you wherever you go." But he said, "Times are evil and you are beautiful. I am afraid lest another trial (ἄλλος πειρασμός) come upon you worse than the first and you do not withstand it and become cowardly (δειλανδρήσῃς)." And Thekla said, "Only give me the seal in Christ (τὴν ἐν Χριστῷ σφραγῖδα), and no trial shall bind me." And Paul said, "Thekla, be patient; you shall receive the water."

*ATh* 25

Scholars have debated the significance of Paul's warning to Thekla in this passage: what in particular does Paul mean by "the first trial"?[42] He appears to be referring simply to her first martyrdom, but he could also be referencing an unmentioned temptation to stay and marry Thamyris—the latter interpretation depends on Paul's mention of Thekla's beauty here. In either case, as Melissa Aubin has noted, this scene in the *ATh* serves to "produce frustration" in the believing reader who has just seen Thekla behave so heroically. It also serves to "discredit" Paul, who here "disenfranchises" his own pupil.[43]

In the *Life*, Paul's hesitancy is softened, and the drama of this crucial scene is intensified and made further to solidify Paul's historical (and theological) unity with Thekla—precisely the opposite implication from the skeptical tone of the original. Instead of a straightforward rebuke, Paul explains at length his reasons for delaying her baptism, and then, pressured by a second wave of Thekla's pleading, finally agrees to baptize her, though he asks her to wait a while, as in the original. Additionally, in the *Life* he invites her to come to Antioch with him, a partiality on Paul's part that is obscured in the *ATh* by the jarring rebuke. The *Life* reads, by contrast:

> "But nothing of the sort will prevail upon me," Thekla said, "for the God who helped me in the fire will always help me, even in other dangers, and even if the enemy will devise more complicated machines against us. Only give me, teacher, the seal in Christ (τὴν ἐν Χριστῷ σφραγῖδα). Armed with this weapon I will crouch before nothing, I will fear nothing, I will triumph over every danger, and I will triumph over every temptation and demon. Only give to me the seal in Christ (τὴν ἐν Χριστῷ σφραγῖδα)." . . . "Therefore," he said, "since this is your opinion, this will be; and now you will join me on the journey, and waiting a little while, you will attain the grace through holy baptism, grace which alone is the irresistible power of salvation, of security, and of faith for those who place all their hope and assurance in Christ."
>
> *Life* 14.26–39

---

[42] E.g. Burrus 1987:54 notes that this scene does not fit the typical structure of the "chastity story," to which she otherwise likens the *ATh*, but it is reminiscent of scenes of female abandonment in the Greek Romance, such as when Chaereas resigns himself to Callirhoe's death in Chariton (sections 6–8). Burrus argues that these dramatic agreements are based on shared oral folktales, but the argument for shared literary imitation of some sort is at least as strong.

[43] Aubin 1998:266–267.

Paul's response here assumes the rest of the story in the *ATh*, and it is through the character of Paul in particular that the author seems to be playing off of a prior knowledge of the legend. Paul's hastily sketched and often ambivalent role in the original *ATh* becomes in the *Life* a crucial authorial device for drawing out and manipulating his reader's narrative assumptions. It is, therefore, through the empty vessel of Paul's character that the author fills in contemporary theological formulations and predicts, or presupposes, Thekla's upcoming triumphs. In the *Life* Paul is a literary vehicle for connecting Thekla's apostolic origins to her status in contemporary faith and practice.

## Thekla in Antioch (*Life* 15–25)

### Intercepted by Alexander

Immediately following Paul's assurance to Thekla that she will be baptized, the *Life* provides a summary statement of the story so far, signaling the conclusion of her time in Iconium. "But these things happened thus in Iconium, and such was their completion. Which things are stronger than human nature, but are not unreasonable miracles of divine power" (*Life* 14.41–44). The author has thus read the *ATh* as a two-setting work, Iconium and Antioch.

The question of whether "Antioch" in the *ATh* is the Pisidian or Syrian city has been thoroughly debated without any resolution, and the various detailed arguments need not be reiterated here. Briefly, the two main points of discussion are, first, in the canonical Acts of the Apostles, Paul proceeds from Iconium to Pisidian Antioch, but, second, Alexander, the town councilor who assaults Thekla in "Antioch," is said to be "Syrian" in several manuscripts.[44]

It is enough to point out that the author of the *Life* recognized this apparent contradiction—later Byzantine editors of the *ATh* did not—and has tried to solve it by overtly conflating the "Antiochs" to Syrian Antioch.[45] Thus

---

[44] Alexander is also called συριάρχης ("Syriarch," i.e. a local wealthy organizer of games) in at least two manuscripts, which may in fact be the original reading since it makes more sense later in the story when he provides beasts for the arena. However, σύρος ("Syrian") is better attested, occuring in six manuscripts (LB 1.253). As noted above, the new critical text in preparation by Willy Rordorf for CCSA is still eagerly awaited. Currently the standard view is represented by Hennecke and Schneemelcher 1992:2.218–220, who also argue for Pisidian Antioch, following Schmidt 1936:115f. Nevertheless, Schneemelcher pleads for some latitude on the question of the redactor's consistency: "Rather is the author of this apocryphal work [the *Acts of Paul*] to a great extent a compiler...The author's purpose is the edification and upbuilding of the community, perhaps also the propagation of a particular 'image' of Paul. We may therefore conjecture that he did not set particular store upon the distinction of the two Antiochs" (219–220).

[45] Dagron 1978:44–47.

the author of the *Life* comments parenthetically in his introduction to the Antioch section:

> When they drew near to Antioch—I speak of the Antioch in Syria, the beautiful and great, where the beautiful and blessed name of "Christians" was first used; and not the Antioch in Pisidia, neighbor to Lycaonia, even though the Pisidians claim it.
>
> *Life* 15.1–4

This conflation serves as another example of the *Life*'s close attention to the details of its source text. It should be clear by now that part of the exercise of this paraphrase was ironing out perceived difficulties in the *ATh*.

Alexander, a libidinous aristocrat of Antioch, succumbs to Thekla's tremendous beauty as soon as the travelers approach the town. Her beauty is not mentioned at this point in the *ATh* but is played up in the *Life* to such a degree that it must be asked whether Alexander could have resisted at all. We have already noticed that a kind of fatalism permeates the *Life* due to its literary character: the paraphrase form naturally anticipates future events of the story because of its audience's familiarity with them.

Despite the honor the author of the *Life* has given to Syrian Antioch by insisting that it was the scene of Thekla's second, and most stunning martyrdom, he has at the same time made it out to be, like every *deme* (ἅπας δῆμος), a center of licentiousness. This reputation is in line with the type of place that would produce, as one of its leaders, the wanton Alexander:

> It reckons its happiness in those who delight it most and make it mad for pleasure . . . so that it revels above all in those who lead it via Bacchic frenzy toward every intemperance and delight.
>
> *Life* 15.21–25

Alexander is essentially evil because he represents the best that the evil-minded citizens can produce. He has the "order" (τάξις) of a town-councilor, but behaves towards Thekla in "disorder" (ἀταξία) and tries to procure Thekla from Paul, as if the latter were her pimp and panderer (μαστρωπὸς καὶ προαγωγός; 15.31–32).

In the original *ATh*, Paul comes off very badly at this point, not defending Thekla in the least, but rather disappearing at her point of greatest need. However, in the *Life* he appears more cunning when he tries to put Alexander off by suggesting Thekla is a boy: "Paul declared that the woman in no way belonged to him—and that he was not even sure that she was in fact a woman" (15.34–36). The first statement echoes the *ATh* (26), but the second is new.

This addition shows an awareness of the poor picture of Paul presented in the *ATh* and represents an attempt at rectifying the original, even though the revising is not as thorough here as it appears elsewhere. Dagron notes that this additional line suggests that Thekla has cut her hair, as she threatened to do above in *ATh* 25.[46] Whether or not she has cut her hair, her appearance is certainly already male to the degree that Paul can reasonably suggest she is not a woman (see *Life* 25.17–19). This is an interesting change to the *ATh*, since in the latter her safe travel from Antioch to Myra, following the second martyrdom, is predicated on her newly adopted male appearance in *ATh* 40. The addition in the *Life*, therefore, foreshadows that later transformation and perhaps also empties it of some of its drama, for the sake of resuscitating Paul in *ATh* 26.

In resisting Alexander's advances, Thekla pleads in the *Life* that her good birth should exempt her from such an outrage. The problem appears to be her aloneness, since Thekla also brings up her abandonment of Thamyris—she could have a husband if she wanted but instead has chosen to travel alone:

> For I am not wandering, as you reckon, between shameful loves fitting for you, trafficking my beauty and offering it up to anyone willing to pay—may it not be! May I not shame myself before God, my protector! May I not forget what I have entrusted to God and render false the pledges (συνθήκας) I made to him through Paul.
>
> *Life* 15.48–54

Her concern is with her own appearance as a solitary woman, not because she may be vulnerable to attack but because she seems to be a prostitute. She thus attempts to appeal to Alexander's aristocratic standing, which has already been duly emphasized in the condemnation of Antioch's moral standards. Aristocracy is also reemphasized in Thekla's response, which is to tear Alexander's *chlamys*, "that imposing and admired garment" and to knock off his "golden crown, brilliant and dazzling" (15.60–62).

Alexander decides, after swaying back and forth between "affection" and "hatred," to rush Thekla to the tribunal, accepting that he had been beaten by the girl. Thekla is thus described throughout this scene in severe masculine terms, which anticipate the male, proto-ascetic disguise that gets her safely to Myra:

> Now the excessively rough (λίαν ἀπηνές) and wild (ἀνήμερον) character of the girl was making her enemy more savage (ἀγριώτερον),

---

[46] Dagron 1978:231n5.

because he was outraged and despised and had completely succumbed to his illegitimate desire.

*Life* 15.79–81

As in the previous court appearances, the "illegitimate" (οὐκ ἐνδίκως) nature of the violence done to Thekla is contrasted with the Roman justice system supporting it. This contrast is not made explicit in political terms, but there is a consistent subversive diatribe in the *Life* against the authorities that side with Thekla's prosecutors like Alexander.

### Tryphaina, Falconilla, and the lioness

In the *ATh* there is no description of Thekla's trial at Antioch, only that she "confessed" and was condemned to wild beasts. In response to the speedy judgment, however, the "women of the city" complained *en masse* to the judge, crying out, "Evil judgment! Impious judgment!" (*ATh* 27). No reaction to this crowd is recorded, but Thekla asks the judge if she could "remain pure until she was to fight with the wild beasts," perhaps having taken encouragement from the pleading women. Again, the judge's response is not recorded, but Thekla appears successful in her request since she is entrusted to "Queen" Tryphaina (βασίλισσα), who not only protects Thekla from violence but who takes consolation in the girl, since her own daughter, Falconilla, has passed away. Tryphaina, later described as a "kinswoman" (συγγενής; *ATh* 36) of the emperor, is a name mentioned by Paul at Romans 16:12: "Greet those workers in the Lord, Tryphaina and Tryphosa." Her connection (perhaps as a freedwoman) to the Julio-Claudian imperial family is debated; but her role in the *ATh* is certainly designed to lend credence to that text's overall verisimilitude.[47]

The *Life*, following the *ATh*, neglects to report on the trial at Antioch, a more conservative approach than we saw with the invented speeches at Iconium. It does insert a comment, however, on Thekla's positive attitude: "Having been handed over, the virgin was nevertheless rejoicing in the trial, and she was already calling the judgment a victory and an addition to her

---

[47] For the identification of Queen Tryphaina with a certain "Antonia Tryphaina" known from first century coins, see references at Hennecke and Schneemelcher 1992:2.222; Dagron is skeptical, however (1978:235n2). He is right to suspect that this is just another expansion on a once-mentioned name in Paul's letters, as seen with "Hermogenes" above. But the title βασίλισσα as a technical term, combined with her being already a convert, does suggest that the *ATh* has attempted to identify the two Tryphainas (i.e. Paul's friend and the "Queen"), even if they were different women, as is likely.

martyrial battles" (16.1–3). This statement fits with the predictive theme apparent earlier in the speeches of Paul.

Tryphaina, Thekla's designated protector, is next introduced as "distinguished by her nearness [in lineage] to the emperor (βασιλέως τε ἀγχιστείᾳ λαμπρυνομένη), proud of her wealth, cultivating virtue in her life and habits" (16.16–17). No explicit contrast is drawn between Tryphaina and Alexander, but the implication is that Tryphaina's aristocratic *romanitas* is both superior to Alexander's local authority and also uniquely ordained by God. Perhaps reminiscent of Paul's appeal to the emperor at Caesarea in Acts 25–26, Tryphaina's involvement with the imperial family in both the *ATh* and the *Life* is understood to be God's ordained means of Thekla's martyrial triumph, as will be seen in more detail later.

Following Tryphaina's reception of Thekla "as a consolation," because her own daughter Falconilla had just died, the martyr is led in a procession with the wild beasts designated to kill her the next day. In the *ATh* Thekla is seated on a lioness, which proceeds to lick her feet to the amazement of the audience. It is reported that the charge under which she is condemned is "sacrilegious" (ἱερόσυλος; *sacrilegium*), the standard Roman legal term for an impious act.[48] The women of the city again make their plea for Thekla: "O God, an unholy judgment takes place in this city." The scene then jumps to Tryphaina receiving a message in a dream from her dead daughter, who tells her to get Thekla to pray so that Falconilla "can come to the place of the just" (*ATh* 28).

The author of the *Life*, in response to this imprecise list of reactions to Thekla's condemnation, chooses the elements he prefers and writes them into a more fluid scene. The lioness receives the most attention, and her affection for Thekla is newly emphasized:

> Then a deed (ἔργον) happened that was miraculous (παράδοξον) and truly worthy of a divine sign (θεοσημείας): for the lioness that was thought the most cruel (πικροτάτη), attached to Thekla, neglected her natural instincts. Like a young maidservant (θεραπαινίς) reared along with the young girl (κόρη), she habitually sat next to her and was fawning over (περιέσαινε) her feet, taking great care with her teeth, I think, lest (even accidentally) she should nibble and damage

---

[48] *OLD* 1675; Berger 1953:688–689. The charge of *sacrilegium* originally applied only to a theft from a temple but expanded in its usage to include any neglect or violation of imperial rule. Accordingly, the term ἱερόσυλος can also mean "temple robber," even in late antiquity, and it appears as such at *Mir.* 22.11, where it is applied to a thief who steals a cross from Thekla's church.

the already evangelical feet (τοὺς εὐαγγελικοὺς ἤδη πόδας) of the martyr. This stunned the entire city, and it struck all the onlookers with a certain speechlessness (ἀφασίας).

*Life* 16.26–34

Both Tryphaina and the lioness are unique accomplices to Thekla's triumph and provide color to the original story. As such, they have clearly taken on a greater importance in the *Life*. Their enhanced profile here points to their broader fame and to the recognition that this part of the earlier story must have had among late antique readers: significantly, the lioness appears as a requisite element of Thekla's iconography on pilgrim flasks from Egypt in this period.[49]

The women of the city, who cry out to God in the *ATh*, are not quoted directly in the *Life*. Instead, their sentiments are summarized and expanded, in a manner typical for this author. He says that they were shouting on the martyr's behalf, not because she was a martyr, but "as a woman suffering pitiably and undergoing an illogical sentence because of her self-control (σωφροσύνη) and dignity (σεμνότης)" (*Life* 16.38–39). The "feminist" strain of the original text is heightened, in contrast to a slight misogynism detected elsewhere in the *Life*.[50]

In the *ATh* Tryphaina asks Thekla to pray for Falconilla "that she may live in eternity, for this I saw in my sleep" (*ATh* 29). Thekla "without hesitation" prays for her daughter, saying, "My God, son of the Most High, who is in heaven, grant her wish that Falconilla may live in eternity." In the *Life* Tryphaina's request is somewhat grander. She asks Thekla to "make Falconilla's soul intimate (οἰκειώσης) to Christ" and "to provide for her what was lacking in [her?] faith (τὸ παρὰ τῆς πίστεως ἐλλειφθέν)" so that Christ might "from his grace give my daughter repose (ἀνάπαυλαν) and eternal life" (*Life* 17.27–31).

Thekla's lack of hesitation in the original is highlighted in the *Life* and transformed into a general exhortation for believers to always be ready to pray, alluding perhaps to Paul's "pray without ceasing" (1 Thessalonians 5:17). Thekla raises "perfectly pure hands" (πανάγνους χεῖρας) to heaven and prays a much enlarged version of her original intercession:

[Tryphaina's] longing (πόθος) is that the soul of that girl be counted (ἐναριθμηθῆναι) among the souls of those who already believe in you, and to have the benefit of the mode of life (διαίτης) and delight

---

[49] Davis 2001:118–119, 164, and illustrations at 216, 234–236 and 231. See also Nauerth and Warns 1981.
[50] See Dagron 1978:38–39.

(τρυφῆς) of paradise. Pay out this reward (ταύτην ἀμοιβὴν ἔκτισον) for her on my behalf, Lord Christ. For behold, as you see, she herself has become a guardian of my virginity (μου τῆς παρθενίας φύλαξ). After your Paul, she has assisted me and has delivered me from the frenzy (οἰστρομανίας) of Alexander. She has comforted me in her bosom after the fright of the wild beasts. For being a queen (βασιλίς) she has humbled herself with me (συνεταπεινώθη μοι), because of the desire and fear she has for you.[51]

*Life* 17.42–51

Several points are worthy of note in this prayer. Not least is the fact that the *Life* is more explicit on the issue of Falconilla's exclusion from "paradise," where she would receive a better "mode of life" and "delight." The latter word in Greek is τρυφή which originally had the negative connotations of "self-indulgence" and "luxury," came also to mean, at least by the Hellenistic period, "satisfaction" or "delight," both in the positive sense.[52] And from very early in Christian Greek τρυφή was synonymous with heavenly bliss.[53] There is also the connection with "Tryphaina" as a name, which is derived from τρυφή and the root-verb θρύπτω, "to refine" or "to break into small pieces."[54] Moreover, the name "Tryphosa," the companion of the Tryphaina greeted by Paul in Romans 16:12, also comes from τρυφή and θρύπτω.[55] This subtlety is not beyond the author of the *LM*: he may have been playing off of Falconilla's mother's name, who, being a believer already, wanted her daughter to receive the same "bliss" that she already possessed. He could also be attempting here to link more firmly the two Tryphainas through some clever wordplay on the name of Tryphaina's New Testament companion.

The next scene, in which Alexander comes to fetch Thekla for her fight with the wild beasts (θηριομάχος), demonstrates how closely the author of the *Life* could, when he wanted, follow the exact wording of the original text. Alexander's address to Tryphaina is almost exactly the same in both texts.

---

[51] The term βασιλίς, while found in Euripides and Plato, is characteristically late Greek and takes on its standard meaning of "empress" in about the fourth century AD, though Philostratus uses it in this way a century earlier (*Life of Apollonius* 1.3). See LSJ and Lampe s.v. "βασιλίς."

[52] For the negative connotations in classical literature, see LSJ s.v. "τρυφή."

[53] E.g. *2 Clement* 10.4; Clement of Alexandria *Paedagogus* ("The Tutor") 1.9; s.v. "τρυφή" (definition 4c) in Lampe. In the Septuagint version of Genesis 3:23, "the Lord God sent Adam out from the paradise of luxury/delight (ἐκ τοῦ παραδείσου τῆς τρυφῆς) to work the earth from which he was taken." The equation of heavenly "bliss" with Edenic "delight" by Syriac writers was common (e.g. Ephrem *Hymns on Paradise* 4.10, 5.5, and passim; see Brock 1990:49–62).

[54] See BDAG s.v. "Τρύφαινα."

[55] See BDAG s.v. "Τρυφῶσα."

51

ὁ ἡγεμὼν κάθηται καὶ ὁ ὄχλος θορυβεῖ ἡμᾶς· δὸς ἀπαγάγω τὴν θηριομάχον.

The governor is seated and the crowd is clamoring for us; give [her to me], so that I so that I can pit her against the beasts.

*ATh* 30

ὁ ἡγεμὼν γάρ, φησί, κάθηται, καὶ ὁ ὄχλος θορυβεῖ· δός, ἀπαγάγω τὴν θηριομάχυν.

"For the governor," [Alexander] said, "is seated and the crowd is clamoring; give [her to me], so that I can pit her against the beasts."

*Life* 18.5–6

Such correspondences demonstrate both that he was paraphrasing a text of the *ATh* very similar to the one that has come down to us and that his theory of paraphrase was such that word for word copying was not inconceivable.

There are further correspondences in this passage, however, which show his small-scale elaborations and changes in diction. For example, the effect that Alexander's demand has on Tryphaina is described in these ways:

ἡ δὲ Τρύφαινα ἀνέκραζεν ὥστε φυγεῖν αὐτὸν λέγουσα·

And Tryphaina put him to flight with a loud cry saying . . .

*ATh* 30

ὡς τὴν Τρύφαιναν ὑπὸ τῶν ῥημάτων τούτων δηχθεῖσάν τε καὶ ἀναφλεχθεῖσαν ἐκβοῆσαί τε πικρὸν καὶ γοερόν, ὡς καὶ εἰς φυγὴν τραπῆναι τὸν Ἀλέξανδρον. οἷα δὲ τὰ ῥήματα Τρυφαίνης·

Tryphaina, stung and inflamed by these words, cried out so harshly and lamentably, that Alexander turned to flee; such were Tryphaina's words . . .

*Life* 18.6–9

These examples serve to show how the seriously author is taking his claim to be making changes to the style and diction of the original text. First there is the insertion of a brief description of Tryphaina's own psychological response: ὑπὸ τῶν ῥημάτων τούτων δηχθεῖσάν τε καὶ ἀναφλεχθεῖσαν. Next, he elaborates the original, simple ἀνέκραζεν with ἐκβοῆσαί τε πικρὸν καὶ γοερόν. And, finally, the simple clause ὥστε φυγεῖν αὐτὸν in the *ATh* becomes the more elegant ὡς καὶ εἰς φυγὴν τραπῆναι τὸν Ἀλέξανδρον. The whole sentence is made up of two result clauses introduced by ὡς, where one would expect the normal ὥστε, as in the *ATh* text. The movement of the passage is thus more vivid and interactive in the *Life*, even if it loses the simple force of the original.

In the *Life* Tryphaina follows Thekla to the arena and complains, in a second speech, about the gross impiety of the Antiochenes in condemning Thekla to the beasts. Thekla's reaction to Tryphaina's wailing is written in the similar terms to Tryphaina's response to Alexander above: "at these words Thekla was stung and pained in her soul" (δηχθῆσά τε καὶ ὑπεραλγήσασα τὴν ψυχήν; 18.41–42). Thekla then prays to God, reminding him of what she has given up to follow Christ and asking that Tryphaina would be comforted. Thekla recapitulates the story thus far, emphasizing Tryphaina's key role in protecting her from sexual violence while awaiting her martyrdom.

> Therefore because of her and her compassion (συμπάθειαν) for me, I have not surrendered my virginity (παρθενίας), and I have conquered the rage (λύττης) of Alexander against me. And I fight with the self-control (σωφροσύνης) dear to me and you, thinking little of the beasts, because you have assisted me from heaven and because she has protected me on earth. This is the result of your providence (προνοίας) for me, that I find a harbor (λιμένος) in the midst of such violent and savage waves (ἐν ἀγρίοις οὕτω καὶ ἀνημέροις κύμασιν), a harbor which rescues me out of this great surging (ζάλης) of the beasts.
>
> *Life* 18.52–59

The decorative additions here, such as the final nautical metaphor, are designed to expose the triangle of devotion between Thekla, Tryphaina, and God. Nowhere is the depth of Tryphaina's faith clearly expressed, but her protection is pious enough for Thekla to want to intercede on her behalf—as she has already done for her daughter Falconilla. Just above this passage, Tryphaina briefly mentions in her prayer to God that she, "evangelized" (εὐαγγελισαμένης) by Thekla, was shown "the true and straight path towards your piety (εὐσεβείας)" (18.17–18).

What is lacking in her expression of faith, however, is a sense of where Paul fits in, since the early Christian person "Tryphaina" is just as familiar from Paul's letters. On one hand, then, there appears to be no attempt in the *Life* to reconcile Tryphaina's appearance in Romans 16 with her character in the *ATh* (assuming that the use of τρυφή above was not signaling this). On the other hand, Tryphaina's inclusion of εὐσέβεια here is significant, and further solidifies her identification with Thekla, as Paul's invented speeches did for his own character at earlier points in the *Life*. Εὐσέβεια has been used by Thekla herself on several occasions as a euphemism for Paul's teachings as a whole. Tryphaina's use of the same word here shows that the image of the passing down of Christian teaching in the *Life* is a linear one—that is, not that of already converted Christians mutually reinforcing one another, as in Paul's closing greetings in Romans. This sense of didactic inheritance is much more well-defined in the *Life* than in the *ATh* and it is reinforced later when Thekla meets Paul at Myra.

### The Antiochene arena

The *ATh* begins the climactic beast-fighting scene at Antioch with a description of how the women spectators were divided in their support for Thekla. Some are anxious for her to see her punished for committing *sacrilegium* (ἱερόσυλον), and others wish to be martyred along with Thekla. The latter cry out, "O that the city would be destroyed on account of this iniquity! Kill us all, proconsul; miserable spectacle, evil judgment!" (*ATh* 32). Thekla is thrown into the arena already stripped, but is given a girdle (διαζώστραν). When the lions and bears are let loose on her, "a fierce lioness" (πικρὰ λέαινα) runs up to meet Thekla and lays at her feet. The text does not explicitly say that this was the same lioness on whose back Thekla rode earlier in the parade of beasts, but that is implied. The lioness defends Thekla against a bear, which it "tears to pieces," but then dies while killing a lion "that had been trained to fight against men" and which "belonged to Alexander" (*ATh* 33). The women, now apparently undivided in their affection for Thekla, mourn the loss of the lioness because she was Thekla's "helper" (βοηθός).

The *Life* follows this order closely, though, as usual, it changes the wording. Thus, the women's plea for the ruin of the city quoted above becomes, "but many others had the thought and desire to be martyred along with Thekla and were also suffering the cruelty and nonsense of the misfortune" (*Life* 19.11–13). Characteristically, what was originally a direct quote from the women in support of Thekla has become in the *Life* a summary statement of their sentiments. Gone is the simple immediacy of the original, though the style of reporting has been heightened. In addition, minor changes are made to the way Thekla's nudity is described: the author has excised the awkward mention of a girdle and has instead chosen to concentrate on her nudity's general effect on animals in the arena. "For beautiful bodies always attract the eyes of beasts" (19.17–18). In order to make firm the connection between Thekla's feline escort in the earlier parade of beasts and the lioness that comes to her defense in the arena, the *Life* uses the same metaphor of a servant-girl (θεραπαινίς) before her young mistress (19.23).

Having thus survived the initial advance of the beasts, Thekla is besieged by many more wild animals. In the *ATh*, after "stretching forth her hands and praying," she notices a large pit of water near her, which is filled with ravenous seals. Before throwing herself into the water, she says, "Now it is time to wash myself (λούσασθαί με) ... In the name of Jesus Christ I baptize myself on my last day (ὑστέρᾳ ἡμέρᾳ βαπτίζομαι)!" (*ATh* 34). The "women and the multitude" weep over this action, as does the governor, because they know it means certain death. The seals, however, "having seen a flash of lightning" are instantly killed and "float dead on the surface." Following this brave act, Thekla is surrounded by a cloud of fire, "so that the beasts could neither touch her nor could she be seen naked."

The *Life* elaborates this climactic scene with a long prayer by Thekla, not present in the original, during which she prays silently to herself in the midst of the arena. The prayer serves as another litany of her exploits up to this point: "while I was just a girl, still shut up in the house, being kept for Thamyris ..." (*Life* 20.7–8). She also considers how God has placed her in the arena, "exercising her faith (καταγυμνάζων τὴν πίστιν)," and she gives thanks to Christ for this opportunity "to be deemed worthy (καταξιωθεῖσα) of your sufferings (παθημάτων) and stigmata (στιγμάτων)" (20.16–17). The force of her prayer is thus a plea for martyrdom and death, and she explicitly requests the latter at the end, alluding to Paul's imagery : "if you approve, clothe me now in death, and through the baptism of death, free me from fear and free these from their toil against me" (20.23–25; cf. Romans 6:3–4). Of course, the (apparently unintentional) irony in all this is that Thekla survives, just as she survived in Iconium: thus, she is never actually martyred, even though that weighty term has been applied to her from the beginning.

In the *ATh* the advance of the beasts continues (35). The women, still mourning for Thekla, throw perfumes down into the arena. The wild beasts are "hypnotized" and leave Thekla alone. Alexander, frustrated in all his attempts on her life, asks the governor for permission to bring out his "terrible bulls" in order to pull Thekla apart. The governor agrees "grudgingly," in imitation of Pontius Pilate (cf. Matthew 27). Even this attack is foiled, however, because the fire that has been applied to the bulls' genitals devours the ropes with which Thekla is bound. Meanwhile, Tryphaina, watching these successive trials from the audience, has a fainting spell. This throws the townspeople into an uproar because they think a kinswoman of the emperor has died. Alexander, fearing that he will be held responsible, asks the governor for mercy and that Thekla may be freed. Following this request the governor examines Thekla on why she survived so many wild beasts.

The changes to this scene in the *Life* primarily deal with issues of consistency. For example, the "plethora of beasts (πλῆθος τῶν θηρίων)" to which Alexander subjected Thekla is paralleled with the "plethora of spices and perfumes (πλῆθος ἀρωμάτων καὶ μύρων)" thrown down by the women (21.2–8). Likewise, the ferocity of Alexander's beasts is contrasted with the modesty of those that God uses (frogs, flies, locusts) to combat human hubris (21.11–17; cf. Exodus 8–10). Intriguingly, Alexander calls Thekla a "demon" (δαίμων) and "possessed by a demon" (κακοδαίμων) during his repentance before the governor, and she is further likened to a "uncouth beast" that is "more shameless than all the other beasts (πάντων τῶν θηρίων τούτων ἀναιδέστερον)" (21.42–44). "Shameless" (ἀναιδῆ) has already been used as an epithet for Alexander himself (21.2), which conveniently undermines his use of it here against Thekla. Their mutual condemnation demonstrates the author's occasional interest in dramatic irony.

Thekla's miraculous triumph

Thekla's questioning by the governor is put off in the *Life* to make way for a programmatic section on miracles in general. The author's focused attention on her miraculous escapes from death in Iconium and Antioch—especially the latter—has much to do with his (as it were) theoretical understanding of miracles and how they are performed. He has already pointed out the power of God to turn beasts against their own nature, as he did the lioness who defended Thekla instead of harming her (16.27 and 19.31). The specific term he uses for this event is θεοσημεία, "divine sign," which was used before his time by Christian writers for many varied miraculous occurrences: angels at Jesus' birth (Origen *Against Celsus* 1.60); the eclipse during the Crucifixion (ibid. 2.35); miracles by Moses and Christian saints (Cyril of Alexandria *Commentary on Romans* 11:30; *Commentary on Nahum* 17); Constantine's heavenly vision (Eusebius *Life of Constantine* 1.28).[56]

The author of the *Life* uses θεοσημεία for other miracles as well: for instance, it is used of Thekla's self-baptism scene generally (21.1, in the plural). The governor himself employs the term in amazement of Thekla post-baptism (23.25). In the latter passage, he seems to mean something specific that has to do with God's self-witnessing through nature: "We have all alike

---

[56] See Lampe s.v. "θεοσημεία."

watched these events, which are many and marvelous, deeds truly worthy of a divine sign (θεοσημείας)" (23.24–26). This passage, read alongside his use of θεοσημεία in the lioness scenes above, suggests that, for this author, the word means the evidence of nature being inexplicably affected, such as beasts miraculously falling asleep in the arena. The term is often paired with words of similar meaning, such as the noun θαῦμα ("wonder" in both senses; e.g. 16.35 and 17.4) and the adjectives θαυμάσιος ("marvelous"; 23.25) and παράδοξος ("extraordinary/miraculous"; 16.26), but θεοσημεία is a programmatic term that proves the divine origin of his topic. He does not use the term in the *Miracles*, thus confining "divine signs" to martyrdoms that can "witness" to God's power. Thekla's miracles are consistently called θαύματα or παράδοξα, and never θεοσημείαι. It is Thekla's renown that is built on θεοσημεία, not her subsequent healings and miracles. Those, like her contests against the beasts at Antioch, attest to θεοσημεία but are secondary to it. Θεοσημεία in this case has to do with anterior reputation. In the story, Thekla's triumphs certainly attest to it, but θεοσημεία is primarily the result of the long-term success of Thekla's legend.

The author of the *Life* goes on to make an explicit comparison between "the miracles of the saints (τὰ θαύματα τῶν ἁγίων)," which he calls "marks of a pious soul (ψυχῆς εὐσεβούσης ἰνδάλματα)," and "the results of some magic or spell," which are what "he who has no knowledge of the divinity" considers Thekla's deeds to be (*Life* 22.6–11). The author firmly separates these two categories of the supernatural and condemns magic because it relies on non-ethical means to achieve its ends:

> A magician (μάγος) desires to work something new (καινουργῆναι) or to perform something extraordinary (παραδοξοποιῆσαι), but he begins with the murder of humans (ἀνδροφονίας) or animal slaughter (ζῳοκτονίας) or some other abominable act. He would not be able to perform any of his strange or unusual signs (τι τῶν ἀτόπων καὶ ἀήθων) were it not for the help of these disgusting acts.
>
> 22.11–15

The author cites "Apollonius of Cappadocian Tyana" as "the most famous (περιφανέστερον) example" of a ancient magician who worked miracles through such means. He calls Apollonius' deeds "witchcraft" (γοητείαν) and includes under this heading "the summoning of gods" (θεαγωγίας), "the summoning of souls" (ψυχαγωγίας), "the calling of demons" (ἐπικλήσεις), and "secret impieties" (λανθανούσας ἀνοσιουργίας). He claims that Apollonius was "not a true philosopher" and was repudiated by the "gymnosophists of Ethiopia and India" precisely because he was known to have "too much to do with the pollution of witchcraft (κατὰ τὴν γοητείαν μιάσματος)" (22.15–25). He includes with Apollonius the more recent "Julianus," "Ostanes," and "Simon," "whom merely to mention is to be filled with pollution (μίασμά τός ἐστι πληρωθῆναι)."[57]

He goes on to set against these unholy magicians five Jewish and Christian figures, who, "adorned with a godly life," lived on prayer and a few words but who did great works all the same. These figures are Elijah, Moses, Peter, Paul, and Thekla (22.27–55). What they asked of God was only "what could be accomplished easily [i.e. without human sacrifice]," such as holding back the rain for three years, parting the seas, raising the dead, and "triumphing over fire, lions, bulls, and marine beasts." Subtly continuing the theme of individual competition between Christian miracle worker and pagan sorcerer, the arch-magician Simon is mentioned among the apostle Peter's exploits (22.46–49).[58]

The story alluded to here, that of Peter "pulling down (κατασπάσας)" Simon from the sky after the latter miraculously flew up into the sky, is from the apocryphal *Acts of Peter*, a text which, on the basis of this allusion, appears to predate the assembling of the *Acts of Paul*.[59] More importantly, however, the use of this story by the author of the *Life* further attests to the broad literary context within which he was attempting to situate his reconstruction of Thekla's received apostolic character. Philostratus' *Life of Apollonius*, not explicitly named but alluded to (τὸν ἐκείνου βίον), is set alongside this somewhat marginal Christian literature as well as famous stories of miraculous deeds from the Old Testament, in a strange patchwork of half-told supernatural tales. On one hand, the author is relying heavily here on previous knowledge of these stories, in much the same way that his paraphrastic changes to the *ATh* require a sense of what happened in the original. On the other hand, he demonstrates an appalling ignorance of the details of Philostratus' *Life* and does not cite what might be regarded as the more sensational scenes of that text, such as the levitation of the gymnosophists or Apollonius' striking, if

---

[57] For Julianus and Ostanes, see references at Dagron 1978:259 nn4–5; on late antique theurgy, see Lewy 1978 with E. R. Dodds's and Pierre Hadot's reviews of the first edition (both reprinted at Lewy 1978:693–720).

[58] For Simon Magus, see Edwards 1997.

[59] The flying scene is from *Acts of Peter* 32 (=*Martyrdom of Peter* 3); see references at Dagron 1978:259n6. For the relationship between the *Acts of Peter* and the *Acts of Paul*, see Elliott 1999:390, citing Schmidt 1936:127–130. It should also be pointed out that the *Life*'s references to Paul's miracles all come from the canonical Acts (9:40 and 12:7–10), as noted by Dagron 1978:258.

few, miraculous exorcisms.[60] Thus, his extended comparison of these texts falls flat and contains little of interest besides the mere mention of Apollonius, a local son, and, as regards narrative, the author's decision to insert such a large programmatic section in the middle of the work's climax. This material seems much more at home in the preface to the *Miracles*, but its use here, at the very least provides further witness to the unity of the work in conception (if also to its desultory deployment in fact).

Following this programmatic section, the narrative of the *Life* continues with Thekla's response to the governor's summons. She reiterates stock elements of earlier speeches—"I am, as you can see, a woman, a girl, and a stranger . . ." (22.56–57)—and she cites another Christological formula: "God is my shield-bearer and champion, and his only begotten Son, the one who is of old, preexistent, and who is perpetually with the Father, but who has recently been seen on earth . . ." (22.57–60). More significant, however, is the narrator's parenthetical comment on Thekla's theological faculties: "[what she said] was much more fitting (μεγαλοπρεπέστερον) and theological (θεολογικώτερον) than standard female reasoning" (22.66–69). This is the only text in the whole *Life* that deals with the difference between Thekla and a normal Christian woman.[61] One implication is that the degree to which she supersedes her gender—"led into the public (ἐν τῷ μέσῳ τε προήγαγες)," as she puts it elsewhere (20.9–10)—is the degree to which she becomes a saint, though this is not spelled out in so many words.

Such programmatic material, however, is generally absent from the *ATh*, to which the author of the *Life* now returns. In the *ATh* Tryphaina leaves her house, having fainted earlier, to come meet Thekla on the way. In the *Life* the scene is written up for the sake of drama. Thekla, having been released by the governor comes to Tryphaina's house with a crowd of people and proceeds to revive Tryphaina from her lifelessness. The *Life* does not explicitly say Thekla raised her from the dead, but this is implied. "Upon hearing these things Tryphaina was refreshed (ψυχωθῆναι), in effect, and immediately came to life again (ἀναβιῶναι)" (*Life* 24.5–6).[62] In both the *ATh* and the *Life* Tryphaina

---

[60] Levitation: *Life of Apollonius* 3.17; Exorcisms: e.g. 4.20, 3.38–40 (the latter by the sages). The author's ignorance of the details of the *Life of Apollonius* is exemplified by his statement that the gymnosophists repudiated Apollonius, which of course is the opposite of what actually happens in the *Life*.

[61] If the audience of this and similar texts was female, as some suggest, a running comparison between Thekla and "normal" women would be expected. Its absence here, and elsewhere, militates against this theory. On the question of female readership of novelistic Christian literature, see Davis 2001:10–13 and references

[62] Both verbs, ψυχόω and ἀναβιόω, have extended meanings in patristic Greek: the former is

next promises Thekla that she will be her inheritor. In response Thekla begins to teach her benefactress and converts her whole household (*ATh* 39; *Life* 24.26–31).

### Thekla seeks Paul at Myra

In the *ATh*, Thekla's success at Tryphaina's home in Antioch does not satisfy her, and, though we are not given the reasons for this decision, she boldly sets off to find Paul, whom she has heard is at Myra. This sudden exit in the *ATh* works because the narrative thus far has been so fast-paced; however, the pace of the *Life* is much slower in general due to its long speeches and expansive description. In line with this practice, its author adds a lengthy descriptive passage on Thekla's mood in Antioch. Thus, despite all the adulation she had received, her memory of Paul was too strong to keep her there:

> The martyr was in awe (ἐτεθήπει) of Paul, and now had no other words but "Paul," and "Where's Paul?," and "Who can point me to this one, whom Christ gave as a guide to me and a teacher in his way of life (πολιτεία) and faith?" For, though she had become widely known and famous from her miracles (θαύματα), she was not now disdainful of her teacher.
>
> *Life* 25.4–7

The image is one of a novelistic heroine, separated from her husband or fiancé, having found success in a far-flung country but still pining for her old, true love.[63] This romantic element has been consciously maintained throughout the *Life*, even at places where the *ATh* seems to have dropped it.[64]

Worthy of note here is that Thekla is described as "in awe" herself, continuing the rhetoric and language of wonder. She says that Paul was her teacher in Christ's "way of life" and "faith." "Way of life" (πολιτεία) is a typically programmatic term that is used very often in saints' Lives to indicate the ethical or ascetic standards offered in the holy person, standards to which the believing readers should aspire.[65] The word has been used elsewhere in the

---

used to describe, among other things, the creation of man (Gregory of Nyssa *On the Creation of Man* 28.1) and the raising of Lazarus (Nonnus *Paraphrase of John* 11.44); the latter term is used of Christ's resurrection as early as *2 Clement* (19.3). For further references, see Lampe s.v.

[63] Such as Callirhoe does in Chariton's novel (bks 2–3). See Johnson forthcoming.
[64] For anti-romantic elements in the *ATh*, see Aubin 1998.
[65] See e.g. Athanasius of Alexandria *Life of Antony* 14; Theodoret of Cyrrhus *History of the Monks of Syria* 1; Palladius *Lausiac History* preface 33; *History of the Monks in Egypt* preface 10. While πολιτεία in this sense is characteristically late antique and Byzantine, the word had taken on

*Life* by both Paul and Thekla to describe the "angelic and heavenly way of life" or the "way of life in Christ" and also appears once in the *Miracles* (*Life* 2.6–7; 13.38; *Mir.* 44.48; cf. *Life* 6.45 by Thamyris).

Next in the original story comes Thekla's famous donning of male attire for her trip to Myra. The *ATh* reads at this point: "And wearing a mantle that she had altered to make a man's cloak, she came with a band of young men and maidens to Myra" (*ATh* 40). The author of the *Life* has not changed the text greatly but he has adjusted the emphasis to correspond to his understanding of why she would wear men's clothes in the first place: "She changed her outfit again to be more male, so as to conceal with this disguise her radiant beauty" (*Life* 25.17–19; cf. Exodus 34:33–35).[66] In the *Life*, the threat to Thekla of being raped is always less important than the excellence of her beauty; in this sense, the roughness of the *ATh*—including the horror of the scene at the gates of Antioch where Paul deserts her—is softened and the attention is consistently drawn to Thekla (*Life* 15; cf. *ATh* 26).

In the same way, Thekla's arrival before Paul in Myra is adjusted to emphasize Paul's shock at her appearance. "When she appeared suddenly, standing before them, she struck everyone stupefied and speechless (θάμβους καὶ ἀφασίας) and filled Paul with fear" (*Life* 25.30–32). This is an elaboration of the *ATh* text, "he was astonished (ἐθαμβήθη) at seeing her" (*ATh* 40). Thus the *Life* linguistically retains the force of the sense but has added texture to this dramatic moment. "Speechlessness" (ἀφασία), of course, is a programmatic term for Stoic philosophy but in this context it indicates the awe with which readers should reflect on the triumphs of the holy people represented.[67] Paul's reaction is, therefore, a model for the readers. As noted above, Paul's rough outline in the *ATh* offers the opportunity for him to be more completely described in the *Life*. Thus, the climactic description of Paul here as "admiring" (ἐθαύμασε) reinforces the role that Paul has come to represent earlier in the text (*Life* 25.38).[68]

---

its basic Christian sense from an early point: e.g. *1 Clement* 2.8; *Martyrdom of Polycarp* 13.2. There are, however, no uses of the word in this sense in the New Testament. See BDAG (definition 3) and Lampe (definition 3d), s.v. "πολιτεία."

[66] That Thekla here changes her clothes "again/back" (πάλιν) to masculine ones, is proof that the author believed her to have done this on the way to Antioch. The *ATh* has her change only here, on the way to Myra.

[67] Cf. Sextus Empiricus *Outlines of Pyrrhonism* 2.211.

[68] It is perhaps also itself imitative of Jesus' amazement at the centurion's faith in Luke 7:9.

## Thekla in Myra, Iconium, and Seleukeia (*Life* 26–28)

Thekla's address to Paul in Myra begins the final section of the *Life*. The address is organized around sixteen uses of the phrase "I learnt through you (ἔγνων διὰ σοῦ)," each followed by abstractions relating to Trinitarian theology. For instance:

> And I learnt through you the ineffable (ἄφραστον), inaccessible (ἀποριστόν), unchangeable (ἀναλλοίωτον), incomprehensible (ἀκατάληπτον) nature of the power (δυνάμεως) that is in the Trinity (Τριάδι). And I learnt through you the consubstantial (ὁμοούσιον) Trinity in the heaven, above the heaven of the heaven, and on earth and under the earth, and everywhere, above everything, and around everything.
>
> *Life* 26.8–12 (cf. 13.27–37)

Unfortunately, this passage shows a large amount of manuscript variation.[69] It would therefore be a mistake to try to demonstrate that the author was quoting from or alluding to a certain source. However, the consistency of authentic Trinitarian formulae throughout the *Life* is still significant for the work's overall tone and apparent theological sympathies. Formulae like these are innocuous and rather pedestrian, but the aesthetic of putting fourth-century technical terms into the mouth of Thekla or Paul is still very striking and the author of the *Life* does not cease to do it, even at the very end of his text. The characters of Paul and Thekla have thus been reconstructed, and their new language fits the author's later, literary vision of their apostolic interactions.

In responding to Thekla's long confession of faith, Paul uses some of the same phrases as his pupil, signaling their unity of thought yet again. Most important is his reiteration of "through me (δι' ἐμου)" in the middle of the passage, in which he is imitating her sixteen uses of "through you (διὰ σοῦ)" above:

> You now lack nothing for apostleship and inheritance of the divine preaching (πρὸς ἀποστολὴν καὶ διαδοχὴν τοῦ θείου κηρύγματος). Therefore, go away, teach the word, complete the evangelistic course (τὸν εὐαγγελικὸν δρόμον), and share my zeal for Christ. On account of this Christ chose you through me (δι' ἐμοῦ), in order that he might move you into apostleship (εἰς ἀποσολήν) and might put

---

[69] Dagron 1978:271n1.

in your hands certain cities yet uncatechized (τῶν ἔτι ἀκατηχήτων πόλεων). For it is necessary for you to multiply your talents.

*Life* 26.61–67 (cf. Matthew 25:14–29)

Paul frames her commission with the term "apostleship" (ἀποστολήν) and additionally employs "succession" (διαδοχήν) as its synonym or complement, highlighting the linear reception of apostolic preaching (glimpsed above in Tryphaina's response to Thekla at Antioch; *Life* 18).

What is being subtly put forward in this lengthy rewritten section is a view of ecclesiastical history and how Thekla fits into it. Thekla takes on a character that she never had in the *ATh*, that of one of Paul's disciples in Acts or in his letters. Despite occasionally being called "protomartyr" in this text, Thekla is consistently, if tacitly, paralleled with the likes of Timothy and Titus rather than the "protomartyr" Stephen.[70] Her commission is ultimately to return to a city in Asia Minor that Paul has already visited, Iconium, just as Timothy is sent to Corinth (1 Corinthians 4:17; 16:10–11) or is given charge over the church at Ephesus (1 Timothy 1:1–3). This much could have been elaborated from the *ATh* alone, where Paul says "Go and teach the word of God" (*ATh* 41). However, Thekla's commission by Paul extends to multiple cities "yet uncatechized," which allows for the future fame of her cult and foreshadows the localized, patriographical rhetoric of the *Miracles*.

At this point comes the end of the *ATh*. Thekla has been commissioned by Paul to "Go and teach the word of God" and has left with Paul the "many things" that Tryphaina sent for "the service of the poor." When she arrives in Iconium, Thekla proceeds to Onesiphorus' house—where she first heard Paul teaching—here she sits, cries, and prays to God. The last paragraph of the *ATh* concerns her testimony to her mother Theocleia and her departure for Seleukeia. This scene is foundational for later elaborations of her legend:

> And [Thekla] found Thamyris dead but her mother alive. And calling her mother she said, "Theocleia, my mother, can you believe that the Lord lives in heaven? For if you desire wealth the Lord will give it to you through me; or if you desire your child, behold, I am standing beside you." And having thus testified, she went to Seleukeia and enlightened many by the word of God; then she rested in a glorious sleep.
>
> *ATh* 43

---

[70] For a brief history of the term protomartyr in early Christian literature, see Bowersock 1995:75–76.

The *ATh* text thus ends by stating that Thekla died in Seleukeia.[71] While obviously attesting to a traditional association between Thekla and Seleukeia, there is (crucially) no elaboration about what Thekla did there or how long she lived.

From this point the *Life* leaves the *ATh* behind and sets out into new territory by offering a description of that city at which Thekla finally settles. "The city [Seleukeia] is situated at the beginning of the boundaries of the East, a first rank place and above every city of Isauria, situated near to the sea and not far from a river; the river's name is the Kalykadnos . . ." (27.27–30). This *ekphrasis* extends to a comparison with Seleukeia's rival, Tarsus, a city which is invoked multiple times in the *Miracles*:

> It contends with the beautiful Tarsus, with regard to size, setting, the mildness of its climate, the abundance of its fruits, the bounty of its merchandise . . . but Seleukeia surrenders its bitter rivalry at one place only, bowing slightly and ceding to the other first place: Tarsus is the homeland and city of the great Paul, apart from whom (it must be said) we would not happen to have our holy virgin.
>
> 27.40–49 (cf. *Mir.* 4.1–13)

This rivalry is expressed in terms that reinforce the revised story he has just told. Paul and Thekla are even more strongly linked, and, moreover, they participate like classical heroes in the founding of cities.

Thekla settles on a hill near Seleukeia "like Elijah on Carmel" or "like John in the desert" and proceeds to wage war against "the *daimon* Sarpedon" and "the warlike *daimon* dwelling on the heights, Athena." These references are to two of the four gods that Thekla conquers in the first four miracles (*Mir.* 1–4). However, Thekla's activities in Seleukeia are not at all limited to the conquering of pagan deities. She has already taken on the character of supernatural miracle worker, and there is no further mention of her martyrial triumphs. She is compared in her apostolic mission—"evangelizing the saving word, and catechizing, sealing, and enlisting many for Christ"—to the apostles Peter ("in Antioch"), Paul ("in Athens and all the nations"), and John ("the great theologian in Ephesus"; *Life* 28.1–5).

Thekla is here being written into competition with these figures, not just nostalgically but in terms of real texts (apostolic legends) which were likely to be in circulation in the fifth century. Given our author's reserved, classical

---

[71] In classical Greek to "fall asleep" (κοιμάω) often means euphemistically "to die" (e.g. Homer *Iliad* 11.241; *IG* 14.1683), and there are several uses of κοιμάω in this sense from the Gospels (e.g. Matthew 27:52; John 11:11). See LSJ and BDAG s.v. "κοιμάω."

literary style, it is impossible to prove that he was reading such texts and employing them directly as models for his project. Nevertheless, such texts were readily available, and there can be no doubt that the *LM* is part of the imaginative inheritance of apostolic personae.[72]

As just noted, in the *ATh* Thekla "went to Seleukeia and enlightened many by the word of God; then she rested in a glorious sleep (μετὰ καλοῦ ὕπνου ἐκοιμήθη)." The author of the *Life* has changed this statement significantly, for the sake of his reinvention of Thekla's legend and subsequent ministry:

> After she had brought everyone to faith, especially through the miracles (διὰ τῶν θαυμάτων μάλιστα), did she die (ἐκοιμήθη)? Absolutely not! (οὐδαμῶς) Just as the most widespread and more sure tradition (ὁ πολὺς καὶ ἀληθέστερος λόγος) attests, she sunk down while alive (ἔδυ δὲ ζῶσα) and went under the earth (ὑπεισῆλθε τὴν γῆν)—the decision of God being that this earth would separate for her and be cleft from below (ὑπορραγῆναι), on the very spot where is fixed the divine and holy and liturgical table (ἱερά καὶ λειτουργικὴ τράπεζα), established in a circular peristyle, shining in silver. This is where she dispenses fountains of healings (πηγὰς ἰαμάτων) for every suffering and every sickness, her virginal grace pouring out healings (ἰάματα) there, as if from some rushing stream, upon those who ask and pray for them.
>
> *Life* 28.5–14

The significance of the words ἐκοιμήθη and οὐδαμῶς in this passage cannot be overemphasized. They represent a conscious overturning of the original legend, as expressed in the text that the *Life* has followed so closely up to this point. Thekla's disappearance is emphatically not death or "sleep," as the *ATh* has it, but rather a "living" (ζῶσα) disappearance.[73]

That this disappearance would be framed immediately on both sides by a description of her miraculous activities is not coincidence. Thekla's posthumous thaumaturgical activity must ultimately depend on her entry into the ground of Seleukeia.[74] More will be said concerning the literary character of

---

[72] No comprehensive study has been made of the reception of legends about famous Old Testament figures and the Apostles in late antiquity; four good studies on New Testament personae are Culpepper 1994 for John, Matthews 2002 for Philip, Thomas 2003 for Peter, and Edwards 1997 for Simon Magus. However, see generally the series *Studies on Personalities of the New Testament*, published jointly by the University of South Carolina Press and T&T Clark.

[73] For ideas as to how this passage contributes to archaeology at the cult site, see Dagron 1978:50–54, 72–73 and Hill 1996:208–214.

[74] Thekla's disappearance into the ground has classical and early Christian literary precedents,

this activity below, but for now it is enough to notice that the author of the *Life* does not try to explain to confused readers why he insists so forcefully that Thekla does not die in Seleukeia. Rather, he simply replaces the original text with this unique rewriting. Placing the disappearance between the two halves of his text—his *Iliad* and *Odyssey*—our author offers a fundamentally new vision of Thekla which lacks the limited horizons of the original *ATh*. The *Miracles* is also his *Posthomerica*—a reinvigoration of the legend in which he attempts to capture all the contemporary phenomena of Thekla's miraculous expression in Seleukeia. By disappearing into the ground Thekla claims the very earth of the place and becomes autochthonous. In this way the *Life* takes on the role of an urban foundational myth and paves the way for a catalogue of the city's golden years in the *Miracles*.

---

though no direct allusion is readily apparent. For instance, Oedipus sinks mysteriously into the ground at the end of Sophocles' *Oedpius at Colonnus* (see lines 1661–1662, 1732, 1760–1763, and 1775). Also, at the end of the *Protoevangelium of James* (see pp. 223–225 below), Elisabeth and an infant John the Baptist flee to a mountain that splits in two (ἐδιχάσθη) and receives them (ἐδέξατο): see §43 in Strycker 1961.

# Chapter 2

## Biblical Rewriting and the Metaphrastic Habit: The *Life of Thekla* within the History of Ancient Paraphrase

### Prologue: Erasmus and the Conflict over his *Paraphrases on the New Testament*

> For a paraphrase is a plain setting foorth of a texte or sentence more at large, with such circumstance of mo [i.e. more] and other wordes as maie make the sentence open, clere, plain, and familiar whiche otherwise should perchaunce seme bare, unfruitefull, hard, straunge, rough, obscure, and derke to be understanded of any that were either unlearned or but menely entreed [i.e. entered=instructed]. And what is this, but a kinde of exposicion, yea and that of the most pithie and effectuall sorte?

This quotation is taken from Nicholas Udall's introduction to the English version of Erasmus' voluminous *Paraphrases on the New Testament* (1548 and 1551–1552), for the first volume of which Udall ("poet, playwright, and some-time headmaster of Eton college") was the general editor.[1] For Udall, the biblical paraphrase was a helpful guide to the hard places of Scripture; this manner of exposition, as he says, could provide a real sense of the meaning of the Bible—which it apparently lacked on the surface—for those with only a basic level of education. Erasmus' *Paraphrases* were not well received in France; the original Latin edition was condemned in 1527, shortly after its first printing.[2] By contrast, the *Paraphrases* were very well received in England and had a discernable impact on early Anglican exegesis and preaching; they have

---

[1] Quoted by Vessey 2002a:7; parentheses are his. For Udall, see Craig 2002:316–322 and n22.
[2] See Bedouelle 2002 on their translation and reception and Rummel 2002 on Noël Béda's condemnation of them.

also been found, perhaps more tellingly, in the library records of hundreds of English parish churches.[3] Therefore, Udall's English edition would appear to have achieved its aims, and, at least in light of its reception, his general assertions about the usefulness of biblical paraphrase were well founded with regard to his contemporary Anglican audience.

As a recent volume edited by Hilmar Pabel and Mark Vessey amply demonstrates, Erasmus' *Paraphrases* were intimately connected with the development of biblical criticism and printing in the early sixteenth century (Pabel and Vessey 2002). The reception of the paraphrases in Reformation Europe, they argue, should be understood from the point of view of the complex intertextuality of the paraphrases and their translations, in which Erasmus' theological commitments and his affected literary rhetoric interweave in a striking fashion. From their initial conception, the *Paraphrases* were Erasmus' attempt to offer, within the biblical text itself, some conclusions of Renaissance exegesis—eventually in octavo (i.e. pocketbook) format—so that (even casual) readers could glean the benefits of advanced biblical criticism. But as Pabel and Vessey point out, the dissemination of the *Paraphrases* was not without interesting twists and turns. As already mentioned, Erasmus from the start met with criticism in France for changing the *ipsissima verba* of the New Testament and introducing foreign (if enlightened) comments into God's Word.[4] Whereas Erasmus claims to have intended that the *Paraphrases* assist believers and congregations in understanding what the Bible really said, as Udall asserted in his translation, several scholars at the time of their publication contended that biblical paraphrase only confuses the reader and, what is more, it adulterates Scripture by introducing ideas that are merely human and thus not divinely inspired.

Erasmus' method of paraphrase would be striking in itself, even if its reception history were less controversial. For each New Testament book he paraphrased, he tried to be conscious of the persona of the author: of each author's style and syntax, of course, but also of the character that tradition had assigned to him. The most interesting example of this method comes from his paraphrase of the Gospel of Luke, to which he prefaced a dedication to Henry VIII.[5] Erasmus presents Luke's Gospel as a drug or medicine that, when

---

[3] For this see Craig 2002 and references, esp. n12 for accounts of the translation of the *Paraphrases* into English. Interestingly, the *Paraphrases* were not on the list of proscribed books issued during Mary's reign: Craig 2002:326–327.

[4] Noël Béda was especially resistant to Erasmus' assertion that some passages of Scripture are not understandable by themselves (Rummel 2002:267); he also condemned the implication that Scripture should be made available in the vernacular (Vessey 2002a:18).

[5] For Erasmus' *Paraphrase on Luke*, see Phillips 2002.

taken (i.e. read), heals the effects of sin and death in the patient. He links this metaphor directly to the tradition of Luke as a physician-historian and emphasizes that the efficacy of the Gospel is based on its historical veracity, as vouchsafed by this educated companion of Paul. Erasmus thus speaks, in his words, *sub evangelistae persona*, taking for himself the traditional characteristics of Luke, the style of his narrative, and his medical authority. Moreover, the two prologues to Theophilus in Luke-Acts provided for Erasmus an exegetical "space" in which to create an audience, not just Henry but all his readers. As Vessey points out:

> Unlike normal commentary, which always declares its supplementarity with respect to the source-text, even when the commentator is merely explicating one biblical passage by another, paraphrase stands up—in its first-person, Erasmian mode, *speaks* up—in the name of Scripture itself.[6]

In this way a personified "Luke-voice," Erasmus' biblical ego, offers the paraphrast an opportunity to discuss the very nature of Scripture: how it works, what it lacks, and what it means; paraphrase becomes Scripture explaining itself, defending itself, and claiming itself.[7] Thus, despite sixteenth-century Catholics in France who resisted Erasmus' free play with the text, the theoretical force of Erasmus' *Paraphrases* is monumental both in their reception among reformed Anglicans as well as, on a more general level, in what they say about the perceived ontology—the malleability—of the Bible.

This debate was also, of course, about the freedom of readers and, consequently, about the degree to which textual criticism should have a say in how the Bible is read. These latter are primarily Reformation issues, which we have inherited, but I would venture to suggest that the battle over Erasmus' *Paraphrases* can be seen, in its essentials, as a battle for cognition as much as for canonicity, since the central question at stake is what, precisely, is necessary for a reader's understanding when he apprehends received texts like the Gospel of Luke? Theories of scriptural cognition are common to all generations of Bible readers, and in this way the key issues in the production and reception of Erasmus' *Paraphrases* can potentially be detected in every paraphrase ever written.

---

[6] Vessey 2002a:14–15.
[7] "Luke-voice" is from Phillips 2002:e.g. 131; the prologue to Luke is expanded into an essay twenty-six times its original length (ibid.).

## Towards a Modern Theory of Paraphrase: Goody, Alter, and McKenzie on the Mutability of Texts

As a way of defending Erasmus somewhat against the charge of literary invention, it is important to make clear—Pabel and Vessey do not attempt this—that biblical paraphrase has an ancient and revered tradition within Judeo-Christian literary history.[8] In choosing to invest so much effort in paraphrasing New Testament books, Erasmus could very well have been inspired by a number of ancient Jewish texts that famously included paraphrased Scripture, such as the Septuagint, Josephus, or the late antique Targums in Aramaic.[9] There is also evidence that he was aware of some early Christian paraphrases of biblical books, which were less numerous but definitely in circulation (in print) by 1520.[10] Therefore, keeping Pabel and Vessey's examination of Erasmus' *Paraphrases* in mind, I would like to consider in this chapter some of the broader issues of biblical paraphrase as it was practiced in antiquity.

I do this in order to contextualize the close reading of the *Life of Thekla* which I presented in the last chapter. As a late antique paraphrase in Greek, the *Life* appropriates the paraphrase tradition as it had been practiced for centuries before and was also currently employed in both Jewish and Christian circles. This tradition clearly flourished at least as much in the eastern Mediterranean as it did in the West, and the eastern side of the tradition

---

[8] Vessey briefly discusses Erasmus' knowledge of earlier paraphrasts and cites Roberts 1985, which explores only the Latin side of biblical paraphrase in late antiquity. Bernard Rousell in his contribution mentions a few ancient paraphrasts, such as Gregory Thaumaturgus and Nonnus of Panopolis, but only in passing; his interest lies in the Reformation paraphrasts subsequent to Erasmus (Roussel 2002:59).

[9] For the Septuagint as a paraphrase, see below. For the revival of biblical languages in the Reformation and some of their political and social implications, see Goldhill 2002:14–57. Erasmus probably knew the first printed edition of the Targums by Felix Pratensis, who printed them in Venice alongside his four-volume edition of the Hebrew Bible (1517–1518). Pratensis was a Jew who had converted to Christianity and was in the employment of Daniel Bomberg, a wealthy Antwerp native who spent his fortune in Venice printing Hebrew (and Aramaic) books—about two hundred in all. On the early printing history of the Aramaic Targums, see Díez Merino 1994, esp. 80–86.

[10] He certainly knew Juvencus, and, "when the *Paraphrases* themselves came under attack, he repeatedly allied himself with that fourth-century Christian poet" (Vessey 2002b:32). It has been argued, however, that he was unacquainted with Proba's *cento* (Vessey 2002b:52n17). There is a good chance Erasmus knew something of Nonnus' *Paraphrase of John*, since editions of the latter had been printed at least twice by this time (Roussel 2002:79n3)—one of these was the Aldine edition of 1501–1504; the other was the 1527 edition by Philipp Melanchthon and Johann Setzer. Vessey makes a useful comparison between the rhetoric of Erasmus' paraphrase program and Jerome's reflections on paraphrase vs. translation (Vessey 2002b:52n13).

was spurred on in late antiquity by the strong influence of Hebrew exegesis. However, most of the important issues raised by the contributors to Pabel and Vessey 2002 have never been addressed in a late antique setting, even though late antiquity was precisely when the eastern Christian tradition of biblical paraphrase was coming into its own. Therefore, in the following sections of the present chapter I attempt to present a brief and selective history of this tradition, beginning with the evidence from the Hebrew Bible and ending with the fifth century AD, when the majority of our earliest (extant) Greek Christian paraphrases were written. I shall also make a brief comparison between this first flowering and the apex of Byzantine paraphrase in the tenth century.

The questions must be addressed at the start, however, of what a paraphrase is and how it seeks to represent the text that underlies it. One could argue that a unique theory of paraphrase must be generated by each individual author, given that the underlying text, its *Vorlage*, can be so determinative of the character of the paraphrase, or "hypertext."[11] One could likewise argue that the socio-cultural contexts of specific paraphrases and rewritings forbid any kind of synchronic examination. To be sure, examples occur in the history of paraphrase that suggest there are interpretive barriers of this kind, and out of regard for such concerns I attempt below to draw attention to the characteristics particular to each paraphrase examined. Despite this need for literary atomism, recent models of textuality and cognition—from the related fields of anthropology, literary criticism, and bibliographical studies—offer opportunities for rewriting to be seen as a project common to human experience and not limited to any one historical or cultural sphere.

In particular, models of "literary" elaboration in oral cultures can, I suggest, provide some help in attempting to analyze the evidence of ancient paraphrase and rewriting. At the head of recent research on literature in oral societies is anthropologist Jack Goody, whose conclusions have become standard fare for anthropologists, as well as for those working on Renaissance book culture, the transition to print, and modern information networks.[12] Goody's numerous publications focus mainly on tribes in West Africa among whom versions of the Lo Dagaa myth of the Bagre were still being recited.[13] Some

---

[11] For theories of "hypertextuality" in ancient literature, see MacDonald 2000:1–14.

[12] For the Renaissance and Reformation, see the standard study of Eisenstein 1980 and, in opposition, Johns 1998; and, for the still disputed significance of our current transition from print to electronic media, see O'Donnell 1998. Both Eisenstein and O'Donnell rely on Goody's formulations. See also the seminal studies of Marshall McLuhan 1962 and Walter Ong 2002, who rely less on Goody.

[13] See his trilogy of major studies, Goody 1977, 1986, 1987, and 2000, which is a convenient summary restatement of his views.

of these tribes had set down written versions of the myth, thus providing a testing ground for explaining the oral-to-written transition. Goody argues (persuasively, for many) that, while the writing-down of myths seems to limit their elaboration, variations among oral versions of myths are actively encouraged. These variations are seen as parts of an ancient whole: the individual teller of oral myth, even if patently inventing a new tale, often sees himself as recovering the lost knowledge of his ancestors. "The Speakers, even at the moment of creation, think of themselves as recovering the irrecoverable."[14] By contrast, when myth is put into text (and only then) variations from it are consistently seen as heterodox. For Goody, cultural memory is thus essentially oral: a vast storehouse of social awareness passed down and elaborated upon by each successive generation. Oral variation is a sign of vitality, whereas the printed versions tend towards stagnation:

> The myth was in a perpetual state of transformation. So we have an infinity of oral versions of the Bagre, which in practice the actors find difficult to compare. But there are now two printed versions, which unfortunately some have begun to take as the truth, as orthodoxy, because of the prestige of writing and because they had been recited by ancestors now dead. A new measure of truth, a new concept of archive, has emerged.[15]

Goody's concept of the decadent "archive" is set in explicit opposition to Jacques Derrida's program of textualizing the spoken word.[16] And Goody insists on the autonomy of the oral in the face of the post-structuralist project to see "inscription" as pervasive, even in illiterate or semi-literate societies. For Goody this is "an irresponsible attitude towards words" and cannot account for the variation found in oral "texts."[17]

Goody accepts a basic "textuality" to social self-definition and power—indeed, he has proudly pointed out that anthropology, in his estimation,

---

[14] Goody 2000:53.

[15] Goody 2000:118.

[16] Goody cites especially Derrida's *Of Grammatology* (1974) but also references discussion of Derrida's work in Culler 1979. It should be noted that Goody's student David R. Olson, has discussed in depth the effect of literacy on cognition, especially in the context of linguistic self-location: "Writing is largely responsible for bringing language into consciousness" (1994: xviii).

[17] Goody 2000:114–115. Goody's commitment to the oral has been followed by many outside his discipline. The classicist Gregory Nagy, for example, has repeatedly emphasized the oral vitality of the Homeric epics. See Nagy 1996; and also his and Stephen Mitchell's new edition of Albert Lord's *Singer of Tales* (Lord 2000).

anticipated the ideas of Derrida and Michel Foucault by a few years.[18] However, Goody's "textuality" is still purely oral, in that he prefers to see the textuality of the written or printed word (in oral or semi-literate societies) as contributing less to the refashioning of literature, history, or social consciousness in general. At a basic societal level, Goody argues, writing cannot supplant oral tradition as a force of change.[19]

Goody, of course, does not view writing as a negative force;[20] he is trying first of all to explain the "interface" between the written and the oral in order to better understand the cognitive processes involved in the transition from one to the other. While his conclusion is that writing and "archives"—the momentary (and thus blinkered) capsulations of a constantly fluctuating discourse—inhibit the creativity of oral literature, he has said many shockingly "textual" things about the character of literary variation and revision within the oral sphere. He has isolated, for example, a trend towards antiquarianism, or "scholarship," among oral composers for whom the language of the people and the language of their tales has begun to diverge.[21] He has also pointed out the tendency for the establishment of an oral canon to stimulate further elaboration of the Lo Dagaa Bagre myth among the tribes he studied.

The picture that emerges from Goody's writings is of a vibrant, unencumbered "textual" culture, that is constantly revising its own "textual" history, encouraging the extension and "rewriting" of the oral myths in every generation. However, he rarely moves beyond the (mainly) oral evidence of the Bagre that he so painstakingly accumulated. By way of extending and problematizing Goody's seminal analysis somewhat, could it not be asked if there is any case where writing does in fact encourage the vibrant literary creativity that Goody has isolated in oral societies?

Paraphrase can arguably be seen as one example of this, and the brief history of paraphrase below seeks to provide evidence from the ancient and late antique Near East. Some studies have been made that already point to this conclusion. In his recent book on the reception of the Bible in modern literature, literary critic Robert Alter has shown (in contrast to Goody) how the

---

[18] Goody 2000:iii.

[19] For a thoughtful critique of Goody on this point, see Bloch 1998:131–151. One could argue that Goody has misunderstood Derrida in that, for the latter, "text" is a metaphor more than a mode of communication. Nevertheless, Goody's seminal conclusions about the cognitive relationship between canon and elaboration still stand.

[20] Goody 2000:151: "writing is a prerequisite, a prerequisite for the development of all the technologies with which our intellect engages."

[21] Goody 2000:21.

institution of a written literary canon almost invariably encourages further elaboration and creativity, in writing:

> The imaginative response to the Bible of writers in a wide variety of languages bears witness to a power of canonicity that is not limited to doctrine or strictly contingent on belief in the inspired character of the texts invoked.[22]

The canon thus serves as a "vehicle" for imaginative literature, which takes its inspiration from Scripture in a wide variety of ways: by mimicking the "earthy" language of a culturally dominant translation (Faulkner); by "wrestling" with biblical self-interpretation (Kafka); by using biblical language to re-present modern paradoxes (Bialik); by "intricately coordinating Scripture with Homer" (Joyce).[23]

The commingling of biblical myth and Homeric epic is characteristic of fifth-century AD Greek paraphrase, as I shall demonstrate below, but it is appropriate to point out here that the attitude of classical writers to Homer and myth in general adds weight to Alter's insights and further enriches Goody's oral model. In her recent study of *Literate Education in the Hellenistic and Roman Worlds*, Teresa Morgan has gathered an impressive amount of papyrological evidence pointing to the manipulation of Homeric texts in a school context. "Texts oscillated between two statuses: that of the particular canonical version of the story, and that of a tool which could be used and altered."[24] Homeric canon could be, therefore, a stimulant to literary activity on a very literal level: Morgan's evidence consists of rewritings of individual words and phrases as well as the wholesale recasting of epic into both prose and verse.[25] On a wider view, the Homeric myths formed an imaginative world for ancient writers, a "site" on which they could play with an ancient, received literary history. Both the incidental details of the myths and the narrative holes left unfilled by the poet became opportunities for expansion. Indeed, as Froma Zeitlin has recently argued at length, ancient patterns of "traffic in Homer" were widespread and varied, often taking the form of imaginative (even visual) reconstructions of the myths and even the persona of the poet

---

[22] Alter 2000:60. Alter is here admittedly building on Alan Bloom's *The Western Canon* (1994), though is critical of its central Oedipal metaphor.

[23] Alter 2000:61.

[24] Morgan 1998:224. She is right to formulate a pair with these two cognitive activities, but whether there was ever, even in literate societies, a "particular version" of the canonical texts is still debated.

[25] On paraphrase in ancient schools, see Morgan 1998:198–226.

himself.[26] In other words, nothing was out of bounds, and almost any aspect of received tradition could become the object of paraphrase. Yet the fact remains that the reception of Greek myth in the Hellenistic period by poet-scholars like Apollonius and Callimachus set an enduring pattern for Roman and late antique elaboration, and there is ample evidence that major Greek poets and paraphrasts of the fifth-century AD, such as Nonnus, were taking direct inspiration from their Hellenistic predecessors.[27] The example of Marianus of Eleutheropolis, an official at the court of the emperor Anastasius (491–518), offers a view from the crest of this trend: according to the Byzantine *Suda* encyclopedia, he wrote iambic paraphrases of the hexameter works of all the important Hellenistic poets—Theocritus, Apollonius, Callimachus, Aratus, Nicander, "and many others."[28]

In Greek, the term for paraphrase one usually finds is μετάφρασις—less often μεταβολή.[29] While μετάφρασις is sometimes mistakenly rendered into English as "translation"—its meaning in Modern Greek—ancient writers typically invested more in the word than "translation" allows. Josephus, for example, parallels μετάφρασις with μεθερμενεύω, "to interpret," when describing his own project of retelling the Hebrew Scriptures in his *Antiquities*.[30] Several Greek writers from the Roman period use the word in this way, and the meaning persists into the Byzantine period when μετάφρασις became a major literary project in its own right.[31]

What, then, is the ancient theory of μετάφρασις? How is a retelling to be understood that is not merely translation or re-presentation? On the basis of theoretical models from anthropology and literary criticism, I have suggested that paraphrase as can be seen as a method of imaginative elaboration. The elaboration is dependent on a canonical or received text, from which it takes inspiration and/or narrative material. The fixity of received texts used for rewriting and paraphrase is less important on a doctrinal or ideological level than on a cognitive one.

---

[26] Zeitlin 2001.

[27] See Hollis 1994 and forthcoming.

[28] Alan Cameron 1965:482; *Suda* s.v. "Μαριανός."

[29] According to a *TLG* search (performed by the author on 28 March, 2005), μεταβολή appears to be a standard Byzantine term for paraphrase from about the tenth century. It only rarely has this meaning in classical and late antique literature (LSJ s.v.). Note, however, that the *Suda* entry for Marianus just cited calls his works μεταφράσεις.

[30] Josephus *Antiquities* 1.5, 10.218. Interestingly, the verb μεθερμενεύω is also used by Josephus when describing the Greek Septuagint "translation" of the Hebrew Bible (12.20, 48); while this usage may seem like contrary evidence, there is good reason to render it also as "to interpret" or "to paraphrase"; for this see Feldman 1998a:44–45.

[31] Writers who use μετάφρασις to mean "paraphrase" include Dionysius of Halicarnassus, Plutarch,

Both Goody and Alter point to the fact that rewriting is necessarily concomitant with any reception of "text," be it oral or written, especially when that text has taken on a dominant, self-defining role in a culture. Whether it is the Lo Dagaa Bagre myth, stories from the Hebrew Bible, or the vast Homeric and related mythologies of ancient Greece, human cognitive response invariably tends towards elaboration and rewriting, sometimes on a very literal level, as in Hellenistic school exercises. The received text naturally becomes, often without any external pressure, a "site" or a locus of rewriting and "play": this play, of course, has as much to do with refashioning contemporary identity as it does with reformulating ancient mythology.[32] In paraphrase the two are inseparably linked; but this play, which Goody would describe as being at root a cognitive activity, occurs whenever a received text is altered, no matter how slightly.

In the context of the copying of ancient manuscripts and codices, Kim Haines-Eitzen has described this cognitive activity in the following terms : "Copying an exemplar meant producing a 'resemblance' not an identity." And she goes on to quote Michel Foucault:

> Resemblance has a "model," an original element that orders and hierarchizes the increasingly less faithful copies that can be struck from it. Resemblance presupposes a primary reference that prescribes and classes.[33]

For rewriting individual words, as much as for paraphrase, the issue of "resemblance" is central: any alteration or elaboration of a received text depends on the original for its new "identity" and, at a secondary level, the re-casted text depends on a pre-existent discourse of classification and power. Exactly how the resemblance is constructed defines the inherent meanings of the text, and, from a structuralist point of view, also describes the society that produced it.

The fifth-century AD *Life and Miracles of Thekla*, the object of the present study, can provide a textual "place" in which to examine these issues. When this text had been previously studied by scholars, the complex issues of paraphrase and textual elaboration have not been addressed. By setting this half of the text in a literary historical framework—and then by doing the same for the second half in Chapter Four—I hope to be able to say more about how the

---

Origen, and Eusebius; see LSJ and Lampe s.v. "μετάφρασις" and "μεταφράζω."

[32] On the refashioning of myth for contemporary political ideologies, see Veyne 1988.

[33] Haines-Eitzen 2000:105–106, citing Foucault 1983:44.

text works internally and, more importantly, how it relates to the culture that produced it.

In a similar vein, the bibliographer Donald McKenzie addressed the question in his 1985 Panizzi lectures of how "textual artifacts" should be treated in an age when the printed word threatens to overwhelm the human ability to process.[34] In a self-conscious attempt to redefine the vocation of bibliography for the new millennium—trying on the label "sociology of texts"—he insisted that scholars should pay close attention to the physical properties of the texts they study, since these properties can tell us as much about what the text means as can the intentions or ideologies that appear on its surface. McKenzie writes:

> My argument therefore runs full circle from a defense of authorial meaning, on the grounds that it is in some measure recoverable, to a recognition that, for better or worse, readers inevitably make their own meanings. In other words, each reading is particular to its occasion, each can be at least partially recovered from the physical forms of the text, and the differences in readings constitute an informative history.[35]

and further:

> If a history of readings is made possible only by a comparative history of books, it is equally true that a history of books will have no point if it fails to account for the meanings they later come to make.[36]

The present study, like McKenzie's new bibliography, takes seriously the changes, the resemblance, of the *Life and Miracles* to its *Vorlage*, the *ATh*. Thus, I examined in detail in the previous chapter the elaborations made by the author in an attempt to highlight and further explain the literary nature of the *Life* on its own.

According to McKenzie's model, however, the *Life and Miracles* would never have existed on its own and, consequently, must today be read through the history of books—more specifically in our case, the history of rewritings and paraphrases—that came before it. The brief history of rewriting that follows is not an attempt to excavate origins or to show direct influence. Rather, it

---

[34] McKenzie 1999 [1986].
[35] McKenzie 1999:19.
[36] McKenzie 1999:23.

discusses the synchronic unity of paraphrastic activity through a diachronic survey. Additionally, I provide at the end a sense of how the tradition continued in Byzantium, post fifth-century, in order to compare an instance where paraphrase, μετάφρασις, became an epoch-defining literary project. Nevertheless, an argument already made explicit in this study is that rewriting (either oral or written) is a basic cognitive activity. Therefore, contrary to previous studies of Byzantine μετάφρασις that insist on its uniqueness to that culture at that time, my study will argue for its near ubiquity in Greek Christian literature.[37] Furthermore, I hope this study can contribute to the larger picture of the process of textual inheritance that has emerged from neighboring disciplines, such as scholarship on the medieval West and the early modern period.

## The "Rewritten Bible" in Ancient Judaism

Christians were, of course, not the first to treat their own Scripture as a site of rewriting. Jewish literary history is particularly rich with paraphrases, and these appear from an early point. Deuteronomy, the ultimate expression of the Mosaic law in the Pentateuch, is largely a rewritten systematization of legal material from Exodus and Numbers.[38] A few centuries later, the postexilic author of the book of Chronicles not only drew material from the Pentateuch, Isaiah, Jeremiah, Ezekiel, and the Psalms, but clearly rewrote substantial sections of the earlier histories of Samuel and Kings, adding, subtracting, and summarizing according to the ideologies of Second Temple Israel.[39] The successful reception of Chronicles as a rewriting is attested, of course, by its subsequent inclusion in the biblical canon, but, interestingly also by its Greek name in the Septuagint, Παραλειπομένων ("the things left out" or "omissions"), a title which suggests that readers in the third to second centuries BC already recognized its unique relationship to Samuel and Kings. Thus, within the biblical tradition itself, rewriting was not seen as a banal or opportunistic activity but could be acknowledged as a legitimate, even "canonical," form of literary endeavor.[40]

Just a few generations before the canon of the Hebrew Bible became fixed (c. 1st century AD), two trends emerged in its interpretative history.

---

[37] Cf. Høgel 2002.

[38] See Alter and Kermode 1987:92–101 and Alter 2004:xv, 869–877, and passim.

[39] See Kugel 1998:2, 6, and the refs at 2n2, esp. Japhet 1997 [1989].

[40] The inclusion of rewrites within the Old Testament canon itself must be of fundamental importance for early Christian conceptions of the validity of paraphrase with regard to their own Scriptures.

One trend was to codify the accepted books (Deuteronomy and Chronicles included, of course) and to comment on the text externally, thus attaching a protected status to Scripture: this is the trend that ultimately resulted in the formation of a "Masoretic" canon as well as influencing the development of rabbinic exegesis.[41] (The mode of rabbinic midrash, i.e. lemma + commentary, also attests to this trend.) Another trend, however, was to continue to mix commentary with received text and thus to perpetuate the interpretive habit of "Rewritten Bible" established by the authors of Deuteronmy and especially Chronicles.[42]

Within this latter tradition, the copyists and commentators of the Dead Sea Scrolls community chose to rewrite biblical books according to the sectarian eschatological vision of their Teacher of Righteousness. The manuscripts found at Qumran are overwhelmingly biblical in their orientation: only one major text (the *Copper Scroll*) is not a biblical manuscript or a work based on Scripture. And every book of the Hebrew Bible was found there, either complete or in fragmentary form.[43] But the biblical texts are not identical with the Masoretic versions: they show a tremendous amount of variation, even between themselves.[44] In addition to these individual changes (both conscious and not) to the biblical text, a striking feature of the Qumran exegetical literature is its extensive interweaving of Scripture and comment on the page, to the degree that often the commentary seems to become Scripture. The fragmentary *Genesis Apocryphon*, a very loose paraphrase, is outstanding in this regard.[45] Surely, this technique (called *pesher* in its standard Qumranic form) is where some of the scribes' own biblical interpolations originated, but what is striking is how pervasive the habit of paraphrase seems to have been at

---

[41] That an importance was attached to the Hebrew text, by the end of the first century AD at the very latest, can be shown from the fact that Aquila's literalist rendering of the Hebrew into Greek was well received by the Jewish community, over and against the paraphrasing Septuagint preferred by the Christians; see Swete 1900:31–42.

[42] The phrase "Rewritten Bible" was apparently coined by Vermes 1975, but others have taken up this concept with vigor. See esp. Kugel 1998, whose conception of the history of Jewish biblical interpretation hinges upon the concept: e.g. "The Rewritten Bible is really the interpreted Bible," and "The Rewritten Bible (whether one is talking about an extended retelling of whole biblical books, or the 'retelling' of a single verse) should be recognized for what it is: the most popular transmitter of biblical interpretation among ancient writers" (Kugel 1998:23).

[43] Vermes 1975:39.

[44] Only a small proportion of these variations are scribal errors. See Vermes 1998:15 on the "extreme fluidity" of the Qumran Bible(s). On the distinctiveness of the Septuagint's *Vorlage* and the Qumran texts, see Tov 1992: "many, if not most of the biblical texts of the third and second centuries BCE were unique ..." (42–43).

[45] See Vermes 1998:448–459.

Qumran across the board. The scribes of this community clearly took a cogni-
tive/interpretative position on Scripture different from those who were simultaneously working to make the Bible inviolable. At Qumran the received text
of the Bible was a book susceptible to modification and elaboration, rather
than the monolithic code it (more or less) became in rabbinic circles.

It is important also to keep in view the parallel history of the ancient
translations of the Hebrew Scriptures, for these translations were at times
paraphrases in their own right and can point to how the tradition of rewriting
was received.[46] To take the most celebrated example, the translators of the
Septuagint (hereafter LXX) significantly modified the original Hebrew text,
adding large sections to certain books, despite the claim to accuracy put
forward in the legendary *Letter of Aristeas*.[47] These changes were significant in
particular because early Christian writers, including the authors of the books
in the New Testament, used the LXX almost exclusively, thereby extending the
life of the translators' rewrites.

A recognition in antiquity of the changes made by the LXX translators
is evidenced by the three important attempts in the first two centuries AD to
bring the LXX back into line with the Hebrew. These are the so-called "minor
versions" or simply "the Three": Aquila's literal translation; Theodotion's less
strict revision of the LXX; and Symmachus' translation in fluid Greek. In addition to these three, Dominique Barthélemy published in 1963 the fragments
of a slightly earlier Greek translation of the Twelve Prophets, which were
found at Nahal Hever in the Judean desert. These fragments, dating to the first
century BC, are part of a literal revision of the LXX that seems to have subsequently influenced Aquila.[48] The importance of these fragments lies in their
showing that a decision to revise the LXX, because of its inaccuracies and elaborations, came even earlier than previously thought.[49]

---

[46] Bernstein 1994:2; Vermes 1975:62–63.

[47] As is well known, the *Letter of Aristeas* records the translation of the LXX by seventy-two
Jewish scholars from Jerusalem invited to Alexandria by the king Ptolemy. In a rather frus-
trating manner the text does not get around to discussing the actual work of the translators
until the very end, and, even then, the details of the process are not revealed. However, what
the *Letter of Aristeas* does make clear, through its rhetoric of superiority and self-justifica-
tion, is that there were competing translations, contemporary with the penning of the *Letter*
(perhaps 1st cent. BC). For the text of the *Letter*, see H. St. J. Thackeray's still standard edition
in Swete 1900:519–574; see also the translation with introduction and notes by R. J. J. Shutt in
Charlesworth 1985:7–34.

[48] Response to Barthélemy 1963 has not been completely positive: Grabbe 1992 argues that
Barthélemy overemphasizes the influence of this earlier revision (the so-called "*kaige* recension") on Aquila's translation.

[49] Brock 1992:303.

There is some scholarly disagreement, however, as to how the translation of the LXX itself should be understood in the context of these subsequent rewrites and translations. Barnabas Lindars, for instance, has argued that a translation of the Hebrew Bible, in whatever form, should be kept distinct from its rewriting in commentaries and the like:

> The Septuagint is essentially a translation and not a targumizing paraphrase. There is a sense in which every translation is a commentary, or contains what might be called linguistic exegesis, because it represents the translator's understanding of the text, and this is inevitably colored by the presuppositions of the time. But this is not the same thing as deliberate modification of the text for the sake of interpretation (which might be designated content exegesis). The aim of the translators of the Septuagint was to give a faithful rendering of the Hebrew.[50]

Lindars's formula, however, depends on a strict a definition of translation; what is "essential" to any translation was contested in antiquity and continues to be so today.[51] If Lindars means the LXX Penteteuch alone, which is more literal than the other books, then he has some room for argument, but it is important to note that most scholars accept that the LXX is conceptually a paraphrase, and it was understood to be so in antiquity. It is because of this ancient understanding that I think it can be argued from a historical point of view that "content exegesis" and translation should not be so artificially separated. As already suggested, it is clear from the subsequent history of the Greek translations that the LXX was considered too loose and needed to be brought back into line, presumably because the "content" had been altered.

Despite the LXX's prominence among Christian writers—even to the level of Luke's imitation of its literary style—later Jewish translators were not satisfied with the text, and Origen, idiosyncratically sympathetic to the Hebrew original, famously put the later Greek versions in parallel columns with the Hebrew and the LXX in his Hexapla.[52] To quote a modern editor of the LXX:

---

[50] Lindars 1992:4–5.

[51] For competing methods of biblical translation in antiquity, see Brock 1992; for a helpful anthology of essays on modern translation theories, see Schulte and Biguenet 1992.

[52] Eusebius *Ecclesiastical History* 6.16. Some Christians, such as Lucian of Antioch in the third century, made their own Greek translations straight from the Hebrew, as Jerome did into Latin over a century later; for a detailed survey of all the biblical versions, see *ABD* s.v. "Versions." However, for most early Christian writers, the approval of Josephus and Philo, in addition to the New Testament, was enough to guarantee the LXX's authority.

> It is clear from the very arrangement of the Hexapla that to [Origen],
> being a scholar, not the LXX, but the original text was the primary
> authority, for he put the original text first, and then had next to it
> the translations of Aquila and Symmachus, since they furnished the
> most accurate renderings of the original text.[53]

In addition, Origen felt comfortable correcting the LXX when he saw fit,
and Hexaplan variants have come down to us that are clearly Origen's own
interpolations.[54] Thus, certainly among biblical scholars in antiquity, there
seems to have been a keen sense of the inadequacy of the LXX alone with
regard to its accuracy—that is to say, some clearly did not consider it a "faithful
rendering," in Lindars's phrase.

A very different approach to the LXX emerged concurrently with the
more literal and idiomatic Greek translations. Jews writing in Greek in the
first century AD, such as Philo and Josephus, continued the tradition of
rewriting (expansively) their received Greek Scriptures. Louis Feldman has
made a sweeping study over several years—in separate articles now collected
in one volume (1998b) and also rewritten into a monograph (1998a)—of
the rewriting, primarily of the LXX itself, made by Josephus in his *Jewish
Antiquities*. Feldman observes that Josephus reworked biblical stories out of
concern for certain factors, including style and narrative quality, the assumptions of his intended readerships, and historiographical tropes—though
apparently not out of concern for the accuracy of the translation. Through his
rewriting, Josephus emerges, according to Feldman, as "no mere copyist or
compiler," but, instead, "his own views—historiographical, political, religious,
and cultural . . . are consistently seen throughout the *Antiquities*, particularly
in the changes which he has made in his paraphrase of the biblical text."[55]
Josephus thus took a comparatively liberal view toward the LXX, introducing his unique vision of the history of the Jews within the biblical text
itself, so that, like the Bible of the Qumran community, his paraphrase is an
inseparable intertwining of text and commentary. Josephus in his *Antiquities*
presented virtually a new Bible, at least in its historical account, and it is
paradoxical that, while the original is all but invisible, to appreciate the argument, irony, and wit of his new text, Josephus' readers even today must be
very well acquainted with the original Scripture, in Greek at least, if not also
in Hebrew and Aramaic.

---

[53] Ralfs 1979:lxii.
[54] Jarick 1990:6, citing Daniélou 1955:133.
[55] Feldman 1998b:539.

Despite his expansive inventiveness, however, Josephus staunchly defended the accuracy of the LXX (interestingly, through his recasting of the *Letter of Aristeas*) and claimed that he himself was only repeating what was in Scripture—both striking comments if one considers how central paraphrase was to his historiographical method.[56] Acknowledging this apparent contradiction, several scholars have pointed out that creativity with the biblical text does not generally entail a lack of respect for the Bible; on the contrary, the opposite is most often the case. The Aramaic *targumim*, for example, are paraphrasing translations, collected in late antiquity and the middle ages, which were originally made from the Hebrew, though which took on an authority of their own in Aramaic.[57] Unlike *midrash*, the *targumim* did not cite the original text but included interpretive material in the text itself, so that the reader or listener would hear only the recast version of the Hebrew: hence, like in Josephus, it is impossible to reconstruct the original text from the *targum* alone.[58] This is in direct contrast to the lemma + commentary mode of the *midrash*.

Despite the conceptual distinctiveness of paraphrase, Josephus and authors of the *targumim* depended on what they considered to be a stable,

---

[56] See Brock 1992:303–310. Josephus *Antiquities* 12.108–109; Philo *Life of Moses* 2.25–44, esp. 40: "... if Chaldeans [i.e. those who read Hebrew/Aramaic] have learned Greek, or Greeks Chaldean [i.e. Hebrew/Aramaic], and read both versions, the Chaldean and the translation, they regard them with awe and reverence as sisters, or rather one and the same, both in matter and words, and speak of the authors not as translators but as prophets and priests of the mysteries, whose sincerity and singleness of thought has enabled them to go hand in hand with the purest of spirits, the spirit of Moses" (trans. F. H. Colson, LCL Philo vol. 6).

[57] Thus, once the rabbis took control of the *targumim* which they inherited, they "were concerned that *targum* should be clearly distinguished from Scripture: the same person could not publicly read the Hebrew and recite the *targum*" (Alexander 1992:330). This is an interesting example of incorporating a paraphrase into a different cognitive system, both to appreciate its teaching as well as to make it submit to a higher textual authority.

[58] Some *targumim* are more paraphrasing than others. For the individual works—Targums Neofiti, Ps.-Jonathan, Onkelos, the Cairo Geniza fragments, etc.—see Alexander 1992, Beattie and McNamara 1994, and Flesher 1995: esp. 40: "This [paraphrasing] approach enables the additions to masquerade as translation, disguising them from all but the most learned. The hidden character of the interpretive material, in turn, enables the targumist to add details, change the meaning, and even rewrite the story without the Aramaic-speaking audience being aware of it. *Targum* authors, then, provided their audience with a text that adhered to the original Hebrew, but at the same time presented accepted interpretations." By whom were these interpretations "accepted"? Apparently, Flesher here means "accepted by the targumist" rather than the audience/congregation generally. I have not been able to find a clear answer to the question of whether a standard Aramaic audience would have recognized, before the rabbis instituted the parallel reading of Hebrew, that the *targum* was in fact a paraphrase. Flesher here suggests they would not have.

authoritative text for their own rewritings.[59] The text Josephus used (primarily) was an interpretative, sometimes paraphrasing, translation in its own right, but it provided a textual "site" where Jewish writers of the Hellenistic and Roman East habitually played with the history and literature that they had inherited and, thereby, tried to make it accessible to a broader audience. In his *Heritage and Hellenism*, Erich Gruen has explored in depth this pervasive characteristic of Hellenistic Jewish writing:

> For Hellenistic Jews writing in Greek, the Scriptures provided stimulus for ingenuity and creativity. The concept of a fixed and unalterable tradition had not yet taken hold. No scriptural "canon" existed. Composition and interpretation proceeded concurrently, and the idea of established texts was still in process of formation. The fluidity of the tradition may frustrate modern scholars. But it gave impetus to writers eager to reshape and revivify narratives long familiar but conveniently adaptable.[60]

Although Gruen is speaking here of a specifically Hellenistic context, the practice of Jewish paraphrase was at least as old as Deuteronomy and continued to be employed in the Roman and late antique periods. Furthermore, as I shall explain in the next section, there is ample evidence that the Christian tradition of biblical paraphrase emerged from this Jewish literary milieu.

However, before proceeding to the Christian paraphrases, there is one more group of Jewish texts that warrants attention—the Jewish novels. The works I have mentioned so far are primarily Scriptural in orientation, and I have suggested that this technique of paraphrase took its inspiration from Scripture—both from the canonical models of paraphrastic writing and, of course, from the literal source material with which the paraphrast worked.[61] Moreover, scholars do not normally see these paraphrases as attempts to

---

[59] It should be noted that there are instances where Josephus uses a revised version of the LXX in his *Antiquities*; e.g. see Ulrich 1978:259, cited by Brock 1992:335n13: Josephus used "a slightly revised form of Old Greek [translations]" for parts of Samuel. As Feldman has shown, there is plenty of evidence that he used Aramaic translations as well, perhaps some of the *targumim* that have come down to us (Feldman 1998a:28–29). The earliest datable *targumim* are first century AD from Qumran: Job 37:10–42:11 and some fragments of Leviticus 16:12–15, 18–21 (ibid.:17).

[60] Gruen 1998:110.

[61] Biblical paraphrase could perhaps be seen as closely aligned to distinct categories or genres, such as commentary (e.g. much of the Qumran material), Jewish historiography (Chronicles and Josephus), or translation (LXX, *targumim*); however, it is not encompassed by any one of these and ultimately transcends genre.

replace Scripture; rather, they represent a kind of homage to Scripture and its imaginative worlds. The extant Jewish novels, while more self-consciously fictional than historical paraphrases like Chronicles, were nevertheless read alongside the interpretative genres in the Hellenistic period and, when they deal with biblical scenes, can arguably be seen as a kind of expanded biblical paraphrase.[62] And the novels themselves went through numerous changes, as is attested by the different recensions that have survived,[63] with the result that the rewriting of the rewriting only further compounds our sense of the pervasiveness of paraphrase and textual elaboration or modification in ancient Jewish literature.

From the texts and fragments that have survived, the Jewish novel seems to have been a particularly successful medium for refashioning biblical stories. James Kugel has argued that, like biblical translators and paraphrasts, Jewish novelists rewrote the stories of the Bible (and added new ones) in response to specific difficulties they found in the text.[64] While this interpretation serves as a productive matrix through which to examine scriptural elaboration, it is probably just as viable to argue that Jewish novelists were inspired by a general flowering of fictional narrative in the Hellenistic Diaspora: works such as *Tobit*, the Greek Esther, *Judith*, and the novelistic extensions to Daniel (*Bel and the Dragon* and *Susannah*) belong to this tradition and were widely known in the late Hellenistic period.[65] These novels and their successors—*Joseph and Aseneth*, Artapanus' *On Moses*, *Third Maccabees*—interacted with the canons of Greek literature more directly than biblical commentary and can perhaps be seen as cross-fertilizing the Greek Romance, which emerged concurrently. There is no doubt that Jewish novels owe a great deal to the Bible itself, but the

---

[62] For the salient characteristics of the Jewish novel, esp. in comparison with the Greek Romance (but not with early Christian literature), see Wills 1995.

[63] Wills 1995:36: "The Jewish novels appear to be composed and recomposed, without the canon of a fixed text but with the canon of a traditional set of plots and characters. The study of ancient novels thus places the scholar in a difficult position between the analysis of oral and written tradition, oral and literary culture. We are addressing neither oral culture nor written culture but 'popular written culture' . . . Comic books, science fiction novels, and drugstore romances occupy a similar position in modern society."

[64] E.g. Kugel 1998:24: "Ancient biblical interpretation is an interpretation of verses, not stories."; see esp. Kugel 1990 for his well-honed, if somewhat idiosyncratic, methodology.

[65] Laurence Wills has produced a helpful one-volume collection of translated Jewish Novels, with introductions, notes, and bibliographies for each (2002); critical texts of these novels are not always available (due to their many recensions), nor easily found if they are—Wills includes a short guide to the disparate texts he used (2002:ix–x). The fragmentary historical paraphrases and novels (such as Artapanus) can be found with text, translation, and commentary in Carl Holladay's four-volume collection, *Fragments from Hellenistic Jewish Authors* (1983–1996).

latter's influence on the novel was less compartmentalized than on standard biblical paraphrase, such as that found in the *targumim* or Josephus' *Antiquities*. Nevertheless, Josephus himself is the conveyer (in the *Antiquities*) of two historical novels—the *Tobaid Romance* and the *Royal Family of Adiabene*—and his juxtaposition of these with biblical paraphrase points directly to the crucial interpenetration of translation, paraphrase, and the novel in ancient Jewish literature.

An extensive treatment of the novels' elaborations is not warranted here, but it should be noted that the novelistic literary style, on display above all in the five major Greek Romances—Chariton, Xenophon of Ephesus, Longus, Achilles Tatius, and Heliodorus—emerged in a potent climate of literary cross-fertilization, a climate in which a key player was Jewish fictional writing in the Hellenistic and Roman periods.[66] Furthermore, this style was, as I have suggested, intimately connected in Jewish literature to biblical rewriting, both from an authorial and an interpretative point of view.[67] Finally, the connection between these literary modes is perpetuated and expanded by Christians in their own tradition of biblical paraphrase. It is to this Christian evidence that we shall now turn.

## Textual Elaboration in Early Christian Tradition: From *Bezae* to *Homerocentones*

### The Gospels amidst Jewish paraphrase

Christians began rewriting their scriptures from the very beginning. The now standard "two-source" theory of gospel composition posits that the authors of Matthew and Luke both used Mark and "Q" (a lost "sayings-source")—in addition to their own material—to construct the narratives of their Gospels. Mark and Q were, in the parlance of New Testament scholarship, "sources" or *Quellen* for the authors of Matthew and Luke. However, modern *Quellenforschung* (or the atomistic separating-out of these strands) seen in the context of the great amount of imaginative rewriting going on in Jewish circles in the first century AD appears, as a methodology, simply stultifying and one-dimensional. By contrast, I would like to try to see Matthew and Luke

---

[66] For the characteristic style of the Greek Romance, see Reardon 1991. For its influence on Christian literature, see Pervo 1987, 1996, Hägg 1983, and Johnson forthcomingb.

[67] On the interaction of novelistic style and Jewish rewriting/interpretation, see Gruen 1998: passim and 2002:part 2, Kugel 1998 (organized according to biblical theme), and, generally, Wills 1995 (a genre-analysis) and 2002 (translations of Jewish novels).

as Christian examples of a habit of biblical rewriting that permeated Judeo-Christian literature in antiquity.[68]

Rather than looking for their sources and origins, it may be more helpful, considering the tremendous amount of evidence for ancient Jewish paraphrase, to see the Gospels as historical "sites" of rewriting where the authors were appropriating a recognizable method of literary activity within their immediate cultural and religious milieu. To be sure, this approach involves a shift of perspective, but it is one that pays dividends. This is true especially when looking at the way late antique prose narratives, such as the *Life of Thekla*, treat earlier Christian literature. The canonical Gospels and Acts became models for how Christian literature was supposed to be written—in language, style, and religious discourse generally—and, despite (or in conjunction with) the persistent influence of classical Greek literature through the educational system, these earliest Christian narratives took on for many later writers a mimetic authority. We have already glimpsed this in the *Life*'s invocation of Luke at the beginning of its paraphrase (see above pp. 18–21).

Looking more closely, however, Luke and Matthew are demonstrably not paraphrases—at least not in the traditional Jewish form exemplified by Chronicles, the Greek Esther, or Josephus. Bypassing summary and elaboration, these writers instead reorganize, moving snippets of Mark and Q around like puzzle pieces. Now that some Jewish examples have been produced above, this method can be brought into relief, especially for the sake of comparison with later Christian literature. On the surface, Matthew and Luke seem to be doing something different, but from a cognitive point of view, I argue, they are treating their source texts in much the same way, or at least producing similar effects on the reader.

Matthew and Luke do not approach Mark as a traditional paraphrast might because they do not see the first gospel as an ancient tradition: to put it differently, not only do we know them as the part of the first generation after Jesus, they recognize themselves as such. As Luke says in his prologue to Theophilus:

---

[68] Another way of seeing the Gospels in more than one dimension is asking, for instance, what is the relationship between Mark and John? This question of genre has been addressed in detail by Wills 1997 which takes a broader view of the question of influence and which points evocatively to a fluid exchange of literary styles and religious language in the gospel-milieu. In particular, Wills argues for a more inclusive definition of "biography" as a classical genre in order to take account of novelistic treatments of hero cults, e.g. the *Life of Aesop*. From the point of view of late antique Greek literature—specifically of the influence that the gospel genre had during that period—Wills's study of the Gospels represents a salutary shift in perspective. Other studies that preceded Wills in this vein are Tolbert 1989, Burridge 1992, and Collins 1992. See Wills 1997:chapter 1 for a thorough discussion of the previous scholarship.

Since many have undertaken to set down an orderly account of the events that have been fulfilled among us (πολλοὶ ἐπεχείρησαν ἀνατάξασθαι διήγησιν περὶ τῶν πεπληροφορημένων ἐν ἡμῖν πραγμάτων), just as they were handed on to us by those who from the beginning were eyewitnesses and servants of the word, I too decided, after investigating everything carefully from the very first (ἔδοξε κἀμοὶ παρηκολουθηκότι ἄνωθεν πᾶσιν ἀκριβῶς), to write an orderly account for you, most excellent Theophilus, so that you may know the truth concerning the things about which you have been instructed.[69]

I have already acknowledged above, in the Prologue to this chapter, the uniqueness among the evangelists of Luke's creation of his own audience. What is also significant is that he claims to have (re)investigated the details again *without* using the "many" (Mark and Q?) who came before him.[70] He acknowledges to Theophilus that he currently has the investigative opportunity to return to "the very first"—presumably he means Jesus' early life, which, of the four evangelists, only he discusses in detail.

By way of contrast, Josephus, in writing his *Antiquities*, recognized the temporal distance between himself and his textual site of rewriting and seems to have felt compelled to emphasize that he was changing nothing that he had received:

At the outset, then, I entreat those who will read these volumes to fix their thoughts on God, and to test whether our lawgiver [Moses] has had a worthy conception of His nature and has always assigned to Him such actions as befit His power, keeping his words concerning Him pure of that unseemly mythology current among others; albeit that, in dealing with ages so long and so remote (καίτοι γε ὅσον ἐπὶ μήκει χρόνου καὶ παλαιότητι), he would have had ample license to invent fictions (πολλὴν εἶχεν ἄδειαν ψευδῶν πλασμάτων). For he was born two thousand years ago, to which ancient date the poets never ventured to refer even the birth of their gods, much less the actions or the laws of mortals. The precise details of our Scripture records will, then, be set forth (τὰ μὲν οὖν ἀκριβῆ τῶν ἐν ταῖς

---

[69] Luke 1:1–4 NRSV.

[70] If the author of Luke means Mark and Q, then he is not telling the truth, for he relied upon them extensively. If he means other accounts than these, then they have not survived. The third and best option is that this statement is simply a necessary aspect of the rhetoric of historiographical prefaces. For the rhetoric of ancient prefaces (specifically Latin), see Janson 1964.

ἀναγραφαῖς προϊών), each in its place, as my narrative proceeds, that being the procedure that I have promised to follow throughout this work, neither adding or omitting anything (οὐδὲν προσθεὶς οὐδ' αὖ παραλιπών).[71]

Elsewhere in the prologue, Josephus claims that Scripture narrated the history of "five thousand years" and that his *Antiquities* "will embrace our entire ancient history and political constitution, translated from the Hebrew records" (1.13). And as he says here, Moses would have had "ample license to invent fictions": is this an ironic gesture to the knowing readers who would recognize that Josephus did anything but "set forth" Scripture "without omitting anything"? Is he employing historiographical convention to add humor to an already weighty prologue? Perhaps this is the case, since Gruen has demonstrated with numerous examples that self-reflective humor was characteristic of Hellenistic Jewish historians.[72]

What is important for the present argument is that, while Luke and Josephus conceive of their temporal distance from the textual site in very different ways—with implications for how they treat their source material—both use that textual "site," the *textus receptus*, to invent a new narrative recognizably different from the original. Prescriptively they are very different but descriptively they are similar. Or, in other words, their approaches, while distinct in conception, nevertheless imply a similar cognitive angle on received texts, an angle which, I would argue, takes its inspiration from contemporary Jewish habits of rewriting more than from Greek historiographical conventions.

## Close elaboration of the New Testament

The habit of rewriting penetrated much of early Christian textual activity, even if not in the style of a formal paraphrase: all of the New Testament Gospels betray some kind of recasting of their source material, and, as I have tried to emphasize, the prevalence of this activity reflects a wider Judeo-Christian metaphrastic mindset. Moreover, as might be expected given the evidence from Qumran, the subsequent copying of these early Christian texts was a particularly fervent locus of rewriting as well.

To take one significant and well studied case, the preeminent witness to the so-called "Western" textual tradition of the New Testament, *Codex*

---

[71] Josesphus *Antiquities* 1.15–17; trans. H. St. J. Thackeray, LCL Josephus vol. 5.
[72] Gruen 2002: chapters 5 and 6.

*Bezae Cantabrigiensis*—a circa fifth-century bilingual (Greek-Latin), uncial manuscript—provides a large number of unique readings for the Acts of the Apostles.[73] In fact, the number of variants is so large that the "Western" text of Acts has been called "virtually an alternative version of the book."[74] In 1966 the New Testament scholar Eldon J. Epp argued that many of these unique readings are conscious attempts to introduce into the text of Acts a rigorous anti-Jewish polemic. For example, the well known "ignorance motif" of the canonical Luke-Acts pair—which intimates that the Jews were not guilty of crucifying Jesus because they were "ignorant" of who he really was (e.g. ἀγνοήσαντες, 13:27)—is consistently written out of the *Codex Bezae* text.[75] The Jews are specifically held responsible in the rewritten Acts, and Christological terminology is re-designed to intensify the divide between Jews and Christians.[76]

Looking beyond Acts, Epp also points out the prayer of Jesus on the cross at Luke 23:34, Πάτερ, ἄφες αὐτοῖς· οὐ γὰρ οἴδασιν τί ποιοῦσιν ("Father, forgive them; for they do not know what they are doing"), is expunged from the *Codex Bezae* text.[77] In addition, there is a consistent "devaluation" of the Jewish element in Christianity and a "positive stress" on the uniqueness of the Christian universalism and the Holy Spirit.[78]

In the time since Epp's seminal study in 1966, several scholars have found in *Codex Bezae* other examples of other conscious changes in the language, rhetoric, and narrative of Acts. Ben Witherington has delineated an "anti-feminist" strain in the *Codex*: at points where the faith of women is applauded there appears to be a coincident attempt to remind the reader of a "gender hierarchy"—γυναικῶν τε τῶν πρώτων οὐκ ὀλίγαι ("not a few leading women")

---

[73] The "Western" tradition is believed to go back to at least the third century: see Aland 1987, cited by Elliot 1996. For *Codex Bezae* generally, see Ammassari 1996 (the text), Parker 1992, and Parker and Amphoux 1996. For the date and origin of *Codex Bezae*, see Callahan 1996:57, 64: "[The scribe] worked in the environs of a Roman colony [perhaps Antinoopolis] in upper Egypt between the fourth and fifth century."

[74] Strange 1992:1.

[75] Epp 1966:41–64. For the "ignorance motif," see also Epp 1962 and, in opposition, Conzelmann 1987:104–105, 146–147, and passim.

[76] Epp 1966:64: "The portrayal of Jewish hostility toward Jesus and of Jewish responsibility for his death in the [*Codex Bezae*] reveals a clearly anti-Judaic attitude. On the other hand, the strong positive emphasis on Jesus as Lord and Christ turns the sword in the wound (so to speak), for by presenting Jesus in bold and heightened tones the heinousness of the Jews' action against him is even more strongly emphasized."

[77] Idem:45. P75 from the third century already contains a truncated version of this verse (Ehrman 1996:111).

[78] Idem: 166. The *Codex Bezae* Acts "seems to 'out-Luke' Luke in its emphasis on universalism" (66).

at Acts 17:4 subtly becomes καὶ γυναῖκες τῶν πρώτων ("wives of the leading men").[79] The text *Codex Bezae* represents is a important example of rewriting (or "close elaboration," as I have termed it) in that it illustrates perfectly that the concept of textual malleability extended to the Christian copying of sacred scripture.[80] No doubt *Codex Bezae* was neither the first nor the only biblical rewriting, but its survival helps demonstrate that this activity is evident at a literal level in the codices of the Bible.

Taking inspiration from Epp and others who highlighted "theological" changes in the *Bezae* text of Acts, Bart Ehrman has attempted to situate these modifications within a competitive cultural milieu.[81] While *Bezae* itself probably originated in fifth-century Egypt, the text it contains is considered by most scholars to reflect a second or perhaps third-century textual tradition.[82] Ehrman has convincingly argued that the revisionist milieu of the second century offers the best interpretative matrix for the Greek text of *Codex Bezae*.[83] Especially with regard to Christological terminology and Jewish-Christian relations, *Bezae* is one dramatic example of a dominant mentality of rewriting that came to the fore in the second and third centuries. However, anti-Jewish interpolators were not the only ones rewriting the New Testament at this time. In response to Docetic, Ebionite, and other forms of Christianity deemed heretical by "proto-orthodox" apologists, the Gospels and Acts were often rewritten to further emphasize, from an orthodox point of view, the doctrinal differences between the heretical and orthodox sides.[84] For instance, against so-called "adoptionist" (e.g. Ebionite) readings of the Gospels that

---

[79] Witherington 1984, cited by Haines-Eitzen 2000:116. "Anti-feminist" is Witherington's; "gender hierarchy" is Haines-Eitzen's. For this and more examples of the "suppression of women" in early Christian manuscripts, see Ehrman 1995:367–368 and 1996:114–116. "Suppression of women" as a label, however, is perhaps too convenient and anachronistic.

[80] Epp makes the important point that *Codex Bezae* is not a completely new Acts of the Apostles but retains "the bulk of the traditional text" (1966:39); however, it does have enough variants for scholars to consider it an attempt to alter significantly the force of the original work.

[81] He rejects Epp's calling these changes "theological," "as if they bore no relation to sociopolitical realities" (Ehrman 1993:274). Of course, the term "theological" does not de jure rule out socio-political realities.

[82] See Parker 1992:261–78 and Ehrman 1994. In the latter Ehrman demonstrates that the text Heracleon used for his commentary on the Gospel of John in the late second century is "a comparable form of the text that was used for the first eight chapters of John by the late fourth-century scribe of *Codex Sinaiticus*" and by "the scribe who produced *Codex Bezae*" (179).

[83] Ehrman 1996.

[84] Ehrman's fullest treatment of this competitive milieu is Ehrman 1993. "Proto-orthodox" means, for Ehrman, those in the first through third centuries whose theological and hermeneutical opinions were positively received by those Christians who first called themselves "orthodox" in the fourth century: see Ehrman 1993:11–15.

argued for the human Jesus' adoption as God's divine Son only at his baptism, the well-attested reading of "You are my son; today I have begotten you" (Υἱός μου εἶ σύ, ἐγὼ σήμερον γεγέννηκά σε) at Luke 3:22 was changed by proto-orthodox scribes to read "You are my beloved son; in you I am pleased" (Σὺ εἶ ὁ υἱός μου ὁ ἀγαπητός, ἐν σοὶ εὐδόκησα). The latter is exactly the text of Mark 1:11, with which the scribes harmonized the former, more difficult passage in Luke.[85] This alteration, which soon gained wide support in the manuscript tradition, seems to be an attempt to remove any opportunity for adoptionist Christians to claim Luke 3:22 in support of their theological agenda. Numerous examples of this process occur in the early textual tradition of the Gospels and Acts: difficult verses that, while not necessarily heretical in themselves, left a door open for heretical *eisagesis*, were rewritten and sometimes significantly expanded (e.g. the variant endings of Mark) to protect orthodox readings of the New Testament.

In her recent book *Guardians of Letters*, Kim Haines-Eitzen has succinctly described the interpolative tendencies found in early Christian manuscripts:

> The discursive debates in the second and third century inter-sected with textual transcription in the activity of copying and the (re)production of texts and creation of new readings. Intentional scribal changes did not occur in a vacuum, nor were they random in nature; rather, they were constrained by the discursive contexts of the scribes themselves.[86]

Thus significant theological arguments within Christian communities, at the time of copying, very often found their way into the texts, even if the divergences have often been read in the past as mere "variants" in the search for an Ur-text of the New Testament.

---

[85] Ibid.:62–67. Attestations to the more difficult reading include *Codex Bezae*, Justin Martyr, Clement of Alexandria, Origen, Methodius, the *Didascalia*, Lactantius, Hilary, Augustine, and several Old Latin manuscripts.

[86] Haines-Eitzen 2000:116. The strength of her overall argument on this point is undeniable and complementary to the present study; however, I would argue for a slightly more moderate formulation. Clearly many of the textual variants in New Testament manuscripts can be shown to be habitual, standard scribal errors, such as dittography and haplography—to name only the most straightforward—and should not be included in an analysis of the discursive networks behind the scribal project generally. Epp argues persuasively for moderation in reacting to Ur-text New Testament scholarship (1966:15–21).

The emergence of a Christian paraphrase tradition: Gregory Thaumaturgus on Ecclesiastes

I hope to have pointed so far to the fact that the habit of rewriting was a part of Christian literature, perhaps especially Greek Christian literature, from an early point and on a very literal level. Some of the most interesting evidence for Christian rewriting is the recasting of the Gospels and Acts from an orthodox point of view. Heretical groups, such as the followers of Marcion, were often accused of altering the New Testament by early Christian apologists, but no substantial evidence of these alterations has survived.[87] Rather, it is the orthodox changes that can be traced with some precision and testify to a thoroughgoing habit of adjusting the received text at its most difficult points. These altered orthodox manuscripts of the New Testament in turn became received texts in their own right, and even the most altered exemplars of this process, such as *Codex Bezae*, were still being copied in the fifth and sixth century—although the alterations contained in *Codex Bezae* appear to belong to a second or third century theological context.

The third century yields a different, perhaps transitional, example of Christian biblical rewriting, this time in the form of the standard biblical paraphrase common to Hellenistic Jewish literature. Gregory Thaumaturgus, the bishop of Neocaesarea in Asia Minor, wrote a lengthy paraphrase of Ecclesiastes that stands out as one of the few patristic commentaries on that elusive book.[88] Originally from a pagan family, Gregory attended Origen's philosophy classes at Caesarea in Palestine during the 230s, to be converted to Christian theology under his tutelage. Taking up the bishopric of Neocaesarea, Gregory was credited with several writings and labeled a wonder-worker in late antiquity, picking up the title Thaumaturgus sometime in the sixth century.[89] His paraphrase of Ecclesiastes is significant as the earliest surviving Christian exemplar of this genre.[90] The paraphrase is in prose and follows the

---

[87] Ehrman 1993:27.

[88] Though, interestingly, Origen and his pupils seem to have had a special commitment to the book: Origen, Gregory, and Dionysius of Alexandria all wrote interpretative works on Ecclesiastes, as did Hippolytus of Rome (Jarick 1990:3).

[89] On Gregory's life and the sources for it, see Van Dam 1982. The main source is Gregory of Nyssa's sermon *On the Life of Gregory Thaumaturgus* (ed. Heil 1990); see also Gregory Thaumaturgus' *Panegyric to Origen*, written on the occasion of his departure from Origen's school c. 240 (ed. and trans. Crouzel 1969). For Gregory's later title, see Telfer 1936:240. On the various writings attributed to him, see Crouzel 1969:27–33.

[90] Text is in PG 10, columns 987–1018 and is conveniently reprinted with translation and commentary by Jarick 1990.

text of the LXX closely. The text shows no sign that Gregory was making reference to the Hebrew, as might be expected from one of Origen's students.[91] A look at the short preface reveals Gregory's intentions to recover this work for Christian believers:

> Τάδε λέγει Σαλομών, ὁ τοῦ Βασιλέως καὶ προφήτου παῖς ἁπάσῃ τῇ τοῦ θεοῦ ἐκκλησίᾳ, παρὰ πάντας ἀνθρώπους βασιλεὺς ἐντιμότατος, καὶ προφήτης σοφώτατος.

> Solomon (the son of the king and prophet David), a king more honored and a prophet wiser than anyone else, speaks to the whole assembly of God.[92]

John Jarick observes in his commentary on the text that, instead of the shadowy Hebrew sage from the original Ecclesiastes, Gregory has named the traditional author of the text, Solomon, and given him his traditional epithet as well, "most wise." The work is here redirected to a Christian audience through the use of "assembly/church" (ἐκκλησία) and its message is brought into the present tense (λέγει), replacing the LXX's aorist (εἶπεν).[93] Throughout the *Paraphrase* there is a conscious effort on Gregory's part to smooth out both linguistic and theological difficulties:[94]

> The recurrent conclusion [in Ecclesiastes] that there is nothing better for a person to do in life than to eat and drink and find enjoyment for himself sounds suspiciously like a certain well known but un-Christian philosophy of life; Gregory tells his readers bluntly that the perfect good does *not* lie in eating and drinking, and that enjoyment is only granted by God to those people who act righteously.[95]

Gregory replaces the "all is vanity" mantra of the original text with a revisionist comparison between those who "see" spiritually and those who do not: "Most people have given themselves over to transitory things, not wanting to look—with the soul's noble eye (τῷ γενναίῳ τῆς ψυχῆς ὄμματι)—at anything higher than the stars."[96] Further, Gregory exchanges the original "the wise person dies,

---

[91] Jarick 1990:310.

[92] Jarick 1990:7.

[93] Ibid.:8.

[94] Jarick 1990:316: "In presenting the Church with this smooth paraphrase of a formerly uncomfortable work, Gregory Thaumaturgus stands firmly at the beginning of a long tradition seeking to remold Ecclesiastes into a more ecclesiastical book."

[95] Jarick 1990:311, citing *Paraphrase* 2.24, 3.12–13, 8.15–17; cf. 3.22.

[96] *Paraphrase* 1.3; Jarick 1990:9, 359n25.

just like the fool" for "the wise person never shares the same fate as the fool," with an emphasis on the moral responsibilities of his Christian congregation.[97]

All of these (and many more) striking changes to the biblical text come in the narrative of the *Paraphrase*, which is (one must keep in mind) ostensibly only the text of Ecclesiastes itself. Towards the end of his *Paraphrase* Gregory gives some hints at how he perceived his role as paraphrast:

> Δώσουσι δέ τινες τὰ σοφὰ ἐκεῖνα διδάγματα, παρ' ἑνὸς ἀγαθοῦ λαβόντες ποιμένος καὶ διδασκάλου, ὥσπερ ἐξ ἑνὸς στόματος ἅπαντες αὐτοῖς συμφώνως δαψιλέστερον τὰ πιστευθέντα διηγούμενοι.

> Some people will pass on those wise lessons which they have received from one good shepherd and teacher, just as if everybody with one voice described in unison and in greater detail what was entrusted to them.[98]

The use of the word "shepherd" perhaps points to Solomon, as the legendary "wisest of all," or perhaps it signals Christ, who will have taught the faithful through the *Paraphrase* the Christian "wisdom" that is communicated therein.[99] Most likely the shepherd is simply Gregory, who portrays himself as communicating age-old wisdom to his young Christian flock—who were in turn previously unaware of the riches of this Old Testament manual. He seems here (like Erasmus) to view the *Paraphrase* as a mode of communicating the deep truths of a difficult text which are not apparent on the surface but which have been nonetheless handed down as pronounced in the chorus of the ages. By adopting the persona of the *Koheleth*—or "Solomon," as he names him— Gregory can bring out those truths in a Christian guise and, most importantly, with the authority of the original author.

*Cento* and the reception of biblical paraphrase in the fifth century

The genre of formal paraphrase continued to be employed in late antiquity, in both prose and verse. Paraphrase in verse found its most talented exponent in the fifth-century Egyptian poet Nonnus of Panopolis, the writer of the lengthy epic poem the *Dionysiaca*, a hexameter account of the Greek god Dionysus' mythical conquests in India. That the author of the *Dionysiaca* would undertake a *Paraphrase on the Gospel of John* is indeed surprising, and

---

[97] *Paraphrase* 2.16, 7.25; Jarick 1990:43, 186, 313.
[98] *Paraphrase* 12.11; Jarick 1990:303, 315.
[99] Jarick 1990:303–304.

many arguments have been marshaled to explain this apparent contradiction in ancient attributions.[100] Some scholars argue that the *Paraphrase* is simply misattributed;[101] others have hypothesized a conversion (or an apostasy) late in Nonnus' career; still others claim that the *Paraphrase* is a distracting exercise, undertaken by (a Christian) Nonnus prior to or even while writing the *Dionysiaca*.[102]

It is not necessary to rehearse here the debates over authorship: detailed studies have been produced by several scholars, including Enrico Livrea, who is overseeing a new edition of the *Paraphrase*.[103] It is enough to observe with Livrea that all attempts to rationalize Nonnus' literary biography suffer from the same lack of internal evidence:

> I dati biographici che emergono da tante migliaia di versi sono così parchi e sfugenti da lasciar aperto il campo alle più contraddittorie construzioni, senza peraltro fornire alcuna sicurreza sull'appartenenza di Nonno al Christianesimo né, tanto meno, su una sua presunta conversione o apostasia.[104]

Despite the surprising dearth of self-revelations in the two texts, Nonnus can be seen, in his immediate literary-historical context, as a "wandering poet," in Alan Cameron's famous description, competing for literary patronage throughout the eastern empire—after the collapse of the traditional games system during the late 4th century—and composing Homeric verse according to the tastes of his disparate audiences. "It was in search of these patrons that our poets moved from city to city, exploiting in turn each center of learning and fashion."[105] Cameron has placed Nonnus in a literary world populated

---

[100] The problem as formulated by Livrea 1989 is that the *Dionysiaca* is "positivamente pagano" and the *Paraphrase* is "positivamente ammaliato dallo splendore del Logos rigeneratore . . ." (21–22).

[101] Sherry 1996; Coulie and Sherry 1995.

[102] Livrea 1989; Hollis 1994:58.

[103] The standard complete edition of Nonnus' *Paraphrase* is Scheindler 1881. Livrea began a new edition (text, translation, and commentary) with the paraphrase of John chapter 18 (1989; cf. Birdsall 1990); since then, he (2000) and his colleagues Domenico Accoriniti (1996; cf. Mary Whitby 1998), Claudio De Stephani (2002; cf. eadem 2004), Gianfranco Agosti (2003; cf. Johnson 2005), and Claudia Greco (2004) have followed with John chapters 20, 1, 5, and 13 respectively. Alan Cameron's evocative studies of fifth-century literary culture are still benchmarks for historical scholarship on the period, though he does little in the way of actual literary analysis (Alan Cameron 1965, 1982, and 2004). Golega 1930 is still the standard stylistic analysis of Nonnus' *Paraphrase*, but see now Hollis 1994 (and forthcoming) in connection with the reception of Hellenistic poetry in the *Dionysiaca*.

[104] Livrea 1989:19.

[105] Alan Cameron 1965:485.

by scores of "scholar poets" now known to us only by name or anonymously through fragments, many of whom were clearly pagan and also had significant connections to the imperial court.[106]

Following Alan Cameron's lead, one of his students, Lee Sherry, has postulated the existence of a "Nonnian school"[107] to explain the difficulties of style and attribution.[108] Sherry has argued that the *Paraphrase* is not by Nonnus at all but by one of his Christian students and is, most interestingly, actually a *cento* of the *Dionysiaca* itself. This possibility was first suggested (tentatively) by Joseph Golega in 1930, though revived by Sherry as a "key" to the problem.[109] However, a formal *cento* of the *Dionysiaca* (idiosyncratic in the extreme) would clearly have to replicate its verses, and the lack of coherency between the metrical patterns of the *Dionysiaca* and the *Paraphrase* is precisely why Sherry attributes the latter to a lesser poet: Golega's suggestion of a *cento* seems meant to be evocative of the close relationship between the two poems, more than a genre analysis per se. Moreover, Golega himself argued that the *Paraphrase* (which he firmly attributed to Nonnus) shows a high level of metrical ability and also concluded that the metrical differences between the poems are due to the paraphrast's *Vorlage*, the Gospel of John.[110] Golega has been confirmed by several subsequent scholars, and Sherry's conclusions have consequently not won wide support.[111]

---

[106] See Alan Cameron 1982.

[107] More specifically centered around Nonnus and his (unknown) students than Golega's *soggenannte Nonnosschüler*, which include Musaeus and the Pseudo-Apolinarian *Paraphrase of the Psalms* (Golega 1960:93–108).

[108] This conclusion emerged out of his 1991 Columbia dissertation on the *Paraphrase*. Note, however, Alan Cameron's and Sherry's conflicting estimates of the literary value of Nonnus' *Paraphrase*—Alan Cameron 1982:284: "Nonnus (if he it was) treated his model with the utmost freedom, producing an elaborate rhetorical masterpiece in the high style scarcely inferior in its way to the *Dionysiaca*"; by contrast, Sherry 1996:411, 414: "Why are there so few testimonia for the *Paraphrase*? I suggest that it is because the poem is not by Nonnus. Since it was not a serious piece of literature and a poem inferior to the *Dionysiaca*, it did not warrant the same attention from readers and collectors . . . Nonnus was too good a poet to produce so lame a paraphrase."

[109] Sherry 1996:414 and n26. See Golega 1930:143: "Und doch weist die Paraphrase fast noch mehr nonnianische Floskeln auf als Musaios, dessen Epyllion ohne weiteres auch in den Dionysiaka Platz finden könnte. Ja man darf die Paraphrase beinahe als einen Cento aus Dionysiakaversteilen und Evangelientext bezeichnen" (29); and "Die sprachlich-stilistische Übereinstimmung zwischen beiden Gedichten ist so groß, daß die Paraphrase fast ein Cento aus Dionysiakaversteilen in Evangelientext genannt werden kann" (emphasis added).

[110] See Golega's *Zussamenfassung* (1930:142–144).

[111] E.g. Alan Cameron 1982:284; Hollis 1994; Mary Whitby forthcoming; Mary Whitby 1998 (review of Accorinti 1996): "a storehouse of ammunition is accumulated against the *cento* thesis."

Sherry's argument about authorship, while widely criticized, has the benefit of suggesting a new way of looking at these texts. In particular, Sherry's suggestion that a mixing of literary forms (*cento* and paraphrase) was even possible in this period reaffirms the need for a much wider discussion of the interpenetration of styles and genres in late Greek literature. *Centones*, typically written directly from the *Iliad* and *Odyssey* and not from recent Homeric continuators, are not extremely well attested but seem to have been a literary entertainment akin to the epigram and often appropriated by magical charm writers: lines of Homer pulled from their context in both a bookish and a religious manner.[112] Likewise, formal Christian paraphrase in late antiquity, in its Homeric forms at least, probably developed directly out of the educational system.[113] As Dennis MacDonald has observed in his study on the Gospel of Mark's imitation of the Homeric epics:

> Quintilian supposed his readers would have taken this activity for granted: "I think we shall all agree that this [paraphrasing] is especially valuable with regard to poetry; indeed, it is said that the paraphrase of poetry [into prose] was the sole form of exercise employed by [the rhetor] Sulpicius." The *littérateur* Philodemus asked, "Who would claim that the writing of prose is not reliant on the Homeric poems?"[114]

Students learned to write through copying and recopying Homer and other canonical authors, a process which instilled in them both the style of the original and a capacity for rewriting. It is quite right, then, that these genres, *cento* and paraphrase, could potentially mingle together in the fifth century, despite appearing distinct in earlier literary history.

Both Homeric *cento* and biblical/Homeric paraphrase presuppose a close attachment to a canonical text, and recomposition is clearly their shared modus operandi. In addition, it appears to be in the fifth century that monastic schools began using the Psalms and certain liturgical texts for basic language instruction, requiring students to memorize large sections of the Psalter and, quite probably, portions of the Gospels as well.[115] That the New Testament texts

---

[112] Usher 1998:2 offers the suggestion that the *cento* is technically not a genre but what he calls simply an "écriture," which, like parody or pastiche, can take various prose and verse forms (citing Verweyen and Witting 1991:172).

[113] See MacDonald 2000:5, with extensive references at 205n14.

[114] Trans. ibid.; Quintilian *Institutio Oratoria* 10.5.4 (cf. 1.9.2–3 and Cicero *On Oratory* 1.154); Philodemus *On Poetry* 5.30.36.

[115] See Browning 2000:868 and passim.

would be subjected to the same project as the Old—and as Homer had been in Greek schools for some time—is not as idiosyncratic to "Nonnus" as Sherry would have us believe in this literary context (which he invoked to begin with).[116] Consequently, any discussion of Nonnian authorship and the development of fifth-century literature should take account of these broader literary and pedagogical movements; the unexplained rise in *cento* and biblical paraphrase exempla in the fifth century is first of all the result of the extant texts (see below), but it was no doubt also part of the germination of a Christian self-consciousness at this time, a self-consciousness which has been shown to owe a tremendous amount to shifting patterns of education.[117]

These two literary forms, *cento* and paraphrase, came together in the famous literary endeavors of the fifth-century empress Eudocia/Athenaïs, empress of Theodosius II (421–460). In her *centones* of the *Iliad* and *Odyssey*, Eudocia retells the Christian story of Fall and Redemption and thus follows the narrative line of biblical history, proceeding from the creation of the world to the ascension of Christ.[118] However, she does so in the "patchwork" form of the *cento*, rewriting the biblical text through Homeric verse; in this striking experiment, she produces what Mark Usher has called "Outsider Art," a reusing of "discarded material" to create new, "other" literary art, in the same manner as, for example, "the magnificently naïve painting of American folk artists" like Howard Finster.[119] Usher, having recently reedited Eudocia's *Homerocentones* (1999) in addition to writing two studies on them (1997; 1998), has brought to the fore some of the complex intertextual questions regarding these works, which, as Gregory Nagy says in his forward to Usher's study, "presuppose a

---

[116] Sherry 1996:420: "The [Nonnian] paraphrase has a unique place in the history of Greek literature. It is not only the sole surviving New Testament paraphrase, but it may well be the only one ever attempted"—a very inaccurate and misleading statement.

[117] Averil Cameron 1998:672: "in so far as a Christian consciousness came into being, it was moulded by scriptural patterns, both inside and outside the Christian élite."

[118] There is no consensus on which recension of the *centones* is Eudocia's: see the succinct treatment in Mary Whitby 2001. This question has been dealt with in depth by Usher 1997 and 1999, Rey 1998, Schembra 1995, and Whitby forthcoming, all with different conclusions. It is possible that none of the recensions is Eudocia's, but most scholars have settled on one or the other manuscript tradition, Usher preferring a longer fourteenth-century manuscript from Athos, Shembra a shorter recension incompletely edited by Ludwich 1897, and Rey accepting multiple authorship in the shorter version—see Mary Whitby 2000 for some of the interpretive implications of this debate. If one accepts Usher's longer recension, then Eudocia's *Homerocentones*, at twenty-four hundred lines, becomes by far the longest of the surviving *centones*. For a list of the other known Homeric *centones* with references, see Usher 1998:3n3.

[119] Usher 1998:16–17. A inspired comparison to be sure, but I hardly think Homer was "discarded material" in late antiquity.

veritable internalization of both Homer and the Bible."[120] Nevertheless, Usher has not placed these *centones* in the literary-historical context of biblical paraphrase, an important and necessary juxtaposition, I believe, if we are to understand the full impetus and the cognitive implications of both Eudocia's and Nonnus' writings.[121]

In addition to the *Homerocentones* Eudocia also wrote hexameter paraphrases of Zechariah and Daniel, the Octateuch (in eight books), and the martyrdom of Saint Cyprian of Antioch (in three books).[122] Only the *Homerocentones* and the paraphrase of Cyprian's martyrdom survive (the latter only partially), but her corpus attests, again, to the combination of biblical paraphrase with other genres in late ancient writing. Specifically, Eudocia as an author reveals the striking union of (Old Testament) biblical paraphrase, the *cento*, and the rewriting (in verse) of early martyr acts. There is no reason not to see all three of these literary projects as coming directly out of a Greek Christian education system in the fifth century.[123] As I have already demonstrated in the preceding chapter, the author of the *Life and Miracles of Thekla* also exhibits the conjunction of these received literary forms in the fifth-century: the influence of biblical paraphrase, the Homeric epics, and early Christian martyr acts. In addition, Photius records a (now lost) verse paraphrase of the *Acts of Paul and Thekla* by Basil of Seleukeia, the fifth-century bishop once thought to have written the prose *Life and Miracles*.[124]

Substantial late antique paraphrasing activity in prose and verse did not go unnoticed by other contemporary writers. The historians Socrates and

---

[120] Usher 1998:ix–x.

[121] This juxtaposition is also suggested in general by Mary Whitby forthcoming—disagreeing with both Alan Cameron 1982 and Urbainczyk 1997, she writes: "One might more cautiously suggest that Theodosius' [II's] combination of educational and pious objectives provided an ideal environment for experimentation with this combination in literature."

[122] Photius *Bibliotheca* 183–184; ed. Henry 1960:2.195–199. The entry for Eudocia in Bowersock, Brown, and Grabar 1999:436 is erroneous in saying that only the paraphrase of the martyrdom of Saint Cyprian has survived, ignoring completely the more significant *Homerocentones* (a belief, if held, that the latter is wrongly attributed should have been noted and defended).

[123] Alan Cameron 1982 has emphasized that the reorganization of schools in Constantinople in 425 should be seen on the background of imperial politics: "After 425 education in Constantinople was in effect the monopoly of a Christian government" (287). This is certainly important, but is it not also possible to see, from a literary-historical point of view, the persistent strength in the fifth century of traditional modes of rhetorical training and biblical exegesis and, then, the contemporary "christianization" of these modes? See n. 121 above.

[124] While both Alan Cameron 1982:282 and Sherry 1996:425n58 rightly (though only in passing) cite the *Life and Miracles* as a comparandum for Nonnus and Eudocia, both appear unaware that its author is not Basil of Seleukeia, accepting the mistaken Byzantine attribution and confusing it with Photius' notice. For the authorship of the *Life and Miracles*, see Dagron 1974.

Sozomen both comment on the writing of biblical paraphrase, though with contrasting conclusions. These fascinating vignettes on Christian literary history are worthy of being quoted here in full:

Socrates:

The imperial law [of Julian] which forbade Christians to study Greek literature, rendered the two Apolinarii, of whom we have above spoken, much more distinguished than before. For both being skilled in polite learning (ἄμφω ἤστην ἐπιστήμονες λόγων), the father as a grammarian, and the son as a rhetorician, they made themselves serviceable to the Christians at this crisis. For the former, as a grammarian, composed a grammar consistent with the Christian faith (τὴν τέκνην γραμματικὴν Χριστιανικῷ τύπῳ συνέταττε): he also translated the Books of Moses into heroic verse (τά τε Μωυσέως βιβλία διὰ τοῦ ἡρωικοῦ λεγομένου μέτρου μετέβαλεν); and paraphrased all the historical books of the Old Testament (καὶ ὅσα κατὰ τὴν παλαιὰν διαθήκην ἐν ἱστορίας τύπῳ συγγέγραπται), putting them partly into dactylic measure, and partly reducing them to the form of dramatic tragedy. He purposefully employed all kinds of verse, that no form of expression peculiar to the Greek language might be unknown amongst Christians. The younger Apolinarius, who was well trained in eloquence (εὖ πρὸς τὸ λέγειν παρεσκευασμένος), expounded the Gospels and apostolic doctrines in the way of dialogue (ἐν τύπῳ διαλόγων ἐξέθετο), as Plato among the Greeks had done. Thus showing themselves useful to the Christian cause they overcame the subtlety (τὸ σόφισμα)of the emperor through their own labors. But Divine Providence was more potent than either their labors, or the craft of the emperor (κρείσσων ἐγένετο καὶ τῆς τούτων σπουδῆς καὶ τῆς τοῦ βασιλέως ὁρμῆς): for not long afterwards, in the manner we shall hereafter explain, the law became wholly inoperative; and the works of these men are now of no greater importance than if they had never been written (τῶν δὲ οἱ πόνοι ἐν ἴσῳ τοῦ μὴ γραφῆναι λογίζονται).[125]

Sozomen:

[Julian] forbade the children of Christians from being instructed in

[125] Socrates *Ecclesiastical History* 3.16.1–7; trans. A. C. Zenos NPNF 2nd series, 2:86–87 (translation altered); cf. ed. Günther Hansen 1995:210. Note also how the technical language for paraphrase appears different here, esp. μεταβάλειν instead of μεταφράζειν.

the writings of the Greek poets and authors and from visiting their teachers. He entertained great resentment against Apolinarius the Syrian, a man of manifold knowledge and philosophical attainments, against Basil and Gregory, natives of Cappadocia, the most celebrated orators of the time, and against other learned and eloquent men, of whom some were attached to the Nicene doctrines, and others to the heresy of Arius. His sole motive for excluding the children of Christian parents was because he considered such studies conducive to the acquisition of argumentative power. Apolinarius, therefore, employed his great learning and ingenuity in the production of a heroic epic (ἐν ἔπεσιν ἡρῴοις) on the antiquities of the Hebrews to the reign of Saul (τὴν Ἑβραϊκὴν ἀρχαιολόγιαν συνεγράψατο μέχρι τῆς Σαοὺλ βασιλείας), as a substitute for the poem of Homer (ἀντὶ μέν τῆς Ὡμήρου ποιήσεως). He divided this work into twenty-four parts, to each of which he appended the name of one of the letters of the Greek alphabet, according to their number and order. He also wrote comedies in imitation of Menander, tragedies resembling those of Euripides, and odes on the model of Pindar. In short, taking themes of the "circle of knowledge" from the Scriptures (ἐκ τῶν θείων γραφῶν τὰς ὑποθέσις λαβὼν τῶν ἐγκυκλίων καλουμένων μαθημάτων), he produced within a very brief space of time, a set of works which in manner, expression, character, and arrangement are well approved as similar to the Greek literatures and which were equal in number and in force (ἰσαρίθμους καὶ ἰσοδυνάμους πραγματείας ἤθει τε καὶ φράσει καὶ χαρακτῆρι καὶ οἰκονομίᾳ ὁμοίας τοῖς παρ' Ἕλλησιν ἐν τούτοις εὐδοκιμήσασιν). Were it not for the extreme partiality with which the productions of antiquity are regarded, I doubt not but that the writings of Apolinarius would be held in as much estimation as those of the ancients. The comprehensiveness of his intellect is more especially to be admired; for he excelled in every branch of literature, whereas ancient writers were proficient in only one.[126]

The Apolinarius the elder whom both writers cite was the father of the Apolinarius the younger whose Christological teaching was condemned at the first Council of Constantinople in AD 381. A *Paraphrase of the Psalms* attributed to Apolinarius the elder has come down to us, though the attribution must

---

[126] Sozomen *Ecclesiastical History* 5.18.1–5; trans. C. D. Hartranft NPNF 2nd series, 2:340 (translation altered); cf. ed. Bidez and Hansen 1995:221–223.

be incorrect due to its dedication to the emperor Marcian (AD 450–457). This text has been analyzed in detail by Golega, who firmly established its date on stylistic grounds to the fifth century.[127]

Clearly Socrates and Sozomen know of even more paraphrasing activity going on in the fourth century, for which we have no texts or fragments, but it is of course reasonable that Gregory of Thaumaturgus' paraphrase of Ecclesiastes in the third century would have had some immediate successors. The length alone of the vignettes quoted above attests to an interest on the part of Socrates and Sozomen in the literary history of the period, but their assessments of the value of these works are strikingly different.

Theresa Urbainczyk has concluded that the lack of a mention of Eudocia's *Paraphrases* in Socrates' *History* is a slight against the empress, since he would have implicitly condemned her writings along with those of the Apolinarii.[128] Urbainczyk's argument seems to assume too much, and the omission has been more successfully and simply explained on other grounds, namely that Eudocia had not published her paraphrases by 439, when Socrates finished his *History*.[129] One remark of Urbainczyk, however, deserves closer scrutiny: "It seems to me that the subject of the work done by the Apolinarii was probably only remembered in the early fifth century because the empress and her friends were repeating the exercise."[130] "Repeating the exercise" is precisely the point, I think, and it highlights the disingenuousness of their reporting: clearly there was a much stronger tradition of biblical paraphrase in the fifth century than either Socrates or Sozomen fully acknowledges.[131]

The Apolinarii, far from inventing the genre, were rather perpetuating a long tradition of paraphrase that could claim a famous proponent, Gregory Thaumaturgus, just a century before. Moreover, Socrates and Sozomen set their notices on the Apolinarian paraphrases in the context of fourth-century disputes over education, precisely the region of knowledge from which Christian paraphrases—especially those in heroic meter—seem to have emerged. The Christian tradition of paraphrase to which these vignettes point confirms the argument of the present chapter: that paraphrase and rewriting, even on a very literal level, was more common, and more integral, to Jewish

---

[127] Golega 1960.

[128] Urbainczyk 1997:33–34.

[129] Alan Cameron 1982:283. Nonnus could have written his *Paraphrase* prior to 439 since it is possible Socrates would not have known it, and there are no known connections between Nonnus and the court; by contrast, the empress Eudocia could presumably not escape notice.

[130] Urbainczyk 1997:33–34.

[131] Though Sozomen's approval of the practice could be read as an implicit acknowledgment.

and Christian textuality than has previously been recognized, or than, most importantly, is represented by surviving exempla.

Even the divergence between Socrates' and Sozomen's histories attests to this habit: Sozomen, writing ten years later (with access to Socrates' *History*), chose to include new and different details of the literary reactions to Julian, in addition to providing a startlingly opposing judgment on the value of those reactions.[132] In this strikingly intertextual way, Sozomen shows himself to be a historiographical paraphrast, and his engagement in this exercise, at the very moment of describing other paraphrasts, highlights further the importance (and ubiquity) of paraphrase in Greek Christian literature.

## Fifth-Century Metaphrastai: Revisiting Rapp on Antiquarianism

In addition to thriving Homeric imitations, the fourth through sixth centuries was a period when apocryphal Acta from the second and third centuries were being rewritten, extended, and embroidered with facility and vigor.[133] In the late antique East this meant that received texts about famous apostolic personages—like Thekla, the apostle Philip, and the apostle John—were the loci of several individual rewritings and extensions. These latter texts testify, of course, to textual competition and the appropriation of the cults for specific sites—Seleukeia for Thekla, Ephesus and Patmos for John—but, more fundamentally, these rewritings are indicative of an indigenous cultural habit of Christian textuality. To be sure, in late antiquity the apocryphal Acta were not Scripture, and textual critics like Ehrman suggest that rewritings of the New Testament were not still occurring on a large scale in the fourth and fifth centuries (at some point between the third and fourth centuries the

---

[132] How do we explain Socrates' harshness in this matter? Besides assuming a distaste for the younger Apolinarius, there is no clear answer. Nevertheless, it is important to note that both historians set the Apolinarii in the same context. They highlight the educational environment from which the paraphrases come and, in their own ways, they obscure the broader tradition of paraphrase through their specific denigrations of Julian's policies.

[133] Bovon 1988:19–20 emphasizes the fact that this vigorous activity was ongoing even in recent times: "At the same time as Konstantin von Tischendorf was preparing his critical edition of the martyrdoms and apocalypses of the apostles, a Greek monk from Palestine [Joasaph of Saint Sabba] was retelling in his own style the same stories which Tischendorf and R. A. Lipsius and M. Bonnet were editing" (see references ad loc.); contrast this observation with the following: "Today no one dreams of publishing interpolated versions of these [canonical] Gospels or of doctoring our holy books" (ibid.)—we have thus inherited a cognitive distinction (formulated sometime between the second and sixth centuries?) between inviolable and violable Christian texts.

manuscript traditions solidified and became more or less stable—attitudes had thus changed with regard to the biblical texts).[134] Nevertheless, the apocryphal Acta were often rewritten at this time with the same goal in mind as the earlier biblical revisions, that is, to purge the texts of opportunities for heretical readings, or of heretical material itself. Following this period of reception and rewriting, which helped spawn new forms of literature, writers like Leontius of Neapolis in the seventh century began to collect and to rewrite more recent (fourth- to sixth-century) saints' Lives in a consciously antiquarian fashion; within a few more centuries, Leontius' antiquarian tendencies found their preeminent expression in the work of Symeon Metaphrastes.[135]

The perceived historicity of the saints' "lives and deeds" (βίοι καὶ πράξεις) was of central importance to the rewriters, but they were also not unaware of the fictional, novelistic, and simply imaginative elements of the legends they received and redacted.[136] This process of collecting, culling, and writing was the modus operandi of late antique "hagiographers" and is often described by them in the self-defining sections of their works. Their antiquarian ethos, which has not gone unnoticed by scholars but is still under-emphasized, depends first, I argue, upon the cognitive classification of the traditions of early saints as historical, received, and authoritative. The early saints were more often than not also apostles, and the names associated with the received texts about them—Paul, Peter, Thomas, John, Thekla—added gravitas to the historiographical vocations of the late antique writers who undertook the antiquarian task of discovering, sorting, and publicizing the previously hidden data, the "apocryphal" deeds of the apostles. This same ethos was extended to the lives of saints contemporary with the antiquarian project, and increasingly, to their current, posthumous activities as well.

The contemporary cultural imperative for this kind of literary activity was as crucial as the historical: the latter depended upon the objective existence of a text, a textual artifact, often consciously given the special status of *textus receptus*; the former depended upon the force of religious habit in late antiquity, the immediacy of sacred, otherworldly holiness in select men and women, and also upon a conscientious respect for the orthodox innovations of the day, notably the ubiquitous cult of the saints and the relics and local stories

---

[134] See Ehrman 1993:17–20: The first attempts to restrict the Christian canon were not voluntary but came only in response to heretical (e.g. Marcionite) canonical definitions. On conceptual distinctions in the second and third centuries between canonical and apocryphal Gospels, see Bovon 1988.

[135] See Høgel 2002.

[136] It is often the case that the novelistic elements are highlighted by these authors as much as the historical. See Hägg 1983 chapter 6 and Pervo 1996.

it generated. This project of exhuming the textual past for cults current in late antiquity was fueled by a recognition of the need to preserve the past (and historical present) for the future.

Within this project, however, authors often sought, or felt compelled, to reclassify, reorient, and purify the textual past for the sake of their audiences and readers-to-come. A cathartic imperative such as this betrays an awareness of the dangerous effects to the soul of an improper interpretation of the past: in particular, the elements of the legends of the apostles that signaled heretical conclusions for Christian morality and practice were expunged. The so-called "Encratites," heretical sectarians who were said to have insisted on (among other things) the necessity of sexual renunciation for salvation, were often accused by late antique heresiologists—antiquarians in their own right—of appropriating to destructive ends what were essentially historical, spiritually nourishing narratives of the apostle-saints.[137] Thus, the "Encratic" elements of early apocryphal acts were removed by late antique rewriters for the welfare of their readers. Interestingly, however, these elements were not seen to have polluted the historical narratives contained in the acts. Subsequent to the purgings, readers were expected to consider the authorized revised versions as true history, and also as beneficial for devotion, prayer, and the Christian spiritual life generally.

It is standard scholarly fare that the earliest Christians, or at least representative writers, considered apocryphal stories concerning Jesus, his family, and the apostles just as factual and authoritative as the canonical New Testament.[138] What scholars of early Christianity have perhaps missed, however, is the inspirational role that apocryphal Acta had on the development of Christian literature. While later generations of writers, particularly in the fourth and fifth centuries, were interested in expunging Encratic elements in these stories—in opposition to the earliest writers who considered such elements authentic?—they were nevertheless enthusiastic about the Acta as received literary tradition. Thus, the apocryphal Acta were not simply bodiless legends about the apostles to be manipulated at will, but they had an

---

[137] The term "Encratites" comes from ἐγκράτεια, "self-control" or "continence"; while this label probably refers to various different sects with Gnostic connections, the second century writer Tatian is often said to be their heresiarch. They are described by Irenaeus (*Against Heresies* 1.28), Clement (*Paedagogus* 2.2.33; *Stromateis* ("Patchwork") 1.15, 7.17), and Epiphanius (*Panarion* ("Medicine Chest") 47.2.3–47.3.1), among others. In addition to sexual continence, they were said to have abstained from wine and meat as well, though it is unclear whether abstinence from these two were also necessary for salvation.

[138] As does in fact appear to be the case when Origen cites the *Acts of Paul* in *On First Principles* 1.2.3 and his *Commentary on John* 20.12 (Elliott 1999:350).

inspirational role as textual encapsulations of these legends. Consequently, a conscious mimesis of the style, structure, and language of apocryphal Acta is very present in Christian novelistic literature from the fourth and fifth centuries. This fact remains underappreciated by scholars of both early Christianity and late antiquity because most saints' Lives in this period have no direct early predecessor but instead describe contemporary holy figures. By contrast, the argument of the present study is that a mimetic motivation could potentially stand behind the authorship of some saints' Lives that have been seen as more or less sui generis. The *Life of Thekla* is very strong evidence that the tradition of Christian biography (or Christian Romance) represented by the second-century apocryphal Acta was alive and well in the fifth century, a hundred years after Athanasius wrote the seminal *Life of Antony*.

In addition to these substantial, and apparently frequent, rewritings of second and third-century Acta, new Acta in the style of the earlier ones continued to be written in late antiquity. While the lack of precise dates for the authorship of many Acta prevents scholars from establishing exactly how late this trend continued, it is nevertheless clear that they were still being written and read in tandem with the first late antique saints' Lives (mid fourth century), and that they were around for a long time after the latter had become widely disseminated. For example, the *Acts of Philip*, recently re-edited by François Bovon and others, was written no earlier than the fourth century and most likely represents an Encratic community of Asia Minor attempting to provide historical documentation for their position in the face of increasing hostility from the ecclesiastical establishment.[139] This hostility came perhaps even from Cappadocian bishops like Basil of Caesarea and Amphilocius of Iconium who participated in the Council of Gangra in Paphlagonia (c. AD 341 or 355), a Council which condemned the extreme asceticism advocated by Eustathius of Sebaste (c. 300–after 377).[140] In subsequent centuries these apocryphal Acta were still widely read and incorporated into homilies, later saints' Lives, and chronographies that dealt with the early church.[141] For instance, it appears that apocryphal acts of James, now lost, were incorporated into a

---

[139] The critical text of the *Acts of Philip* is Bovon, Bouvier, and Amsler 1999; French translation, Amsler, Bovon, and Bouvier 1996. On the religious community that produced the *Acts of Philip* see the references at Bovon 2001:140n10, esp. Slater 1999.

[140] On the Council of Gangra in the context of the extreme eastern asceticism of the fourth and fifth centuries, see Caner 2002, esp. chapter 3; in addition, see the references in *ODCC* s.v. "Gangra, Council of" and "Eustathius," esp. Gribomont 1957, 1980, and Barnes 1989, and, for the text of the Council (20 canons in Greek and Latin) with a French translation, see Joannou 1962–1963:1.2.83–99.

[141] On the Byzantine reception of early Christian apocrypha, see Patlagean 1991.

sermon by Nicetas David of Paphlagonia, who shows a very detailed knowledge of that tradition.[142] The apocryphal Acta thus survived, and surely cross-fertilized, the flowering of the traditional saint's Life in late antiquity and, moreover, continued to be considered legitimate historical literature concerning the apostles. While it is not clear precisely how late these Acta continued to be written in the style of the second-century ones, they are found as late as the fifth and sixth centuries and, not insignificantly, they were mined by homilists and historians of Byzantium for their own creative writing on the early saints. The Acts of John by Pseudo-Prochorus (fifth or sixth century) stands as perhaps the latest surviving Greek exemplum of this tradition,[143] but the sixth and seventh century translations of the apocryphal Acta into Syriac and Armenian attest to their continued popularity in non-Greek early Byzantium.

In her article "Byzantine Hagiographers as Antiquarians, Seventh to Tenth Centuries," Claudia Rapp has analyzed the tendency of middle Byzantine authors to rewrite (μεταφράζειν) saints' Lives, to collect their legends into practical compilations—μενολόγια, συναξάρια, and the like—and to treat the earlier legends as textual artifacts of a distant past.[144] Underlying this tendency was, she says, "the melancholy insight that the age of the saints has irrevocably come to a close" (31). Along the literary-historical continuum of Byzantine hagiography Rapp locates this paradigm shift in the seventh century, during which works like the Life of John the Almsgiver by Leontius of Neapolis and the Miracles of Saint Anastasius the Persian projected onto the saints an innovative antiquarian consciousness: both John and Anastasius are said to have themselves enjoyed reading the Lives of saints (τὸ ἐντυγχάνειν τοῖς βίοις τῶν ἁγίων πατέρων; 35 and n12). Also in the seventh century came the "first flourishing" of μεταφράσεις: Leontius' "stylistic downgrading" of John's original Life by Sophronius of Jerusalem and John Moschus anticipated the later, massive project of rewriting by Symeon the Logothete, nicknamed "Metaphrastes" (36–37).[145]

---

[142] Bovon 1999a argues against Lipsius 1883–1890:2/2.233, who said that a later use of this lost apocryphal material on James, by the Byzantine historian Nicephorus Callistus Xanthopoulos, is taken from Nicetas. Bovon argues that they both independently attest these lost Acta, demonstrating that standard versions were in circulation for a considerable time.

[143] Critical text: Zahn 1975 [1880]:3–165. See Krueger 2004:216n15 for references to modern translations.

[144] Rapp 1995.

[145] See Høgel 2002. Between Sophronius and Symeon comes, of course, Nicetas David of Paphlegonia in the ninth century, mentioned above in relation to the lost acts of James the brother of Jesus (Rapp 1995:35–36).

As Rapp shows, it was not until the ninth century that hagiographic compilations first appeared: Theodore the Stoudite produced a proto-μενολόγιον, the πανηγυρικὴν βιβλίον, which in the next century was the inspiration for a much larger compilation, the famous μενολόγιον of Constantinople, also by Symeon. This is the literary history that for Rapp is most indicative of an antiquarian tendency: that is, an increasing awareness of the use and spiritual profit of saints' Lives in the seventh century, then an early interest in compiling in the ninth, culminating in a very substantial intensification of rewriting and compilation in the tenth century, commissioned by Constantine Porphyrogennetos and spearheaded by Symeon Metaphrastes.[146] She has shown how many writers before Symeon were engaged in reconfiguring and preserving older Lives, and she has argued convincingly that Symeon's metaphrastic collections should thus be seen as the culmination of a tradition rather than as a historically isolated project of "inventorizing" in the tenth century.

Rapp has thus delineated this significant trend from the seventh to tenth centuries, but what I hope to have shown is that μετάφρασις, a constituent element of Greek Christian textuality, was embedded in Christians' responses to their texts, including the New Testament, from much earlier. Did the Byzantines recognize earlier μετάφρασις? They certainly did with regard to the apocryphal Acta—Symeon is aware of multiple versions of apocryphal apostolic narratives, some of which are closer than others to the revisionary style he advocates and employed in his compilations.[147] On this basis, I would conclude that Rapp's argument is further strengthened, if significantly revised, by pushing the continuum back into earlier Christian literature. Rewriting and paraphrase are central to Greek literary history (classical, Jewish, and Christian) and provide a cognitive thread which can be traced through the whole first millennium of the Christian era.

## Conclusion: Metaphrasis in Late Antiquity and Beyond

The brief survey just presented offers an opportunity to consider synchronically a literary activity that, by the fifth century AD, had been ongoing for a very long time in Jewish and Christian literary traditions. It is probable, though most likely impossible to prove, that the evidence of μετάφρασις in the

---

[146] It should also be noted that the metaphrastic trend continues for several centuries after Symeon as well: see Talbot 1991, cited by Rapp 1995:36n24.

[147] Høgel 2002:89–126.

received texts of both religions—e.g. the canonical books of the Chronicles—provided the initial impetus for the receivers (Jews or Christians) to engage in that activity themselves. Scholars would, of course, be arrogant to assume that early Christians were unaware of something of the metaphrastic relationships among the synoptic gospels: the fascinating, if elusive, example of Tatian's *Diatessaron* is already suggestive of such an awareness. Through the reception of texts and rewritings of those texts, as well as through the reception of the project of rewriting (as a kind of institution), μετάφρασις became a literary vocation and proceeded to cross-fertilize new and influential texts, such as the disparate group of writings broadly labeled as "hagiography."

Concerning a topic as big as rewriting there will always be new evidence to cite and new syntheses to be made. However, I have tried in this chapter to point to commonalities among the examples cited above in an attempt to center the scholarly discussion of rewriting on the processes involved. The investment of contemporary ideology or polemic is visible in all of the rewritings, even if not always as pronounced as in the Qumran community's eschatological anticipations. The presence of the paraphrast in the "hypertext"—*sub evangelistae persona*—is also a common feature, though often less self-conscious than in Erasmus' dedication of his *Paraphrase on Luke* to Henry VIII. Further, *Vorlagen* could be changed almost beyond recognition, as in the *Genesis Apocryphon* or Eudocia's *cento* of Christian redemptive history; however, subtle changes also point to a similar process of reception and modification, as evidenced by *Codex Bezae*.

Jack Goody's model of endless elaboration by oral myth tellers—especially among the "scholars" that elaboration produced—is suggestive in its "textual" outline of a cognitive imperative of rewriting inherent to human textuality or story-telling in general. Ancient paraphrase and rewriting, it has been argued, could provide an extension of his oral evidence. Donald McKenzie has suggested something like this in his controversial attempt to redefine bibliography as a twenty-first-century discipline.[148] In addition to pointing out the importance of ascertaining physical changes to texts through time—as an entrée to pursuing their full meaning diachronically—he has emphasized the synchronic inevitability of a text becoming a "site" for later rewritings.

In other words, not only does the physical history of a text "make up" its meaning, but the dissemination of a text (oral, visual, or written) "lets out" its meaning to be reconstructed by as many as come into contact with it. McKenzie has formulated this argument not to relativize textual meaning as

---

[148] McKenzie 1999 [1986]; see Chartier 1997 for differing reactions to McKenzie's seminal lectures.

much as to historicize it, and to provide a firmer basis for the work of textual criticism in the age of textual deconstruction:

> History simply confirms, as a bibliographical fact, that quite new versions of a work which is not altogether dead, *will* be created, whether they are generated by its author, by its successive editors, by generations of readers, or by new writers.[149]

My argument in this chapter takes inspiration from McKenzie in that I have tried to forge a link between rewriting and paraphrase in practice (as examined in Chapter One above) and the literary history of biblical and apocryphal paraphrase. Such a link is not primarily about authorial intention but about how texts are inevitably changed by their receivers. This may seem at first glance to be a banal point in an age when every phenomenon in human experience comes under the academic designation "text." However, with regard to the history of Greek literature in late antiquity, the important connections between paraphrase as a literary form, literate education, and the way Jews and Christians read their "Bible" (or the history of their institutions in general) suggest that a link between minute changes to received Scriptures and the wholesale rewriting of formative texts, canonical or apocryphal, needs to be made and explored.

In her analysis of the *Paraphrase of Ecclesiastes* by Gregory Thaumaturgus, Françoise Vinel has concluded that biblical paraphrase as a genre performs certain tacit operations on its audience. First, within a Jewish or Christian context it conflates interpretation with Scripture to the degree that what originally was text now becomes a kind of prohibitive intertext. "La *metaphrasis* comme la paraphrase interdit par définition ce mouvement entre le texte original et sa lecture."[150] More forbidding than in a sermon, an interpretation that is made in a paraphrase sticks with you because it has become the very Scripture you are reading or hearing, and it thereby affects your apprehension of other parts of the Scriptural or imaginative whole.

While it has not been the concern of this chapter to deal with the complex allusions of the paraphrases cited above, the allusive quality of paraphrase must be kept in mind—and perhaps this is a point at which paraphrase, as a genre, diverges from literal rewritings of scriptural texts.[151] However, Daniel Boyarin has argued for the intertextuality of midrash to be seen as inspired

---

[149] McKenzie 1999:37, citing Doctorow, Wittock, and Marks 1978; emphasis is McKenzie's.
[150] Vinel 1987:213.
[151] See Pucci 1998 for a recent restatement of the value of allusion in late antique literature.

by, or as the direct result of, the intertextuality of Scripture itself.[152] And one might assume that individual changes to Scripture would also play off of these inherent allusions. As demonstrated in Chapter One, the author of the *Life of Thekla* appropriates for the contemporary cult the history of the apostles and their personae (particularly Thekla, Paul, Stephen, and Luke). This appropriation, however, requires the author to take seriously any dominant, received legend concerning the earliest period of Christian history.

The seriousness with which the author of the *Life of Thekla* has taken the received testimony of her apostolic status is evident in every one of the changes that he makes to his source text, the *ATh*. His cognitive appreciation of that text's authority is dependent on its received, quasi-canonical status in his contemporary situation. His appreciation is strengthened and intensified by his spiritual relationship to Thekla herself and by her local activities at the shrine in Seleukeia. Both the past and the present thus serve as motivations for the *Life and Miracles* as a whole—and, as will be shown, so does the future. With this in mind it is time to look closely at the second half of his text in order to see how he transforms Thekla the apostolic saint into Thekla the late antique miracle worker.

---

[152] Boyarin 1990:15.

# Chapter 3

## History, Narrative, and Miracle in Late Antique Seleukeia: Thekla's θαύματα and their Collector

### Introduction: Herodotean Precedent and the Autobiographical Rhetoric of Miracle-Collecting

T HE SHORT HISTORY OF PARAPHRASE presented in the last chapter was not designed to be comprehensive but only to point to the widespread use of the form in early Christian and late antique literature. The issue of form is central, I argue, to a right understanding of the whole *Life and Miracles* as well as to the development of Byzantine genres such as the saint's Life and the miracle collection. Biblical and Homeric paraphrase, as well as related literary forms like the *cento*, provide a literary historical context for the rewriting of the *Acts of Paul and Thekla* in the fifth century. Both paraphrase and *cento* can be seen, at least in their late antique forms, as developing first out of educational systems and, subsequently, out of a habit of rewriting characteristic of early Christian textuality. That the author of the *LM* situates himself amongst "une dynastie de professeurs" at Seleukeia comes as less of a surprise once the paraphrase genre is invoked as a literary background.[1]

In this third chapter the role played by the literary aspirations of the *LM*'s author will come to the fore. In an attempt to show how he has molded his materials with a definite theme or purpose in mind, the social reality which has been so often associated with local, Asclepian (or simply indigenous) healing must be queried. In no way should the results of this examination diminish our access to the reality "on the ground" in Seleukeia. Instead, these

---

[1] Quotation from Dagron 1978:129; the whole gamut of professions is represented: γραμματιστής, σοφιστής, and ῥήτωρ (*Mir.* 38–40). See Kaster 1988 for the grammarian's profession (passim), the meaning of γραμματιστής compared with γραμματικός (447–452), and, most importantly, his prosopographical entries for the individuals named in the *Miracles*: Alypius (239; no. 5), Isocasius (301–302; no. 85), Olympius (321; no. 108), and Solymius (431; no. 259).

results should enhance that access by bringing into focus the way reality is shaped by the author of the text. What I hope to make clear is that it is only through making a close examination of the *Miracles*, our chief conduit to that Seleukeian reality, that we can hope to achieve the social or anthropological high ground that a text like this one seems to offer.

With this in mind, I would like to begin by examining the rhetorical position adopted by the author in his preface to the *Miracles*. The author opens the *Miracles* (after a brief proem) with a citation from Herodotus, the father of classical historiography. This citation is the oracle given to Croesus in Book 1 of the *Histories*: "In crossing the Halys river Croesus will destroy a great kingdom" (*Mir.* preface 50; compare Herodotus 1.53). This oracle is used by the author of the *Miracles* to illustrate the opacity of pagan oracular wisdom. As he says, "in puzzles and riddles lies the whole honor of the oracles" (preface 36–37). He then proceeds to compare these devious oracles to the "healings and oracular sayings (ἰάματα καὶ θεσπίσματα)" of the saints, which he says are "wise, true, complete, holy, perfect, and truly worthy of the God who has given them" (preface 75–77).

The author clearly misunderstands how Herodotus uses the oracle in the course of narrating Croesus' defeat and the sources of war between Greece and Persia.[2] However, what is most interesting about this Herodotean citation is that the father of history is not himself being called into question. Instead, he is reverentially called "the sweetest" (τὸν ἥδιστον) and brought onto the scene to corroborate the assertion that pagan oracles are false and misleading. Herodotus' account of Croesus's hubristic misinterpretation and subsequent defeat by Cyrus is considered genuine and authoritative, as is the brief mention of the prophecy about the mule (Herodotus 1.55), which Croesus also did not understand correctly. Herodotus' reporting is thus not impugned here, and it matters little that the author of the *LM* has not grasped the overall import of Herodotus' message.

Once the *Miracles* is set within a literary historical context of paradoxography (Chapter Four), it will become clearer why it is that the author's chief interlocutor, at least in terms of programmatic rhetoric, is Herodotus: as discussed below, Hellenistic paradoxography self-consciously aligned itself with the "natural wonders" side of classical historiography, which includes Herodotus, as well as Theopompus of Chios and others.[3] Yet, the choice of

---

[2] Suffice it to say that at *Histories* 1.91 Herodotus himself explains that the oracle was only misleading because Croesus was not clever enough to ask which empire would be destroyed.
[3] See pp. 175–179.

Herodotus is not just significant because of his association with paradoxography: it is through the frequent rhetorical appeals to "authenticity," "truth," and to his sources, as well as the process of collecting, that the author of the *Miracles* places himself alongside Herodotus in the historiographical fold.[4] And it could be cited as further proof of this historiographical bent that Herodotus is singled out in this programmatic section over and above Homer, even though the latter is cited by name at many points throughout the text of the *Miracles*.[5]

Herodotus' authorial persona is, therefore, at the forefront of the *Miracles*. This imitation, perhaps more properly called "emulation" (ζῆλος/ ζήλωσις),[6] shows up as much in the organization of the miracle narratives as in the programmatic description of his project. His method of organization, placing story after story ad infinitum, is also characteristic of paradoxography, which shares this format with the *Miracles* and Herodotus, as will be shown in Chapter Four.[7] Without venturing now into a detailed comparison of these three, it is enough to note that the method of framing individual units of narrative has also been acknowledged for some time now to be a primary organizing principle in Herodotus' *Histories*. As Henry Immerwahr explained in his 1966 book *Form and Thought in Herodotus*, Herodotus employs anticipating and summary statements at the beginning and end, respectively, of narrative units—a simple, "paratactic" style that has the potential to produce a complex overall narrative.[8] In Immerwahr's words:

---

[4] Perhaps it is best at this point to refrain from categorizing the *LM* as historiography per se, since its author—by his own admission a writer and public speaker (*Mir.* 41)—is clearly drawing on multiple sources for inspiration, perhaps especially on unnamed or altered biblical texts. On this latter point, see Dagron 1978:156–157.

[5] For a selective list of references to Homer in the *Miracles*, see Dagron 1978:157. It should be noted that the author of the *LM* does acknowledge Thucydides in the preface to the *Life* (preface 29), though the latter seems to have had little if any influence on either the *Life* or the *Miracles*, unless one considers the invented speeches of the *Life* to be specifically Thucydidean. It is more likely, however, that those speeches stem simply from a general historiographical self-consciousness on the part of our author.

[6] For the various meanings of the terms ζῆλος or ζήλωσις in classical Greek, see LSJ s.v. The idea of ζῆλος as "rivalry" or "imitation," and not its basic meaning of "jealousy," is found in Plato (*Menexenus* 242a) and Aristotle (*Rhetoric* 1388a30), but its uses in the Second Sophistic come closer to the practice suggested above: e.g. Pseudo-Longinus 13.2 (cf. Maximus of Tyre 7.9) and Hermogenes *On Types of Style* (213–214, trans. Russell and Winterbottom 1972:562).

[7] In addition to sharing the language of "wonder" (θαῦμα).

[8] Paratactic is the adjective from "parataxis" (παράταξις), which is the arrangement of sentences or narrative units side by side rather than in subordination to one another (ὑπόταξις): see Smyth 1956:485–487 and Immerwahr 1966:46–78, with standard references to Norden, Fraenkel, and others.

It is by a simple system of external repetition (and to some extent internal repetition as well) that Herodotus has created a large unified work. Throughout this work descriptions of single events reach out to find connections with other events, especially at the beginning and end of the story. Thus Herodotus' style everywhere exhibits the single chain rather than complex interweaving.[9]

This literary style serves as a method of organization which turns a mass of unrefined material into a manageable whole. It also serves the function of propelling the reader from one story to the next: without realizing what is happening, the reader is whisked away to another story, another country even, and only later realizes the important connections between the narrative units.

The *Miracles* employs a similar paratactic style in the formulaic introductions and conclusions found in each miracle. A key phrase for the introduction is something like the following from the opening of *Mir.* 42: "I should mention (μνημονευτέον) this miracle, of which I obtained the remembrance (μνήμην) only with some difficulty." Likewise, these story-units often have formulaic closings, which serve to conclude the miracle as they push the reader on to the next one. For example, the conclusion to *Mir.* 13 (31–38) reads:

> While I am still dazzled by the splendor of this miracle, another dazzling miracle, which happened once, astounds me (καταπλήττεται) by its beauty and persuades me to move quickly onto to itself, as beautiful as it is, as lovely as it is, and since, much more than the other miracles, it is able to enchant its listener and to proclaim more openly the grace and power of the martyr. Therefore, we should not delay, and to the miracle impatient that we spring forward, let us gratify it with swiftness. Of what a sort is it?

This pattern of formulaic beginning and formulaic ending does not occur so explicitly in every miracle, but the author is very regular in his framing of the stories. I will draw more attention to this technique again when I treat individual miracles in subsequent sections of this chapter.

Having thus shown how both Herodotus and the author of the *Miracles* achieve this paratactic style through similar means, let us consider other ways in which the model of Herodotus' *Histories* could be at work in the writing of the *Miracles*. First, the author of the *Miracles* emulates Herodotus in the way he cites sources for the miracle stories. As noted in a recent article by Carolyn Dewald, Herodotus employs an "expert's persona" which allows him to present

---

[9] Immerwahr 1966:59.

a "polyvocal" narrative from an authoritative position: "[Herodotus] sets up a division between what he knows and says in his own voice because he knows it, and the *logoi* or stories of others."[10] This description could be accurately made of the author of the *Miracles*. For instance, *Mir.* 34 is a story about two thieves from Eirenopolis (in Isauria) who attempt to rape a virgin attached to the shrine at Seleukeia, and they attempt this in the very gardens of the holy shrine. When Thekla reaps punishment for this act of drunken hubris (since they were also drunk at the time, celebrating a recently stolen gold piece), the two thieves meet their end. In the final paragraph of this miracle the author appeals to the authority of his sources: "I learned this story from [the thieves'] fellow citizens, perhaps even from their own relations (τάχα δὲ καὶ [παρὰ] συγγενῶν)" (34.56–57). His appeal to the testimony of the thieves' families promotes the sense of direct access to the authentic work of Thekla. At the same time, however, this appeal distances him from the testimony and allows him to report on the event as if he were a third, disinterested party. Like Herodotus, the author of the *Miracles* is highlighting at the same time both the quality of his testimony and the trustworthiness of his reporting.

So much for the incorporation of sources and others' eyewitness testimony. How, then, does the author of the *Miracles* attempt to integrate Herodotus' claim to autopsy and personal experience? This question proves to be somewhat more difficult to answer because Herodotus' own practice varies throughout the *Histories*. In the middle of Book 2, for instance, Herodotus declares, "up to this point my narrative is the result of my own direct observation, reasoning, and research (ὄψις τε ἐμὴ καὶ γνώμη καὶ ἱστορίη)" (2.99). As John Marincola has pointed out, Book 2 of the *Histories*, the Egyptian λόγος, is by far the most "autobiographical" of all nine books, and for two reasons in particular: 1) we know Herodotus was attempting to supersede previous histories of Egypt, like that of Hecataeus, whereas there is no evidence that any other writer had written a history of the Greek war with Persia; 2) autopsy was impossible to achieve for the whole of the war itself, whereas the ethnography of Egypt found in Book 2 is much more geographical and anthropological—most significantly, Herodotus claims that Egypt has more "marvels" (θαυμάσια) than any other country (2.35).[11] Does this mean that Book 2 is essentially a different kind of ἱστορία than the rest of the *Histories*? In the sense that both the tools and subject matter seem to be different, the answer according to Marincola is definitely "yes": in Book 2 Herodotus is polemicizing

---

[10] Dewald 2002:269. See also an earlier article on this topic, Dewald 1987.
[11] Marincola 1987.

against prior writers on Egypt and also attempting something more ethnographic or digressional which is less concerned with the overall narrative of the war between Greece and Persia.[12]

Concerning the *Miracles*, there are a few points to note from Marincola's analysis of Herodotus. First, it is reasonable that an emulator of Herodotus like the author of the *Miracles* might decide to choose between the political history of the Persian war and the more "autobiographical," autopic ethnography of the Egyptians in Book 2: the combination of styles of inquiry in Herodotus is idiosyncratic and clearly continues to challenge even modern scholars.[13] Second, the paratactic structure of Book 2, as explained by Immerwahr, has already been noted and shown to be similar to that of the *Miracles*. Third, the *Miracles'* emphasis on "wonders" (θαύματα) focuses our attention on the ethnographic part of the *Histories* and highlights the conduit of Hellenistic and Roman paradoxography between Herodotus and the *Miracles*.[14] Fourth, and most importantly, Marincola has noted that the "personal involvement" which Herodotus displays in Book 2 is different from his authorial persona in the rest of the *Histories*. To quote Marincola on this point, "Herodotus here and only here occupies simultaneously the position of narrator and character. We see him everywhere in [Book 2] as the initiator, guide, and discoverer of information."[15]

This last point has important repercussions for how we understand the *Miracles'* author participating in the discovery of information about Thekla's healings in Seleukeia and its environs. There are a number of autobiographical comments strung throughout the course of the *Miracles*, which, when examined in this historiographical light, serve further to solidify the rhetorical connection that the author is trying achieve between his work and that of Herodotus. For instance, in *Mir.* 31 Thekla appears to the author to encourage the progress of his miracle collection (συλλογή). This short miracle deserves to be quoted in full:

> At the very moment when I was writing (ἐποιούμην γραφήν) about this miracle (θαύματος)—it is not good to keep silent any longer about what the martyr granted me—the following happened to me.

---

[12] For an attempt to integrate Book 2 more closely with the rest of the *Histories*, see Benardette 1969.

[13] Myres 1953:96–97 simply refuses to attempt to incorporate Book 2 in his overall structural analysis. For a more positive solution, see, again, Benardette 1969.

[14] But in a sense paradoxography is not necessary for this argument, since the author of the *LM* has already cited Herodotus in the prefaces of both halves of his work.

[15] Marincola 1987:127.

I had been neglectful in collecting (τοῦ συλλέγειν) and committing these events to writing (γράφειν αὐτὰ ταῦτα), I confess, and lazily did I grasp a writing tablet (δέλτου) and a stylus (γραφίδος), as if I had given up on my inquiry (ἔρευναν) and collection (συλλογήν) of miracles. It was when I was in this state and in the process of yawning (χασμιῶντι) that the martyr appeared to my sight (ἐν ὄψει) seated at my side, in the place where it was my habit to consult my books (πρὸς τὰ βιβλία ποιεῖσθαι συνουσίαν), and she took from my hand the notebook (τετράδα), on which I was transcribing (μετεγραφόμην) this latest story (ταῦτα) from the writing tablet (δέλτου). And she seemed to me to read (ἀναγινώσκειν) and to be pleased (ἐφήδεσθαι) and to smile (μειδιᾶν) and to indicate (ἐνδείκνυσθαι) to me by her gaze (βλέμματι) that she was pleased (ἀρέσκοι) with what I was in the process of writing, and that it is necessary for me to complete this work (πόνον) and not to leave it unfinished—up to the point that I am able to learn from each person what he knows and what is possible [to discover] with accuracy (ἀκριβείᾳ). So, after this vision (ὄψιν) I was consumed with fear and filled with desire once again to pick up my writing tablet and stylus and to do as much as she will command.

Of course, this type of supernatural experience is not at all what one reads in Book 2 of Herodotus, but the point to be made is that the author is, like Herodotus, placing himself at the center of the very subject matter he has set out to describe. As Gregory Nagy has commented on Herodotus' narrative: "The search for original causes motivates not just the events being told but the narration itself."[16] The quest for the history of Thekla's miracles at Seleukeia is distinctly portrayed as a quest for the completion of the miracle collection, with the author's role in that quest at the very center of the portrayal. The suggestion in the passage above is that, if the author had continued to delay the completion of his literary task, then the *Miracles* would never come to light. Rather than simply declaring that this is a divinely ordained task, the author incorporates his own personal experience as the miracle collector (supernatural as it may be) into the history of the events he is recording. This autobiographical mode of historiography is undeniably Herodotean: the Egyptian λόγος in Book 2 of the *Histories* is here considered to be a model worthy of emulation.

---

[16] Nagy 1987:184.

Herodotus is invoked, therefore, as a literary precedent in several different ways by the author of the *Miracles*.[17] To recap, first, at the beginning of the *Miracles* Herodotus is cited as a trustworthy account on a point of polemic: Croesus was the recipient of a devious oracle which led to his demise—what kind of god would intentionally trick his adherents? The fact that this is a misreading of Herodotus hardly matters. What matters is that Herodotus' name is front and center at the beginning of the *Miracles*, a position which, from a literary point of view, signals to the attentive reader that Herodotus is going to be an interlocutor for this author. Second, the paratactic style of Herodotus' narrative, especially Book 2, is repeatedly invoked. While it is important to note that by late antiquity there was an established sub-genre of historiography called paradoxography, which took this paratactic style as its modus operandi (see Chapter Four), the author of the *Miracles* has signaled his allegiance to Herodotus already in the preface to the *Life*, so the reader should be sensitive to the outworking of the author's historiographical self-consciousness throughout the work. Finally, the author places himself at the center of the history of Thekla's deeds and, consequently, at the center of their collection and promulgation, since Thekla's activity is bound up with his efforts as well. This autobiographical mode of history writing is also characteristic of Herodotus and, as John Marincola has shown, particularly Book 2 of the *Histories*.

I would like to turn now to an examination of Thekla's character in these miracles. Over the next several sub-sections I shall be examining closely two groups of miracles in particular: 1) the miracles which are primarily concerned with Thekla's divine power, as displayed in her confrontations with local pagan gods as well as in her miracles of vengeance; and 2) the miracles of healing. This latter group is the one that usually attracts separate attention among scholars, but I hope to show that (despite my division for the sake of analysis) there is no good reason to divide the miracles from one another in any formal manner whatsoever. In other words, miracles of healing may be distinct from the vengeance miracles in terms of content, but there is no overarching structural difference between the two groups, either in terms of narrative or the overall picture of Thekla that is offered.

---

[17] As mentioned above, Homer is variously invoked throughout the *Miracles*, and Dagron has suggested on this basis that the *Life* and *Miracles* is its author's *Iliad* and *Odyssey* (1978:19). The comparison is not without good evidence, though the *Miracles* fits the *Odyssey* much better than the *Life* fits the *Iliad*. The point to be made, however, is that these classical models of major literary undertakings—*Iliad*, *Odyssey*, and Herodotus' *Histories*—are assumed points of contact with the ancient world. The same analogy could be made, with equal or greater significance, for the canonical pair of Luke-Acts, which is cited twice in the preface to the *Life* (though admittedly absent from the preface to the *Miracles*).

# Thekla's Miracles of Divine Power: Supremacy, Vengeance, and Humanitarian Aid under the "All Seeing and Divine Eye" of the Martyr

## Rhetorical conventions

While the *Miracles* has often been read as a book about incubatorial healing in the Asclepian style, the majority of Thekla's *Miracles* are not about healing at all.[18] A full 26 of 46 miracles (56%) deal with her divine power and authority over Seleukeia and its environs and contain no mention of sickness or healing. Thus, the reader sees her overcoming pagan gods (*Mir.* 1–4), meting out well deserved punishments upon hubristic groups (such as Isaurian brigands) and upon sinful individuals (e.g. *Mir.* 28, 35), and performing various acts of compassionate protection and instruction, such as teaching a woman named Xenarchis how to read (*Mir.* 45). On this basis it is important to note that the *Miracles*, when taken as a whole, is not concerned primarily with describing the process and experience of late antique healing, at least not in the way the *Miracles* of Artemios is two centuries later.[19] Instead, I shall argue, its author had a much broader and complex vision of how Thekla was at work in Seleukeia and in his own career.

To begin in the middle of the *Miracles*, an arresting description of Thekla's divine power comes in *Mir.* 22, one of the shortest miracles in the collection. The miracle begins with a framing sentence: "Thekla displayed (ἐπεδείξατο) the next miracle concerning one of her own treasures." Then the author explains that a thief stole one of the consecrated crosses from her shrine and, ferreting it some distance away, hid it in a tree. Thekla's joking reaction to the theft is telling: "The martyr took this action against her as grounds for laughter, since the best thieves would not neglect her, even if it were possible to escape her all-seeing and divine eye! (τὸ πανδερκές τε καὶ θεῖον ὄμμα)" (22.4–7).[20] Next, the martyr visits (ἐπιφοιτήσασα) one of her attendants and reveals where the stolen cross is hidden. A brief summary statement, according to the author's typically terse style, closes the miracle: "For the one who reckoned that he

---

[18] I quote here a standard interpretation of the *Life and Miracles*: "The most spectacular instance of the Christian appropriation of Asclepius is found in the mid fifth century in the cult of Saint Thecla in Seleucia . . . Thecla wore the mantle of Asclepius, now in the guise of a female saint" (Cox Miller 1994:117; quoted in full on p. 173 below).

[19] Crisafulli and Nesbitt 1997. Cf. Déroche 1993.

[20] For πανδερκής as an attribute of divine/heavenly vision, see also ὀφθαλμὸς κραδίης πανδερκής at Nonnus *Paraphrase of John* 12.41 (referring to Isaiah's vision in the temple; Isaiah 6).

possessed the cross, this was the only profit: being called 'temple-robber' (ἱερόσυλον)."[21]

While it is unusual that the martyr is the subject of the abuse—this only happens in one other miracle (*Mir.* 28)—in other ways this short miracle exhibits shared rhetorical characteristics of all of the miracles. The most important is the description of Thekla's "all seeing and divine eye." This epithet could be taken as representative of the way Thekla's presence in Seleukeia is understood by the author of the *Miracles*: she never stops watching and never stops working miracles. As the author says later in the collection, "The final miracle, this will never come; there will never be a final miracle of the martyr" (*Mir.* 44.2–3). In the words of *Mir.* 22, this is because Thekla is always "watchful." Interestingly, this unceasing gaze is only once described in terms of shepherding or assisting the helpless—orphans show up in *Mir.* 35—a tone or characterization which could have easily drawn upon biblical motifs from the Psalms, Isaiah, and the Gospels. Instead, Thekla's gaze is directed at everything that is "her own" (cf. John 10:27). In the case of *Mir.* 22, "her own" takes the form of the consecrated "loot" (τὸ φώριον), but in human terms the impact of the theft would have fallen upon "her attendants and servants" (ὑπηρέται καὶ πάρεδροι), exactly whom she "visits" (ἐπιφοιτήσασα) to reveal the location of the stolen cross. Elsewhere, Thekla's "own" is defined as the individuals who seek to honor her, such as the author of the *Miracles* himself: "she knows to help with the greatest gifts (τὰ μέγιστα) those who honor her a little (μικρά)" (*Mir.* 41.7–8).

Thus, her principal focus is upon defending and protecting those who are attached to her in some way: in *Mir.* 22 this means her "assistants" (presumably priests and virgins attached to her shrine), but in *Mir.* 44, it means the author, whom we know, from *Mir.* 12 and elsewhere, is not a monk (though he appears to become a priest in *Mir.* 41; see below). While her gaze is omnipotent in its scope, it focuses on those who are connected to her: in other words, there is a correspondence between those who need her, who honor her, and whom she looks out for. For the author of the *Miracles* this correspondence is one-to-one between his text and the assistance that Thekla provides for him.

---

[21] As noted in Chapter One, ἱερόσυλος is applied to Thekla in the Iconian arena (*ATh* 28) in its broader, later sense of Roman *sacrilegium*, as opposed to the more restricted, original meaning of "temple-robber" here.

Dominance in Seleukeia

Related to this correspondence between those who need Thekla and those whom she helps is Thekla's authority over the region of Seleukeia and Isauria/Cilicia generally. The verb ἐπιφοιτάω ("to visit, haunt") is the most common verb used of Thekla's activities "on the ground." Thus, as in the passage quoted from *Mir.* 22 above, she "visits" her assistants directly after and in response to her "watching" the thief steal and hide the cross. In the *Miracles* there is a causal relationship between her omnipotent, divine vision (sometimes "listening": e.g. *Mir.* 45.20–21), and the practical "haunting" which she performs, either visibly (as herself or in the guise of another), or in dreams.

The most programmatic examples of her visiting "in person," so to speak, are the four miracles at the beginning of the work, in which she encounters and conquers four local gods: Sarpedon (literally, "the Sarpedonian"), Athena, Aphrodite, and Zeus. The first and fourth of these miracles are the longest, and their length is related to the prominence of Sarpedon and Zeus in the author's conception of the pagan pantheon: Sarpedon, in particular, because he was a local (originally Lycian) deity to whom local residents would appeal for healing. Thus, the *Miracles* begins with Thekla's most serious competition for the faith of the people of Seleukeia: "No one is ignorant of the Sarpedonian, for we knew (ἔγνωμεν) the most ancient mythical narrative (μυθολόγημα) concerning him from histories and books (ἱστοριῶν καὶ βιβλίων)."[22]

The author of the *Miracles* takes pains to de-mythologize this ancient narrative, before bringing Thekla onto the scene to defeat Sarpedon. Instead of recalling the prominent role that the Trojan Sarpedon (son of Zeus and Laodameia) plays in the *Iliad* (e.g. 5.628–672; 12.290ff.), including his death at the hands of Patroklos (16.419–683), the author of the *Miracles* presents a much less grandiose history of Sarpedon's arrival in Cilicia:

> Some people are aware that he was once a stranger...wandering in search of his sister and putting in by sea at these parts here, and in ignorance of the territory and in ignorance of the current ruler—this was Kilix, his uncle and his father's brother—he was killed because he had caused some pain and attracted the hostility of the inhabit-

[22] Dagron 1978: 291n2 suggests this is either hendiadys, as translated above, or an opposition between oral and written sources (thus, "inquirers and books"). Μυθολογεύω is used by Homer (*Odyssey* 12.450) and μυθολόγημα is used by Plato (e.g. *Laws* 663e); thus, both are standard Greek terms. However, the verb μυθολογέω is used by later authors to speak of specifically Homeric myth-telling (Longinus 34.2). The use of μυθολόγημα here most likely retains the resonance of the latter verb.

ants, and he was buried by the breakwater at this shore. Thereafter, he received the name of *daimon*, and the reputation of an oracle and prophet, and on account of this was considered among foolish people to be a god.

*Mir.* 1.5–10

The author of the *Miracles* clearly has no gift for mythologizing.[23] Indeed, he summarizes his iconoclastic approach to ancient mythology with the following statement: "the long passage of time produces many such ideas, and people accept them uncritically and create gods out of fables" (1.12–13). While it is true that in other mythological traditions Sarpedon does not die at the hands of Patroklos but lives on, long enough at least to settle in Asia Minor (Apollodorus 3.1.2; Diodorus Siculus 5.79.3; scholia on *Iliad* 16.673),[24] the author of the *Miracles* seems intentionally to eschew any details that would bring some repute to Sarpedon, and perhaps his habit of calling him "the Sarpedonian" serves as a polemical aside on popular opinion.[25]

However, as Dagron notes, the association between Sarpedon and Apollo is very close in the *Miracles*, to the degree that when the rhetor Aretarchos is healed of an infection of his kidneys in *Mir.* 40 he attributes the miracle to "Sarpedon or Apollo" (40.30–31). According to Dagron, this attribution helps to interpret the statement from *Mir.* 1 quoted above "thereafter he received the name of *daimon*," by which the author means that Sarpedon's local character was coincident with Apollo's. If this is correct, then a proper interpretation of "the Sarpedonian" should not be as a substitute for the proper name "Sarpedon" but should be extended to mean "the Sarpedonian version

---

[23] As Dagron notes (1978:86), the author makes Europa, who is Sarpedon's mother according to Apollodorus, into his sister, making Sarpedon the nephew of Kilix (i.e. the eponymous founder of Cilicia). Thus, if he knows this later version of the myth (see below), then he is here intentionally drawing the attention away from Lycia (Sarpedon's traditional homeland) to Seleukeia.

[24] Of course, the tradition that Sarpedon came from Lycia is in the *Iliad* itself (e.g. 12.310–321), and Gregory Nagy (1990:122–142) has demonstrated that the language used to describe Sarpedon's death and subsequent retrieval by Death and Sleep (at the command of Apollo and Zeus) has its roots in the Anatolian (Hittite) and Indo-European traditions of immortalization, specifically as it relates to the verb ταρχύω (*Iliad* 16.456 = 16.674).

[25] Other instances of Σαρπηδόνιος include *Mir.* 11.12, 18.30, and 40.15 (cf. 40.30). As an adjective modifying a noun, Σαρπηδόνιος shows up as early as Aeschylus (*Suppliants* 869: Σαρπηδονία ἄκρα), but as a substitute for a proper noun, either for "Sarpedon" or "Sarpedonian Apollo," it does not occur until the first century AD, when Diodorus Siculus claims (32.10.2) that there is a temple (ἱερόν) to "Sarpedonian Apollo" at Seleukeia. This usage is also found in Zosimus (1.57.2): "in Cilician Seleukeia they made use of the temple/oracle (ἱερόν) of Apollo called 'Sarpedonian'."

of the oracle of Apollo."[26] This interpretation has the benefit of reinforcing the author's list of Apollo's shrines in the preface to the *Miracles*—he lists Delphi and "the waters of Kastalia" (i.e. Parnassus, as if the two were different places)—but, on the other hand, the "Sarpedonian" is not included in this list and makes no appearance until *Mir.* 1.

Thekla's attack on the Sarpedonian takes the form of re-conquering a physical area of Seleukeia which had for some time been in the wrongful hands of the pagan god and his followers. As is well known from the classical geographers, the cape on the southern coast of Asia Minor, just below Seleukeia and the mouth of the Kalykadnos, was called in antiquity "the Sarpedonian."[27] This usage should not be kept separate from the personalized usage in *Mir.* 1, since the connections between the two are abundant. First, one should connect the statement above that "the Sarpedonian" was buried at the shore with the following assertion: "As soon as Thekla arrived in this country, reached its borders, and occupied this peak [i.e. Hagia Thekla], she demoted him back [to being a just a man] and she silenced him" (1.14–16). The author is clearly associating Thekla's spiritual battle against Sarpedon with her conquering of the territory over which he held sway. The sense of the passage is not that she is invading and conquering a wild pagan land but that she is reconquering her own homeland. Accordingly, Sarpedon is treated as an upstart who has to be turned "back" (αὖθις) into what he was before he was a god, that is, just a man. Thekla thus restores the natural, divine order as it was before the invasion of the pagan gods.

Her final act against Sarpedon is to "silence him"—in fact the act quotes her direct speech: "Silence! Shut up!" (1.18)—a speech-act which accomplishes the spiritual work of the miracle. In concluding his account of Thekla's attack on Sarpedon the author of the *Miracles* comments that the god simply "left," abandoning those at his shrine ("whether one wants to call it a tomb or a *temenos*") who patiently waited on him "devoting themselves to prayers and supplications." Thus, the inability of Sarpedon to fulfill the hopes of his suppliants—essentially because he is an upstart man, not a god—is contrasted with Thekla's authority in recapturing a land that was originally her own

---

[26] For this argument, see Dagron 1978:85–87.

[27] See Strabo 14.5.4, as noted by Dagron 1978:86n3. Also noted by Dagron (86n4) is the following passage, interesting for the light it sheds on Sarpedon's shifting associations: "In Cilicia there is the temple (ἱερόν) and oracle (μαντεῖον) of Sarpedonian Artemis" (Strabo 14.5.19). Of course, another "Sarpedonian" shrine could have existed elsewhere in Cilicia or Isauria other than the one mentioned in the *Miracles*. Nevertheless, the number of separate references to Sarpedon's Cilician connections point to his lasting association with this region over a millennium (i.e. Aeschylus to the *Miracles*).

possession. Finally, just before moving on to the second god to be dispatched (Athena), the author of the *Miracles* closes with a typical summary statement, which underlines the completion (and narrative autonomy) of this miracle: "This was the prelude of the miracles of the martyr, which no one disbelieves any longer, but instead those who are here see it, and all everywhere are amazed (θαυμάζουσι)" (1.23–25). The paratactic style, evident here in the very first miracle, emphasizes the one-to-one correspondence between the miracles that Thekla accomplished and those that are recorded in this collection.

The demise of Sarpedon's sanctuary at the Sarpedonian cape, south of Seleukeia, is followed in *Mir.* 2 by Thekla's conquering of the mountain sanctuary of Athena just to the north. With these two miracles Thekla acquires military dominance over the intermediary plain between the cape and the mountains, that is, the lowland area where the ancient city of Seleukeia and the hilltop shrine of Hagia Thekla were located. Thus, there is a very important theme being established in the first miracles: Thekla is autochthonous in Seleukeia, a status which mutually confirms and is confirmed by her divine power. As noted above (p. 65–66), it is the supernatural event of Thekla's disappearance into the ground which provides the narrative transition between the *Life* and the *Miracles* halves of this work. By beginning the *Miracles* with these mythological, or even patriological, stories about Thekla's physical dominance over the coastal territory of Isauria, the author is only continuing a theme which he began in the "previous composition" (τὸ προλαβὸν σύνταγμα), as he calls the *Life* in the preface (*Mir.* preface 7). From a narrative point of view, the exertion of her divine power in overcoming Sarpedon and Athena is only a logical outworking of the claim that she placed on this territory when it supernaturally opened up for her to disappear into, at the end of the *Life.*

The mountain on which Athena has her sanctuary was, as the author of the *Miracles* points out, originally called Mt. Kokusion (Κωκύσιον),[28] an indigenous name which was changed after "Kanetis" Athena took over: "as if the mountain were a sanctuary of Athena!" (2.3–4).[29] Once again, the author is

---

[28] The change from the name Kokusion ("the mount of shrieking"; κωκύω?) can be dated, according to Dagron (1978:84), to he reign of the Hellenistic monarch Seleukos I Nicator (after c. 295 bc), to whom the town of Seleukeia owes its name as well (Cohen 1995:369–371). However, the reference to Kokusion here must be the cause of local memory, since the name Κωκύσιον does not appear anywhere else in Greek literature according to the *TLG* (search performed by the author on April 15, 2005). Dagron's evidence is numismatic and epigraphic (1978:84n3) and is thus not contained in the *TLG*.

[29] As Dagron notes (1978:84–85), the epithet κανίτις or κανῆτις (genitive κανήτιδος at *Mir.* 2.3) is a local title for Athena probably derivative of κανής ("mat of reeds"). Thus, this iteration of Athena's persona is as the divine protector of "basket weavers," the regional equivalent, Dagron

appealing to Thekla's connections to the region: it is she who has respect for the original onomastics of the region and seeks a return to them—the pagan myths are the innovators, not Thekla. Underlining the swiftness with which Thekla exerted her divine power over Athena, the author remarks, "And this mountain was snatched away from the *daimon* and was placed under the mastery of Christ, exactly as it was before (ἄνωθεν)" (2.4–6). In the place of Athena now are "martyrs," "holy men" who occupy Athena's temple, "just as some high citadel might be occupied by generals and military men" (2.6–8).[30] Thus, Thekla's dominance extends to the most warlike female goddess, who "cannot hold up at all against the assault of the unarmed maiden, one who is both a stranger and defenseless (literally, 'naked')" (2.9–10). Thus, between Sarpedon and Athena, Thekla dispatches, in the first two miracles, the two most recognizable pagan/indigenous divinities in the area, both of whom had a temple which occupied an important, distinct part of the territory around Seleukeia.

Unlike these two very programmatic battles, the next two gods whom Thekla encounters, Aphrodite and Zeus, are much less significant in terms of their direct relationship to local religion. The author of the *Miracles* appears to make use of Aphrodite only to show off his talent at Homeric allusion, claiming that the bishop Dexianos was armed by Thekla—as her own Diomedes—to do away with the "presumptuous maidservant" of a god (*Mir.* 3).[31] The allusion is to Books 5 and 6 of the *Iliad* where Athena grants Diomedes extra strength in his attacks on the Trojans, and he ends up wounding Aphrodite herself who comes into the fight to protect her son Aeneas. What is most striking about this allusion is the fluidity with which the author appropriates classical litera-ture: Thekla is, of course, being likened in this passage to the very goddess that she has just done away with in the previous miracle! Thus, *Mir.* 3 has little

---

posits, of the Athenian κανηφόροι, girls who carried woven reed baskets in religious proces-sions. It would be more helpful, however, if this epithet could be linked with the perennial, indigenous name for this region, Κῆτις (*Life* 27.31; *Mir.* 19.3; cf. Ramsay 1890:363–367), but these two names appear philologically distinct, the former being exclusively Greek and not Hittite or Luwian in origin, as is the latter.

[30] Dagron assumes this means that the church on the site of Athena's sanctuary held relics of the martyrs (1978:293n2), but since relics are not mentioned elsewhere in the *LM*, it is perhaps better to understand this Christian occupation in a literary sense and to link it, as I have done, to Thekla's physical (and epic) conquering of the region for Christ. A relic of Thekla's is mentioned in a late antique, Greek extension to the *ATh* (see Appendix 1), so there is no doubt that relics were present at the site—all the more reason, perhaps, to draw attention to the significant absence of relics in the *LM*.

[31] Dexianos was bishop of Seleukeia in the 430s and is elsewhere characterized as an upright man and a friend to the author and to Thekla herself (e.g. *Mir.* 7, 8; cf. *Mir.* 32).

to offer in comparison with the local significance of the first two miracles, especially in that it does not continue the theme of Thekla conquering specific areas around Seleukeia.

The fourth and final miracle which spotlights Thekla's divine superiority over local gods is the miracle in which she attacks Zeus, "the very chief of the *daimones*" (4.1). Zeus is described as a "usurper" (τύραννον) and a "brigand" (ἀλιτήριον), generic terms of abuse which the author of the *Miracles* uses elsewhere to speak of fifth-century political and military turmoil in Isauria. As with the attack on Aphrodite, there is no mention of a specific area in the region of Seleukeia, such as the Sarpedonian cape or Mt. Kokusion. The author does mention, however, a temple, presumably in Seleukeia itself, which Thekla took away from Zeus and made into a "residence" (καταγώγιον) for her "teacher" (διδάσκαλος), the apostle Paul.[32]

There are two important aspects to this aside about Paul. First, calling Paul her διδάσκαλος is reminiscent of the description of their relationship in the *Life*: Paul is consistently invoked in that earlier work as Thekla's teacher rather than as her "companion" (as in the second-century *ATh*). Thus, it is important to note that Paul's distinctive character in the *Life* is carried into the *Miracles*. Second, mentioned along with the setting up of the temple in Seleukeia is that fact that Paul's "own city" is Tarsus. As the author comments:

> Paul is a guest of the Seleukeians, and the virgin Thekla a guest of the Tarsians. And great was the competition (ἅμιλλα) between these two cities—either one would travel up to the Apostle Paul for his panegyris, or would similarly go from there to the Apostle Thekla for her festival. Great was the rivalry (ἔρις) on this topic that was born among all of us. It was excellent and perfectly suitable for the Christian children and townspeople.
>
> *Mir.* 4.8–13

This passage also continues a theme begun in the *Life*, but only in its concluding chapters (especially *Life* 27). In that earlier passage the author of the *LM* sets Seleukeia in comparison with Tarsus for the beauty of its surroundings and the quality of its people. However, here the emphasis is, as we might expect, on Thekla's ownership (so to speak) of Seleukeia, in parallel with Paul's ownership of Tarsus. The author jokes that this competition is all in good fun,

---

[32] Archaeologists claim to have found a temple to Zeus in Seleukeia proper (modern Silifke), but their attribution rests solely on the "evidence" of this miracle (Hild and Hellenkemper 1990:404; Hill 1996:241; cf. Dagron 1978:82–83).

but the literary purpose of this aside is clearly to establish further the current theme, which is definitive for Thekla's relationship to Seleukeia. Her divine power is linked to her control over the region, and, as becomes increasingly apparent as the reader progresses, the extent of Thekla's power in the region corresponds to the extent of coverage the author of the *Miracles* gives her.

The author's proof that Thekla conquered these gods is simply that the *daimones* are no longer in possession of the property they once controlled, an ex post facto argument which offers little hard evidence for the "christian-ization" of the region.[33] Sarpedon has been removed from his sanctuary on the southern coast, Athena has been driven from her mountain to the north, and Zeus' temple in the city of Seleukeia is now a church. The author appeals to this obvious fact of the gods' demise: "For who could deny what happened before the eyes of all, that it was like this or that it came about in this way?" (4.16–17). Further, in concluding this miracle about Zeus, he clarifies that Thekla was "assigned" (τασσεῖν) this region by God, just as he has given "some cities and places to some saints and others to other saints" (4.21–22). This is a very important clarification to make, since any careful reader of the *LM* could point out that Thekla's hometown was not Seleukeia but Iconium in Lycaonia. Unlike Paul, therefore, she was not "assigned" the town with which early Christian history most associated with her birth. Instead, she is assigned the city which is associated with her death (or disappearance), a further reinforce-ment of Thekla's protection of and spiritual work in Seleukeia.

As proof that the author is aware of this problem, there is the miracle that Thekla performs on behalf of Iconium (*Mir.* 6). The author's introduction to that miracle reads as follows:

> But the virgin has not so exclusive a relationship [literally, "was not such"] concerning this city Seleukeia—that she would be its defender, protector, mother, and teacher—but at the same time be indifferent concerning other cities. She also rescued Iconium, the city that was so insolent to her and lit against her the exceedingly evil fire, but which had come into similar dangers as Seleukeia.
>
> *Mir.* 6.1–5

Her compassion for Iconium is described as almost a stretch of her good character, since this city had already shown itself to be disreputable through

---

[33] Nevertheless, as mentioned above, Sarpedon is given credit by characters in the *Miracles* on two occasions (*Mir.* 11 and 40), over and against Thekla, who was the true source of their healing. This suggests an ongoing struggle (or confusion) between Sarpedon and Thekla for control of the locals' thaumaturgical imaginations.

how it treated her in the *Life* (see pp. 40–42 above). Nevertheless, she condescends to visit it and delivers the city from a band of Isaurian brigands. This passage is reminiscent of the end of the *ATh* and the *Life* when Thekla returns to Iconium from meeting Paul in Myra. Instead of setting up residence there and converting her home city to Christianity she only visits her mother briefly, then pushes on to Seleukeia. There appears to be no wavering in this tradition—in other words, there is no alternative legend that has her staying in Iconium. Like the passage just quoted from *Mir.* 6, Thekla's visit to Iconium at the end of the *ATh/Life* is almost a formality, and one which serves mainly to fix the reader's attention on her much closer relationship with Seleukeia. Iconium is used in the *Miracles* as well as at the end of the *Life* only for the sake of contrast with the city she calls her own.

What emerges, therefore, from these first four miracles is that Thekla's divine power is linked to her affiliation with, "assignment" to, or even owner-ship of Seleukeia and its environs. Thekla's power extends only to this area, which corresponds to the area covered by the *Miracles* itself. In taking posses-sion of this land from the pagan *daimones*, Thekla is characterized as taking back possession of a region which the author accords to Christ from a deeply rooted past. In his mind the pagan gods are intervening innovators who have arrived on the scene recently and need to be removed from power. How far back in time their rule is meant to extend is unclear. The author is primarily concerned with Thekla's triumph and setting things aright: he only notes that "as soon as" (ἅμα) she appeared in Seleukeia, she defeated Sarpedon (*Mir.* 1.14). Beyond this the reader is not invited to inquire further into the muddy "past-times" history at work in the background. In contrast, however, the two main literary arguments of these initial stories appear unambiguous enough: 1) the autochthonous nature of Thekla's character and 2) her power to contend with even the most revered and ancient of the pagan gods.

Hubris and its just punishments

Despite the programmatic nature of the first four miracles in the collection, Thekla's power is not confined to those divine beings who might be considered her equal. Often throughout the *Miracles* she is portrayed as meting out justice on groups or individuals whose hubris leads them to act against a city, a church, or an individual whom Thekla considers her own. In a number of miracles Thekla defends cities and churches from the brigands for whom the Isaurian mountains were famous throughout classical and late antique history. Alongside these city-defense miracles stand a group of vengeance stories in which individuals are vindicated for wrongs that they have suffered. The narrative focus in these latter miracles is on how the offenders meet their (often violent) deaths. Both groups, city-defense and individual-vindication, employ the rhetorical conventions noted above, but each shares certain internal characteristics as well, which it will be worthwhile to examine in more detail.

A pair of two city-defense miracles begins just following the miracles against the pagan gods. In *Mir.* 5, Seleukeia is protected against a surprise attack by the brigands. In *Mir.* 6 Iconium is preserved by Thekla when faced with a similar danger. Another pair, *Mir.* 26 and 27, concerns the defense of two Isaurian cities, Dalisandos and Selinous, which were beset by sieges also perpetrated by brigands from the mountains. In *Mir.* 28 one of Thekla's churches, presumably the shrine at Hagia Thekla, is pillaged but is restored to its former glory once Thekla wreaks punishment on the brigands. This latter miracle demonstrates a combination of elements from the city-defense and individual-vindication miracles.

To begin with *Mir.* 5, the author opens this miracle by noting something rather curious, namely that Seleukeia at this time was not very well defended. "All that was necessary," he says, "was for the brigands to desire her, and she would be in their hands" (5.4). Usually, as in *Mir.* 27, the city is already very well defended but comes under an impenetrable siege. In the case of *Mir.* 5, however, the author takes pains to describe the Seleukeians' lackadaisical attitude and its consequences:

> The inhabitants of the city tended to disbelieve most of the rumors circulating at that time, either sleeping or taking their leisure at the theater, and never suspecting at all that there was any immediate danger. Their enemies, on the other hand, were awake, passing the night without sleep, and were all but sharing already the possessions and slaves (σώματα) of Seleukeia's inhabitants.
>
> *Mir.* 5.4–9

If the defenselessness of the city is somewhat unusual, the picture of the uncivilized brigands biding their time while they feast their eyes upon their prey is a common description not just in the *Miracles* but also in most of the descriptions of Isaurian brigandage which have survived from the period. In 1990 Brent Shaw published a long study of the history of brigandage in Isauria and came to the conclusion that there was a very consistent picture of the brigands (or "bandits") from this region:

All of them fit a pattern of appearance, of presentation. They are all portrayed as huge and impressive in their physical size and demeanor, and they put this hugeness into action in feats of some-times unbelievable strength and violence.[34]

Having established this "pattern of appearance, of presentation" through numerous examples from Roman, and especially late antique, literature—such as Ammianus Marcellinus and the *Miracles* itself—Shaw comments that these literary *Leitmotive* should not be understood as mere rhetoric but have some basis in the self-presentation of the brigands on the ground. As he says, "They make perfectly good sense as essential attributes required of any man who wished to become a 'leader' in the sort of social structure that prevailed in Isauria throughout antiquity" (Shaw 1990:259–260).

In terms of the miracle currently under examination, *Mir.* 5, Shaw's conclusions ring true in the sense that those who feared the brigands person-ally or who viewed them from afar (as represented by historians of the period) were defining their role mutually with the brigands themselves. The latters' banditry in the plains of Isauria and the surrounding area was definitive for the self-presentation of the region. It was always known, from Roman occupa-tion forward, as an autonomous and wild place, a reputation which appears to have been of consequence for the rise of the Isaurian emperor Zeno in the latter fifth century.[35]

Yet, what is naturally missing from Shaw's social analysis is how the role of the brigands fits into the literary agenda of the *Miracles*.[36] Most importantly, when the reader comes to *Mir.* 5, it is not the brigands but Thekla who is in control of the Seleukeian plains. Surely any close reader must realize that the brigands' authority in the region is being (to some degree) simply replaced by Thekla's, and the description of the brigands' actions, however authentic according to Shaw, is primarily serving the literary purpose of supporting the specific image of Thekla which this author is presenting. To take an example, once the enemy is rebuffed by Thekla's miraculous defense of the walls in *Mir.* 5, the brigands are described as dumbfounded at their failure. Yet, crucially,

---

[34] Shaw 1990:259. Lenski 1999 argues that Shaw is incorrect that Isauria resisted Roman control throughout antiquity. From the mid first century to the mid third century AD, according to Lenski, Roman influence can be seen in Isauria in many different aspects of social life.

[35] Shaw 1990:252–255.

[36] Of course, this is not the goal of his essay, but there is a mishandling of some essential details from the *LM*—e.g. on page 245: "The compilation, usually attributed to Basil of Caesarea ..." should read "Basil of Seleukeia," who is also named in *Mir.* 12 in an adversarial scene (for issues of authorship see, again, Dagron 1974); and "Thekla, a Cilician woman" should read "a Lycaonian woman" or "an Iconian woman."

they know who it is who defeats them. As the narrator says, "And out of that blood-stained phalanx there are still some who highly praise the martyr in these events" (5.25–27). While the characterization of the brigands earlier in the miracle is indeed as a fearsome enemy that wields "the engines of war," the emphasis of the miracle as a whole (and especially at the end) is on the brigands' miraculous, vocal respect for Thekla after the fact. Indeed, in other miracles, the conversion of the offender (or bystander) is often described as "even more miraculous" than the miracle itself (e.g. *Mir.* 17). This rhetoric makes use of the brigands as a topos but eschews the responsibility of telling the complete truth. More important than comprehensive description for this author is making sure his readers know about the divine power of Thekla to overcome siege works.

Similar rhetoric is at work in *Mir.* 6, in which Thekla saves her home city of Iconium from the same type of attack. Yet the emphasis there is on the swiftness and pervasiveness of Thekla's rebuttal. As the author says, "all [the attackers] were subject to the same danger and ruin. 'No messenger escaped alive,' as one might say in parody of Homer (ὁμηρίζων)" (6.10–12). The brigands are so utterly destroyed that it is almost as if they never existed. They are a prop for displaying Thekla in action, even while, as a locus of societal trepidation, they have an important role to play in communicating Thekla's empathy to a local audience. Further, the miraculous works of Thekla in saving these two cities from certain demise are explicitly equated at the end of *Mir.* 6: "the one trophy is not much more common than the other, for both are the work of a sole hand, thought, and ability" (6.13–15). Thekla's power is given no bounds. Like with the "all seeing and divine eye" which always watches over her region and people, the author of the *Miracles* is invoking again a sense of uniformity among Thekla's miraculous activities. The paratactic structure serves to reinforce this uniformity in its pairing of equivalent or near equivalent miracles (e.g. *Mir.* 5 & 6; 26.47–53 & 27) and its repetitive method of framing stories of Thekla's divine power.

In addition to defending cities, Thekla is also portrayed as a defender of her churches. For instance, in *Mir.* 28 the brigands (ἀλιτήριοι) completely take over her church at Seleukeia (literally, "temple"; ναός) and take as loot all of the "consecrated goods" (τὰ ἱερὰ χρήματα). (Sometimes, he says, the brigands perform less serious looting, "in the manner of enemies" [ἐν πολεμίων μοίρᾳ], but other times they take over the entire region "like despots and tyrants" [ἐν δεσποτῶν τάξει καὶ τυράννων]; 28.11–14) The image here is one of Thekla's church being forcefully raped and plundered. The rape is followed by the brigands retreating with the holy loot to their homeland, which is called

Laistrygonia (Λαιστρυγονία).[37] As in *Mir.* 5, the brigands are characterized as knowing exactly who it is they have just pillaged: "they were rejoicing on two counts: first, that they had conquered the martyr and, second, that they had all of a sudden become rich" (*Mir.* 28.17–19).

All of this scene-setting serves to focus the narration on the main point of action, which is Thekla's reversal of the brigands' newly found fortune. The climax is told succinctly but not without reinforcing the sense that Thekla is fully in control of the region, despite appearances:

> But the virgin, letting their boldness have sway a little—in allowing them to sail in, gather up and remove the holy adornment, load it up, disembark, and head home—this is how she played the game against them.
>
> *Mir.* 28.19–22

The conclusion to *Mir.* 28 presents the brigands in a much weakened state, having been handed over by Thekla to a company of "Roman" soldiers which then proceeds to cut their throats. These soldiers are also fully aware of the role that Thekla has played in the capturing of the looters. According to the text, the soldiers sing and rejoice in triumph and then replace the stolen ornaments in Thekla's church (even though Thekla has supposedly already done this in preceding paragraph). Their reaction is perhaps intended to offer an example of how the reader should react to the *Miracles* in general: "they reconsecrated the ornaments that belonged to the martyr, while also marveling (θαυμάζειν) and struck (καταπεπλῆχθαι) that she did not endure for long at all the boldness (τόλμης) of those brigands and offenders" (28.37–40). Thekla's unwillingness "to endure" the hubris of her enemies is essential to the author's conception of her role in Seleukeia: she always responds swiftly. This is because, first, the crime is worthy of a proper response and, second, her swiftness is concomitant with her power and ability to set wrongs right, especially when it concerns something dear to her (as all of these miracles do). The reaction of the witnesses is one of dumbfoundment—in this case, both the brigands and the soldiers were reduced to speechlessness due to their awe of Thekla's power.

The appositeness of their response is highlighted at the end of the miracle. The author brings this story from the past into present day reality:

> Do not endure them now, nor allow them to bring an attack in their great hubris and foolhardiness against us your infants (τροφίμων).

---

[37] On Laistrygonia, see Dagron 1978:121n1 (cf. *Odyssey* 10.80–132).

For our misfortunes are unbearable and intolerable. Already we all have inclined toward destruction and utter ruin. Churches (ἐκκλησίαι) have bowed the knee (κεκλίκασι), and also cities, fields, villages, and homes have bowed. Everyone everywhere mourns—all have turned towards the one hope still remaining: your intercession (πρεσβείαν) and the help of your bridegroom and king, Christ.

*Mir.* 28.40–48

As has been demonstrated by Shaw and others, the period from the late fourth to the early sixth century was a time of major upheaval in Isauria: from the insurgencies described by Ammianus, to the rise of Zeno, the revolt of Illus, and the wars of Anastasius I, southern Anatolia changed hands numerous times and was a source of frustration for the imperial army.[38] The author of the *Miracles* is clearly aware of these struggles and their effect on the people of Seleukeia. The picture he paints is a dismal one, of churches and towns being put under subjection, one after another. His description of the situation is apocalyptic. He calls the faithful inhabitants "us your infants (τρόφιμοι)," perhaps in reference to apocalyptic passages in the Bible where the infant is an image of utter helplessness.[39] Rhetorically speaking, he has placed this flourish at a strategic point in the narrative: the story he has just told about Thekla's swift, definitive vindication of her pillaged church should give the reader hope that Thekla will certainly act when provoked. "The enemies attacked and they were overturned, with not even one person being allowed to remain to tell" (28.53–56). Referring again to the passage from the *Iliad* (12.73) which he quoted in *Mir.* 6, he underlines the completeness of Thekla's punishment: "No messenger escaped alive" (6.11–12). This also serves to confirm the uniformity of the punishment miracles, so that the shared rhetorical or literary features of this group appear well defined from the beginning to the end of the collection.

Having thus considered the depiction of Thekla's power in defending cities and in protecting and vindicating her churches, it remains to examine how she punishes and vindicates individuals. Miracles in this category extend

---

[38] Shaw 1990:259: "The clear and unmistakable implication of all these imperial measures is that Isauria remained, till the mid seventh century, a zone of permanent dissidence within the empire and hardly, as some would have it, a region now brought within the confines of imperial power." He is referring to A.H.M. Jones's assertion that Anastasius I was finally able to pacify the region in the late fifth century (Jones 1964:1.230–231).

[39] Later in this miracle (28.61–65) he alludes to the biblical stories of Jonah and Nineveh (Jonah 3) and Sodom and Gomorrah (Genesis 18–19), further solidifying the prophetic tone that he adopts in this passage.

from the lighthearted restoration of a stolen girdle to a bride on her wedding day (*Mir.* 21) to the physical mutilation of a man named Pappos, who had the audacity to disenfranchise a dead friend's orphan children of their inheritance (*Mir.* 35). Also a part of this group are miracles concerning the clergy of Seleukeia, such as the Arian Symposios, who conspires to deface the local inscription of a Trinitarian creed (*Mir.* 10)—presumably the creed of the first Council of Constantinople (AD 381).[40]

In the latter miracle, Symposios is not at all successful because, as the narrator says, "the undefiled and immaculate hand of the virgin was clearly protecting and guarding those letters like imperial seals (βασιλικὰ σήμαντρα)" (10.15–17). While this is surely another ex post facto interpretation, it is confirmed rhetorically by the vengeance of Thekla which follows her confounding of the erasure: "In the end [the worker Symposios had hired], who waged war against the godly letters fell off his ladder, broke his bones, and all at once paid the penalty for his audacity" (10.19–21). Thus, Symposios receives a harsh, immediate punishment from the martyr—in the form of the broken body of his hired worker. Without delay, the punishment inflicted on this worker serves to provoke Symposios' conversion to the orthodox faith: "Immediately at that moment, having exchanged his false opinion, Symposios pronounced, breathed forth, confessed, publicly and visibly proclaimed, and was teaching the very formula [of the inscribed creed] which he had formerly attacked: the consubantial Trinity" (10.21–25).

Within the space of two or three sentences the author of the *Miracles* has set up the story, described Symposios' misdeed, shown how Thekla swiftly brought punishment, and, finally, concluded the miracle in the most miraculous way possible, with the offender's own conversion. This pattern evokes the punishments of the brigands, who themselves testified to Thekla's power (e.g. *Mir.* 5). One difference, however, between those group miracles and this one concerning an individual is that the groups are not usually converted but only bear witness to the identity and the supernatural power of the one performing the miracle. The benefit of focusing the narrative on an individual is that the author can more convincingly draw the miracle to its best possible conclusion: the offender himself is converted to Christianity.

---

[40] As for the formula which had been inscribed, the author of the *Miracles* says only the following: "the letters are affixed in fine pebbles of gold, proclaiming to all men the consubstantiality (τὸ ὁμοούσιον) of the holy and superlative Trinity" (10.6–8). Elsewhere, however, the author speaks of the Trinity in distinctive language characteristic of the Cappadocian Fathers (*Mir.* 14.55–65; see also pp. 32–35 above).

Some punishments of individuals, however, do not end with such a pleasant finale. The punishment of Pappos, for example, appears very harsh by comparison. In *Mir.* 35 Pappos is described as a βουλητής, a provincial administrator in charge of grain distributions to the military (35.1–3). His partner in this, Aulerios, suddenly dies, leaving a moderate inheritance to his children. Out of greed, however, Pappos seizes the inheritance and leaves Aulerios' orphan children destitute. As the author poignantly observes, "Their misfortune was thus double, becoming orphans as well as loosing the few possessions that still belonged to them" (35.9–11). At this point Thekla intervenes, appearing to Pappos in a grim nightmare. She claims that Aurelios presented himself before Christ in heaven, "the emperor above all," and condemned Pappos, pleading for divine retribution. In the end, Thekla proves to be both the messenger and agent of justice, as she predicts that one week from that day Pappos will die (35.15–26).

Pappos is not portrayed as indifferent to this news. On the contrary, he is stupefied by the nightmare (as are the brigands and Roman soldiers in *Mir.* 28), and in the end he finds the strength to repent of his "oppression" (συκοφαντία; cf. LXX Ecclesiastes 5:7 [5:8]). Nevertheless, without hesitation, on the appointed day Pappos meets his end (10.39–40). The author cannot resist concluding with a comment on the story's widespread fame: "no one of those in our city, nor anyone in theirs [i.e. Isaurian Eirenopolis], was ignorant of the fate that comes from injustice (μετ᾽ ἀδικίας)" (10.41–42).

A few important points need to be observed regarding the conclusion of this miracle. First, the miracle takes place in Eirenopolis, approximately sixty-five miles to the west of Seleukeia. The author underlines the unity of reporting both there and in Seleukeia with regard to Pappos' punishment as meted out by Thekla. Thus, by setting the miracle in Eirenopolis, the author projects a uniformity of opinion over the whole region. This narrative strategy makes the knowledge of the people correspond to the regional boundaries of Thekla's spiritual activities: the cognitive uniformity between the individuals described and the collection itself cannot be emphasized enough, as it is central to the self-presentation of the *Miracles* as a whole. Second, Thekla's divine power to extinguish the life of an offender like Pappos is complete and effective. Even though, as the narrator remarks, Pappos turned in the end (during his week of reprieve) to "ill-timed philanthropy" (ἄκαιρον φιλανθρωπίαν), his earlier greed was superlative and deserving of the punishment that he received.

Why would the author of the *Miracles* not take the opportunity here to make something out of Pappos' conversion following his vivid nightmare? One answer is, of course, that the author recorded simply what he thought had happened, but an author as concerned as he is with the consistency of Thekla's portrayal surely has some idea of how each miracle connects to Thekla's spiritual nature (even if it proves to be only a hazy conception). A better answer would be that the intended effect of *Mir.* 35 is to show the lengths to which Thekla will go in displaying her divine power and authority over the region. Confirmation of this comes at the end of the miracle in a framing section designed to push the reader on to the next miracle:

> But come, turn away—I need to repeat this—from depressing miracles to more cheerful ones, from the oppressive ones to the more charming, in order that we might uplift our souls tense from fear, and we might warm them up with some stories (τισὶ διηγήμασιν) both sweeter and gentler. Therefore, let me again publicize (εἰς μέσον ἀγάγωμεν) the things which I have learned.
>
> *Mir.* 35.43–48

In this passage the author categorizes his miracles into those that are depressing and those which are cheerful. Of course, as it is part of a framing device, this formulation should not be taken as definitive for the whole of the *Miracles*. Nevertheless, the author demonstrates a crucial awareness of the spectrum of responses that these miracles might bring, responses which are in turn related to the degrees of Thekla's wrath as presented in the *Miracles* itself.

When taken as a whole, the vengeance miracles evince several defined rhetorical and literary characteristics. First, from a literary point of view, the vengeance miracles are related to the author's depiction of Thekla's divine power over the whole region of Isauria, as established through her epic battles with the pagan gods in *Mir.* 1–4. Essential to this depiction is the direct control Thekla exhibits over the cities in the plains between the mountains and the ocean—particularly Seleukeia (*Mir.* 5), but also Selinous (*Mir.* 27), Olba (*Mir.* 24.5), and the otherwise unknown Dalisandos (*Mir.* 26; see below). Yet a reader could assume that Thekla's victory over Athena's "Mt. Kokusion" is symbolic for Thekla's ability to protect also cities like Iconium (*Mir.* 6) and Eirenopolis (*Mir.* 34 and 35), both of which are located some distance from the coast, within and beyond the mountains that were so infested by the brigands. Thus, among the vengeance miracles, the reader is offered a much wider compass for Thekla's activities, yet it is a compass which is predicated on her symbolic victories over the pagan gods—the ultimate expressions of her power, perhaps—which are presented at the very beginning of the work.

Second, the characterizations of those on whom Thekla metes out her punishments are very stylized. This stylization is used to great effect: it focuses the narration on the action which really constitutes each miracle. For example, in *Mir.* 35 Pappos' stunned reaction to the nightmare in which Thekla condemned him to death is a device which builds the tension of the miracle. The reader wonders whether Pappos is going to be let off the hook or whether he will die on the day appointed, as Thekla predicted. Ultimately, maintaining the consistency of Thekla's resolve is more important rhetorically to this author than any gain from Pappos' repentance (which the author claims "was not by choice, but by necessity"; *Mir.* 35.38). The effect is to focus the narration on Thekla's promise coming true, which proves so harsh and emotionally cold in the telling that the author must acknowledge the difference between Thekla's action in this miracle and her more charming, compassionate work elsewhere.

Third and finally, there are important correspondences drawn between the collection itself and the events taking place in the miracles. For instance, in *Mir.* 28 the soldiers are amazed (θαυμάζειν) and astonished (καταπεπλῆχθαι) at the swiftness with which Thekla dealt with the brigands. Besides being a subtle aside on the inefficiency of the soldiers in real life to deal with the local insurrections threatening Seleukeia, this comment presents to the reader a model for the appropriate reaction to the telling of Thekla's *Miracles*. The word θαῦμα and its cognates are programmatic for the *Miracles* as a whole, and there is some indication in the preface of the *Miracles* (preface 10) that θαύματα is to be considered the official title of this second half of the *LM*.

In addition, there is a correspondence between the area covered by Thekla's divine power in her defense of cities and her vindication of individuals (or their orphan children). Only once does the author mention an episode in which a city or region outside Isauria is attended to by Thekla: this comes in the very idiosyncratic *Mir.* 12, which concerns the author's own excommunication— Thekla says she "must hurry on to Macedonia to help a woman in danger."[41] Thus, in the great majority of cases Thekla's power is very localized. Moreover, the author is not unaware of his own role in the circumscribing of this power to Seleukeia and its environs: as shown above, he considers the *Miracles* to be the natural outworking of the divine power she has exhibited before the eyes of those in his immediate vicinity, even in his own time and before his own eyes. Indeed, her power is described as achieving the collection at a number of points

---

[41] For this reference to Macedonia, see p. 163–164 below. There is also one brief miracle that occurs in Constantinople (*Mir.* 9.71–87), but this is in protection of a priest who had gone to the imperial city on official Seleukeian business.

(e.g. *Mir.* 31), and in the epilogue the author invokes her power one last time to achieve the post-publication success of the work she inspired (epilogue 8–11).

Humanitarian causes

Included in the *Miracles* are around six or seven stories in which Thekla is allowed to demonstrate her power to help people in ways beyond effecting their vindication following some misfortune. The group of vengeance miracles just discussed is much larger than this "humanitarian" group, by about two-to-one, yet the two groups are linked through the author's depiction of Thekla's power to produce unforeseen or supernatural outcomes in straightened circumstances. For example, in *Mir.* 15 a "well born and faithful" Cypriot man comes with his family and servants to Seleukeia to celebrate Thekla's annual panegyris. They leave their boat at the dock, guarded only by two boys. Without warning, a fierce storm arises and pulls the boat out to sea, with the two boys still on it, trapped and with no means of escape. In a miraculous show of power and compassion, Thekla appears on the boat—"storm-tossed and about to be sunk"—seizes the helm, unfurls the sail (not something one would normally do in high winds!), and brings the boat to safety, while at the same time "reproving the storm" (15.26–33). She docks the boat at the very place from which it was pulled loose, and in the end, when the Cypriot man and his family return, they do not realize that anything has even happened until the two boys explain their adventure and Thekla's intervention, and the pilgrims go away "marveling" (θαυμάζοντας) at the martyr and "glorifying" (δοξάζοντας) her (15.42–50).

It is important to recognize in this miracle the absence of any immediate personal need relating to an individual, either in terms of sickness or in terms of harm done by someone else. While it is true that the lives of the two boys are at stake, the miracle is performed, according to its narration, out of respect for the faithful Cypriot man (15.35–36). He comes to Thekla's shrine at Seleukeia to pay her honor, so Thekla ensures that everything is as he left it when he returns to the dock from her panegyris. Yet, the conclusion of miracle shows there is more going on than Thekla's concern for that one man. The boat, the locus or site of the miracle-working itself, appears to be the very means by which the boys return to Cyprus and report the miracle to their fellow Cypriots—though all that is explicitly said is that they reported it both in Seleukeia and Cyprus (15.42). In any case, this miracle is symbolic of Thekla's power to insure that her own fame is widely spread: the miracle-working she does in Seleukeia effects its own dissemination, in the city and abroad.

A characteristic of these humanitarian miracles is that their narration is often more elaborate and exciting than those of the punishment-vengeance type. This is true in the case just cited: the wind and waves of the storm in *Mir.* 15 are described in detail, which increases their perceived menace to the boat and the two frightened boys. A provisional interpretation of the typically intensified emotional component of the humanitarian miracles is that there is less "action" than in the vengeance or healing miracles. By action I do not mean Thekla's appearances as much as the overturning of a helpless situation or the cure of a hopeless disease, the real meat of the *Miracles* in terms of its narration.

A different, literary interpretation might be that the humanitarian miracles are devices meant to tie the larger structure together: for instance, *Mir.* 15 comes between a very long, complicated miracle about the healing and conversion of Hypsistios and a series of shorter healing miracles involving disconnected individuals. *Mir.* 15 thus serves as an interstitial miracle which transitions from a long narrative to a series of shorter paratactic narratives and brings variety to this series of miracles which is otherwise dominated by healing.

Another miracle that serves a similar purpose is *Mir.* 26, which concerns Thekla's panegyris at the town of Dalisandos.[42] At the end of this miracle comes a typical city-defense story, already cited above, in which Thekla protects the citizens of Dalisandos from a siege by brigands (26.47–52).[43] Before that, however, comes a very detailed and evocative description of Thekla's annual appearance at the festival. In introducing this miracle the narrator calls the events "even more extraordinary (παραδοξότερα)" than those he has just recounted. Indeed they are, for the chief event of this miracle is Thekla's appearance in the sky over Dalisandos driving a fiery chariot. The narrator's recommendation is that a pilgrim should ascend the peak of a neighboring

---

[42] At the beginning of *Mir.* 30. the author presents a topographic etymology of the name Dalisandos: according to him it is a contraction of Damalisandos/Damalisanda, formed from the pair Δαμαλίς and Σάνδας/-ης/-ων. The latter is the name of a Cilician deity known to Ammianus Marcellinus (14.8.3) as the founder of Tarsus, assimilated to Heracles on local coins from the city (Agathias 2.24.8). Δαμαλίς was known to have been a female heroine associated with Heracles. For these and more references to this toponym, see Dagron 1978:371n3.

[43] The exact location of ancient Dalisandos is unknown. Dagron suggests, on the basis of epigraphical studies, that it was in the valley of the Kalykadnos, just to the northwest of Seleukeia, thus deeper into the Isaurian mountains and away from the coast (Dagron 1978:357n1). Also to be noted, however, is that the author of the *Miracles* remarks that Dalisandos has been lost to the historical record in his own time: "Dalisandos is a city, or rather, is only the image and name of a city that has been discarded into obscurity and anonymity, but it at one point gained notoriety for itself on account of the martyr" (26.2–3).

mountain the night before and "keep his back to the East and face the West" at dawn to catch a glimpse of this "paradoxical" event (26.8–13).

This story should be classed among Thekla's humanitarian miracles because her appearance at Dalisandos is described as a tribute to the public devotion the city showed on her behalf: "just as the city magnificently honors her, it obtains from her a miracle which was even more magnificent" (26.3–6). In fact, the miracle verges on becoming an *ekphrasis* of the city of Dalisandos:

> For in it there are many lofty, thick, blossoming trees with beautiful fruit, where many very lovely springs (πηγαί), and of very cold water, run out from under each plant and rock, so to speak, and which run down and encircle the temple itself; and there is a sweet breeze to the place, both crisp and delightful; and the song of the birds from above: [all of which] is both exceedingly marvelous (μάλα θαυμασία) and sufficient to enchant (ἱκανὴ καταθέλξαι).
>
> *Mir.* 26.17–23 (cf. *Odyssey* 10.213)

In narrative terms, this evocative and deliberate digression serves very well to connect three healing miracles dealing with diseases of the eye (*Mir.* 23; 24; 25) to three miracles of protection dealing with Isaurian brigands (*Mir.* 26.47–52; 27; 28). As noted, the end of *Mir.* 26 provides the first of these city-defense miracles. *Mir.* 26, therefore, confirms the interpretation offered above that the humanitarian displays of Thekla's power—here couched in explicit terms of performance and display—offer a rest for the reader, something to unify distinct sections of the work, as well as delighting and distracting from the occasional monotony of vengeance and healing.

Other examples of this humanitarian group include two miracles at the end of the *Miracles* which seem to have been added in a very late editorial change. These are *Mir.* 45 and 46, both of which concern women devoted to Thekla at her shrine. Incidentally, female monasticism does not play the role one might expect for a mid fifth-century work in a hagiographical vein: in fact, monastics of either sex are barely mentioned in the *Miracles*—priests, bishops and academics, on the other hand, receive the lion's share of Thekla's benefactions. This is in contrast to the picture one reads in the travelogue of the pilgrim Egeria, who visited Seleukeia and Thekla's shrine at Hagia Thekla in May of AD 384. As quoted in the Introduction, she claims that "round the holy church there is a tremendous number of cells for men and women" and she goes on to mention a "deaconess" named Marthana, whom she met as a pilgrim in Jerusalem. Marthana, as Egeria explains, was now the "superior of some apotactites or virgins."[44] The only stories in the *Miracles* which may directly involve some of these virgins are the two at the work's very end.

As just mentioned, they appear to have been added as an afterthought. This is because the work has a strange aborted miracle at *Mir.* 44 (concerning a "Dosithea") which is taken over by what seems to be the first draft of a conclusion. At the end of this conclusion—not nearly as conclusive as the final conclusion in the epilogue[45]—the text continues with the two miracles just mentioned: in the first Thekla teaches a woman named Xenarchis how to read (*Mir.* 45), and in the second she sleeps alongside a virgin named Dionysia (*Mir.* 46). Instead of performing the function of tying narrative units together, as with *Mir.* 15 and 26 above, these humanitarian miracles can be interpreted as summing-up certain literary motifs running throughout the work.

In *Mir.* 45 concerning Xenarchis, Thekla gives the remarkable gift of literacy, and by doing so is presented primarily as a helper for someone in need—the narrator says that Xenarchis "pleased the martyr" and that it was Thekla who "listened and acted," emphasizing again Thekla's attentiveness to those who are devoted to her. Secondarily, Thekla's power is invoked as something which works instantaneously and without warning:

> Some pious person, whether man or woman I'm unable to say, made a gift of a book to Xenarchis, bearing it by hand. The book was the Gospel...She untied the book and, opening it, she bent over it, as if to contemplate it or perhaps to kiss it. As soon as she trained her eyes on the letters, she began to read, and so fluently and without hesitation that all the women around her were astonished (ἐκπλαγῆναι) and invoked that passage from the Gospel: "How does she know letters without having learned them?"
>
> *Mir.* 45.5–7; 15–19 (cf. John 7:15)

Thekla's divine power is instantaneous, and once again the reader sees the correct model for response modeled before his eyes. "Astonishment" (ἔκπληξις) is, in the *Miracles* at least, the result of a supernatural occurrence, but, more specifically, it is the result of the completeness, swiftness, and

---

[44] For Egeria's visit to Seleukeia, see pp. 1–4 above.

[45] In fact, the syntax of the author's final sentence of this first conclusion is very convoluted and not at all comparable to the more inspired rhetoric of the epilogue. The first conclusion serves mainly as a litany of holy persons whom the author is embarrassed that he has not had time to speak about. Perhaps he ultimately found the time and decided to add the miracles about Xenarchis and Dionysia, the latter of whom is named in *Mir.* 44 as one of those he had thus far failed to mention. In any case, the author is more concerned about "holy people" in these final three miracles than he has been up to this point.

"unhesitating" nature of Thekla's acts of divine power. Thus, the appearance of the supernatural in nature is not, in itself, the catalyst of this response; rather the catalyst is the specific way in which Thekla manifests her concern for those under her care. The "astonished" reaction of the Roman soldiers in *Mir.* 28 to the swiftness with which Thekla dispatched the brigands is uniform with the reaction of the bystanders here in *Mir.* 45.

Furthermore, their astonishment is, in the passage quoted above, given the imprimatur of the Gospel: the bystanders at the Feast of the Tabernacles in John 7 were amazed (ἐθαύμαζον) at Jesus' "learning" (literally, "letters"; γράμματα). Is this allusion to be read as merely decoration for the miracle story or are we to assume this is direct imitation and that the miracle is modeled on the Gospel? There is no simple answer since the literary relationship between the two texts is complex. First, Thekla has been shown in the rest of the *Miracles* to work wonders which can only be the result of authoritative, divine power, and she is said to have been assigned this region by Christ himself. Yet the citation from John is applied to Xenarchis: it is Xenarchis that is being likened to Jesus, not Thekla. There is no question that this example shows the facility with which the author employs scriptural motifs, which has been noted by Dagron.[46] However, there is more going on here than the author making a show of his scriptural knowledge. Note in particular that the author's emphasis in *Mir.* 45 is not on the one-to-one relationship between the Xenarchis (or even Thekla) and Jesus. Instead, his emphasis is on the proper response that a bystander should have to what is clearly an authentic display of divine action in natural, even circumstantial, experience. The reader is, I would argue, supposed to appropriate the allusion to John 7 in an empathetic way: in other words, those astonished by Jesus' learning are, in an effectively modeled fashion, correct in their wonder. This is, of course, an unsophisticated reading of John in the sense that the Jews at the Feast of Tabernacles are being derided in that passage for recognizing Jesus' authority but not acknowledging his divinity. Nevertheless, the resonance appropriated in *Mir.* 45 of the correct, popular response to divinity and divine miracles crosses literary boundaries: "wonder" (θαῦμα) and "astonishment" (ἔκπληξις) are the only responses available when Thekla's divine power is at work in the world.

In concluding this section, let us consider the final miracle in the whole collection, *Mir.* 46, which concerns a woman named Dionysia. In one important concern, this miracle can be read as atypical of the stories in *Miracles*: Thekla never actually performs a miracle. In this way it could be linked with

---

[46] Dagron 1978:156 and passim.

her flying across the sky in a chariot in *Mir.* 26. Both are exhibits of Thekla's divine power but through display rather than action. However, a distinction should be drawn between them in that the display of Thekla's power in *Mir.* 46 is very intimate and personal, witnessed only by one person, whereas the chariot scene in *Mir.* 26 is theoretically open for all to see (though the author emphasizes that it is only those willing to climb the mountain who will catch a glimpse of her).

Mir. 46 begins with Dionysia having just "renounced" (ἀποτάττεσθαι) her husband, children, household,—"in a word, everything"—to become a female monk and live at the shrine of Thekla. The night after she does this Thekla is said to "sleep with her (συγκαθευδῆσαι) and embrace her [literally, 'grasp her tightly'; περιδεδρᾶχθαι] for the duration of the night" (46.1–4). The only witness to this event is a certain Susanna, the "bedmate" (σύγκοιτον) of Dionysia, who the author claims is the one who told him this miracle. Susanna relates that when she saw Thekla sleeping alongside Dionysia, "sleeping in-between them," she was "amazed" (θαυμάζειν) and "astonished" (καταπεπλῆχθαι) out of fear of the martyr. Once again, the emphasis of this miracle is on the proper response to Thekla's divine power: Susanna, a trustworthy source for the details of the miracle, also exhibits, in her very testimony, the cognitive, emotional, and even physical characteristics of so many individuals and groups in the *Miracles*.

It would be wrong, I think, to interpret this miracle in a sexual way: if anything *Mir.* 46 serves as an example of Christian female companionship of the sort that one sees at work, on the male side, in John Moschus' *Spiritual Meadow* (c. 600). Nevertheless, there is a clear sensuality in how the miracle is retold by Susanna, ostensibly in her own words (46.6–7). During the night Susanna sits up several times in bed, "leaning on her elbow and gazing at the martyr" (46.8–9). Likewise, the martyr's presence makes her "lost in her thoughts—for she was carefully watching her" (46.11–12). The visual theme is continued when Thekla finally leaves their bed: at the end of the night Susanna saw the martyr "slink off (ὑποδραμοῦσαν) back to her bedchamber (θάλαμον), where it is said she sunk down (καταδῦναι)" (46.14–16).

The latter reference is an allusion to the very end of the *Life* when Thekla disappears bodily into the ground, instead of dying as in the original *Acts of Paul and Thekla* (*Life* 28.8–11). This reference serves, therefore, as a bookend to Thekla's activities in the *Miracles*. For, while she continues today to work miracles in Seleukeia (as the author insists at various places; e.g. preface 81–91), there is a definitiveness to the collection which the author has constructed through literary means. Moreover, the fact that she sleeps in the earth—if that is in fact what is being suggested in this passage[47]—further solidifies the author's contention in *Mir.* 1–4, and at numerous other points, that Thekla holds the region of Seleukeia physically in her power. It is as if disappearing into the ground has given her authority over the earth. (This is further confirmed when she instructs Aba, an ill suppliant, to rub the "clay from the Cilician coast" on her injured foot in *Mir.* 18.)

*Mir.* 46 provides, therefore, a convenient point for summation because it has certain characteristics common to the miracles of divine power. To reiterate, these miracles comprise the majority of stories in the *Miracles* as a whole and they have nothing to do with illness, incubation, or healing. Instead, they are meant to display the supernatural, divine power or authority of Thekla over the region and people of Seleukeia and its environs. They emphasize the appropriate response to both the miracles experienced in the text and the *Miracles* as a text to be read. In fact, one of the most intriguing elements of this collection is the repeated, sometimes subtle assertion that the *Miracles* and Thekla's miraculous activities in Seleukeia are coterminous. This is at the very least true in a spatial sense, but there are indications—such as the bookends of Thekla's disappearance in *Life* 28 and *Mir.* 46—that it is true in a temporal sense as well. "Wonder" and "astonishment" are repeatedly invoked not just on account of the events themselves but on account of how rapid, complete, and effective Thekla's power proves to be: there is a tone of the superlative in all of these miracles.

Finally, the appearances of Thekla in person are common. This is an important point for the sake of comparison and contrast with Asclepian literature, but it is also important for understanding this author's conception of Thekla's presence in Seleukeia. In *Mir.* 46 Thekla appears in as intimate a fashion as possible; she sleeps alongside one of her own and embraces her. Yet in *Mir.* 26 she is depicted in very distant, impersonal, and lofty (even mythical) terms riding like Apollo on a fiery chariot across the sky over Dalisandos. In this dichotomy there is a clear, perhaps subconscious, invocation of the union of two natures, divine and human, in Christ—despite a demonstrable resistance on the part of this author to equating the miracle working of Thekla and Jesus (e.g. in *Mir.* 45). Thekla, in her divine power and authority, can also appear (significantly, at the very end of the *Miracles*) in the most personal and physical form possible.

---

[47] The suggestion may be, instead, that she sleeps in the church that was built over the spot where she disappeared, as described in *Life* 28.

## Narrative Healing: Thekla as Healer-Evangelist and Patroness-*littérateur*

### Healing by prescription

The healing miracles begin with *Mir.* 7, which follows the first four miracles against the pagan gods and two city-defense miracles (*Mir.* 5 and 6). Picking up on a reference made in *Mir.* 3 (Thekla's attack on Aphrodite), *Mir.* 7 concerns the bishop Dexianos, who in that earlier miracle is likened to Thekla's "Diomedes" (see p. 127–128 above). In *Mir.* 7 Dexianos is highly praised: he is a "holy man," a "high priest" (i.e. bishop), and "a man truly worthy of the honor conferred on him." The story of the miracle which happened to him is a bizarre one, unlike anything else in the *Miracles*. During the night Dexianos gets up to go to the toilet, only to encounter a "savage and raving demon" sitting beside him in the darkness.[48] This demon utters a horrible sound which frightens Dexianos so severely that he slips his neck out of joint. To quote the narrator at this point, "the cervical vertebrae were dislocated with one another. His head was trembling and shook with frequent movement, so that there was general mourning among those who saw him" (*Mir.* 7.15–18). Dexianos' condition is thus described in desperate terms, and the bystanders who are observing him and mourning over his misfortune are clearly, though not explicitly, unable to ease his suffering.

By contrast, Thekla is described in the next paragraph as observing all that the demon does to Dexianos yet as obviously unperturbed. The text begins by noting that she "immediately removed his malady (τοῦ πάθους)" and only then goes on to describe the remedy. This is typical of most of the *Miracles*, in both healing and vengeance stories: the reader is assured of the outcome up front, and only later told the details (if there are any). In this case the details amount to a substantial narrative about Thekla "visiting" (ἐπιφοιτήσασα) Dexianos in a dream in order to reassure "her assistant" (πάρεδρον) not to "lose heart" (ἀθυμεῖν). In the dream she instructs him "to use as a remedy (πρὸς θεραπείαν) the oil that continually preserves the nocturnal flame at her own place (χῶρον), namely the holy bema" (7.23–26). Without any more instructions than this, Dexianos "anoints" (χρισάμενος) himself with the "fragrant" (μυρωθέντι) oil, about which the author comments, "clearly Thekla herself

---

[48] I have translated δαίμων here as "demon" (instead of "*daimon*" as I did with the pagan gods in the last section) because the supernatural being that the author is describing is in this miracle is very obviously of a different nature and rank.

provided this" (αὐτῆς δήπουθεν καὶ τοῦτο ἐργασμένης; *Mir.* 7.29).⁴⁹ The cure works immediately and effectively, and Dexianos rejoices in the gift. Indeed, the cure works so well that he continues to make use of it as an apotropaic device "on another dangerous occasion" (7.31–34), an attack which occurs in the following miracle.

*Mir.* 8 thus also concerns Dexianos, though it is told in a very different way from *Mir.* 7. The two provide an instructive contrast between different styles of narration within Thekla's healing miracles. In this miracle Dexianos is riding on a skittish horse that bucks the bishop off, a fall which results in his broken leg. Once again, the reader is immediately assured that Thekla provided him with help, this time because "she had great care for our man" (8.4–5). The pairing of *Mir.* 7 and 8 is further solidified by the author's statement that in both cases Thekla accomplished "the exact same miracle (θαῦμα)." As in the vengeance miracles, the uniformity of Thekla's miracle-working activity is once again underlined in this passage.

However, in *Mir.* 8 the source of the cure is not explicitly mentioned, though the oil has been signaled already in *Mir.* 7. Instead, the statement that both miracles were "identical" (ἴσον)—ambiguous as it is—leads to a comment on how Thekla makes use of common materials in her cures. The oil is thus clearly in mind when he concludes his accounts of Dexianos with this more theoretical passage:

> These events were not the result of any complicated drug, which is exactly the reason she is admired (θαυμάσειε)! When she makes known what those who are suffering must do, she does not lead her suppliants to rare and expensive remedies (φαρμακείας); instead, to common and readily available remedies, so that effecting their salvation (σωτηρίαν; i.e. healing) comes even easier than the procuring of the remedy prescribed (τοῦ μηνυθέντος) is speedy. The result is that her power is exhibited in the use she makes of common ingredients, and efficacy is rightly reckoned to the one handing out the prescription rather than to that which is prescribed (τοῦ προσταχθέντος).

> *Mir.* 8.6–14

This passage seems to be a comment on the methods of ancient doctors, who were known for their elaborate and extreme methods (cf. *Mir.* 12). It is difficult

---

⁴⁹ On the use of the imagery of smell in liturgical poetry from this period, see Ashbrook Harvey 2002 and Johnson 2002b.

to gauge the precise import of this rhetoric since we obviously do not have the writings (if there were any) of the doctors in Seleukeia competing with Thekla for patients. Yet, in the context of the *Miracles* as a whole, the statement at the beginning of this passage that Thekla deserves to be admired (θαυμάζειν) for her preference for readily available ingredients fits well with the rhetoric we have observed thus far. Thekla achieves the miraculous using as little effort (in human terms) as possible: in fact, the less effort she can be shown to have used in a particular cure or act of vengeance, the more divine her status in the eyes of this author. According to his rhetoric here, the lack of fancy prescriptions is actually a sign of Thekla's superiority in the game of healing. This is, of course, a reversal of ancient logic, and one wonders whether the author is here consciously polemicizing against Aelius Aristides' *Hieroi Logoi*. Perhaps local medical practices were still relatively isomorphic with what Aelius describes, so that the *Miracles* can be said to be engaging real practices on the ground in Seleukeia. *Mir.* 12 would seem to confirm this hypothesis, since it describes the author's own experience, but the rhetoric here in *Mir.* 8 (as well as in *Mir.* 12, as we shall see) is highly argumentative and selective, so it is very difficult to tell how accurate his picture of ancient medicine really is.

The miracles that lead up to that supremely programmatic *Mir.* 12 all concern priests and bishops. Thus, *Mir.* 7 through *Mir.* 11 deal with the various difficulties and resolutions of Dexianos, Menodoros, Atlantios, Symposios, and Aurelios. The last of this group, Aurelios, is healed in *Mir.* 11 of a very specific disease, "hog's bumps" (χοιράδες), which appears to be the ancient name for the glandular disease Scrofula.[50] Aurelios, a fellow citizen and kinsman of Symposios (*Mir.* 10), caught this disease when he was just a boy. According to the story, the bumps seized his neck and grew "to an immense size" as they proceeded almost to choke him (*Mir.* 11.7–10). Continuing the polemic against medicine begun in *Mir.* 8, the author here includes the salient information that the doctors (ἀσκληπιάδες) attempted to apply their knowledge to the disease but only in vain, since the malignancy of the disease was too great. Next, that "excellent physician of physicians," Sarpedon, was called upon by Aurelios' grandmother, yet even he, the text says, was unable to provide a remedy (θεραπεία) for the boy. In typical fashion, Thekla now comes onto the scene and her assistance is assured:

> The martyr, the true help (ἀληθῶς ἀρωγός), the effective assis-
> tant (ἐνεργὴς βοηθός), who is always zealous regarding every good
> service, first mocked the old woman, then took pity on the boy as

[50] See LSJ s.v.

even her own nursling and as a child of faithful parents—as was her custom—and she hastened on to the remedy (θεραπείαν).

*Mir.* 11.17–21

Thekla is characterized in this passage as a surrogate mother—presumably the parents of the boy were dead—which is a unique role for her in the *Miracles*, especially considering her war-like persona in *Mir.* 1–6. Yet her "mocking" attitude is not unique and appears elsewhere, such as in her taunting of Sarpedon in *Mir.* 1, and the author's description of her "haste" in completing the remedy is so common, as noted above, that it should perhaps be considered a standard element of every miracle, more significant in its absence than its inclusion.

However, as normal as *Mir.* 11 is in its use of certain stock features from the *Miracles*, the author goes on to expand this story of healing to include a sequence in which Thekla offers a prescription to the boy's grandmother. This is similar to what happens in *Mir.* 7, but the prescription for Dexianos occurred in a dream sequence; *Mir.* 11 is expressly not a dream. Furthermore, in *Mir.* 11 Thekla's prescription is much more involved. Thus, first, Thekla's appearance to the old woman is put in typical terms of her visitation or haunting of Seleukeia—ἐπιφοιτάω is once again the verb of choice for her activities—but the narrator specifies clearly that Thekla "visits" the grandmother directly, instead of appearing to her in a nighttime vision. Next, Thekla advises the woman to weave a length of soft wool which measures to the boy's height. Then, the old woman is told to burn it and collect the ashes. Finally, Thekla instructs her to apply the mixture directly to the inflamed area. The old woman's response is in keeping with her original hopes: she accepts the cure but is disappointed that it did not come from Sarpedon. Crucially, however, the author notes that the grandmother recognized who it was that gave her the prescription because Thekla resembled her daughter, the mother of Aurelios, who intriguingly was also named Thekla (11.33–35).[51]

Before examining how the success of the poultice is described, there are a few points to make about the prescription itself. Most important is the emphasis on proportionality and direct contact. The wool equals Aurelios' exact height and, consequently, can serve as a something like a substitute for the boy—yet pure, healthy, and untainted. The physical husk of this substitute,

---

[51] This passage could reasonably be compared to the secret, spiritual naming of Macrina as "Thekla" before she was born, as told in Gregory of Nyssa's *Life of Macrina* (2.21–34, ed. Maraval 1971:144–148). Davis 2001:201–208 collects the namesakes of Thekla in late antique Egypt, both Greek and Coptic.

the wool, is then burnt away, leaving only its essential elements. Finally, the potion is applied directly to the infected area, as if the poultice were simply replacing the inflamed area, reconstituting a healthy neck. The correspondence between the sick boy and the poultice is therefore one-to-one.

Despite this proportionality and direct application, the poultice is not completely effective: the "hog's bumps" keep popping up on one part of Aurelios' neck after another. Such an incomplete result of Thekla's swift prescription is very surprising, but what is even more surprising is that Thekla does not provide the solution to this secondary problem (at least not directly). The narrator describes the persistent illness and its resolution in the following passage:

> It was just like some race between dogs and deer, of those chasing on one hand, and of those fleeing on the other; until the excellent doctor (ὁ βέλτιστος ἰατρός), whoever he was, made a lot of this potion—it was the martyr, I think, who put this idea into his head—and covering the whole neck with this, he compelled the shameless "bumps" to descend to the belly, and from there to flow out through the bottom. We know this story from the one himself who suffered and was healed; he tells the story often and gives thanks to the martyr for what she did.[52]

*Mir.* 11.44–51

The role of the martyr is very limited here: the attribution of the doctor's common sense to Thekla's "inspiration" is a much weaker claim than Thekla's epiphany before the grandmother. Even still, the author of the *Miracles* has the testimony of the boy, now an adult, to back up the report.

This endorsement of a single doctor's ability to solve a serious medical problem runs counter to the other appearances of doctors in the *Miracles*. As already noted, the doctors at the beginning of *Mir.* 11 are unsuccessful, as is Sarpedon. Likewise, in *Mir.* 18 a pagan (literally, "Greek") woman Aba, who broke her leg riding on a mule, was disappointed by "some Jews," "some enchanters" (ἐπαοιδοί; related to the "doctors"?), and even "Sarpedonios," none of whom were able to heal her leg. Yet, "either on their own counsel or by her own prompting," as the text says, the woman was moved to the shrine of Thekla, where she was healed. (At the end of this miracle comes another

---

[52] The epithet βέλτιστος frequently appears in the *Miracles* as an ironic reference to an individual's standing in the community. It is used for Sarpedon, the old woman, and the doctor in this miracle, as well as for the Pythian Apollo (*Mir.* preface 63) and others. It is a tool for distancing the author from the reputation of his characters in the community.

denunciation of "expensive" and "precious" remedies [18.38–41].) In addition, at the beginning of *Mir.* 38, the grammarian Alypios is described as being
"abandoned" by the doctors and "himself reckoning the illness stronger than
any human assistance." In this hopeless state, he seeks out the martyr's shrine,
whom he considers to be "the only place of refuge for illnesses of this kind,"
that is, illnesses which have no human solution (38.1–8). Finally, in a miracle
concerning a little boy whose eye is filling with pus (*Mir.* 24), Thekla's remedy
(slicing open the eye) is compared to the skill with which a doctor would use
a scalpel (24.41–42). However, instead of wielding a scalpel herself, she has an
angry crane puncture the boy's eye with its bill. Not unaware of the different
registers of miracle-telling, the narrator claims that this was accomplished "in
sport rather than in earnest" (24.21).

The latter miracle highlights an underlying theme in all of the miracles in which Thekla offers a prescription or trumps local doctors. Namely,
Thekla's healings of sick individuals are effortless for her. They require no
strain or discomfort on her part; in fact, she appears to make no sacrifice at
all (except perhaps the one she already made in her two abortive martyrdoms in the *ATh*). The prescriptions can be very brief, such as the one for
Dexianos in *Mir.* 7, or they can be elaborate, such as the one given to Aurelios'
grandmother in *Mir.* 11. Additionally, the application of the prescription can
be told with varying degrees of detail. In Dexianos' case that detail is very
limited, especially for his broken leg in *Mir.* 8, where the cure is not discussed
at all: "these two were identical." In *Mir.* 11, however, the application is more
involved and is complicated by the fact that the grandmother appears to
have made too little of the poultice. The doctor's role is not directly related
to Thekla's appearance to the grandmother, and there is no mention that the
doctor gave credit to Thekla.

This is, in fact, atypical among the *Miracles*: in nearly every miracle in
which bystanders or third-parties are involved, such as the Roman soldiers in
*Mir.* 28 or Aurelios' grandmother in *Mir.* 11, they acknowledge that it is Thekla
who accomplish the miracle, thereby reconfirming the testimony of the
collector. The absence of the doctor's recognition of Thekla's work is possibly
related to the fact that Thekla appeared to the grandmother in person, instead
of in a dream, the validity of the latter being more open to challenge than a
direct epiphany. In other words, this miracle contains so direct a manifesta-
tion of Thekla's presence that the doctor's verbal or notional affirmation is
rendered unnecessary. Nevertheless, despite this lack of formal acknowledgment, the narrator remarks parenthetically, "it was the martyr, I think, who

put this idea into his head" (τῆς μάρτυρος οἶμαι καὶ τοῦτο ἐπὶ νοῦν ἀγαγούσης; *Mir.* 11.46–47). Clearly an ex post facto device, this remark serves the purpose of keeping the martyr's presence firmly in the reader's mind, even though her direct action has not been logically linked to the doctor's handiwork. From a literary point of view the lack of logical coherence may be considered a fault of the text, but the complexity of *Mir.* 11 adds depth to the miracles by prescription while still maintaining a sense of consistency (albeit imposed) about Thekla's healing work in Seleukeia.

## Healing leading to conversion

The miracles by prescription just discussed are a unique group in the *Miracles* as a whole because they include a description of the special method by which Thekla accomplishes each miracle. This is not true for many of the miracles: as we have seen, some she simply accomplishes by willing them (e.g. *Mir.* 8). These less detailed miracles serve the rhetorical purpose of reinforcing in a short compass the picture painted by the longer miracles and programmatic passages, the preface and epilogue in particular. However, among the healing miracles there is another subgroup which might be called "healing miracles leading to conversion." This group is notable for its additional narrative goal, that of bringing superior praise to Thekla for converting people to Christianity. This is a small group of miracles in total number simply because Thekla is most often depicted caring for those already under her care or petitioning her for help, such as Dexianos in *Mir.* 7–8, Bassiane in *Mir.* 19, Pausikakos in *Mir.* 23, and the author himself in *Mir.* 12, 31, and 41. The group of miracles leading to conversion nonetheless has special significance for the *Miracles* because conversion is more than once lauded as the supreme miracle which Thekla accomplishes.

For example, *Mir.* 17 concerns Leontios, a Christian craftsman who was decorating the interior of a wealthy gentleman's house in Syrian (not Pisidian) Antioch.[53] While "exercising his talent," as the text says (17.9), setting marble slabs (μαρμάρων καὶ πλακῶν) around the walls, the scaffolding collapses, and he shatters his leg so badly that he was reckoned as dead (17.13–15). (Indeed, the text says that the others who fell with him died immediately as a result of their fall—he was the only one to survive.) Maximinos, Leontios' patron, is grieved by this fall not only because of the loss of Leontios' art but because Leontios himself was "a good, excellent, and peaceable man" (17.15–18). In a desperate state, Leontios asks Maximinos if he can travel to Seleukeia to seek

---

[53] For the location, see Dagron 1978:25, 110–111.

the help of Thekla at her "martyrion." Maximinos allows this but smirks as if he doubts in the power of Thekla to do anything.[54] When Leontios arrives in Seleukeia he is healed within three days at the martyrion: "Leontios was delivered of his illness and his foot was returned to strength—the broken bone was again rejoined" (17.25–26). Without delay Leontios returns to Antioch to show Maximinos that he has been healed. As he gazes (θεασάμενος) at Leontios' reformed leg, Maximinos is "astonished" (ἐκπλαγῆναι), "not only at the miracle itself (τὸ θαῦμα μόνον)," the text says, "but at its swiftness (τὸ τάχος)." On account of this miracle Maximinos himself becomes a Christian, which was "the intention of Thekla in accomplishing the miracle (θαῦμα)" (17.32–33). Finally, to end the miracle, the author tells how Thekla effected Leontios' cure (θεραπεία). The scene returns, therefore, to Seleukeia and to Thekla's martyrion. During the night, while Leontios was sleeping, he martyr visits him (φοιτήσασα) and steps on his injured leg, "very forcefully" the text adds. Leontios leaped up at the pain and began walking, then running, and immediately he returns to Antioch (17.36–45).[55]

A number of points could be made about this miracle in terms of how it fits in with the other miracles in the collection. The absence of any (initial) description of the cure itself, for example, is typical in the sense that several miracles are told without graphic details, but it is atypical in the sense that most miracles which happen explicitly at the shrine (here "martyrion," else-where "temple" or even "*temenos*") do normally include at least a moderate amount of detail regarding the cure (e.g. *Mir.* 23 and 24). In other words, if the set-up is told in detail, then there is usually a detailed narrative of the climax. This formula comes true at the end of the miracle, in the conclusion to the author's modest attempt at ring composition: Leontios' experience in Thekla's martyrion is told in excruciating detail. Unlike Thekla's prescription miracles, in this case she takes matters into her own hands. Very few of the healing miracles, in fact, are accomplished through direct contact with the patient, a characteristic of the *Miracles* which is in contrast to many of the Asclepian texts that will be discussed below in Chapter Four (esp. pp. 197–210). This direct, physical mode of healing is much more typical of the seventh-century *Miracles of Artemios*, for example, in which the saint is often depicted grabbing

---

[54] As Dagron notes, Leontios' request suggests that he was Maximinos' slave, or at least bound to him in some way (Dagron 1978:337n4).

[55] The text says that he returned to Antioch by land, "saying farewell to the sea, to boats, and to waves" (17.44–45). Dagron groups this with other comments in the *Miracles* about preferring land travel to sea travel, the shining exception being the Cypriot pilgrim in *Mir.* 15 (Dagron 1978:110–111).

or treading on the infected testicles of his suppliants.[56] Finally, *Mir.* 17 is also atypical in the way it describes Maximinos' doubt in Thekla's abilities: usually the doubter will attribute the miracle to Sarpedon (e.g. *Mir.* 40). But the use of dramatic irony in this passage, with its description of Maximinos' knowing (yet ignorant) grin, is certainly one of the more effective uses of any literary device in the *Miracles*.

Crucial to the argument of *Mir.* 17 is Maximinos' conversion, which occupies the central place within the ring composition of Leontius' healing. It is clear from its placement as well as from the way it is told that Maximinos' miraculous acceptance is preeminent, even though Leontios' experience is (in the end) told in more detail. Maximinos' response of "astonishment" at Leontios' renewed leg is common for bystanders of every miracle, as demonstrated in numerous examples above. What is new in this case the narrator's comment that Thekla "took care ahead of time" (προμηθουμένη) to bring Maximinos to conversion (17.32). In this way it is revealed Thekla's chief purpose behind Leontios' healing is to lead this wealthy citizen of Syrian Antioch to Christ, which was her intention from the beginning (17.32–33). Once again there is a correspondence between Thekla's miracle working and the text itself. The centrality within *Mir.* 17 of Maximinos' conversion is emphasized by the author through its placement at the center of the two narratives about Leontios; but it is also Thekla's stated opinion in the miracle that Maximinos was her a central part of her aims in healing of Leontios. Thus, in the very telling of a miracle which places Maximinos at the center, Thekla is "overheard" (so to speak) to have intended Maximinos to be at the center all along. The practical/literary and notional/spiritual coincide in his conversion.

Maximinos' centrality brings up an important, general point about many of the stories in the *Miracles* as a whole. The majority of the miracles are accomplished by Thekla for wealthy or otherwise prominent individuals in Seleukeia and neighboring cities. This category of persons represented in the *Miracles* includes contemporary (now barely known) ecclesiastical figures such as Dexianos (bishop of Seleukeia; *Mir.* 7–8, 32), Menodoros (bishop of Aigai; 9), Symposios (10), Aurelios (11), and Marianos (bishop of Tarsus; 29). It also includes men with imperial positions, such as the general Satornilos (i.e. Saturninus; *Mir.* 13),[57] the "imperial messenger" Ambrosios (16), and the

---

[56] See Crisafulli and Nesbitt 1997.

[57] Saturninus was the *comes domesticorum* under Theodosius II. The emperor sent Saturninus to Jerusalem to execute, in AD 444, the companions of the exiled empress Eudocia-Athenaïs, namely, the priest Severus and the deacon John. The latter two were charged with professing

"*bouletai*" Aulerios and Pappos (35); as well as illustrious women like Tigriane and Aba (*Mir.* 18), Bassiane (19), the unnamed wife of Bitanos and Gregorios (20), and Kalliste (42). Finally, classed with these eminent individuals are the grammarians and rhetors: Eusebios and the recently deceased Hyperechios (*Mir.* 30), Alypios and his son Solumios (38), Isokasios (39) and Aretarchos (40).

This crucial concentration of the author of the *Miracles* on the prominent members of society will be discussed further below. For now, the latter two of the miracles just listed are worth paying some extra attention because they concern Thekla's stated interest in converting the non-believers involved in her miracles, either directly or as bystanders. The premise of both miracles, which are treated as a narrative pair, is that Isokasios and Aretarchos were non-believers but still received healing from Thekla anyway. What is even more paradoxical for the author is that they have remained non-believers even to that very day, but to him Thekla's work is still worth recording and worthy of praise. In fact, he quotes from Plato at the beginning of *Mir.* 39 in a subtle jab against the rhetors' wisdom: "The responsibility is that of the chooser, as the amazing (θαυμαστός) Plato says somewhere, but the martyr remains innocent (ἀναίτιος)" (39.4–5).[58]

Isokasios' healing is told in a very straightforward, typical style for the *Miracles*: he falls ill (no details); he seeks out a place of "tranquility" (ἠρεμία), which he only finds at Thekla's shrine; while sleeping she brings him a prescription (again, no details), which he carries out and is healed. At the end of the miracle, however, the point is clearly made: "While chastising his unbelief, she did not withhold her assistance" (39.13–15). Thus, Thekla's failure to convert Isokasios is rhetorically transformed into a positive quality of hers: she refuses to withhold help from those who seek her out. There are too few examples in the *Miracles* of individuals who do not know Thekla prior to her assistance to prove whether this quality of Thekla's character holds true all the time. One assumes it does not, since Pappos repents after being chastised by Thekla in *Mir.* 35 but is killed anyway for his sin against the orphaned children of Aulerios. Nevertheless, the point is made clearly enough in this and the following miracle that Thekla's compassion extends (in principle, at least) to those who are not Christians to begin with, and even to those who choose not to become Christians after their healing (unwise as it is).

---

heretical doctrinal views. As Dagron notes, some sources claim that Eudocia avenged their deaths by killing Saturninus himself (Dagron 1978:323n2).

[58] Plato *Republic* 10.616e (as noted by Dagron 1978:395n1).

Aretarchos' healing in *Mir.* 40 is somewhat different in narrative quality because there is more detail and the story is more complicated. It is similar to but ultimately distinct from *Mir.* 11, in which Aurelios' grandmother beseeches Sarpedon and gets Thekla instead (afterwards sulking ungratefully that her chosen *daimon* was unresponsive). In this case, Aretarchos is healed by Thekla but ultimately gives the credit to Sarpedon. He acknowledges that it was Thekla who treated him (with lamp oil from her shrine, like Dexianos in *Mir.* 7), but he claims that Sarpedon instructed him to seek her out. In the words of the author, "Thus he obtained healing (ἴασις), but not deliverance from irreverence (ἀσέβεια)" (*Mir.* 40.12–13). In a rare use of literary apostrophe, the author breaks into direct speech to Aretarchos: "O wisest and most sensible of sophists (σοφώτατε καὶ ἐμφρονέστατε σοφιστῶν)! You who reenact (ἀναπνέων) for us Gorgias himself! That one [Sarpedon] who has delivered you to someone else, if he were able, would he not supply [your need]?" (40.16–19). In this rare verbal outburst and counterfactual expression, the author of the *Miracles* draws attention to Aretarchos' refusal to acknowledge the power of the martyr. Once again, the author lightly adds a Platonic reference as a jab against the wisdom of this so-called "sophist."[59]

Finally, in concluding the miracle, the narrator attempts to draw the reader's attention back to the work of Thekla: "I assign (λογιούμεθα) this healing to the power of the martyr, but your attribution I assign to your foolishness (ἀμαθία). But, this latter point is to me of little importance compared to the former" (40.31–33). The author's rhetorical coup de grâce in *Mir.* 40 is to undercut his own attacks on Aretarchos' lack of wisdom and to reemphasize the work of the martyr in healing a serious illness. For the reader this provides the continuity he has come to expect in terms of miracle-framing: this passage performs the role of a closing summary. Moreover, to reinforce his emphasis on the martyr's work in *Mir.* 40 the author includes, as *Mir.* 41, a healing which Thekla worked for himself: she heals his ear at a critical time right before he is supposed to speak publicly at her panegyris. Thus, his criticism of an ungrateful sophist in *Mir.* 40 is contrasted with the self-conscious modeling of the correct response to Thekla's compassionate healing in *Mir.* 41. Both concern prominent pubic speakers, but, of the two, only the author has the wisdom to assign the work to the omnipotent martyr. Furthermore,

---

[59] The sophist Gorgias (c. 485–c. 380 BC) was very influential in classical Greece as a thinker and a stylist. His style is parodied by the character Agathon in Plato's *Symposium* (194e–197e), and he was considered generally to be a skeptic on the communicative power of words. See *OCD* s.v. "Gorgias (1)."

the author depicts himself as engaged in the work of praising Thekla herself, whereas Aretarchos has the air of both narcissism and idolatry.

Compared to some of the punishment miracles, in which Thekla is often depicted as severe and unyielding (e.g. *Mir.* 35), the martyr's response to Isokasios and Aretarchos, as prominent unbelievers, is very tolerant and even tacitly condoning (despite the author's antagonistic rhetoric). Two points should be emphasized: 1) she still heals them and 2) the author of the *Miracles* still includes these miracles. Nevertheless, *Mir.* 39 and 40 have the rhetorical value of showing Thekla at work outside her normal role, yet still within the Seleukeia region: this underlines her spiritual dominance, even if some individuals still cling to powerless *daimones* like Sarpedon.

By way of concluding this section on healing leading to conversion, mention should be made of *Mir.* 14, the only miracle in which Thekla actually compels someone to convert to Christianity. Thus far we have seen two methods of dealing with conversions in the *Miracles*: the first, most normal and proper method is that a bystander like Maximinos in *Mir.* 17 will witness Thekla's work and be so "astonished" that the only open recourse is to convert; second is the tolerance Thekla shows to those who are unrepentant, such as Isokasios and Aretarchos—even though they remain unbelievers, Thekla is to be praised because she healed them anyway (more a rhetorical use of conversion than a description of how it happens). The third and final method by which the author of the *Miracles* deals with conversions to Christianity is to show Thekla as an inflictor of disease and suffering for the very purpose of bringing a non-believer to Christ. This is what happens in *Mir.* 14 when the devoted Christian wife of Hypsistios, a "noble and illustious" man from neighboring Claudiopolis, prays earnestly to Thekla that her husband would become a Christian.[60] The text says that Thekla marveled (θαυμάσασα) at her faith and proceeded to accomplish the miracle out of pity. She accomplishes Hypsistios' conversion first by bringing disease upon him, which was designed to "soften the ignobility (τὸ ἀγεννής) and relentlessness (ἀμείλικτον) of his soul" before she applied the remedy (θεραπεία; *Mir.* 14.19–21).

Once the disease has taken its effect and the doctors have proved themselves useless (14.26), Thekla comes to the man "in a waking vision (ὕπαρ)"; and "not in a dream (ὄναρ)," the narrator hastens to add. She appears in the form of a "little girl" (εὐσταλὴς κόρη), a comment which serves to introduce a digressive *ekphrasis* on Thekla's appearance (14.33–45). Leaving aside the

---

[60] Hypsistios' wife's prayers are compared to Hannah's in 1 Samuel 1:1–20, though the author of the *Miracles* characterizes praying for children as "the demand of Jewish vulgarity."

author's digression for the moment, her epiphany before Hypsistios is told in a swift novelistic style: she enters the room and sits on his bed; Hypsistios only notices her when she makes "a slight noise with her foot"; he shouts at her and asks who she is; then she boldly announces herself and commands him to get baptized if he wants to end the sickness. The command to be baptized is followed by a litany of doctrinal statements additionally to be believed if Hypsistios wants to get well:

> Since you have learned who I am, and having already paid enough of a penalty for your faithlessness, stand up, go out, be baptized, participate in the mysteries, worship, confess the Father, Son, and Holy Spirit, the uncreated and consubstantial Trinity that created all things, either known (νοητά) or perceived (αἰσθητά) or seen or unseen, that bears and drives all these things, that manages and rules all things. Confess in addition to these things the divine presence in the flesh (μετὰ σαρκός) and the sojourn of the only-begotten (I am speaking of his taking-on-of-flesh (σάρκωσιν; i.e. incarnation) and birth through the virgin and Theotokos Mary), the cross, the death, the resurrection, and the ascension. Straightaway you will cleanse your body along with your soul, and you will inhabit well this earth, and you will live well, and well you will migrate (μεταστήσει) to heaven, where you will view Christ the king thereafter in great immediacy (σὺν πολλῇ τῇ παρρησίᾳ).
>
> *Mir.* 14.55–68

As has been noted already (e.g. pp. 33–35), Trinitarian language of this type is scattered throughout the *LM*. Incarnational language, such as in the second half of this passage, is less common but obviously reflects better the contemporary debates surrounding the councils of Ephesus (AD 431) and Chalcedon (AD 451). What is important in narrative terms here is that the author has taken the opportunity of the ill Hypsistios to offer a litany of theological terminology which he clearly believes is central to faith. This includes a reference to the Theotokos, as well as to his eschatological vision of the afterlife as a vision of Christ "with great immediacy" (cf. 1 John 4:17 for eschatological παρρησία).[61] At

---

[61] The reference to the Theotokos here is surprising given that the author has demonstrated his apathy towards contemporary theological issues elsewhere in the *LM* (see pp. 221–226 below). He adds nothing to these debates, except to tie the term to Christology, which was its fifth-century setting (see Lampe s.v., definitions C–D). Thus, the appearance of the term Theotokos here is primarily significant as a demonstration that the author is not unaware of contemporary Christological issues, though he chooses elsewhere not to involve his text in them.

the end of the miracle, the author emphasizes the completeness of Hypsistios' experience after Thekla has disappeared: he gains "faith," "grace," "initiation," and "to be good health on top of all these" (14.71–73). These features of his new found strength in Christ are described as the gifts that Thekla left him with, the most important of which, the text says, is "becoming a Christian" (χριστιανὸν γενέσθαι).

In *Mir.* 14, as also in *Mir.* 17, the conversion of Hypsistios (Maximinos in *Mir.* 17) is the central narrative goal of Thekla's healing work. Unlike *Mir.* 17, however, Hypsistios is inflicted with his disease by Thekla, who elsewhere is always depicted as the healer. However, Hypsistios is healed at the end of the miracle, and Thekla makes it clear earlier in her speech that he deserves his disease because she has "always been mistreated and abused" by him, though the reader learns nothing else about these abuses. Yet, despite these caveats, the implication of the miracle is that Thekla has the power not just to remove sickness but also to inflict it. Once again, *Mir.* 35 concerning Pappos serves as a touchstone because, even though he repented of his sin, Thekla still killed him without mercy.

Thus, the miracles about healing leading to conversion all have a different message, but at the same time they can be grouped together because they employ the rhetorical commonplace of conversion. *Mir.* 14 is unique in the group because of its length and it is in direct contrast to the tolerance she shows Isokasios and Aretarchos (*Mir.* 39 and 40). One gets the sense that the latter two may have been too prominent (or too close to the author?) to receive a waking vision of Thekla such as what appeared before Hypsistios. In any case, the topic of conversion proves to be fruitful for the author of the *Miracles* because it provides the narrative structure for two of the longest miracles in his collection (*Mir.* 14 and 17) as well as the necessary locus for sophistic antagonism in *Mir.* 39 and 40, which in turn propels a key story in *Mir.* 41 concerning his close relationship with Thekla. It is appropriate at this point, therefore, to consider the miracles that happened to the author himself and how they reinforce the picture of Thekla's literary patronage which he established in the *Miracles*' preface.

Authorial encounters with Thekla

There are two miracles, *Mir.* 12 and 41, in which the author himself figures prominently as the subject of Thekla's power to heal. *Mir.* 12 is the longer of the two and is made up of a complex series of two independent stories spread over three dream sequences. *Mir.* 41 is more straightforward and concerns the healing of the author's ear just before he is about to speak at Thekla's panegyris. Both miracles make implicit arguments for Thekla's approval and patronage of the author's project of publishing her miracles. Like the programmatic passages in the preface and the epilogue, these two miracles serve to orient the reader with regard to Thekla's involvement with the collection: both emphasize that without her assistance the author would not have succeeded in collecting and presenting the *Miracles*. The afflictions which the author suffers in these two stories impinge directly on his ability to communicate the message that she has inspired and commissioned him to communicate. Moreover, at the same time as the author is arguing that his collection of Thekla's miracles is the result of her miraculous intervention, he is also arguing that, in order for Thekla's miracles to achieve their goal, they must be collected and disseminated. Furthermore, he insists in his preface and epilogue that this dissemination also depends on her divine power. Thus, the correspondence between the *Miracles* as a literary collection and Thekla's power to work θαύματα is reinforced multiple times in different rhetorical contexts, not least in the healing miracles which concern the author directly.

As just noted, *Mir.* 12 is composed of two independent stories spread over three successive dream sequences. In the first story, the author is healed of an inflammation of his index finger (12.1–40). The inflammation is called "anthrax" (literally, "coal") and proves too malignant for the doctors (ἰατροί) to cure by their "art" (τέχνη) and their "drugs" (φάρμακα). Instead, they decide that to save his life they must amputate the offending finger, and they promise to return the next day to do just that. In between their decision and the impending amputation—in a state of "terror and tears"—the author has his first dream (ὀνειροπολέω). In this dream he is sleeping in the atrium of the healing shrine when a swarm of wasps appears and begins to attack him "brandishing their stingers like spears." Suddenly Thekla appears and, taking hold of the edge of her cloak and wrapping it around her hand, chases the wasps and tramples them under her feet. The author wakes to find that he has been miraculously healed from his inflammation. The doctors' response is a conflicted one, as the texts explains:

> The doctors arrived with zeal and they held the knife in their hands, and they were discussing amongst themselves, as is typical, but they went away marveling (θαυμάζοντες) with me at the martyr, singing her praises, and possibly discreetly complaining about her, because,

> on account of her examination (ἐπίσκεψιν) and cure (ἰατρείαν), they
> were unpaid.
>
> *Mir.* 12.35–40

Several points could be made about the author's depiction of the doctors in this passage. Most important for the present discussion, however, is the narrative progression of the miracle: the doctors' inability to effect a cure results in a drastic prescription on their part which Thekla's compassionate intervention renders unnecessary. Moreover, this passage is unique in the *Miracles* because Thekla's work appears to imitate that of the doctors instead of simply being more effective. The actual miracle of physical healing, fantastical in its dream-narration, is by the end of the story couched in traditional, pragmatic medical terminology: Thekla has made her "examination" (ἐπίσκεψις) and she has effected a "cure" (ἰατρεία). In addition, the passages scattered throughout the *Miracles* which condemn the complicated and expensive remedies of the doctors should also be brought to bear on an interpretation of this miracle. Most importantly, the picture of the failure of the doctors' φάρμακα here reinforces the rhetorical stance taken in those other, more directly polemical passages. This miracle is not very polemical towards the doctors at all but is consistent nonetheless with the author's comparisons between their φάρμακα and Thekla's simpler prescriptions, such as clay from the Cilician coast (*Mir.* 18). As noted earlier in this chapter, such comparisons are meant to heighten Thekla's divine status: the power of the healer is in inverse proportion to the sophistication and expense of the remedy.

With regard to the author's first dream sequence, his mention of sleeping in the atrium of Thekla's church is probably a reference to the practice of incubation, in the classical, Asclepian style.[62] Intriguingly, however, the author is not in fact sleeping in her church but only dreaming of sleeping in her church—incubation at a remove.[63] Likewise, in his other two dreams from *Mir.* 12, the author appears to be sleeping at home, not in the church. This is a clue,

---

[62] See pp. 197–210 below.

[63] Nevertheless, two points should be noted: first, as I emphasized in the Introduction, most of Thekla's miracles are not about healing at all; second, incubation is not the standard method of healing for Thekla when she does chose to heal a suppliant. Regarding the latter point, take for instance *Mir.* 12, 38, and 39, three miracles which involve local Isaurian or Cilician literati and which appear to present scenes of incubation. None of these explicitly takes place in an incubation setting, even though visions, healings, and prescriptions are variously invoked. Thus, 1) in *Mir.* 12 the author of the *LM* only has a dream that he is sleeping in the church; 2) it is unclear whether Alypios in *Mir.* 38 does in fact sleep in the church; and 3) Isokasios' healing in *Mir.* 39 does not take place in Seleukeia. Therefore, despite superficial connections with incubatory healing, it could be argued that the *LM* has nothing to do with incubation at all.

I would argue, that in order to understand the healing of the author's finger, it is necessary to consider how the rest of the miracle is told, including the two other dream sequences. For it is clear that *Mir.* 12 is being told as a reminiscence and not as a recent, immediate experience on the author has just had: the rest of the miracle confirms this point of view.

In the second dream of *Mir.* 12 the author is approached by "some black manikin" (ἀνθρωπίσκος τις αἰθίωψ) named Zamaras and handed a dark bronze tremissis. He states that this dream seemed to forebode something: "I took this [tremissis] unwillingly and not with pleasure, I confess; for this dream (ὄναρ) seemed not a prophecy (μάντευμα) of anything good at all" (*Mir.* 12.62–63). The author wakes up to find out he has been excommunicated by the local bishop, Basil, whom he claims had it in for him all along and whom he earlier slanders by calling him a "youngster" (μειράκιον; 12.44) and "little boy" (παιδάριον; 55). He finds out by means of "a white Zamaras" (i.e. Basil himself, whom he now openly calls a drunkard). This Zamaras/Basil comes to him and excommunicates him personally, but without even a single co-accuser present (and with a "foul and rude phrase, I do not lie"; 14.71). The author claims that the public reaction to his excommunication was vociferous, with several prominent individuals coming to his defense, including a certain saintly "Thomas" and the author's own parents (14.76, 85). In the midst of this clamor and confusion, however, he comes to the realization that the events of his dream about Zamaras were "symbols (σύμβολα) and a premonition (προάγγελσις) of the present events" (*Mir.* 12.89–91).

In the third dream, which happens on the second day of his excommunication (ἀκοινωνησία), the author is visited again by Thekla, this time dressed as a young girl "in a white *tribonion*, wrapped around her from the back to the chest and fastened again at the back" (12.95–98). She places something in his hand which turns out to have an exceedingly sweet smell. She then speaks a few words to him: "Hold this and take courage, child, and know that I must hurry on to Macedonia to help a woman in danger" (12.99–101).[64] As Dagron explains in a footnote, Eucharistic bread is often described in patristic texts as

---

[64] This is an allusion to Paul's dream in Acts 16:9: "At night a vision (ὅραμα) came to Paul. A Macedonian was standing, exhorting him, and saying, 'Come to Macedonia and help us!'" The author of the *Miracles* adds the phrase "it befitted her since she was in a hurry" perhaps to forestall the charge of plagiarism, emphasizing the reality of the situation over his skill at allusions (Dagron 1978:323n17). Yet, in the context of Thekla's association with Paul in the *Life*, plagiarism was probably not a serious concern for this author: her quick disappearance has more to do with the pace of the narrative and the author's desire to press on to his vindication and the resolution of the story. As seen in the first miracle recounted in *Mir.* 12, he could dwell at length on Thekla's dream-activities when he so desired.

having a sweet smell.[65] Accordingly, when the author awakes from this third and final dream he has been miraculously re-communicated. As he describes the situation, Thekla forced Basil, against his will, to restore the author to fellowship. The details of Basil's change of mind are not offered, only a reiteration that Thekla accomplished this "wonder-working" (θαυματουργία) on the author's behalf.

These two dream sequences that deal with the author's excommunication at the hands of Basil are fascinating for their portrayal of an ecclesiastical struggle in such hostile (and personal) terms. With regard to the relation of the author's excommunication to the healing of his index finger in the first dream sequence, Derek Krueger has recently argued in his book *Writing and Holiness* that the emphasis on "hands" in *Mir.* 12 (as they feature in each of the three dream sequences) draws attention to the author's writerly piety and the sanction that Thekla places on his vocation and literary project.[66] I would add to Krueger's interpretation that, in narrative terms, the placement of the healing at the beginning of *Mir.* 12 predisposes the reader to believe that Thekla is on the author's side. Or, to put it in terms of the vengeance miracles discussed in the previous section, the author is one of "Thekla's own," for whom she cares and whom she vindicates as the situation may require. The reader is thus alerted to a prior history of Thekla's intervention on the author's behalf before the excommunication is even mentioned. The author's reputation is strengthened by this narrative progression, which is an appropriate rhetorical strategy since the mention of excommunication could potentially bring doubts to a reader's mind.[67]

In addition, the very structure of the miracle confirms Thekla's protection of the author. The middle dream, in which the black Zamaras places a pebble of excommunication in the author's hand, is framed by two dream sequences in which Thekla appears to and helps the author. Thus, the evil that

---

[65] Dagron 1978:321n16. See also Ashbrook Harvey 2002.

[66] Krueger 2004:79–92.

[67] For the sake of a fruitful interpretation, one must insist that the author is in control of the amount of biographical material that he allows to be known in *Mir.* 12—unless he is somehow incapacitated or being careless. Therefore, it is appropriate to assume that the rhetorical value of Thekla's healing, as told at the beginning of the miracle, was strong enough in the author's mind to offset the negative effects of the rest. Of course, as readers we do not have to assent to the success of this wager. Thus, another plausible interpretation might be that he is too obviously trying to restore a damaged reputation, with the prominence of Thekla's healing being an overt use of the rhetoric of patronage. While I think this latter interpretation (basically Krueger's) is to a great degree true, the narrative logic of *Mir.* 12 exhibits more sophistication than has previously been noticed.

is done to the author by Basil is surrounded by Thekla's favor, in reality as well as in narrative structure. Her intervention on his behalf is consequently never in doubt, even during those dark three days of his excommunication.[68]

Moreover, once this narrative structure is taken into account, it is not even clear at the end of the miracle that the grim vision of the black Zamaras is to be taken as a portent of evil. As the author remarks just before his culminating third dream, the events of the second dream were "symbols" and a "premonition" of what actually happened. Indeed, he goes on to say that, on the basis of his reappraisal of the second, foreboding dream, that the events of that dream "would eventually relieve the evil" (12.90–91).

The narrative of *Mir.* 12, therefore, is told both as a circle and as a progression. It is told as a circle in the sense that Thekla's healing of the author's finger and her vindication of his rightful position in the Seleukeian church frame the actual injustice done to the author: in other words, Thekla's attention to his personal needs is both the starting and ending point of his excommunication narrative. At the same time, *Mir.* 12 is told as a progression in the sense that the author only comes to realize the significance of the second, middle miracle once its events have come true. The validity of the "premonition," as he calls it, thus encourages him that Thekla is ultimately behind these events. Of course, the narrative purpose behind both the circular (or ring) structure as well as the psychological progression of the author's cognizance is to emphasize that Thekla was never very far away from these events. While there is no hint of what we might call Providence in *Mir.* 12, the portrayal of Thekla is consistent with (and perhaps paradigmatic for) the other miracles in his collection, both of healing and vengeance. In particular, the assumption that no event escapes her "all seeing and divine eye" (*Mir.* 22) is cleverly worked into this miracle using a complex series of two miracles told over the course of three dream sequences. All the while the author is also making use of multiple structural patterns. Moreover, the author makes use of his own healing as an internal topos to speak about something else, namely Thekla's patronage of his project and the omnipotent and pervasive power of Thekla against sickness and evil. Like when Leontios is healed in *Mir.* 14 for the sake of Maximinos' conversion, *Mir.* 12 is not an isolated healing story but one which points the reader to a larger argument about the character of Thekla. *Mir.* 12 is also very significant for this overall project, not just because it programmati-

---

[68] The "three days" as a reference to the time Jesus spent in the tomb is rhetorically valuable for the author's self-presentation as suffering for a righteous cause. Furthermore, this allusion highlights the literary nature of the miracle itself.

cally concerns the author's own authority in the community, but because it is the longest and most sophisticated attempt, narratively speaking, to represent a specific vision of Thekla, which is carefully constructed throughout the whole of the *Miracles*.

Turning now to a much less sophisticated miracle that concerns the healing of the author, *Mir.* 41, I would like to show in conclusion how his unique vision of Thekla comes to the fore later in the collection, once all the facets of Thekla's divine power to punish and heal have been met by the reader. *Mir.* 41 comes at the end of a four-miracle grouping that concerns the dealings of Thekla with local literati. This grouping is introduced by a transition in *Mir.* 37 in which the author personifies "Letters" (οἱ λόγοι) and claims that they are complaining about having been ignored in the previous miracles.[69] This literary device provokes three healing miracles dealing with Alypios the grammarian (*Mir.* 38), Isokasios the rhetor (literally, "sophist"; *Mir.* 39), and Aretarchos the rhetor ("sophist"; *Mir.* 40). The latter two miracles have been discussed at length above. What is important to note is that this series of literati culminates with the author of the *Miracles* in *Mir.* 41 being healed of an ear infection just before Thekla's annual panegyris, at which he is slated to speak. Thus, the progression of the miracles just prior to *Mir.* 41 places the attention on the author as part of (perhaps as the chief of) a prominent coterie of literati and public speakers in Seleukeia and neighboring cities. Moreover, while Alypios in *Mir.* 38 is clearly a believing Christian, the intervening miracles concerning Isokasios and Aretarchos make it clear that both refused to convert to Christianity, and Aretarchos even attributes his healing to Sarpedon. *Mir.* 41, therefore, emerges as the capstone of a series of "literary" miracles that are bookended by two longish healings which happen to devotees of Thekla, framing in turn two healings performed by Thekla for pagans. The author's comparison and contrast method of collection is clearly visible in this arrangement, with his ultimate emphasis being placed on his own experience as Thekla's chosen conduit for the dissemination of her *Miracles*.

The healing itself is told in the simpler style of Dexianos' healing from *Mir.* 7, with just a brief dream sequence in which Thekla appears to the supplicant. The description of the illness, however, is somewhat more expressive: "My whole ear was inflamed, but it was producing strong pains internally and pushing vigorously against the very base of my skull, on account of

---

[69] He also states somewhat cryptically in *Mir.* 37 that "Letters" are worthy of the blessing of the "institution of the chorus" (χοροστασία; perhaps "public recitation"?). The meaning of this statement is unclear since there are no other indications that these miracle were designed to be read out.

which it was causing a loud internal throbbing" (41.10–13). The author writes in addition that the illness (τὸ πάθος) was so severe that it might have cost him not only his speaking engagement but perhaps also his life (41.14–15). At this point Thekla intervenes, appearing (ἐφιστῆσαι) at night and shaking his ear vigorously with her hand. "She brought the whole affair to an end," as he says, "when a little pus [flowed out]" (41.19).[70] Because of Thekla's timely intervention, the author is able to go ahead with his speech. He says that he made his appearance at the "tribunal" (δεκτήριον), "which is what one calls the place where the orators (οἱ λέγοντες) appear, otherwise called the ambo or the speaker's platform (ἀκροατήριον)"[71]—indeed, he spoke from this platform, he says, because he was not yet (οὔπω οὔτε) numbered "among those who speak in the churches" (41.19–24). This is a reference, most likely, to a certain lay-reader status in the Seleukeian church, a status to which he refers in the epilogue as well (epilogue 31–41), and the δεκτήριον appears to have been a platform set up outside the church where lay *encomia* could be presented at the panegyris.[72]

The miracle ends with a very important summary of the author's perception of his relationship with Thekla. In the end, she made it possible for him to give the speech on her behalf, a speech during which he garnered admiration (θαῦμα) for what he said, even though he modestly acknowledges that it was not an admirable (θαυμαστός) speech (41.24–27). He claims that at some point (perhaps after the speech?) he was judged worthy to become a member of "the council of elders (τῆς ἱερατικῆς γερουσίας) and the catalogue (τοῦ καταλόγου) of preachers and teachers," and during his tenure in this esteemed company Thekla was constantly present alongside him (41.27–29). He says that she continued "almost constantly" to "appear" to him (ἐπιφαινομένη) "at night" (νύκτωρ) and was in the habit of offering him (ὤρεγεν) a book (βιβλίον) or a papyrus (χάρτης). Each of these gifts, he says, appeared to be "a sign (σύμβολον) of her absolute approval (πλείστη εὐδοκίμησις) of me" (41.30–31). He adds at the very end of *Mir.* 41 that if he is going to speak but Thekla does not appear to him in this way, then the inverse meaning—that she disapproves—is just as clear. Yet, despite this final self-effacing caveat, the emphasis

---

[70] The author at this point makes a rather sacrilegious analogy, as Dagron notes (1978:399n6), between the unblocking of his ear and the stone rolled away from Jesus' tomb in the Gospels (e.g. Matthew 28:2).

[71] In Christian texts the term ἀκροατήριον is employed as meaning both "speaker's platform" (see Lampe s.v. where this text is cited as evidence) and "audience hall" (for which see Acts 25:23 and BDAG s.v.).

[72] As noted by Dagron 1978:399n7.

in *Mir.* 31 on the author's patron-client relationship with Thekla is as explicit as at any other place in the *Miracles.*

In fact, this assertion of "absolute approval" recalls the short *Mir.* 31 in which Thekla appears to the author to encourage him to press on in his work. As discussed above, Thekla indicates her approval in *Mir.* 31 by taking a notebook (τέτρας) from his hand and reading it (ἀναγινώσκειν); she also smiles and indicates with her "gaze" (βλέμμα) that she is pleased (ἀρεσκεῖν) with his work. By contrast, in *Mir.* 41, which comes only five miracles from the end of the work, Thekla is depicted as handing him a book instead of taking one away. Admittedly the context is different—the former relates to his miracle collection, the latter to his public speaking—but it might still be argued that this subtle change is perhaps a symbol that the author knew that he was nearing the completion of his work. The taking of the τέτρας in *Mir.* 31 could thus symbolize the unfinished state of the text which needs Thekla's miraculous intervention to produce the finished product, now a βιβλίον, delivered by Thekla herself in *Mir.* 41.

From a narrative point of view, however, this interpretation falters on the organization of the collection—why would he not place *Mir.* 41 right at the end of the *Miracles,* instead of before a few (more or less) inconsequential miracles? Therefore, in place of this more grandiose picture of the construction of the *Miracles,* the narrative unit of *Mir.* 41 requires the reader keep close together the healing of the author's ear, on one hand, and the general approval of his speech at her panegyris on the other. Of course, *Mir.* 12 offers a model for this more modest interpretation: the healing comes at the very beginning, highlighting by its narrative sequence Thekla's prior approval of the author, and only later offering details about the author's public role and relation to the ecclesiastical authorities in Seleukeia. When taken together, therefore, the two miracles that deal with Thekla's direct healing of the author, first his finger (*Mir.* 12) then his ear (41), self-portray an author who is conscious of the ever-shifting status that he has with relation to the "bishop" (*Mir.* 12) and the "elders, preachers, and teachers" (41). Indeed, at times he can be explicitly nasty towards some of these figures: Basil as a "youngster" (μειράκιον) in *Mir.* 12 and Porphyrios as an "ill-mannered bear-pig (ἀρκόχοιρον) of low birth" in the epilogue (epilogue 24–25).[73] Nevertheless, the literary inspiration he draws from Thekla's personal healing miracles on his behalf is immense. In both *Mir.*

---

[73] The term ἀρκόχοιρος is a neologism meaning "bear-pig," not in the sense of invoking a mutant animal but in the sense of combining descriptively the viciousness of the bear and the ignobility of the pig (Dagron 1978:411n3).

12 and 41 the healing is linked through the internal narrative structure of these miracles to the author's self-confidence among those who would seek either to exclude him from the church or who may in some way be his competition, like the pagan rhetors of *Mir.* 39 and 40 or perhaps the other speakers at Thekla's panegyris.

## Conclusion: Literary Collection and Spiritual Correspondence

The two healing miracles that concern the author himself demonstrate more clearly than any other parts of the *Miracles* that the miracle collection and Thekla's divine power to heal and wreak vengeance are, in the final analysis, corresponding entities. This correspondence appears in the *Miracles* in a number of ways.

First, the author's programmatic rhetoric in the preface, the epilogue, and *Mir.* 31 display the *Miracles* as a quest for its own completion. The role that Thekla plays for the author is to encourage the publication of his work as well as to propel its dissemination afterwards (*Mir.* epilogue 8–15). The paratactic style serves this quest very well in its ability to move the reader speedily on from one miracle to the next.

Second, the author places himself at the center of the *Miracles* through the autobiographical literary mode that he adopts in *Mir.* 12, 31, and 41. In emulation of Herodotus, the author uses these autobiographical miracles to buttress his claims elsewhere that the testimony on which he relies is trustworthy. Thus, by combining the first person account of Thekla's healing of his finger and his ear (*Mir.* 12 and 41) with the third person "omniscient" accounts of others' experiences of Thekla's miraculous power, he weaves a web of authenticity in which the alternating first and third person modes reinforce one another. The authenticity and comprehensiveness of his reporting strengthens the correspondence between the miracles Thekla accomplished and the miracles he has included: in other words, "what you see is what you get."

Third, and finally, the author has chosen a specific physical area and type of person which he intends to cover in the *Miracles*. By no small coincidence, this is the same area over which Thekla achieves mastery in performing miraculous feats of vengeance and healing for her suppliants. Topographically speaking, Thekla reclaims in the *Miracles* her divinely assigned authority over the whole region around Seleukeia: from the Sarpedonian cape and shrine in the south (*Mir.* 1), to Mt. Kokusion in the north (*Mir.* 2), and to numerous cities extending as far to the west as Eirenopolis (*Mir.* 19 and 34), and as far to the east as Tarsus and even Antioch (*Mir.* 29 and 17). Thus, the coastline of southeastern Turkey, and especially the estuary of the Kalykadnos, is safely under her watchful eye. In terms of suppliants she only really helps those in prominent positions—the reader is never told why. Only occasionally does she work a miracle for someone who is explicitly poor (e.g. *Mir.* 23). Moreover, it is intriguing that these occasional *pro bono* miracles always include a statement about how Thekla cares for the poor. Surely this rhetorical stance means that the *Miracles* itself was intended for an educated, elite audience: all the miracles deal with wealthy or prominent people except for those which are labeled otherwise. Those whom Thekla helps are the very people intended to read the collection.

This multi-faceted and subtle correspondence highlights the artificiality, or simply the literary quality, of the text, especially in its organization and subject matter. Thus, there are clear groupings of miracles, such as the opening fights against *daimones* (*Mir.* 1–4) and the closing miracles for the literati (*Mir.* 38–41). These groups show the author moving from one theme to another, not very systematically but, nonetheless, in a way that eschews any idea that this is a "random sampling" of Thekla's miracles in Seleukeia. Likewise, the choice of location and class of people generally points to a special interest on the part of the author. This is not at all to say that he simply wrote the *Miracles* from scratch—there are enough narrative anomalies in the stories and a healthy variety of narrative patterns which suggest that he truly was making a "collection" (συλλογή). Rather, the correspondence between the *Miracles* as a text and

Thekla's spiritual activity in Seleukeia underlines the author's role in shaping the source material into what is ultimately an audacious and complex literary work aimed at drawing together multiple strands of experience and legend for the benefit his home city.

What needs to be emphasized most of all, from this point of view, is that the author's choices in rewriting and organizing the (now lost) sources of his collection have a distinctive, literary impact on the view of Seleukeia with which a reader, ancient or modern, is presented. The author attempts to offer that reader a consistent picture of Thekla, and crucial to reading the text aright is understanding that her consistency depends on the author's conception of her role in the production of the collection itself. When a reader is confronted with so intimate a relationship between author and saint, he or she must keep in mind that the saintliness of Thekla is bound up with the author's conception of his own career and literary work. Thekla and the author of the *Miracles* mutually construct one another: the author in showing his devotion by collecting and publishing her "life and works"; Thekla in showing her approval through vindicating, healing, and encouraging the author in his pious endeavor. The *Miracles of Thekla*, therefore, offers a distinctive portrait of its author while attempting to present a new and distinctive portrait of his patron saint. The literary choices summarized and explained above do, in fact, offer a window on the plain of Seleukeia in late antiquity, but this window is the one through which the author himself has decided that we should look.

# Chapter 4

## Greek Wonders: Classical Models for Christian Miracle Collections[1]

### Introduction: Mistaking Content for Form

T HE QUESTION OF WHETHER CLASSICAL LITERATURE had a formative influence on the genre of the Christian miracle collection in late antiquity was left unaddressed by André-Jean Festugière's well known selection of translations, *Collections grecques de miracles: Sainte Thècle, Saints Côme et Damien, Saints Cyr et Jean (extraits), Saint Georges—traduits et annotés* (1971). Likewise, Natalio Fernández Marcos found the similarity of content between Sophronius' collection of saints Cyrus and John and Asclepian ἰάματα suggestive enough to preclude any further inquiry in his *Los Thaumata de Sofronio: Contrabución al estudio de la incubatio christiana* (1975).[2] By contrast, the four main sections of Chapter Four will argue that the standard scholarship on late antique miracle collections has tended to confuse the form of these writings and their content and by doing so has failed to explain adequately the literary history of Christian miracle collections in Greek. In particular, a false sense of security with Asclepian healing has predominated, which has in turn hindered further investigation of the significance of the Christian collections for late antique literary history.

---

[1] This chapter is an expansion and revision of a communication delivered at the Fourteenth International Conference on Patristic Studies in Oxford (Johnson 2003).

[2] The word ἰάματα (literally "remedies" or "healings") is used by scholars as a shorthand for a wide range of votive inscriptions carved and set up for display at ancient Mediterranean healing shrines dedicated to the Greek god Asclepius, principally at Pergamon and Epidaurus (Herzog 1931; LiDonnici 1995; Girone 1998). These texts exhibit significant variations between sites and periods, to the degree that it proves difficult to regard those which have survived as a standardized genre. Nevertheless, the standard shorthand term ἰάματα will be used in this chapter with reference to the corpus as a whole, unless otherwise specified. In addition, the compositional structure of these texts (however various they may be) often betrays literary

This association between Christian miracle collections and Asclepian ἰάματα is made on the background of what seems to have been genuine cultural continuity in the realm of faith healing, between the ancient world and the early Christian. Thus, while Fernández Marcos did not pursue the links between Christian miracle collections and classical literature (including the ἰάματα) as regards the form of these texts, he did produce one of the most thorough and important studies to date of religious continuity in the ancient world. Other scholars have taken this type of analysis even further, linking Greco-Roman and Christian cultural institutions through meta-concepts such as "dreams" and "imagination." The leading study of this type has been Patricia Cox Miller's *Dreams in Late Antiquity*, in which she exposes the broad overlays of cultural creativity among Greco-Roman pagans (or polytheists) and Christians from the second to fifth centuries. As regards healing, Cox Miller has insisted, like Fernández Marcos, on the unity of cultural practice during this period. In fact, she has pointed to the cult of Saint Thekla as the preeminent example of the continuity of the practice of incubation from the ancient world:

> The most spectacular instance of the Christian appropriation of Asclepius is found in the mid-fifth century in the cult of Saint Thecla in Seleucia . . . She healed by appearing in dreams to the sick who were sleeping in her church. Proficient in the application of miraculous medicine, Thekla wore the mantle of Asclepius, now in the guise of a female saint. The conviction that dreams can heal was too deeply embedded in the cultural imagination for it to succumb to the vagaries of religious rivalry. In the figure of Thekla, oneiric aspirations to health lived on.
>
> 1994:117

This statement represents, therefore, a broader conclusion on the development of culture within the history of late antiquity, a conclusion which emphasizes the similarities of cultural institutions and deemphasizes the distinctions between those institutions.[3]

The argument of the present chapter takes a different approach to the textual material which has survived from late antiquity. In particular, while Asclepian healing miracles do appear at a socio-cultural level to have much in

---

characteristics, as Lynn LiDonnici has shown (1995:20–39). On that basis, it is reasonable to compare their literary character to that of Thekla's *Miracles*.

[3] The word "guise" in Cox Miller's formulation is precisely the metaphor which obscures the complex relationship between form and content in religious literature from this period.

common with the "christianized" practice of incubation, the literary form of the miracle collection as employed in the fifth-century AD *Miracles of Thekla* can be shown to work on a different model. Namely, the form of the *Miracles* shares most of its salient characteristics, not with Asclepian ἰάματα, but with ancient literary collections and miscellanies, and particularly with the ancient genre of paradoxography.

Paradoxography was understood to be a sub-genre of history writing in antiquity and took a peculiar view on the value of historical information, a view which is expressed partly through its form and partly through what we can glean from ancient writers about the theory of paradoxography. This view corresponds, in its essential aspects, to what the poet and playwright Louis MacNeice called "the drunkenness of things being various."[4] More specifically, the view highlights what was seen in antiquity to be a typically Herodotean style of history writing, in which anthropological and (eventually) supernatural phenomena are reported in an episodic style that has little or no overarching narrative. This is, of course, a very simplistic view of Herodotean narrative which ignores the complex structure of his *Histories* (see pp. 113–120 above). Nevertheless, the ancient paradoxographers saw themselves as Herodotus' heirs and they did so particularly in comparison with the more overtly political narratives of Thucydides, Polybius, and others.

When Asclepian ἰάματα are looked at carefully, they do not meet the demands of the genre of paradoxography, and paradoxographers generally eschewed the inclusion of healing miracles among their παράδοξα and θαύματα. What one sees in late antiquity, however, is a significant recycling of the paradoxographical form of literature—often considered to be an essentially "popular" mode of writing—but with different content. As I will show, the literary influence of the New Testament is partly the cause of this. Late antique Christian miracle collectors were thus filling old wine skins with new wine. What this convergence means for literary history is that these later writers were more sophisticated in adopting, manipulating, and re-presenting received literary forms than has previously been acknowledged. In addition, it means that any analysis of Christian miracle collections which remains solely on the socio-cultural level is ignoring a great deal of evidence which can bring out the character of the period and the nature of Christian interaction with the Greco-Roman and early Christian past.

To support this thesis, I will offer evidence from the earliest Greek Christian miracle collection to have survived, the *Miracles of Thekla*. Like

---

[4] Quotation taken from Peter Green, *TLS* October 3, 2003.

the literary history of ancient paraphrase presented in Chapter Two, the present chapter will attempt to situate the *Miracles* in a literary historical context primarily for the sake of interpreting the text more accurately and more completely and, broadly speaking, for understanding the development of Christian literature in late antiquity and Byzantium. The close analysis of the *Miracles* made in Chapter Three above is based on the conviction that the form of the collection has much to do with the material being presented. To read the *Life and Miracles* primarily as a source text for social history, or for the sake of displaying the continuity of cultural and religious practice, is no doubt profitable—and the present study builds on previous work in those areas—but scholars of late antiquity are increasingly aware that research of those sorts does some injustice to literary works as they stand. Moreover, late antique and Byzantine writers' preoccupation with form has been recently identified as an important explanandum for the discipline to move forward alongside contemporary critical and theoretical issues.[5] I intend in this chapter, therefore, to contribute to a more holistic reading of the *Miracles of Thekla* by situating the text within a plausible literary history. From this literary history, conclusions can be drawn about the *Miracles'* contribution to the history of Thekla's cult and, more generally, to the religious thought and literature of late antiquity.

## The Heirs of Herodotus: Paradoxography as Literary Tradition

### Paradoxography from Callimachus to Damascius

First attested in the third century BC, paradoxography was closely associated with the ethnographic current of ancient historical writing and was, consequently, associated with Herodotus and somewhat at odds with the political history of Thucydides and Xenophon.[6] Emilio Gabba's statement that paradoxography was "a strand of literary activity of the greatest importance" in the ancient world is justified by two opposing testimonia: 1) Thucydides tellingly distances himself from proto-paradoxographical writing, which he criticizes for its lack of historical discernment (1.29); and 2) despite

---

[5] I am thinking particularly of recent work by Averil Cameron on the nature of late antique heresiology (2003a; 2003b)

[6] The major studies of ancient paradoxography are Ziegler 1949; Giannini 1963, 1964, and now Schepens and Delcroix (1996); the standard critical text of the paradoxographers is Giannini 1966, which collects all the fragments and cross-references those that appear in later collections; the term παραδοξογράφος is a Byzantine coinage: Tzetzes *Histories* 2.35.154, ed. Leone 1968:49; cf. Schepens and Delcroix 1996:381.

Thucydides' protest, the fragments that have survived suggest a vast quantity of paradoxographical literature from the third century onwards.[7]

For the paradoxographers, θαύματα ("wonders") were discrete instances of strange and notable natural phenomena which on their own required no historical explanation. Accordingly, these writers organized their stories into individual segments with no collective thesis or unifying narrative. Sometimes they would order the segments alphabetically or by region, or group them into thematic books, but normally the discrete units follow no pattern at all. The earliest paradoxographer on record is Callimachus of Cyrene (3rd century BC), poet and librarian of the Museum of Alexandria. In addition to his erudite poetry and the Πίνακες—the famous 120-volume catalogue of all books on the shelves of the Museum—Callimachus also wrote a Συναγωγή θαυμάτων τῶν εἰς ἅπασαν τὴν γῆν κατὰ τόπους (*Collection of Wonders from the Whole Earth Arranged by Locality*).[8] This book dealt with such esoteric (yet characteristically authenticated) data as "Megasthenes, the author of a treatise on India, reports that there are trees which grow in the Indian Ocean."[9] The *Collection of Wonders* was only one of Callimachus' many antiquarian books; others, such as the Πίνακες and his Ἐθνικαὶ ὀνομασίαι (Local Nomenclature), were similar reference books, no doubt inspired by having all of Greek literature under one roof in Alexandria.[10] While notably preeminent in the history of paradoxographical literature, Callimachus was only the first of many writers to collect arcane and marvelous stories in this way.

In the late third century BC Antigonus (perhaps of Carystus) wrote his own Συναγωγή ἱστοριῶν παραδόξων (*Collection of Marvelous Researches*) which paraphrased and synthesized Callimachus' *Collection* and replaced the geographical order with a topical arrangement.[11] He seems also to have added

---

[7] Gabba 1983:14; Ziegler 1949:1139. Ephorus (c. 405–330 BC), Aristotle (384–322), and Theopompus of Chios (c. 378–320) all have paradoxographical fragments attached to their names. However, Ziegler 1949:1140 is convinced that these are pseudepigraphical collections written after Callimachus, and Giannini 1966:222–313 concordantly labels Ephorus' Παράδοξα and Theopompus' Θαυμάσια as *opera dubia*; Pseudo-Aristotle's Περὶ θαυμασίων ἀκουσμάτων is printed as a complete, but pseudepigraphical, collection.

[8] See Giannini 1966:15–20 for the testimonia; and Jacob and Polignac 2000:92–95 for analysis and historical context. The title of Callimachus' text (from the *Suda*) is somewhat corrupted: Schepens and Delcroix 1996:395nn68–69.

[9] Jacob and Polignac 2000:92–93.

[10] On the library of Alexandria, its history, and book collections, see Robert Barnes 2000.

[11] On paradoxographical organization, see Schepens and Delcroix 1996:394–399 and Hansen 1996:5. For a study of Antigonus' technique of collection, see Jacob 1983. It should be noted that there were a number of writers named "Antigonus" from the Hellenistic period on: Antigonus the paradoxographer, Antigonus the biographer, Antigonus the historian of art and sculptor,

significantly to the collection, citing weighty ancient writers, such as Ctesias (late 5th century BC), Theopompus of Chios (c. 378–320), and Theophrastus (c. 371–287) in support of his remarkable stories. Two typical examples of Antigonus' collection read as follows:

> The same writer [i.e. Theophrastus] says concerning stones: the one that is found among the Bottiaioi in Thrace, when hit by the sun fire ignites from it. In that place the stones perform the function of coal, but they endure incorruptibly, and even if someone extinguishes them, as has been attempted, they retain the same energy.[12]

> The Ichneumon [weasel], when he sees the asp snake, does not make an attempt on it before calling others to help; and they plaster themselves with mud [as a defense] against the bites and stings; [this is why,] having wetted their bodies, they roll around in the dust.[13]

This juxtaposition of authenticated celestial and geological knowledge with observed habits of the animal kingdom is a defining characteristic of Hellenistic paradoxography.

Yet, despite their rhetoric of natural observation, the primary organizing principle for Callimachus, Antigonus, and the many later paradoxographers is ultimately the compiler's own reading. This bookish, encyclopedic style has led Guido Schepens to comment that "the guided tour around the wonders of the world . . . was essentially a tour within the walls of the library."[14] In this case the library is not a metaphor but a tangible place in Alexandria which seems to have served as the catalyst for paradoxography as a literary endeavor. Callimachus' model proved valuable on a number of counts: first, the form of the collection, resembling the library itself, gathered in one place knowledge that had previously been disparately located; second, the short notices of natural wonders were easily digestible; and third, the material was entertaining and immediately engaged the reader without the added weight of historiographical gravitas. In addition, the open-endedness of these early, paradigmatic collections offered

---

Antigonus the poet and the author of the Περὶ λέξεως. Willamowitz 1881 famously identified them all as the same Antigonus of Carystus on Euboea. Since that study the fragments have been often reorganized, and the traditional identification is consequently much less secure. See now the critical text of Antigonus the biographer by Dorandi 1999:xi–xxxii, with full bibliography. Another recent critical text of note is Musso 1985, which contains the paradoxography only.

[12] Text, Giannini 1966:104.
[13] Text, Giannini 1966:50.
[14] Schepens and Delcroix 1996:382–399.

inspiration for further accumulation of θαύματα and παράδοξα, as seen in the case of Antigonus. To cite Christian Jacob on this point: "Such collections were open structures, inviting elaboration each time they were read. They were a response to intellectual curiosity as well as a certain aesthetic pleasure. They juxtaposed a brevity of formulation with an infinite possibility of expansion."[15] Paradoxography in its Hellenistic form is, therefore, a system of organization and one with its skeleton exposed: it provides immediate and easily referenced access to otherwise hidden, or effectively lost, knowledge and it offers a textual site for extension, epitomization, and reorganization by its eschewing of the fixed boundaries of traditional narrative.

Early paradoxographies like those by Callimachus and Antigonus appear from the surviving fragments to be mainly pseudo-scientific works in terms of their content: the stories are about bizarre plants, geographical formations, and the like. Gradually, however, the content became more fluid, including social customs and sexual oddities. Phlegon of Tralles, a paradoxographer of the second century AD, records a number of stories about the supernatural in his collection of thirty-five marvels.[16] Many of these stories involve ghosts or grotesque accounts of human malformation, such as the following example:

> A child was brought to Nero that had four heads and a proportionate number of limbs when the Archon at Athens was Thrasyllus and the consuls in Rome were Publius Petronius Turpilianus and Caesennius Paetus.[17]

The historiographical tone of this selection is belied by its fantastic subject matter; nevertheless, it shows how these collections could present material of different levels of believability through the same narrative structure and style. The tendency for paradoxographers to write other collections on different topics is exemplified also by Phlegon, who wrote in addition to his paradoxography Περὶ τῶν παρὰ Ῥωμαίοις ἑορτῶν (*On The Festivals of the Romans*), Περὶ τῶν ἐν Ῥώμῃ τόπων καὶ ὧν ἐπικέκληται ὀνομάτων (*A Topography and Onomasticon of Rome*), Περὶ μακροβίων (*On Long-Lived Persons*), and Ὀλυμπιάδαι (*Olympiads*).[18] The first two of these works are now lost, but

---

[15] Jacob and Polignac 2000:93.

[16] Text, Giannini 1966:169–219; English translation, Hansen 1996 and Hansen 1998:249–258 (selections). See also Ziegler 1949:1157–1159; Giannini 1964:129–130; Schepens and Delcroix 1996:430–432.

[17] Trans. Hansen 1998:256.

[18] Titles: *Suda* Φ.527 (Φλέγων, Τραλλιανός). In the *Suda* entry, Phlegon's *On Long-Lived Persons* is coupled with the *Book of Marvels* as one work; this goes against the manuscript tradition, which prints them as separate compositions (Hansen 1996:17–18).

the last two survive (the *Olympiads* only in fragments).[19] As William Hansen has remarked, "linearly organized collections of information on different themes is probably a fair description of Phlegon's literary output."[20]

Thus, it seems clear that throughout the Hellenistic and Roman periods paradoxographers maintained a self-conscious literary tradition which corresponded to a broader interest in the form of the collection. Exponents of this tradition retained as their modus operandi the related processes of "excerpting" (ἐκλογή) and "arrangement" (συναγωγή), with a particular emphasis on the authority of their textual sources.[21] While many of the later paradoxographers are known only through fragments or their titles, their literary tradition appears to have continued until at least the sixth century AD when Damascius, head of the Academy at Athens and the author of the *Life of Isidore*, wrote a paradoxography of his own.[22] According to Photius—who elsewhere applauded Damascius' style and grouped him (as a novelist) along-side Lucian, Achilles Tatius, and Heliodorus—this work contained 372 marvels, arranged in four books according to their kind: fictional stories (παράδοξα ποιήματα), histories of gods (παράδοξα περὶ δαιμονίων διηγμάτων), ghost stories (παράδοξα διήγματα περὶ τῶν μετὰ θάνατον ἐπιφαινομένων ψυχῶν), and natural wonders (παράδοξα φύσεις). Regrettably, Damascius' text is now lost, but its very composition (if Photius can be trusted) shows that paradoxography was a vibrant and lasting literary form which proved amenable to many different types of marvel.[23] It is a significant comment on taste that the cross-fertilization of the novel and paradoxography in the Hellenistic and Roman periods, evident in the very "Second Sophistic" writers cited by Photius, continued to be felt in ninth century Byzantium.

## Literary collections in the Roman empire

The genre of paradoxography is only the most specific outworking of a pervasive trend towards collection in later classical literature which finds its best surviving exponents writing under the Roman empire of c. 200. This trend was certainly influenced by the paradoxographical (and other) collections

---

[19] See *FGrHist* 257 for all the remains of Phlegon's other works. Hansen 1996 includes a translation of *Long-Lived Persons* and the two most substantial fragments of *Olympiads*.

[20] Hansen 1996:17.

[21] Schepens and Delcroix 1996:382–389.

[22] For Damascius and the *Life of Isidore* (or the *Philosophical History*), see now Athanassiadi 1999.

[23] For Photius' notice on Damascius' paradoxography, see *Bibliotheca* cod. 130, ed. Henry 1959–1977:2.104; for his notice on the *Life of Isidore*, see codd. 181 and 242, ed. Henry 1959–1977:2.189–192 and 6.8–56.

pioneered by scholars such as Callimachus and Antigonus. However, it finds its expression in genres, such as the natural encyclopedia and the miscellany, which are related to paradoxography but less specifically defined in terms of their content. These two genres in particular find important exemplars in both Greek and Latin from Pliny the Elder (AD 23/4–79) and Aulus Gellius (125/8–after 180) to John Stobaius (c. 500) and Stephanus of Byzantium (6th cent.).

Indicative of the popularity of this literature in the ancient world is a passage from Gellius' preface to his Latin *Attic Nights* (c. 180) where he names the titles of a number of collections similar to his own:[24]

> And since, as I have said, I began to amuse myself by assembling these notes during the long winter nights which I spent on a country-place in the land of Attica, I have therefore given them the title of *Attic Nights*, making no attempt to imitate the witty captions which many other writers of both languages have devised for works of the kind. For since they had laboriously gathered varied, manifold, and as it were indiscriminate learning, they therefore invented ingenious titles also, to correspond to that idea. Thus some called their books "the Muses" (*Musarum*), others "Woods" (*Silvarum*), one used the title "Athena's Mantle" (Πέπλον), another "the Horn of Amaltheia" (Ἀμαλθείας κέρας), still another "Honeycomb" (Κηρία), several "Meads" (Λειμῶνας), one "Fruits of my Reading" (*Lectionis suae*), another "Gleanings from Early Writers" (*Antiquarum lectionum*), another "the Nosegay" (Ἀνθηρῶν), still another "Discoveries" (Εὑρημάτων). Some have used the name "Torches" (Λύχνους), others "Tapestry" (Στρωματεῖς), others "Repertory" (Πανδέκτας), others "Helicon" (Ἑλικῶνα), "Problems" (Προβλήματα), "Handbooks" (Ἐγχειρίδια), and "Daggers" (Παραξιφίδας). One man called his book "Memorabilia" (*Memoriales*), one "Principia" (Πραγματικά), one "Incidentals" (Πάρεργα), another "Instructions" (Διδασκαλικά). Other titles are "Natural History" (*Historiae naturalis*), "Universal History" (Παντοδαπῆς ἱστορίας), "the Field" (*Pratum*), "the Fruit-Basket" (Πάγκαρπον), or "Topics" (Τόπων). Many have termed their notes "Miscellanies" (*Coniectanea*), some "Moral Epistles" (*Epistularum moralium*), "Questions in Epistolary Form" (*Epistolarum quaestionum*), or "Miscellaneous Queries" (*Confusarum*), and there are some other titles that are exceedingly witty and redolent of

---

[24] The standard critical text of Gellius is Marshall 1990; see also the classic (newly revised) study of Holford-Strevens 2003.

extreme refinement. But I, bearing in mind my limitations, gave my work off-hand, without premeditation, and indeed almost in rustic fashion, the caption of *Attic Nights*, derived merely from the time and place of my winter's vigils; I thus fall as far short of all other writers in the dignity too even of my title, as I do in care and in elegance of style.[25]

Many of the titles that Gellius' mentions are known to have been famous works in his time: for example, the Παντοδαπὴ ἱστορία of Favorinus and the *Pratum* of Suetonius.[26] More to the point, however, in this passage Gellius is associating himself with a wide range of literature and speaks directly to the popularity of various kinds of collections in this period. Yet he intends to dissociate his own book from the above titles because of their pretentiousness—"Attic Nights" is a more "rustic" title than the others. Moreover, just following this passage he criticizes collections that are too capacious, pointing out that his book does not go into too great of depth but is meant merely to inspire study in its readers (*ad alendum studium*, preface 16).

Gellius' argument, therefore, is that the *Attic Nights* intentionally falls short of comprehensiveness—taking him neatly out of competition with Pliny the Elder—yet it is selective enough so as to point the reader in worthwhile directions. Gellius is keen to carve out of a specific literary niche for himself, but, amongst works that seem so similar to his, his positioning only emphasizes how competitive the market for topical collections must have been in the late second century.[27] Moreover, at a later point in the *Attic Nights* Gellius expresses openly his enthusiasm for paradoxographical collections:

When I was returning from Greece to Italy and had come to Brundisium, after disembarking I was strolling about in that famous port ... There I saw some bundles of books exposed for sale (*fasces librorum venalium expositos*), and I at once eagerly hurried to them. Now, all those books were in Greek, filled with marvelous tales, things unheard of, incredible (*libri Graeci miraculorum fabularumque pleni*); but the writers were ancient and of no mean authority: Aristeas of Proconnesus, Isigonus of Nicea, Ctesias and Onesicritus,

---

[25] *Attic Nights* preface 4–10, ed. Marshall 1990:1–2; trans. Rolfe 1946–1952:2.xxvii–xxxi. Many of the titles Gellius mentions here are known from other passages in the *Attic Nights* or from entries in Photius' *Bibliotheca* or the *Suda*.

[26] On Favorinus, see *OCD* 590; on Suetonius' *Pratum*, an influential collection of his *opuscula*, see Schmidt 1994.

[27] On Gellius' rhetorical self-positioning, see Holford-Strevens 2003:28–29, 34–35, 38, 165.

Philostephanus and Hegesias. The volumes themselves, however, were filthy from long neglect, in bad condition and unsightly (*habitu aspectuque taetro*). Nevertheless, I drew near and asked their price; then, attracted by their extraordinary and unexpected cheapness, I bought a large number of them for a small sum, and ran through all of them hastily in the course of the next two nights. As I read, I culled from them, and noted down, some things that were remarkable (*mirabilia*) and for the most part unmentioned by our native writers (*scriptoribus fere nostris intemptata*); these I have inserted here and there in these notes (*his commentariis*), so that whoever shall read them may not be found to be wholly ignorant and ἀνήκοος, or "uninstructed," when hearing tales of that kind . . . These and many other stories of the kind I read; but when writing them down, I was seized with disgust for such worthless writings (*tenuit nos non idonae scripturae taedium*), which contribute nothing to the enrichment or profit of life . . .[28]

There are a number of points that could be noted in this passage, not least of which is its fascinating description of the book trade in Brindisi. However, for our purposes, most important is Gellius' citation of six ancient authors of renown, all of whom were read in the late classical period as belonging to the paradoxographical and antiquarian fold. Aristeas (of Proconnesus) was a semi-legendary historian whose Arimaspea Herodotus relied upon for his description of the Scyths but who also reported stories of magical feats, including his own disappearance and reappearance two hundred forty years later.[29] Ctesias (of Cnidus) was a doctor at the court of Artaxerxes II in the late fifth century BC who wrote a history of the Persians, made up mainly of romantic stories, and was considered a fabulist even in antiquity.[30] Onesicritus (of Astypalaea) was a pupil of Diogenes the Cynic and wrote an encomium on Alexander the Great, a text reputed by ancient readers to be fictionalized but which described geographical and ethnographic features of India.[31] Hegesias (of Magnesia) also wrote on Alexander in the third century BC and was maligned as an "Asianist" by later Atticists.[32] Philostephanus (of Cyrene) was a pupil of Callimachus and the writer of an antiquarian handbook (Ὑπομνήματα;

[28] *Attic Nights* 9.4.1–4, ed. Marshall 1990:1.1–12; trans. Rolfe 1946–52:2.161–167.
[29] See Bolton 1962 with testimonia at 207–214.
[30] *OCD* 411–412.
[31] *OCD* 1068.
[32] *OCD* 674.

*Memoirs*) as well as various works of geography.[33] Finally, Isigonus (of Nicea) was a well known paradoxographer who wrote his Ἄπιστα (*Unbelievable Things*) in two books sometime in the first century BC or AD: he seems to have known Varro in Latin and is cited by Pliny the Elder.[34] Several fragments of Isigonus survive in later paradoxographies, especially the anonymous late second-century Paradoxographus Florentinus.[35] As Gellius says in the passage quoted above, these writers were "of no mean authority" even though their works were *miraculorum fabularumque pleni*. His initial enthusiasm for their wonders, however, eventually subsided, and he became filled with disgust (*tenuit nos non idonae scripturae taedium*) when he examined their content in earnest.

I would suggest Gellius' aversion here to paradoxographical stories is something of a red herring.[36] The process he describes of culling (*carpere*) and noting down (*notare*) the parts that most interested him seems typical of both paradoxography and the miscellany, as well as many of the works noted by title in his preface. Other well known writers can be associated with the methods of literary collections, such as the Christian writer Clement of Alexandria, who also wrote a Στρωματεῖς or "Patchwork" (c. 200–202)—a title mentioned by Gellius (preface 7) and employed by Plutarch in a lost work (Eusebius *Evangelical Preparation* 1.7).[37] Clement's Στρωματεῖς is more thoroughly organized than the paradoxographies or the *Attic Nights* but it nevertheless retains the desultory style that its title suggests. As Clement remarks on the character of his text:

> There is a promise, not to give a full interpretation of the secrets—
> far from it—but simply to offer a reminder, either when we forget,
> or to prevent us from forgetting in the first place. I am very well

---

[33] *OCD* 1171.

[34] Ziegler 1949:1155–1156.

[35] Giannini 1964:135–136; 1966:146–148; Ziegler 1949:1161–1162; Schepens and Delcroix 1996:426–428.

[36] *Contra* Schepens and Delcroix 1996:424, it does not follow that Gellius' apparent distaste for paradoxography is indicative of the genre's decline; if anything this vignette suggests a much broader circulation of these texts than one might assume (that is, if the story is not fictionalized to begin with: Schepens and Delcroix 1996:421–422).

[37] The full title of Clement's work is *A Patchwork of Notes* (ὑπομνήματα) *of Revealed Knowledge in Accordance with the True Philosophy*. His use of ὑπομνήματα, while standard Greek, also recalls collections by Hellenistic writers such as Philostephanus and Parthenius of Nicea; for various uses of the term as a literary title, see Lightfoot 1999:217–222. On *commentarii*, the closest Latin equivalent to ὑπομνήματα—as used by Suetonius in his *De grammaticis et rhetoribus* ("On Grammarians and Rhetors")—see Kaster 1995:101, 145. *Commentarii* is also used by Gellius in the passage from Book Nine quoted above, as well as by Augustine in Book 22 of the *City of God* with reference to miracle stories from Hippo and Carthage (on which see pp. 210–215 below).

aware of how many things have passed away into oblivion in a long lapse of time through not being written down. This is why I have tried to reduce the effect of my weak memory, by providing myself with a systematic exposition in chapters as a salutary *aide-mémoire*; it has necessarily taken this sketchy form.[38]

Clement considers his work a depository of select information, the truth of which, as he says elsewhere, appears differently in different places (1.15.1). There is also a sense in which the Στρωματεῖς is a work that has an open structure, like paradoxography, and could continue to be added to or adjusted later, by Clement even by someone else.[39] This may be the reason the book has no definite ending, and Photius records that the Στρωματεῖς has seven books, when in fact the work has come down to us in eight without any clear evidence of tampering.[40] Thus, the form of the collection served similar purposes for Clement as it did for the Hellenistic and Roman paradoxographers, and all these collections together share literary characteristics, even though the content was quite different between them.

In fact, the early third century AD was especially fruitful for collections of various sorts, and several of them have survived more or less intact. Athenaeus' voluminous Δειπνοσοφιστής (*The Sophist at Dinner*) and Aelian's Ποικίλη ἱστορία (*Historical Miscellany; Varia historia*) and Περὶ ζῴων ἰδιότητος (*On the Characteristics of Animals*) are important Greek miscellanies all written around AD 200.[41] Pliny the Elder's *Naturalis historia* (*Natural History*; AD 77) has already been mentioned as a touchstone for Gellius, but we know it also served as a sourcebook for other Latin miscellanists from this later period, such as Solinus, whose *Collectanea rerum memorabilium* (*Miscellany of Memorable Things*; also c. 200) is made up chiefly of excerpts from Pliny as well as from Pomponius Mela, the famous geographer who wrote the *De chorographia* (*On the Description of Countries*; AD 43–44).[42] Likewise, Diogenes Laertius' Βίοι καὶ γνῶμαι τῶν ἐν φιλοσοφίᾳ εὐδοκιμησάντοι (*Lives and Opinions of Eminent*

---

[38] Clement of Alexandria *Stromateis* 1.14.2 , trans. Ferguson 1991:32.

[39] There is, of course, a large scholarly bibliography devoted to Clement's writings; I would point in particular to the recent study of Emmett 2001, who situates him with regard to the rhetorical climate of the Second Sophistic.

[40] See Ferguson 1991:11–12, who suggests that the work is unfinished.

[41] For Athenaeus, see now Braund and Wilkins 2000; along with the critical texts of Kaibel 1887–1890 and Peppink 1936–1939 (the *Epitome* only); and see the translation of Gulick 1927–1941. For Aelian, see Philostratus *Lives of the Sophists* 2.31; along with the critical texts of Dilts 1974 (Ποικίλη ἱστορία) and Hercher 1864 (Περὶ ζῴων ἰδιότητος); and the Loeb translations of Wilson 1997 and Scholfield 1958–1959, respectively.

[42] *OCD* 1218.

*Philosophers*; c. 200) and Philostratus' Βίοι σοφιστῶν (*Lives of the Sophists*; c. 230–238), while not technically miscellanies, certainly would have derived some benefit from readers' acquaintance with the collective form: they both exploit earlier writings and collections and string together short narratives about the numerous intellectuals they describe.[43] Similarly, several lexica are known to have been produced in this period which collect together arcane linguistic knowledge and present it in a (more or less) readable format. Pollux of Naucratis' Ὀνομαστικόν (*Vocabulary*), Phrynichus' Σοφιστικὴ προπαρασκευή (*Sophistic Preparation*) and Ἐκλογὴ ῥημάτων καὶ ὀνομάτων Ἀττικῶν (*Selection of Attic Verbs and Nouns*), Moeris' Ἀττικιστής (*Attic Lexicon*), Herodian's Περὶ μονήρους λέξεως (*On Anomalous Words*), and Pseudo-Herodian's Φιλέταιρος all date from the late second and early third centuries, though some are better preserved than others.[44] The authors of these Second Sophistic *instrumenta studiorum* (among others) all share with the paradoxographers a taste for order, economy, and esoteric knowledge. Their various productions also share a similar literary form, which further links them, with paradoxography, to a post-Callimachean impulse to collect, organize, and publish.

## Late antique collections, chronographies, and anthologies

This substantial tradition of collection, represented by various types of writing, did not cease after the high water mark of c. 200 but it continued through late antiquity into the sixth century and from there became institutionalized in the medieval world, both East and West. Moreover, in its distinctly late antique forms, it seems to have served as the basis or inspiration for Byzantine encyclopedism in the ninth through eleventh centuries, and many Latin collections were used in the West as teaching tools for monastic communities. These later literary phenomena fall outside the purview of the present survey, which only discusses the high points of a very rich and wide-ranging literary movement up to the time of the *Life and Miracles of Thekla* in the mid fifth century.

---

[43] It should be noted that Diogenes Laertius' and Philostratus' texts are arranged more or less chronologically and thus retain something of an overall narrative, guided by the progress of time. As such, they would perhaps be less open to extension or manipulation than the paradoxographers or miscellanists. Compare, however, the following statement on Diogenes Laertius from *OCD* 475: "In 10.138 Diogenes speaks of giving the finishing touch to his entire work; but the book is such a tissue of quotations industriously compiled, mostly from secondary sources, that it could have been expanded indefinitely."

[44] For Pollux, see Bethe 1967. For Phrynichus, see de Borries 1911 (Σοφιστικὴ προπαρασκευή) and Fischer 1974 (Ἐκλογή). For Moeris, see Dirk Hansen 1998. For Herodian see Lentz 1965. For the Φιλέταιρος, see Dain 1954.

To begin where the last section left off, a comprehensive prosopography of the grammarians from the period AD 250–600 has been made by Robert Kaster (1988:233–440), a study which shows in its 281 entries that the *grammatikos'* vocation in late antiquity was vibrant, attractive, and integral to late antique society. While not all of the individuals he describes wrote treatises on Greek or Latin grammar, many of them did. Most of the extant texts are collections of grammatical and often lexical information, certainly more structured than a paradoxography, but nevertheless firmly within the Hellenistic and Roman tradition of compilation. Most of these grammarians are dated in Kaster's prosopography to the fourth and fifth centuries, but one significant example from the third, who shows the continuity of this tradition, is the grammarian Lupercus of Berytus (born or flourished before AD 268/70).[45] According to the *Suda* he wrote (among other things) a treatise in three books Περὶ τοῦ ἄν (*On the Particle* ἄν), an Ἀττικαὶ λέξεις (*Attic Vocabulary*), a Τέχνη γραμματική (*Manual of Grammar*), and a work in thirteen books Περὶ γενῶν ἀρρενικῶν θηλυκῶν καὶ οὐδετέρων (*On the Male, Female, and Neuter Genders*)— "in (all of?) which he is more esteemed than Herodian," in the words of the *Suda*.[46] While none of these works has survived, the testimony of their titles, as well as Lupercus' reputation in Byzantium, suggests that the form of these writings was comparable to Herodian's Περὶ μονήρους λέξεως or other productions from the second and early third century. Lupercus is an important example, therefore, of the continuity of the grammatical side of literary collections, which was recognized in Byzantium, and presumably in his own time as well, as influenced by or perhaps competing with the earlier generations of grammarians. In fact, were Lupercus' texts extant, it would not be a surprise to find in them citations of earlier grammatical and lexical collections nor (and more to the point) excerpts and epitomations of previously collected material.

Less structured than these *instrumenta studiorum* were the miscellanies, which grew up in the same post-Hellenistic environment of the high Roman empire, as seen in the cases of Aelian and Athenaeus above. To take an important example, also from the third century, the Κεστοί (*Charms*) of Sextus Julius Africanus (c. 180–250) was an encyclopedic miscellany in fourteen (some witnesses say twenty-four) books containing entries on natural history, military science, magic, and various other subjects.[47] According

---

[45] Kaster 1988:305, no. 91.

[46] *Suda* Λ.691 (Λούπερκος), ed. Adler 1933:2.285.

[47] *ODCC* 913. The fragments of the Κεστοί have been critically edited and published with a French translation (Vieillefond 1970). See also the study of Thee 1984 on the magical content of the Κεστοί, with an English translation of the fragments. (Note that the bibliography on Africanus

to Syncellus's ninth-century *Chronicle*, Africanus dedicated the Κεστοί to Alexander Severus.[48] The work survives now only in fragments, but Photius records (not unexpectedly) that the Κεστοί was recycled in later compilations, and in particular as a source for Vindanius Anatolius of Berytus' collection of agricultural pursuits.[49] He also names as sources for Vindanius the writings of Apuleius and Florentius and the παράδοξα of Diophanes, thereby indicating similar material between the Κεστοί and paradoxographical collections.[50] The Κεστοί is also cited in Fulgentius' *Mitologiae* (c. 500), a compendium of allegorical interpretations of various classical myths.[51] Fulgentius, interestingly, calls Africanus "a professor of medicine," a reputation which preceded him in Byzantium as well—according to Francis Thee, Africanus is also cited in at least two Byzantine medical collections, the *Hippiatrica Graece* and the *Geoponica*.[52] Zosimus Panopolitanus (c. 300) also cites Africanus as an authority in his treatise Περὶ τοῦ ὅτι πάντα περὶ μιᾶς βαφῆς ἡ τέχνη λελάληκεν (*On All that the Craft has Said on Unique Dyeing*).[53] All of this evidence suggests that the Κεστοί easily crossed boundaries of scholarship and literary genres, and its reception-history reinforces the picture of the fragments which have survived: namely, that Africanus' miscellany was a repository of many types of information, often paradoxographical or magical in character, and had an open structure which allowed easy quotation and reference. Like Callimachus' paradoxography, therefore, the Κεστοί was a touchstone text which could be endlessly invoked and recycled.

Julius Africanus is best known in modern scholarship as a key contributor to the early development of the chronographic tradition in late antique and medieval literature.[54] Another of his collections, the famous, five-book Χρονογραφίαι (now lost) was potentially (though not certainly) influential on Eusebius of Caesarea's Χρονογραφία and Χρονικοὶ κανόνες (*Chronological*

---

at *OCD* 778 is out of date and deceptively incomplete: the PG text is no longer standard for *any* of Africanus' surviving writings.)

[48] Syncellus refers to the book as having nine volumes; he must have known an epitome instead of the full text (ed. Mosshammer 1984:439).

[49] Photius *Bibliotheca* cod. 163, ed. Henry 1959–1977:2.134.

[50] On paradoxographical and astronomical works ascribed to Apuleius (c. 125–c. 170 AD), see Harrison 2000:29, 37.

[51] For Fulgentius and grammatical discourse in late antiquity, see Hays 2002.

[52] Thee 1984:29–30, 59–62 (with appropriate reservations about the *Geoponica's* authenticity).

[53] *CAG* 2.169, lines 7–8; see Vieillefond 1970:313.

[54] For Africanus' role in this tradition, see Gelzer 1880–1898, Mosshammer 1979:146–157, and Croke 1982. Both Gelzer and Mosshammer argue that Africanus' direct influence on Eusebius was minimal; though both Africanus and Eusebius were hugely influential on the Byzantine tradition (Croke 1990).

*Tables*; c. 325) and subsequently on Jerome's updated translation of the Κανόνες (*Chronicon*; c. 380).[55] From the few fragments that survive, Africanus' Χρονογραφίαι seems to have been organized in a very basic chronological pattern with collected tables of the Greek and Oriental rulers from the time of Adam, listed not synchronically according to each year but separately and diachronically (thus not a "universal" chronicle in the Eusebian sense).[56] In Africanus, therefore, we see a combination of collective genres, the miscellany and the chronicle, each arranged according to their own principles but similarly easily referenced and aiming at something like comprehensiveness. Of course, the fragmentary state of both works prevents a close analysis of their literary forms, but we know that Africanus was acquainted with Origen's school at Alexandria, and he would thus already have at hand a model for compilation in Clement's Στρωματεῖς.[57] Moreover, that the early tradition of the chronicle was bound up with the Christian appropriation of the classical miscellany form is further exemplified by the abbreviated universal history that Clement presents in section 1.21 of the Στρωματεῖς itself.[58]

Origen, in fact, proves to be an important link between Africanus and later Christian writers in this tradition.[59] Not only was his physical library at the catechetical school of Caesarea passed on to Eusebius via Eusebius' mentor Pamphilus, but he too wrote a Στρωματεῖς, which is unfortunately now lost.[60] More importantly, Origen's interest in scholarship on the Bible—exemplified by voluminous commentaries and the innovative *Hexapla*—serves to highlight the literary historical connections between Clement, Julius Africanus,

---

[55] See Helm and Treu 1984 for the critical text of Jerome's translation; for Eusebius' (mostly lost) text, see now Burgess 1999. Eusebius' Χρονογραφία appears to have been the first volume, or at least a preparatory work, of the Κανόνες. It survives (nearly) complete only in an Armenian translation (Karst 1911), but many excerpts can be found in later chronicles. In form it appears much more in the style of Africanus, including separate lists for each nation rather than amalgamating them synchronically according to Olympiadic, accession, or consular dates: see Burgess 1999:31n11.

[56] Croke 1982:196. Interestingly, Eusebius disagreed with Africanus' willingness to discuss Paradise and antediluvian chronology, deciding instead to begin his *Canons* with Abraham (Mosshammer 1979:148). Africanus was himself unwilling to discuss the events of the first day of creation, so did not write his chronology *ab origene mundi* but rather *ab anno Adam* (Adler 1989:46).

[57] On Africanus' *Letter to Origen* and Origen's response, see Harl and de Lange 1983:471–573.

[58] For a detailed literary history of the chronicle tradition up to and including early Byzantium (i.e. Malalas, Theophanes, and Syncellus), see Adler 1989, Mosshammer 1979, and Croke 1990a; 1990b; and now 2001 (chapter 5).

[59] On Origen's school of Caesarea as an important conduit of chronological information for Byzantine chroniclers like Malalas, see Croke 1990b.

[60] Eusebius *Ecclesiastical History* 6.24.3; Jerome *Letters* 33.4; 70.4; Nautin 1977:293–302.

Eusebius, and Jerome.[61] While, on one hand, all of these writers were direct inheritors of a Hellenistic Jewish tradition of scholarship on the Bible and "Universal History," they nevertheless sought out distinct literary technologies through which to convey the received information. One product of their interest, as argued here, was an appropriation of the Hellenistic and Roman tradition of the collection. Cited as evidence are the miscellanies by Clement and Africanus; the latter's Χρονογραφίαι, Eusebius' Χρονικοὶ κανόνες, and Jerome's translation and extension; likewise, Eusebius' collection of martyr acts, the *Martyrs of Palestine*, and Jerome's *De viris illustribus*—the latter explicitly taking its impetus from Suetonius' own biographical compendium *De viris illustribus*.[62] In addition, collective biography also shows its influence in Eusebius' mini-biographies (often substantiated by authoritative sources) from his *Ecclesiastical History* (e.g. Theophilus of Antioch, 4.24). And finally, further evidence is Eusebius' study of biblical topography in Palestine, the Περὶ τῶν τοπικῶν ὀνομάτων τῶν ἐν τῇ θείᾳ γραφῇ (*Biblical Onomasticon*), which has numerous predecessors in the literary history of Hellenistic and Roman geography, such as Pollux, mentioned above.[63] All in all, the scholars connected in various ways with the biblical studies tradition represented by Alexandria's Christian legacy and Origen's school at Caesarea produced a sizable corpus of collective writing, employing various versions of the form for different purposes. Some texts were, of course, more thoroughly edited and arranged than others, but the appropriation of the collective form exemplified by writers of the Hellenistic period and the Second Sophistic is clear enough.

However, collections of classical literature in the Hellenistic model continued to be produced, despite what might seem to be a dominant tradition of biblical studies during the fourth century. For instance, Julius Obsequens composed a collection of divine portents from Livy in the fourth or fifth century, organized according to consulships from 190–12 BC (that which is extant).[64] A typical entry reads like the following:

---

[61] See the forthcoming book on Origen's contribution to biblical scholarship by Anthony Grafton and Megan Williams.

[62] Jerome (*De viris illustribus* preface) cites "[Suetonius] Tranquillus" as the model for his collection (*ad cuius nos exemplum vis provocare*). Suetonius' *De viris illustribus* now only survives in one part, *De grammaticis et rhetoribus*: see Kaster 1995. The narratives of his biographies of Roman emperors were much longer and of a different style yet were themselves published as one collective work, the *De vita Caesarum* (AD 117): see Wallace-Hadrill 1995:1–2 and passim. Richardson (1896) is the standard critical text of Jerome's collection; see also the recent Italian translation and commentary by Ceresa-Gastaldo 1988.

[63] For Eusebius' *Onomasticon*, see Klostermann 1902.

[64] A critical text of Obsequens can be found at Rossbach 1910:149–181; see also the study of Schmidt 1968.

> Cn. Domitio C. Fannio coss. [632 AUC/122 BC]
>
> In foro Vassanio androgynus natus in mare delatus est. In Gallia tres soles et tres lunae visae. Vitulus biceps natus. Bubo in Capitolio visus. Aetnae incendio Catina consumpta. Sallyes et Allobroges devicti.[65]
>
> Gnaeus Domitius and Gaius Fannius consuls.
>
> In the forum at Vassanium a hermaphrodite was born and subsequently driven away in the sea. In Gaul three suns and three moons were seen. A calf was born with two heads. An owl was seen on the Capitoline. Catina was consumed by the fire of Mt. Etna. The Sallyes and Allobroges were conquered.

This excerpt demonstrates Obsequens' persistent interest in paranormal births, but also evident is his propensity for epitomization, economy of expression, entertainment, and arrangement. In these aspects his text resembles, for example, Phlegon of Tralles' paradoxography, which deals with portents in much the same way, offering no historical explanation or interpretation but instead assuming that the salacious and miraculous material (gleaned from an ancient, authoritative writer) will stand on its own.[66] Obsequens' interest in chronology is also significant, especially in the context of its popularity among Christian writers of the period. But, once again, Phlegon of Tralles shows a propensity for this brand of collecting as well, in his work called the *Olympiads*, fragments of which include tabular lists of athletic champions, Pythian oracles decreed at the games, as well as (not unlike Obsequens) world events arranged according to Olympic year.[67] Indeed, a fascinating conjunction of the legacy of chronography, paradoxography, and the miscellany is found in George Syncellus' *Chronicle*, who cites Phlegon, Africanus, and Eusebius to authenticate a point of New Testament reporting: according to Syncellus, they all three independently corroborate the testimony of the Gospels that the sky went black at Jesus' crucifixion (e.g. Matthew 27:45).[68]

Zosimus of Panopolis, the alchemist, has already been mentioned as a witness to the Africanus' Κεστοί. His own Ὑπομνήματα γνήσια περὶ ὀργάνων καὶ καμίνων (*Genuine Notes on Implements and Kilns*; c. 300) has come down to us

---

[65] Obsequens 32 [92], ed. Rossbach 1910:162.

[66] Hansen 1996:18 on Phlegon.

[67] Text, *FGrHist* 257, fragments F.1–34; English translation (fragments F.1 and F.12 only), Hansen 1996:58–62.

[68] Syncellus, ed. Mosshammer 1984:391, 394. The historicity of this event is also emphasized by Origen and the late antique Neoplatonist John Philoponus (Jeffreys 1990:190). John Malalas also quotes Phlegon and Eusebius on this point: 10.14, ed. Thurn 2000:181–182.

as the most significant alchemical collection of the period.[69] The Ὑπομνήματα deals primarily with "the role of alchemy in the process of spiritual purification" and he has been associated by modern scholars with the treatises contained in the multifarious corpus called the "Hermetica" or simply "Hermes Trismegistus," after its eponymous divine author.[70] Interestingly, Zosimus organized his collection alphabetically (κατὰ στοιχεῖον), if his *Suda* entry can be trusted.[71] He was not the first to do this, but alphabetical arrangement is not nearly as common in the ancient world as one might assume.[72] One of the first alphabetical collectors, also a writer on alchemy, was Bolos Mendesios ("the Democritean"; 2nd cent. BC), whose literary corpus contains a wide variety of magical and paradoxographical texts. According to the *Suda* he wrote Περὶ τῶν ἐκ τῆς ἀναγνώσεως τῶν ἱστοριῶν εἰς ἐπίστασιν ἡμᾶς ἀγόντων (*On Matters from [our reading around in] History that Compel Us to Make Inquiries*), Περὶ θαυμασίων (*On Wonders*), Φυσικὰ δυναμερά (*Potent Spells*), Περὶ συπαθειῶν καὶ ἀντιπαθειῶν λίθων κατὰ στοιχεῖον (*On the Sympathies and Antipathies of Stones in Alphabetical Order*), and Περὶ σημείων τῶν ἐξ ἡλίου καὶ σελήνης καὶ ἄρκτου καὶ λύχνου καὶ ἴριδος (*On Portents from the Sun, Moon, Ursa Major, the "Lamp," and the Lunar Rainbow*).[73] Bolos' corpus thus exemplifies many of the common topics investigated by the collectors mentioned above (paradoxography, chronology, astronomy, etc.) and serves as an early example of the alchemical collection tradition. In fact, many sections of alchemical collections put together in late antiquity, such as the *Kyranides*—which also claims Hermes Trismegistus as its author—have been traced back to Bolos.[74] As Bolos' example attests, the recycling of alchemical work in late antiquity became commonplace—work which was divorced from its original author and assigned to a divinity, in a catch-all manner. The received material became, in its individual pieces, building blocks for larger and more comprehensive corpora. As in the case of Damascius' paradoxography mentioned above—and

---

[69] Critical text, French translation, and detailed introduction: Mertens 1995.

[70] Fowden 1986:120–126; Festugière 1944–1954:1.260–282. The Hermetica, or the works attributed to Hermes Trismegistus, do not seem to have been collected in the form we have them today until the eleventh century, though the individual treatises were obviously circulating much earlier than that, and forty excerpts (of varying length) were included by John Stobaius (c. 500) in his *Anthology* (Copenhaver 1992:xlii). Garth Fowden (1986:3–4), however, notes that philosophical (as opposed to "technical") Hermetica did in fact circulate on their own in antiquity, as a comment by Cyril of Alexandria attests: "the man who put together at Athens the fifteen so-called Hermaic books" (*Against Julian* 1.548bc).

[71] *Suda* Z.168 (Ζώσιμος, Ἀλεξανδρεύς). See Mertens 1995:xcvii–ci.

[72] On alphabetization, see Keaney 1973.

[73] *Suda* B.482 (Βῶλος, Μενδήσιος). See Festugière 1944–1954:1.197–200.

[74] Copenhaver 1992:xxxiv–xxxv; Festugière 1944–1954:1.201–216.

as with medical and magical literature in general—alchemical and Hermetic textbooks were large compositions which could accommodate multiple topics impinging on one central theme.[75] Because of this literary characteristic, the collections also tended to grow in size during late antiquity as they were manipulated and added onto, and as the methods of compilation became more widely dispersed.

Alchemical and medical writings served also as a paradigm for Christian writers, who played on their titles and form but substituted different content, as part of their literary polemics against heresy.[76] Thus Epiphanius of Salamis (c. 315–403) wrote his Πανάριον (*Medicine Chest*) in the late fourth century, in which he collected numerous types of exotic heresies, many of which were gleaned from earlier collections such as the Ἔλεγχος καὶ ἀνατροπὴ τῆς ψευδωνύμου γνώσεως (*Adversus Haereses*; *Against Heresies*) of Irenaeus of Lyon (c. 130–c. 200), and the Ἔλεγχος κατὰ πάσων αἱρέσων (*Refutation of All Heresies*; or the Φιλοσοφύμενα) and the (lost) Σύνταγμα πρὸς ἀπάσας τὰς αἱρέσεις (*Treatise Against All the Heresies*) of Hippolytus (c. 170–c. 236).[77] Theodoret of Cyrrhus (393–466) continued this literary tradition—which became institutionalized in Byzantium—with his own Ἐπιτομὴ αἱρετικῆς κακομυθίας (*Compendium of Heretical Myths*), distinguished from the earlier collections in that it replaced the genealogical system of arrangement with a topical one.[78]

---

[75] The similarity between magical, medical, and alchemical writing is illustrated by shared titles in the Byzantine literary catalogues, but the cross-pollination of thought and argument in these occult fields can be seen as early as the Hellenistic period; Festugière 1944–1954:1.189: "La connexion entre les diverses branches de l'occultisme est bien antérieure à la Renaissance ou même au Moyen Age. Elle remonte à la période hellénistique."

[76] Rebecca Lyman has argued that the choice of the form of the medical handbook is evidence of an intra-Christian "assertion of theological authority" by Epiphanius of Salamis (2000:154–155). While the compendium certainly holds natural rhetorical value, one should be aware that this form increased in popularity in all areas of literary production during late antiquity. Therefore, Epiphanius' *Panarion* (e.g.) could very well be seen as a typical product of late antique literature, at least much as an idiosyncratic (or just individual) response to the exigencies of the orthodoxy/heresy debates of the time.

[77] On the nature of Christian heresiological writing in late antiquity and Byzantium, see now Averil Cameron 2003a, with full bibliography; and Averil Cameron 2003b on the categorization of Jews in heresiology. See the critical text of Irenaeus' *Adversus Haereses* (with the Latin versions) in Rousseau and Doutreleau 1965–1982. The standard critical text of Hippolytus' *Refutation of All Heresies* is Wendland 1916; Marcovich 1986 is more recent and has a complete apparatus, but the text contains several editorial conjectures. For Hippolytus' complicated literary corpus and reception history, see Loi 1977; and on the famous statue, now in the Vatican library, which ascribes (in a later inscription) various works to Hippolytus, see Guarducci 1977. For the remains of Hippolytus' lost Σύνταγμα see PG 10.868–869, where the full title is given in a citation by the *Chronicon Paschale*.

[78] Averil Cameron 2003a:478, citing Sillet 2000. Text of the Ἐπιτομὴ αἱρετικῆς κακομυθίας at PG

What has not been sufficiently emphasized in scholarship on heresiological catalogues is that both Epiphanius and Theodoret were the authors of other collections, several of which are non-heresiological in nature. Epiphanius, of instance, wrote a short work *On Weights and Measures*, which tries to define what biblical words for weights and measures mean in contemporary terms.[79] The text is comprised of a list of the biblical words, each accompanied by a short description of its value for contemporary readers and, in some versions, a description of the relationships between the terms. Epiphanius also wrote a treatise on the twelve stones in the breastplate of Aaron (*De xii gemmis*), an idiosyncratic work (and surviving complete only in a Georgian translation) but one which ties him again to the tradition of biblical scholarship and also to the large corpus of ancient mineralogical writing.[80] Much of this writing in antiquity took the form of collections like Epiphanius', and it is not hard to believe he was acquainted with that literary tradition.[81]

In 447 or 448 AD, just prior to the completion of the *Life and Miracles of Thekla* (c. 470), Theodoret published the final edition of his *Eranistes*, which takes the form of a dialogue between "Orthodoxos" and "Eranistes," Theodoret's own position being argued by the former.[82] The work consists of

---

83.336–556. It should be noted, however, that Theodoret had literary precedent for this arrangement in the ἐπιτομή of heretical opinions which Hippolytus included at the end of his Ἔλεγχος κατὰ πάσων αἱρέσων (10.9–29, ed. Wendland 1916:268–284): "But in addition we will first set forth in epitome (ἐπιτομῇ) the [opinions] of the heresiarchs, so that the opinions of all being thereby easy to discern, we may display the Truth as clear and easy to discern also" (10.8, trans. Legge 1921:2.153). These summaries are presented just in front of a statement on the true faith which closes the book (10.30–34, ed. Wendland 1916:285–293). This presentation—i.e. heretical compendium + closing statement of orthodoxy—also appears in Epiphanius and Theodoret (Averil Cameron 2003a:477–478), a literary alignment which further illustrates the long tradition of heresiology, and the importance of Hippolytus as a literary model.

[79] The Syriac version of this text is understood to be the oldest surviving (Dean 1935); the original Greek survives only in fragments (*CPG* 2, no. 3746); there are also versions in Armenian (Stone and Ervine 2000:78–81, 103–108) and Georgian (van Esbroeck 1984), both of which show different attempts at rendering biblical values in contemporary terms. *On Weights and Measures* contains other treatises on popular themes in ancient biblical scholarship, such as the names of the translators of the Septuagint: "Indeed, the work contains much material that has no relation to weights or measures, and it could much more appropriately be called a Bible handbook" (Dean 1935:3).

[80] For textual information on the *De xii gemmis* see *CPG* 2, no. 3748.

[81] Admittedly, the ancient "lapidary" tradition lacks Epiphanius' biblical focus. For mineralogical writing in the ancient world, see *OCD* s.v. "mineralogy"; for late antique "lapidaries" (writers of semi-mystical collections on gems), see Halleux and Schamp 1985: "les lapidaires sont toujours des compilations" (xvi).

[82] Text, Ettlinger 1975; English translation, Ettlinger 2003. The name *Eranistes* is thought to come from ἐρανισάμενοι ("collectors") and describes those who would weave together various opinions, just as one sews scraps of cloth together (*Eranistes* 61.21–62.7): see Ettlinger 1975:5n2.

three dialogues, each of which is followed by a section of *florilegia*. The *florilegia* are theological quotations that defend the argument of Orthodoxos and are taken from authoritative writers (all bishops) from Ignatius of Antioch to John Chrysostom.[83] Cyril of Alexandria had previously used the technique of *florilegia* in his disputes with Nestorius, subsequently influencing a whole generation of theological and polemical writers and inaugurating what would become a standard form of theological argumentation in Byzantium.[84] The *florilegia* in the *Eranistes*, therefore, stand at the beginning of a literary tradition of collecting the wisdom of the biblical, and especially patristic, writers for contemporary theological concerns. As a compendium of easily referenced and authoritative information, the *Eranistes* shares essential elements of late antique collections across the board. Moreover, it shares this form—that of the collective *florilegia*, not of the dialogue—with another of Theodoret's literary collections, the Θεραπευτικὴ ἑλληνικῶν παθημάτων (*Remedy for Hellenic Maladies*), which is a systematic compendium containing self-standing entries on topics of metaphysics and moral philosophy.[85] And, as with Eusebius a century or more earlier, one could even associate the biographical *Historia Religiosa* (*History of the Monks of Syria*) with Theodoret's more academic collections: particularly in that the *Historia Religiosa* collects together short biographies of famous Syrian monastics with little to unify them except the overall theme announced by his title.[86] Again, like parts of Eusebius' *Ecclesiastical History*, Theodoret's mini-biographies are often substantiated by documentary accounts and historiographical autopsy, are easily referenced, and are even entertaining.

On the basis of the broad literary corpora of Epiphanius and Theodoret—two of the most virulent heresiologists of late antiquity—it could be said that the technique of literary compilation was not a tool of "christianization," as argued by Hervé Inglebert, as much it was simply a common means of literary expression, shared by writers of different religious commitments.[87] In fact,

---

[83] Interestingly, Theodoret also includes substantial quotations from condemned heretics, Apollinarius and Eusebius of Emesa; for the role of these quotations in the *Eranistes*, see Ettlinger 1975:25–26.

[84] On Cyril's importance for this tradition, see the references at Ettlinger 1975:24n2. See also Averil Cameron 1990: "The doctrinal polemics which raged throughout the period [of Iconoclasm], especially in its later phase, focused a tendency already in existence to codify views of the past into competing sets of approved and authoritative versions" (207). In the sense that Theodoret and Cyril were on opposing sides of the Council of Ephesus (and after), this tendency was in existence by the early fifth century.

[85] Critical text and French translation, Canivet 2000–2001.

[86] Critical text and French Translation, Canivet 1977–1979; English translation, Price 1985.

[87] See Inglebert 2001a. While I am resistant to Inglebert's unqualified invocation of "christianiza-

what is most distinctive of the catalogue or compilation form in late antiquity is that it was not religiously affiliated at all, but was suitable for scientific, medical, scholarly textbooks, as well as (when the occasion arose) polemical and religious discourse.

## Paradoxography as exemplar of collection

The literary history of Hellenistic, Roman, and late antique literary collections is rich and important, principally because it reveals a substratum of ancient literature that is rarely talked about on its own. Instead, these texts are usually mined by scholars for the otherwise lost information they contain about the ancient world. The present chapter, however, is designed neither to present its own comprehensive catalogue of ancient collections nor to argue that treating collections as sourcebooks for philology and social history is bad scholarly practice. Rather, I have tried to offer only a glimpse of the broad literary historical context within which the fifth-century *Miracles of Thekla* is best situated.

Further, within that broad field of late ancient literary collections, I have suggested that the genre of paradoxography, which originated in the Museum library of Hellenistic Alexandria but which continued until the sixth century, is the best single candidate for the origins of the form of the *Miracles of Thekla*, out of all the collective works surveyed above. There are several reasons for this. The intimate relationship between the paradoxographies of Callimachus and Antigonus shows an awareness of an understood generic tradition. Likewise, the many citations by later paradoxographers of these early figures is evidence of the continuity and reception of this tradition—as is, in particular, the association of paradoxography with Herodotus and the ethnographic strain of ancient history writing. That Herodotus is invoked at the beginning of the *Miracles* as a figure for *emulatio* comes as much less of a surprise when the paradoxographical tradition is evoked as a context for the collection (see pp. 113–120 above).

Additionally, the vocabulary for paradoxography remains very consistent over time, and it is shared by the *Miracles of Thekla*. As I will show in

---

tion" in explaining the rise of heresiology, I have no disagreement with the following statement: "La conversion au christianisme se traduisit dans l'Antiquité tardive non tant par le passage d'une culture à l'autre, que par la réorientation de l'ancienne culture dans un sens chrétien" (2001a: 125). However, it still remains to be worked out what this means in a broader literary historical sense. While he has begun this project with an important study (Inglebert 2001b), he has not sought to explain the pervasive influence of the compendium form across religious, linguistic, and cultural boundaries.

the next section, the terms the author of the *Miracles of Thekla* uses for Thekla's supernatural activities are θαύματα and παράδοξα, not ἰάματα as in Asclepian inscriptions, nor σημεῖα and τέρατα as in the New Testament. I am ready to admit that the semantic range of θαύματα and παράδοξα has been extended from the Hellenistic and early Roman world by the time of the fifth century. But I would suggest that the genre of the paradoxography has also been extended, so as to cover healing miracles as well as natural wonders. θαύματα and παράδοξα always retain the sense of "something extraordinary" throughout their long usage, but even by the time of Phlegon of Tralles, these words are able to describe portentous births of mutant humans and stories about ghosts—in addition to the natural wonders of Hellenistic tradition. Moreover, only about half of Thekla's miracles are actually about healing—this fact of the text has been underappreciated. Many of her θαύματα are displays of divine or supernatural power, often with consequences for the natural elements (see pp. 123–146 above). I would submit that the flexibility in late antiquity of θαύματα and παράδοξα, and therefore of paradoxography as a genre, is exemplified foremost by the variety of "wonder" that one reads in the *Miracles of Thekla*.

The final reason for considering paradoxography as the specific example of collection most worthy of associating with the *Miracles* is that other types of collections tended to grow more and more technical during late antiquity.[88] Paradoxography, however, does not exhibit this trend, nor does Thekla's *Miracles*. Both paradoxography and the *Miracles of Thekla* are more casual in their approach to collection, arranging their material with no real structure or overarching argument. In this sense both paradoxography and the *Miracles* show genuine affinity with the genre of the classical miscellany. Aelian's Ποικίλη ἱστορία and Julius Africanus' Κεστοί both stand out as essential comparanda for the rise of the Christian miracle collection.

It is never wise to reduce the author's choice of literary form to a question of origins. Reductionism of this sort denies the value of differences, even small ones, between his text and the tradition, differences which can often be an indispensable guide to the creative success and discursive practices of a given author. Nevertheless, in order to achieve an understanding of that success (or failure) one must be able to measure somewhat precisely the distance from

---

[88] For instance, one sees in the sixth century (not covered in the present study) an increased usage of alphabetization: e.g. in Stephanus' Ἐθνικά or in the epitome of Harpocration's *Lexicon* (Keaney 1973). One also sees, either an intense thoroughness on the part of the collector (Stobaius and Stephanus), or an increased specialization in his chosen topics (John Lydus), the latter trend perhaps mimicking the specialization of grammatical writers of all periods.

forebears and competing authors. Genre, while easily fetishized in scholarship, is a necessary tool of literary history and analysis. Fortunately, the genre of "the collection" as described (more synchronically than diachronically) in this chapter is broad enough to allow the Miracles to have multiple sources for comparison within one literary field.

As argued here the genre of paradoxography offers a number of points of correspondence with the Miracles. In fact, the correspondence is sufficient enough to suggest that the author of the Miracles was familiar with the paradoxographical tradition and its internal identifiers and literary characteristics. At this point, it is necessary to explain how the text relates to its traditional dialogue partner, the Asclepian ἰάματα.

## Asclepian *Iamata*, "Priestly Redaction," and Aelius Aristides

### The terminology of wonder

As illustrated in the previous section, the historical trend over time within the tradition of paradoxography was away from technical pseudo-science and towards the fantastic and supernatural—"teratology" in its specialized definition. The increasing interest in portents is exemplified by Phlegon of Tralles in the second century AD, who was one of the first of several authors to incorporate sensational stories into his collection. Other later exemplars were Damascius, who included "Ghost Stories" (παράδοξα διήγματα περὶ τῶν μετὰ θάνατον ἐπιφαινομένων ψυχῶν) as one of four sections in his paradoxography (according to Photius) and John Lydus, whose De ostentis comprised a concise but thorough collection of earthquakes and celestial phenomena for the purpose of predicting the future. What had essentially changed about paradoxography by the sixth century was its interest in the divine and supernatural. Callimachus in the third century BC had been chiefly interested in those natural phenomena which went against what one expected from nature—παράδοξον, after all, means "contrary to expectation"—but there is nothing especially supernatural about the Hellenistic paradoxographies which have survived. By contrast, Lydus called his work on celestial phenomena Περὶ διοσημειῶν (On Divine Portents), indicating a changed sense of their relationship to natural expectations. One now expected to be surprised from above or outside nature, rather than perplexed within it.

The term "teratology" comes from the Greek τέρας (or τέρατα in the plural) and in antiquity was applied in its various Greek forms (τερataλογέω, τεραταλογία, τερατaλόγος) to writers or writings which displayed a penchant for the paranormal. Thus in Philostratus' *Life of Apollonius of Tyana* the word τεραταλόγος is used as an Egyptian slander against the Greeks, in parallel with μυθολόγος, and emphasizes a stereotypical addiction to fantasy.[89] Τέρας in its root meaning of "wonder" or "portent" goes back to Homer but retains, through the Hellenistic period, a separate existence from παράδοξα and θαύματα.[90] The word appears frequently in the New Testament, where it is often used for the "signs" or "portents" that vouchsafed the ministries of Jesus and the apostles.[91] Even more familiar from this literature, perhaps, is the term σημεῖον (or σημεῖα), with which τέρας is often paired. For instance, in Peter's speech at Pentecost in Acts 2:

> You that are Israelites, listen to what I have to say: Jesus of Nazareth, a man attested to you by God with deeds of power (δυνάμεσι), wonders (τέρασι), and signs (σεμείοις) that God did through him among you, as you yourselves know.
>
> 2.22

and then again, just following Peter's speech:

> Awe came upon everyone, because many wonders and signs (τέρατα καὶ σημεῖα) were being done by the apostles.
>
> 2.43[92]

This exact language is shared by paradoxography in the Roman period, and many scholars have connected the Gospels and Acts to a paradoxographical literary milieu.[93]

However, despite this evidence of shared vocabulary, many of the New Testament τέρατα καὶ σημεῖα are miracles of healing, indicating a disjunction of content with the paradoxographers. Paradoxography, as shown above, never included healing miracles. It veered increasingly towards the para-

---

[89] *Life of Apollonius* 3.32. The *Miracles*, in fact, also employs this stereotype in its programmatic introduction (*Mir.* preface).

[90] LSJ s.v. "τεραταλογέω."

[91] For the interactions of τέρας, σημεῖον, and δύναμις in the New Testament, *TDNT* s.v. "τέρας" (8.113–126, esp. 124–125; article by K. H. Rengstorf). For the word τέρας in classical literature, see Stein 1909.

[92] Trans. NRSV; τέρατα καὶ σημεῖα: Matthew 24:24; Mark 13:22; John 4:48; Acts 2:19; 2:22; 2:43; 4:30, 6:8, 7:36, 15:12; Romans 15:19; 2 Corinthians 12:12; 2 Thessalonians 2:9; Hebrews 2:4. On miracles in Luke-Acts, see Kee 1980:194–220. See also Achtemeier 1970 for the miracle collections underlying the Gospel of Mark.

[93] On the literary relationships between the Gospels, ancient biography, the Greek Novel, aretalogy, and paradoxography, see Burridge 1992, Wills 1997, Beck 1996 (cf. Merkelbach 1994), and the classic studies of Reitzenstein 1906, Weinreich 1909, and Söder 1932.

normal but never arrived in the realm of physical healings. Instead, these were the domain of what some scholars have labeled "aretalogy." According to a standard view, the best surviving examples of aretalogy are the inscribed cures (ἰάματα) performed by the god Asclepius, especially at his pilgrimage and healing shrines, such as Epidaurus and Pergamon.[94] These inscriptions were set up on votive stones (στῆλαι) of various sizes, beginning from the fourth century BC, within the sanctuary area (τέμενος) of Asclepius' temple. The inscribed στῆλαι were post-healing offerings, paid for by grateful recipients; though the stories they tell, of their ailments and healings, are communicated through the skills of paid artisans, who inscribed the stones on site.[95]

The cultic context would therefore lend itself to be compared to Christian miracle collections such as the *Miracles of Thekla*, since cult and text go together in both cases. Yet, there are several problems with this association. First, the terminology of the *Miracles* is very much in the paradoxographical tradition. Second, no collections of ἰάματα have survived in textual form; rather, they seem meant only to be read on site and were not distributed.[96] Third, the literary style of the inscriptions on the στῆλαι is not high, but the *Miracles*, on the other hand, is written in educated Attic Greek. Finally, only about half of Thekla's θαύματα are miracles of healing, and many are wonders of divine power, some even highlighting her divine control over the natural elements. Given all of these difficulties, it is safe to say that the literary relationship between the ἰάματα and the *Miracles* is a very complicated one, if there is one at all. It is also the case that the problem has never been addressed in any detail in the scholarship—instead, as mentioned above, an association between Asclepius and Thekla has been more or less assumed on the basis of these texts (but without close analysis). What follows below is therefore a provisional attempt to understand the thorny overlap between paradoxography, Asclepian ἰάματα, the New Testament, and early Christian miracles.

[94] On aretalogy, see Chaniotis 1988:19–23; in relation to New Testament scholarship, see Smith 1971 and references. Winkler 1985:235–238 rightly emphasizes the division between an *aretalogus*, who told stories and "miracles" (ἀρεταί) of the gods for entertainment (Suetonius *Augustus* 74; Juvenal 15.16; Ausonius *Letters* 13), and the genre ἀρεταλογία, for which there is little evidence in ancient literature: "what we are describing is an activity and an ability ... rather than a formal religious office or a genre with fixed rules of style and content" (236–237; cf. Reitzenstein 1906). As something less than a genre, such flexibility contrasts even more with the accepted, paratactic structure of paradoxography and Thekla's *Miracles*. On the title *aretalogus*, see Aly 1935 and Smith 1971:174–176.

[95] On the *stelai* see LiDonnici 1995—Epidaurus only, but with analysis—and Girone 1998—all the inscriptions, no analysis.

[96] Some aretalogies *may* have circulated in a form similar to paradoxography; however, the evidence is not certain and none of these texts has survived. Smith 1971:177n27 lists ancient testimonies to written (not inscribed) aretalogical collections.

Thekla's miracles between paradoxography and Asclepian votives

It is important to consider first the way the *Miracles of Thekla* signals and employs its own form in order to identify as much as possible the formal consciousness of its author. This analysis will suggest some ways in which he has passed over other genres and adopted a method of organization that most resembles paradoxography. It will also point out how the experience of healing can be described in multiple ways, even among Asclepian "aretalogies": the spectrum of miracle telling in the ancient world was a broad one.[97]

First, in terms of vocabulary, the author of the *LM* does use σημεῖα and τέρατα, known from the New Testament, and ἰάματα, the key term of Asclepeian aretalogies. However, σημεῖα and τέρατα are mainly confined to the first half of his text, the *Life of Thekla*, and are used in reference only to the deeds of Jesus and the apostles.[98] Thekla herself does not work any miracles in the *Life* until she has already arrived in Seleukeia at the end of that text, and those miracles (θαύματα) are designed to "lead everyone to faith" (potentially an allusion to the σημεῖα of divine power in Acts).[99] Moreover, it is only after her mystical disappearance into the ground and her adoption of a spiritual, ghost-like nature that Thekla actually begins to perform healings (ἰάματα) in the Asclepian style: that is, through incubation and dreams.[100] Thus, there are three stages represented in the vocabulary of the *Life*—pre-arrival at Seleukeia (σημεῖα), in Seleukeia (θαύματα), and post-disappearance (ἰάματα). One could therefore postulate, within the *Life* itself, a development of vocabulary which imitates the development of Thekla's career: she begins by working "portentious" signs imitative of Jesus and the apostles but culminates in healings of physical ailments imitative of Asclepius. However, once the reader gets to the *Miracles*, something unexpected happens. Instead of continuing this aware-

---

[97] As an aspect of ancient and late antique religion, this breadth of representation could potentially illustrate a wide diversity of practice. But it certainly means that we should be careful about associating too closely the social practices of cults across different cultures and practices of writing. Nevertheless, as I will emphasize in the next section, the striking unity of collective forms in the post-classical world provides a space for investigating junctions and disjunctions between religious literatures.

[98] Τέρατα and σημεῖα: e.g. *Life* 26.25 (cf. *Miracles* preface 24).

[99] *Life* 28.5–6: καὶ διὰ τῶν θαυμάτων μάλιστα πάντας ἐναγαγοῦσα πρὸς τὴν πίστιν.

[100] This is by way of contrast to other contemporary versions of her sojourn at Seleukeia, which have her healing the sick during her lifetime (see LB 1.271–272 and Appendix 1 below). On incubation at Asclepius shrines, a practice still understood only in its general outlines, see the classic studies of Deubner 1900 and Hamilton 1906; and now Dorati and Guidorizzi 1996; see also shorter studies by Fernández Marcos 1975:23–86; Edelstein and Edelstein 1998 [1945]:2.145–158; and Dodds 1951:110–121.

ness of ἰάματα signaled at the end of the *Life*, the author instead reverts to calling all of Thekla's miracles (including the ones of healing) θαύματα and παράδοξα—precisely at the point when she is at the height of her career as a divine healer.

Compare, for instance, the use of ἰάματα at *Life* 28.11–12, "[In the place where she disappeared] Thekla dispenses fountains of healings (πηγὰς ἰαμάτων) for every suffering and every sickness," with θαύματα at *Mir.* 4.14, "Of such a kind were the wonders (θαύματα) of the martyr against the *daimones*." Likewise, compare the use of παράδοξον at *Mir.* 15.43–44, where it is used synonymously with θαῦμα: "In this way the island of Cyprus was filled with this miracle (θαύματος), and our city Seleukeia was not ignorant of the marvel (τὸ παράδοξον)."[101] This use of terminology thus highlights from the start that Thekla's miracles are not necessarily, nor perhaps primarily, conceived of in terms of physical healing. Additionally, the adjectives ἄπιστος, ἴδιος, and ξένος, which are used often in traditional paradoxography to refer to the wonders themselves, are used throughout the *LM* in relation to outsiders, or perceived outsiders, such as of Paul by the persecuting citizens of Iconium (e.g. *Life* 3.50). Admittedly, the valence of these words in the *Life and Miracles* is different from their use in the paradoxographies (except ἴδιον at *Mir.* 36.26); nevertheless, they testify to a persistent interest in concepts such as "foreign" and "disbelief" which the paradoxographers associated with Herodotus.[102] In the end, therefore, the author of *Miracles*, though clearly aware of the terminology of classical healing, as he showed at the end of the *Life*, prefers instead the terminology of natural wonders and historiography. And it should be noted by contrast that the healings described in Asclepian inscriptions are always called ἰάματα and never παράδοξα.[103]

An even more significant point of comparison is the fact the Asclepian inscriptions retain their own unique formulae, which do not correspond to the formulae of natural wonders and do not even agree among themselves. In fact, it is difficult to point to one inscription as typical of the Asclepian corpus as a whole. For instance, on the same *stele* (α) at Epidaurus can be found the following two inscriptions:

[101] The latter miracle concerns a Cypriot boat full of pilgrims coming to her festival. Thekla saves the boat from crashing on the rocks of the Isaurian mainland in the midst of a surprise thunderstorm; see p. 140 above.

[102] For these concepts in Herodotus see Rosalind Thomas 2000. The word ἄπιστος does occur on an Epidaurian *stele* as an epithet of a skeptic who is subsequently himself healed (α.32; LiDonnici 1995:86).

[103] For ἰάματα in Asclepian inscriptions, see LiDonnici 1995:84 (α.2), 88 (α.35), and 144–155 for her "glossary"; see also Girone 1998:79 (3.1.2).

Once a man came as a suppliant to the god who was so blind in one eye that, while he still had the eyelids of that eye, there was nothing within them and they were completely empty. Some of the people in the sanctuary were laughing at his simple-mindedness in thinking that he could be made to see, having absolutely nothing, not even the beginnings of an eye, but only the socket. Then in his sleep, a vision appeared to him. It seemed that the god boiled some drug, and then drew apart his eyelids and poured it in. When day came he departed with both eyes.[104]

Nicanor, lame. When he was sitting down, being awake, some boy grabbed his crutch and ran away. Getting up he ran after him and from this became well.[105]

Almost nothing unites the formulae of these two Asclepian inscriptions except the basic transition from sick to well. They share neither a cultic terminology nor a style of narration. Whereas the god appears and acts in the first, he is completely absent in the second. The first is several sentences long and includes a personal vision; the second is very brief and secondhand. In the first, a radical cure is needed to heal a blind man whose infirmity is noted even by other suppliants; in the second, we are left in doubt as to whether Nicanor was even really lame to begin with. An interesting fact should be noted about this juxtaposition: the accepted discourse of the healing shrine was clearly loose enough to allow this broad variation in inscriptional texts. Nevertheless, this brief comparison suggests that Asclepian ἰάματα, at least in their inscribed form, were not internally consistent enough to serve as a model for the formulaic narration that we find in Thekla's *Miracles*.

To press the point a little further, the latest inscription from an Asclepian shrine has been dated to the fourth century, and that is on a *stele* from Athens, not from Pergamon or from Cilician Aigai.[106] The latter is by far the closest shrine to Seleukeia at around 200 km but it has thus far yielded no inscriptions at all.[107] It is therefore likely that the author of the *Life and Miracles* had

---

[104] *Stele* α.9, ed. and trans. LiDonnici 1995:92–93.

[105] *Stele* α.16, ed. and trans. LiDonnici 1995:96–97.

[106] Girone 1998:36–38.

[107] Inscribed votives were not standard at every shrine; e.g. Epidaurus appears to have been the only predominately "textual" site from mainland Greece (LiDonnici 1995:42). For the shrine at Cilician Aigai, which was famously destroyed by Constantine in 326 and perhaps restored by Julian ("at the expense of the bishop"), see Edelstein and Edelstein 1998 [1945]:1.196, 418–421; and for the archaeology, see Hild and Hellenkemper 1990:1.160–164.

never seen an ancient Asclepian votive inscription in situ, unless he had traveled widely and was acquainted with much older inscriptions. This is despite his awareness of the shrines' existence and their popularity throughout the world. Thus, at the beginning of the *Miracles* he writes:

> The spokesmen and servants of the prophecies (χρησμολόγων) of the demons, the interpreters of Pythian portents (τερατευμάτων)—I am speaking of those of the chattering Zeus at Dodona [in Epirus], and of the Pythian Apollo at Delphi, and also of the one who makes his divinations (τὰς μαντείας) beside the waters of Kastalia [i.e. Parnassus = Delphi], and of Asclepius, either in Pergamum, Epidaurus, or nearby Aigai. They have put into writing, at many times and about many people, oracular responses and remedies for sufferings. Some are myths (μῦθοι), fictions (πλάσματα), and the ingenious inventions (κομψεύματα) of those who wrote them down, who desired to confer upon demons a certain energy, strength, and foreknowledge. Others are plausible responses (πιθανά) and are often nearly authentic prophecies, but are full of much ambiguity and equivocation, so that those who receive their prophecies are without fail overcome by perplexity (ἀπορίας), and they are not able to make use of the oracles they received, or, in making use of them, they perish utterly (συναπολομένους ἄρδην) in these same oracles (θεσπίσμασι) and divinations (μαντεύμασι). For in puzzles (αἰνίγμασι) and riddles (γρίφοις) lies all the distinction (φιλοτιμία) of the oracles (τῶν χρησμῶν).[108]

*Mir.* preface 23–38

The author's knowledge of pagan religion is thus limited to the following facts: it is demonic, it is deceptive (even to the most earnest of suppliants), there are certain sites in the world where it flourishes, and the oracles' honor is undeserved. With regard to the last point, the author shows by reference to the story of Croesus, which he places just after the quotation above, that he has gleaned much of his knowledge from Herodotus, who also highlights

---

[108] All of the representations of pagan religion in the *LM* are formulaic; they are literary appropriations of earlier Christian polemic and should not be read transparently as representing active Christian-pagan conflict at Seleukeia in the fifth century. (Cf. Dagron 1978: "Le paganisme, ses dieux, ses adaptes, reviennent comme un thème constant dans les *Miracles*, prouvant que la victoire officielle du christianisme n'a pas entraîné la suppression immédiate de toute dévotion et de toute culte anciens." [80]) Theodoret's claim that some locals still worshipped Asclepius in secret appears less formulaic than the *Life and Miracles* (Edelstein and Edelstein 1998 [1945]:1.10–12).

the instability of oracular pronouncements. If anything, the connection between the *LM* and pagan religion is historiographical and literary historical, not coming directly from Asclepian religion but instead through the lens of Herodotus and his successors (see pp. 113–130 above).

Given this situation, one might reasonably expect to see the paradoxographical form serving as a model for the narrative style of Thekla's *Miracles*, and this expectation is proved true by the text. As noted above, θαύματα and παράδοξα are normally narrated by the classical paradoxographies in discrete chapters and they do not connect to an overarching theme or progression: they effectively serve as a theme unto themselves. Likewise, in the *Miracles*, there is little or no narrative development between these isolated stories. Once the author has achieved his rewriting of Thekla's early history in the *Life*, and established Thekla's revised character as a spiritual being who works physical healings, the story of Thekla has finished. The *Miracles*, then, are individual glimpses of that already established character from the very end of the *Life*, but nothing ties them together in the *Miracles* beyond Thekla herself.

The most significant narrative features shared between paradoxography and Thekla's *Miracles* are the rhetoric and organization of the individual miracle units. First, they share a simple, patterned, paratactic order that repeats itself in each story. After a brief introduction naming the source of the story or giving some reason for mentioning it, there follows a narrative (of varying length); this narrative without fail ends abruptly after its climax; and there sometimes follows a very brief conclusion. A typical short example from paradoxography is provided by Phlegon of Tralles:

> The same authors relate that in the land of the Lapiths a daughter was born to King Elatos and named Kainis. After Poseidon had had sexual intercourse with her and promised to fulfill any wish for her, she asked that he change her into a man and render her invulnerable. Poseidon granted her request, and her name was changed to Kaineus.[109]

This pattern of short introduction, story ending abruptly with its climax, and very short conclusion—here, the changing of the name—is repeated throughout paradoxographical texts and fragments and is also characteristic of the *Miracles of Thekla*.

Asclepian inscriptions, by contrast, exhibit much more variety in the telling and do not follow this pattern. I have already quoted two distinctly

---

[109] Phlegon of Tralles *Book of Marvels* 5.1–3; ed. Giannini 1966:198; trans. Hansen 1996:38.

different examples from *stele* α at Epidaurus.[110] Consider also the latest Asclepian *stele* found by archaeologists, dated to the fourth century AD, from Athens:

> Ἡγέμαχος
> Κραταιμένο(υ)ς
> Λαμπτρεὺς
> Ἀσκληπιῶι.
> Δεινὰ παθὼν καὶ πολλά
> ἰ]δὼν σωθεὶς ἀνέθηκεν
> ἐπὶ Θεοφίλου ἱερέω[ς
> Ἀσκληπιῶι Ὑγι[είαι
> Εὐρυμέδων Ἡγεμάχου.[111]

Hegemachos, son of Krataimenes of Lamptra to Asclepius. Having suffered many terrible ills and seen many visions, [and] having been saved, Eurumedon, son of Hegemachos, dedicated [this] to Asclepius [and] Hygieia, under the priest Theophilus.[112]

By contrast, paradoxographical tales and Thekla's *Miracles* are both almost always told in the third person. The only first person examples are in the case of autopsy or, at two points in the *Miracles*, when the author himself is healed.[113] However, as in the inscription just quoted, Asclepian ἰάματα are usually in the first person. They are temple votives offered in gratitude by individuals for their own healing—and one cannot always expect a description of what the suffering and visions actually were![114] This is in contrast to paradoxography and Thekla's *Miracles* which always describe the salient details, even if heavily abbreviated. (A good example of this habit is Phlegon's

---

[110] For further intra-inscriptional comparison, see the elaborate Epidaurian inscription at Girone 1998:58–70 (2.4, an account of healing by prescription) and one of the smaller ones from Tiber Island in Rome, such as at Girone 1998:154–156 (5.1, dedication of a votive).

[111] 1.2, ed. Girone 1998:36–38.

[112] As Girone notes, the translation could read differently: "Hegemachos, son of Krataimenes of Lamptra to Asclepius. [Who], having suffered many terrible ills and seen many visions, [and] having been saved, dedicated [this] to Asclepius [and] Hygieia, under the priest Theophilus. [And] Eurumedon, son of Hegemachos." But this reading means that Eurumedon is syntactically dissociated from what comes before (Girone 1998:37n20).

[113] *Mir.* 12 and 41. This proves to be a special case in which the author is further solidifying the image of Thekla as literary patron which he has developed elsewhere: see pp. 160–169 above.

[114] Maria Girone comments on this inscription, "ma l'insistenza sull'estrema gravità dei mali e su un'intensa attività onirica (lines 5–6: δεινὰ παθὼν καὶ πολλὰ ἰδὼν) è di chiara marca aretalogica" (1998:36).

notice on Kainis/Kaineus quoted above.) Therefore, to reemphasize the point, paradoxography and the *Miracles* almost always behave in a standard historiographical manner; the ἰάματα almost never.

An important exception to this rule should be noted, however. If ever the third person is used in the Asclepian inscriptions it shows coincident evidence of what Lynn LiDonnici has termed "priestly redaction."[115] Priestly redaction is actually not much different in conception from what is going on in the para-doxographies and Thekla's *Miracles*: some of the Asclepian texts themselves attest to a prior collecting process (though they still do not exhibit any extra-inscriptional distribution). Redaction in this context means a loose unity of stories—collected orally or from earlier *stelai*—based on a central theme or style of narration, such as "action at distance," as LiDonnici describes tales 1–5 on *stele* β at Epidaurus.[116] However, it is difficult to prove priestly redaction because the texts do not exhibit nearly the level of unity one would expect in such cases. LiDonnici sums up the problem as follows:

> It seems improbable that a project as important as the composition of the most visible and important literary statement of the sanc-tuary "self-definition" would have been deliberately conducted in a manner haphazard and careless enough to account for the incon-sistencies in the preserved *Iamata* inscriptions. A model of one-time redaction requires us to envision not only a general "free-for-all" in terms of rephrasing, selection, and arrangement; but in terms of change and variety in letter size, format, and layout on the finished *stelai* as well.[117]

She argues instead for a collective process that went through several stages and cycles, perhaps initially coincident with the reorganization of the temple complex in the early third century BC but continuing on for some time. The record of smaller *stelai* not included in these larger redactional projects could have come from earlier stages, or they could instead be contemporary with the priestly redaction, sometimes accepting the (impenetrable) ideology represented by the collections but sometimes indicating separate, individual artisanal agendas of language and description. In the end it would prove impossible to determine exactly which literary evidence belongs to which stage in the redaction process. More importantly for our purposes, LiDonnici's

---

[115] For "priestly redaction," "artisan composition," and a unifying "Asclepian theology" found in one series of inscriptions at Epidaurus, see LiDonnici 1995:64–69.

[116] LiDonnici 1995:67; texts and English translation, LiDonnici 1995:101–105.

[117] LiDonnici 1995:66.

analysis underlines the hazards of ascribing to any one inscriptional center a clear statement of the prescribed literary form of Asclepian religion. Further, it should be remembered that the majority of Asclepian *stelai* retain a naive, immediate tone suggesting that there was little mediation between the recipient of Asclepius' favor and the text that has survived.

## Aelius Aristides and his diary

While Asclepian *stelai* ("aretalogies" to some) are the most direct route into what scholarship has identified as standard Asclepian healing in the ancient world, there are other examples of this phenomenon which differ significantly in form from the inscriptions. Most notable among these are the Ἱεροὶ λόγοι (*Sacred Tales*) of the orator and author Aelius Aristides (AD 117–c. 181).[118] In the sense that the Ἱεροὶ λόγοι are an attempt to narrate multiple experiences of divine healing within a precise literary form, they can be said to be similar to the *Miracles of Thekla*.[119] However, the similarity extends only this far, since both the content of the Ἱεροὶ λόγοι and their specific form—which has few ancient parallels before or after—attest to an idiosyncratic organization of religious and medical knowledge.[120]

For the most part, the Ἱεροὶ λόγοι take the form of a diary, in which Aelius describes the ailments he suffered and the cures prescribed by Asclepius for that day. In the preface he explains his choice of form, claiming that it would be "impossible" for him "to speak or write" about his all experiences since they are so many. For this reason he has previously demurred in

---

[118] Text, Keil 1898 vol. 2; English translation, Behr 1981. Edelstein and Edelstein 1998 [1945]:2.143 make the point that before the Epidaurian *stelai* had been discovered Aelius was the main source for scholarship on temple medicine. Once Epidaurus was excavated, however, and the findings published, certain scholarly intuitions about the delusional nature of Greek temple medicine were given free rein: "The Epidaurian tablets were published [in 1883]. They seemed unrestrictedly to confirm the verdict of the skeptical scientists. It was now obvious to all that these so-called cures had been trickery and mere fraud." In contrast to this latter conclusion, Edelstein and Edelstein proceed to explain incubational healing more convincingly than anyone before them and they do it precisely by trying to understand Asclepius' role in ancient medicine and cult religion (1998 [1945]:2.145–180).

[119] On healing pilgrimage among Asclepian devotees in the second century AD, see Petsalis-Diomidis 2001.

[120] On the literary form of the Ἱεροὶ λόγοι, see Weiss 1998:17–30, where Aristides' text is associated with the ancient genre of ἐφημερίδες (diaries/memoirs); examples of this genre may include the (tendentious) journal written by Alexander's chief secretary, Eumenes (OCD 528), or the travelogue written by Hadrian on his tour of the provinces, or even the *Meditations* of Marcus Aurelius. Philostratus links Aelius' Ἱεροὶ λόγοι to the ἐφημερίδες explicitly at *Lives of the Sophists* 2.9 [581] (Weiss 1998:19).

the face of pressure from his friends to do so. Instead, he now offers "to speak like Homer's Helen," who in Book Four of the *Odyssey* did not tell of all the "toils of stouthearted Odysseus" but rather concentrates on one deed alone.[121] For Aelius, the experience of Asclepius was so ever-present that any attempt at collection would be mere pretension. An alternative for him is the form of a daily diary:

> For each of our days, as well as our nights, has a story, if someone, who was present at them, wished either to record the events or to narrate the providence of the god, wherein he revealed some things openly in his own presence and others by the sending of dreams, as far as it was possible to obtain sleep. But this was rare, due to the tempests of my body. In view of this, I decided to submit to the god, truly as to a doctor, and to do in silence whatever he wishes.[122]

There is, of course, a sense in which Aelius' programmatic statements are very similar to those of a collector. His refusal to present a comprehensive catalogue is a rhetorical commonplace, employed by no less than the *Miracles of Thekla*. The author of the latter writes:

> For this reason, without too much thought and toil, we compiled (συνελεξάμεθα) her miracles that happened here and there and we published them (ἐξεθέμεθα) in a little prose composition (διὰ μικροῦ συγγράμματος)—not every miracle, nor even the majority of them, but just the smallest number, and only those that happened in our day and in a little before us.

> *Mir.* preface 8–13

Only Pliny the Elder was confident enough to assert that his collection encompassed the whole world (see p. 215 below). Instead, most writers of catalogues use comprehensiveness as a foil: a logical impossibility which all readers can understand is the ideal but which is humanly speaking unreachable, especially when one is dealing with the divine.

The resulting diary-catalogue of Asclepius' radical prescriptions to Aelius seems very incongruous with the Epidaurian *stelai*. By the same token, in his study of Aelius' devotion to the god, Charles Behr sets out three different types of physical healing practiced in the ancient world: 1) the god operates on the patient directly in a dream (e.g. most of the *stelai*); 2) the god prescribes a cure

---

[121] *Odyssey* 4.241.
[122] *Orations* 27.1.3–4, trans. Behr 1981:2.278.

in a dream, which the recipient then has to perform in real life; 3) ancient physicians, who called themselves the "Sons of Asclepius" (*Asklepiades*), perform the surgery or offer prescriptions themselves in real life.[123] Aelius' *Sacred Tales* generally fall into the second type, dream prescriptions, which included (in his rather extreme case) harsh regimens of freezing cold baths and physical evacuations of various sorts. The nature of his diary entries are, therefore, necessarily distinct from the *stelai*: he narrates the dream, as they often do as well, but he also describes his own efforts at carrying out the task set for him. Further, his entries over time elucidate the development of his relationship to the god, and frequent flashbacks to earlier stages of his spiritual journey, as well to previous ailments, punctuate the story, which by the end one has realized is an important literary endeavor in its own right.

Consequently, the dissociation between inscriptional evidence and Aelius' *Sacred Tales* is a necessary one, based on 1) the nature of the healing being described, 2) Aelius' idiosyncratic picture of his physical well-being, and 3) the literary aspirations and effects of the text itself. This last element of the distinction is an important comparandum for the *Miracles of Thekla* since the imposition of the collector's literary vision is very much at the forefront of both texts, and it is this important aspect of miracle collecting which I shall take up in the next section. For now it is enough to acknowledge that Aelius' natural distance from the inscribed ἰάματα, which are ostensibly reporting very similar phenomena from the same cultic contexts, is instructive for a cautionary reading of healing texts. Not only is his diary distinct from the collective form of the *Miracles*, but it also differs significantly within the broader corpus of Asclepian texts.

Text, cult, and cultural continuity

Even a brief analysis of the ἰάματα and Aelius Aristides' Ἱεροὶ λόγοι demonstrates the variety of textual responses to this cult in the ancient world. There was certainly no one accepted way of writing about Asclepius. Given this fact alone it would be difficult to postulate a simple imitation or appropriation of Asclepian healing by Christian writers.

---

[123] Behr 1968:35–40. Edelstein and Edelstein 1998 [1945]:2.169–180 point out that the number of operations doctors could perform competently was so small, and the operations themselves so expensive, that it was natural for many people to seek out Asclepius' help, and often, especially when the need was severe. On the relationship between physicians and religious/magical medicine in the ancient world, see Edelstein 1968:205–246.

As I have tried to argue, the texts from which we learn about these divine figures do not share an overarching textual form. This should give us pause, since the content of these texts could potentially be responding to genre requirements, and producing in the process false resemblances to our modern eyes. In addition, there is no reason to think that the organization of religious knowledge—especially in a collective form like the *Miracles*—is not responding to intra-religious and societal needs more than to meta-movements like the spurious concept of "christianization." Moreover, the similarity between Asclepius and Thekla is hardly borne out in the narrative handling of the *Miracles*, and there are a number of instances where Thekla seems to be completely outside the matrix of Asclepian thought: for instance, when she is seen struggling with the natural elements (see p. 140 above). At these times she has much more in common with the Gospels' visions of Jesus than with Asclepius, and the author's declaration in the preface to the *Life* that he is following in the footsteps of Luke the Evangelist begins to look more and more plausible (see pp. 18–21 above).

There is no doubt that the figure of Asclepius was important to both the Gospels and late antique Christian biography—though the relationship of the former pair is much more difficult to assess. Why, however, must we see Thekla as a christianized Asclepius? And what would "christianized" mean in the context of cultic texts anyway? I suggest instead that, while looking to Asclepius for the answers can be instructive, an over-reliance on the Asclepius-Thekla association is ultimately injurious to the literature as it has survived. The search for links between the two healers requires trying to read past their textual particularities, and there is no doubt that such a search has prevented the *LM* from being set in its proper literary historical context.

## Conclusion: Archives and the Semiology of Collecting

In the preceding sections of Chapter Four, I have explored the ways in which language and form provide indicators for the literary historical setting of the *Miracles of Thekla*. In this regard, the *Miracles* presents itself as sharing many more features with the classical genre of paradoxography than with texts about Asclepian healing, even though culturally speaking there seems to have been an important overlap in the larger continuity of religious and medical practice. I have also attempted to set paradoxography in an overarching collection movement, beginning more or less with Callimachus but extending back in its ethnographic and comparative-religious interests to Herodotus, and perhaps even to the *Odyssey*, in the perception of later collectors.

There are, however, a number of theoretical points which have not yet been addressed in the provisional literary history and brief analysis presented above. First among these is the question of the author's unique vision for his collection. How is it intellectually possible for a miracle collector in late antiquity to present a collection that shares more in common with the literary tradition of Hellenistic and Roman collections (broadly speaking) than with his own immediate interests in the community for which he is writing? This is a particularly important question for cultic literature since the Asclepian texts and the *Miracles of Thekla* are the most tangible evidences of underlying cultic practices.

In attempting to answer this question, it may be instructive to consider an early and explicit account of the collecting process in late antiquity, an account which frames one of the first Christian miracle collections to have survived in Latin.[124] In Book 22 of the *City of God*, Augustine tells of a prominent lady of Carthage, who had been personally healed by the relics of Saint Stephen. However, when she refused to publicize this miracle, Augustine chastised her for what he perceived to be apathy, ingratitude, and a neglected opportunity for evangelism:

> When I heard this story I was full of wrath that in that city, when that woman, certainly no obscure person, was concerned, so great a miracle was so unknown. Indeed, I thought she should be admonished, if not rebuked. When she answered that she had not failed to tell about it, I asked the women who happened to be with her then, and were very close friends, whether they had known the story before. They answered that they had never heard of it. "Well," I said, "that's the way you tell about it—so that not even these women who are your best friends hear about it!" And since I had questioned her only briefly, I made her relate the whole story from beginning to end just as it took place, while the women listened and marveled greatly (*multumque mirantibus*) and glorified God.[125]

The woman's status in the city made her silence all the more unpalatable for Augustine. If the people of Carthage could be offered a vision of aristocratic

---

[124] I am of course not unaware of Paulinus of Nola's (353/5–431) important verse miracle collection on Saint Felix, the *Natalicia*, which has been interpreted to great effect in Peter Brown's *The Cult of the Saints* (1981: chapter 3); see also the English translation of these poems in Walsh 1975. However, I am concentrating here on the early prose collections, which I believe exhibit important unifying characteristics, particularly the shared rhetoric of collecting.

[125] Augustine *City of God* 22.8, ed. Dombart and Kalb 1981:2.571; trans. Green et al. 1957–1972:7.223.

devotion and gratitude, not to mention the important lesson that God's favor depends not on human distinction but falls upon the rich and poor alike, faith would be confirmed and the gospel could be further proved true (and publicly). Augustine, however, unwittingly reveals in this ethical vignette an important discontinuity between religious practice and religious literature: the values of private recipient and public writer are distinct.

With this story in mind, it could be said that the Asclepian inscriptions at Epidaurus and elsewhere are all the more unique because of their immediacy. It is very surprising, in fact, not to find much more "priestly redaction" than has survived—and, instead, to find that which has survived in such a muddled and inconsistent state. For miracles of healing to have achieved the unity of book form at all requires the transfer of the miracles' essence from personal experience to authorial agenda. Knowing this, the ancient sick, like the prominent matron of Carthage, were less willing to divulge their stories than the literature often suggests.

This is no less true today than it was in fifth-century North Africa, as Candace Slater has shown in her study *Trail of Miracles* (1986), where she transcribes and analyzes stories of miracles attributed to the Brazilian priest Padre Cícero. In her experience, female residents of Joazeiro, Padre Cícero's pilgrimage site in northeastern Brazil, were often reluctant to tell the local priests about the healings Cícero had done on their behalf. She describes their uneasiness with men in a story-telling context:

> For the purposes of this study it was helpful to be a woman. First, my sex assured me a certain degree of trust. "I wouldn't tell Saint Peter the things I am telling you," an old woman once confided. It would have been difficult, if not impossible, for a man to walk in and strike up a conversation.[126]

An instructive diffidence is shared by Augustine's reluctant Carthaginian and Slater's old woman. The experience of healing was a private matter, and the healed have every reason to want to keep these experiences to themselves. One could understand, especially at a bustling pilgrimage site like Joazeiro or Seleukeia, where the normalization or domestication of miracle narratives was constantly at work, that a believing resident—vis-à-vis the pilgrims—would consider their individual experience to be a personal treasure. Unwilling to have the local priest spend that treasure on more propaganda, even if it could

---

[126] Slater 1986:15–16.

promote the welfare of the community, the resident instead keeps the story secret.

Given such an important window on the pitfalls of the miracle collecting process, is this then the matrix through which we are to understand all Christian miracle collections? Should we assume that only the runt of the litter, so to speak, is represented in the texts, and that the unique, individual, or even the most authentic miracle stories have been lost to time, more precious to the recipient than the fame of publication? These rhetorical questions may not be far from the truth, especially if Slater's experience could be taken to be in any way normative for miracle collecting across the board. Nevertheless, Slater repeatedly highlights the fact that clear narrative distinctions can be drawn between resident and pilgrim miracles, demonstrating that perhaps some of the more individualized stories may be getting through the net.

In fact, the distinction is a stark one: miracles shared by both pilgrims and residents at Joazeiro are almost always miracles of vengeance and divine power; by contrast, the miracles told primarily by residents most often concern personal healing and show a wider variety in the telling.[127] Additionally, in specific cases it can be shown that there is literary influence from the Gospels at work in these tales—not a surprising event, perhaps, but important for discerning certain miracles from others.[128] In sum, the Joazeiro miracle stories reflect multiple perspectives, all recorded by Slater orally and in situ. Her research method thus offers an unparalleled opportunity to isolate different spheres of miracle telling from one another, and she has, in addition, traced the effects of overlap and interaction between these spheres, showing how both draw on shared ideas about the past, sacred space, and pilgrimage to produce their narratives.

The primary difference, however, between Slater's research into the miracles worked by Padre Cícero and Thekla's *Miracles* is the state of the collection. Slater heard the miracles first hand, and produced a collection herself, making theoretical notes as she went. Moreover, she was able to elicit from reluctant women tales that, she insists, would not have been told otherwise. The *Miracles of Thekla* is, by contrast, a text, and the collection process which produced it has been completely shrouded from us. Augustine's picture, therefore, may be a better model for the *Miracles*, especially given the shared late antique context: the collector is a redactor, whose external interests—

---

[127] Slater 1986:88–97 (both residents and pilgrims); 97–100 (residents). Miracles told primarily by pilgrims have a heightened dramatic element, including dialogues and the journey of pilgrimage (100–103).

[128] E.g. miracle no. 23, a raising from the dead *à la* Lazarus (Slater 1986:99).

whether for the publicity of the cult, or as evidence of supernatural activity—dominate the project. This authorial enthusiasm naturally limits the kind of miracle he may find, since many pilgrims or residents may not be at all sympathetic. There is very little a modern interpreter can do with ancient texts to produce (in good conscience) the individual, anthropological familiarity that is so arresting in Slater's book. Such is the impasse one faces when attempting to analyze a miracle collection. Do these represent what is actually going on at the site? If so, which miracles are more authentic than the others? Is it possible to penetrate the vision of the redactor even for a moment?

All is not lost, however. Certain miracle collections, such as that of the *Miracles of Saint Artemios* (7th century), seem to short-circuit such questions in their very telling.[129] That collection in particular retains an immediacy, even a naiveté, which cannot but represent to a great degree the actual words of the miracle recipients on site.[130] Moreover, the *Miracles of Artemios* boldly claims its own performance space: each Saturday evening an all night vigil was held at the church of the John the Baptist ("the Forerunner") in Constantinople, during which (besides the liturgy itself) the hymns of Romanos ("the humble") were sung and miracle stories were presumably also read aloud.[131]

Yet, the *Miracles of Thekla* is a very different text. Written in the uniform language of educated Greek, it is difficult to imagine it being read aloud at an all night vigil before an uneducated audience. The register of Greek is simply too high. Additionally, the text never mentions any specific context for reception. On the contrary, all indications point to a very literary-minded author and one who is writing solely for his literate peers. Thus, dissociating the *Miracles of Thekla* from its literary character proves almost impossible, and Augustine's discussion of the collection process, from the collector's point of view, is most helpful in warning modern readers not to take these miracles as transparent views of Seleukeian society in the fifth century. In fact, we have no a priori guarantees that the collector of Thekla's *Miracles* was not even less successful than Augustine at wrenching authentic stories away from reluctant recipients. Instead, its anonymous author may be offering us very heavily revised versions of miracles circulating at the shrine.

My close analysis of the *Miracles* in Chapter Three above attempted to nuance considerably this harsh judgment, and I have suggested that, as in Slater's experience with the Padre Cícero miracles, the influence of the

---

[129] Crisafulli and Nesbitt (1997). Cf. Déroche 1993.

[130] Crisafulli and Nesbitt 1997:27.

[131] Vigil: Crisafulli and Nesbitt 1997: "general index," s.v. "all-night-vigil of the Forerunner"; hymns of Romanos: 114–115; miracle stories: 27.

Gospels on the author is an important link between private experience and literary narrative. There is obviously a certain amount normalization, but that process always includes liturgical and communal elements of belief. And the fact that both Joazeiro and Seleukeia were major pilgrimage centers in their regions allows them to be more readily compared with one another, over North Africa, which, according to Augustine himself, had not yet achieved the fame of other places at the time of the writing Book 22 of the *City of God* (AD 426–427).[132] Augustine's treatment of the Carthaginian matron comes in the context of his trying to promote the newly founded shrine of Saint Stephen. This background may explain Augustine's intensive approach to miracle gathering, and could thereby make his testimony unrepresentative of other, long-standing centers.

For now, it is only necessary to note a few literary characteristics arising from the collective form in writing, which may help in understanding the organization of Thekla's *Miracles* and its effects on the reader in late antiquity. The fact that the *Miracles* might be called "literary" (for many synonymous with "impenetrable") does not automatically sequester it from the kind of anthropological or sociological analysis which has been attempted before with this material. Yet, as highlighted above, the various attempts to establish firm connections between Asclepius and Thekla required scholars to look beyond the texts, simply because the texts themselves prove to be so different from one another. What would happen, instead, if one considered the collective form to be integral to the religious and cultural vision at the heart of the miracle stories? What if collection itself was a source of cultural meaning? Further, perhaps the unity of collective writing in antiquity can provide a locus for explaining the similarities and differences between different religious literatures.

This is, of course, the argument underlying the survey of collective literature above, and it finds proponents among theoretical writers who have dealt with categorization and archival texts in other cultures and historical circumstances. A classic analysis of the pre-modern tendency towards encyclopedism is that of Michel Foucault in the second chapter of *The Order of Things* (1989

---

[132] Augustine *City of God* 22.8; trans. Green et al. 1957–1972:239: "It is not yet two years that the relics [of Saint Stephen] have been in Hippo Regius, and though I am certain that there are many miraculous events of which no report has been published, those published at the time of my writing have almost reached the number of seventy. But at Calama the relics were earlier in existence and reports are published more frequently, so that their number is far greater." He goes on to describe how he has encouraged other colonies—including Uzali, which had a shrine "before any other city"—to begin publicizing their own miracles, even if it was against their custom.

[1970]). Foucault argues that encyclopedias and collections in the sixteenth century (and presumably before) depended on an idea of proportional correlation between the sign (the encyclopedia entry) and the thing signified (the natural phenomenon itself).[133] In this way, alchemical and magical collections, as much as natural histories, mimic in the world in their totality and point to hidden natural sympathies through their incessant juxtaposition of unexpected (and wondrous) catalogue entries. While he argues wrongly (ignoring the late antique and Byzantine evidence) that alphabetization is necessarily an arbitrary method of organization—and thus modern, and antithetical to a semiology of resemblance—he nevertheless has identified one central factor in ancient collections as a group: all collectors exhibit a complicit affirmation of the value of comprehensiveness, which is based not on the system of organization itself but upon a cosmological view of the comprehensiveness of the world. One could add that Pliny the Elder was preeminent in this regard, being one of the only collectors to claim *imitatio* explicitly—but presumably the others took it for granted.[134]

In the sense that human experience of the macrocosmic world is made up of infinite microcosms, catalogue entries could be added ad infinitum. There is no limit to the size of the collection, simply because there is no limit to the iterations of the natural world. This may explain the gargantuan collections that were written throughout late antiquity: for example, Stephanus of Byzantium's Ἐθνικά in sixty volumes, which almost instantly, and perhaps even under his own direction, went into an abridged one-volume version. These collections were, therefore, much more about the future than the past, since they were by nature open-ended literary constructions. As Jacques Derrida has noted in his book *Archive Fever* (1996:68):

> How can we think about this fatal repetition, about repetition in general in its relationship to memory and the archive? It is easy to perceive, if not to interpret, the necessity of such a relationship,

---

[133] Foucault 1989 [1970]:17–44, esp. 25: "By means of this interplay, the world remains identical; resemblances continue to be what they are, and to resemble one another. The same remains the same, riveted onto itself."

[134] I have not attempted a survey of work on Pliny the Elder, since his Latin *Natural History* falls outside of this study's purview. However, I would like to point to two recent studies which take up the question of form in Pliny's catalogue: Carey 2003 and Murphy 2004. They both cite the survey *Encyclopedism from Pliny to Borges* by Anna Sigridur Arnar (1990), a catalogue of a 1990 exhibit at the University of Chicago Library (a catalogue which, incidentally, only deals with western material and ignores Byzantium altogether). On Pliny's claim to *imitatio*, see Carey 2003:passim, esp. 19: "Through this relationship between structure and content, a particularly literary presentation of the world can appear directly to reflect the world itself."

at least if one associates the archive, as naturally one is always tempted to do, with repetition, and repetition with the past. But it is the future that is at issue here, and the archive as an irreducible experience of the future.

Derrida isolates here the indeterminate character of the collection, or the "archive" as he calls it. The metaphor of the intellectual storehouse, on this basis, is deceptively simple in its appeal to antiquity and to the antiquarian enterprise. In reality, the archive is a sophisticated attempt to place a stamp on the future; the collection is an arbiter or gatekeeper of knowledge for coming generations.

The collection is not, however, simply a play for literary immortality; it is more complicated in its literary aims and effects. On one hand the archive destroys what it is trying to memorialize. It does this by never capturing it in its completeness, or never capturing all the iterations of the subject. In this way "archivization" is generally characteristic of Derrida's concept of "inscription": no matter what the individual circumstances, whenever something is written down, some of its meaning as a thought or as speech necessarily escapes; and this "seepage" of content and meaning can be seen as one of the archive's defining characteristics. On the other hand—and this is what Derrida tries to point out in *Archive Fever*—the archive also always refuses to signify that which it does contain; by its nature it leaves the door open to a future increase of data and to becoming a larger and different sort of archive, in essence, to reinventing itself and to offering itself to conflicting interpretations and meanings. Thus, on the surface the archive appears to signify, because it is a collection, but it ultimately refuses to, because of its necessary indeterminacy. In Derrida's (typically poetic) wording, "it grasps without grasping, comprehends without taking" (1996:58).

Likewise, the author of a modern day paradoxography, Jorge Luis Borges in his fantastical collection *The Book of Imaginary Beings* (2002 [1970]:12)—very much inspired by the ancient tradition—has also insisted (almost in parody) on the open-endedness of collective writing:

A book of this kind is unavoidably incomplete; each new edition forms the basis of future editions, which themselves may grow on endlessly. We invite the eventual reader in Columbia or Paraguay to send us the names, accurate descriptions, and most conspicuous traits of their local monsters.

Borges' knowing characterization of mythological collecting thus winds its way through remarkable and wondrous beasts: everything from the familiar Greek centaur, to medieval Trolls and Valkyries, to "Jewish Demons," to the South-African "Hochigan," and even up to "an animal imagined by Kafka" and "an animal imagined by C. S. Lewis." Despite this comprehensive variety, Borges acknowledges at the outset, so conversant as he is with the genre, that any given iteration of the *Book of Imaginary Beings* is only ephemeral and that reader-response is critical to the collection's form and future value. In fact, the book has already been through several revised editions and translations since it was first published in Spanish in 1957.

When looked at through this lens, the *Miracles of Thekla* exhibits very similar characteristics. For instance, at the very end of the *Miracles* Thekla is invoked as the insurer of the future success of the collection. In his epilogue to the *Miracles* the author prays:

> Further, it is for you [Thekla] to work now this further miracle after the others: to receive (δέξασθαι) these small and feeble [tales], offered to you from small and feeble hands, and to show them (δεῖξαι) to be great and miraculous (θαυμαστά).
>
> *Mir.* epilogue 8–11

There is no doubt that this is a rhetorical topos; dedicating a hagiographical work to the saint it describes is quite common in this period.[135] However, I would argue that there is never such a thing as "mere rhetoric," especially in a text that betrays so much self-consciousness in terms of style and form. Rhetoric is always "performative" as much as it is "constative," in J. L. Austin's well known formulation (Austin 1975). Scholars of Byzantine history have, of course, always struggled with this aspect of post-classical Greek literature: it appears, like Byzantine icons, to be so formalized and so reliant on rhetorical topoi that creativity, or imagination, is lost in the process. Few today, however, would continue to argue such a limited position for Byzantine visual art, yet hesitations about engaging the creative, or simply literary, side of Byzantine texts still linger on.[136] I would argue, therefore, that the author of the *Miracles* is saying something very important about the collection as a

---

[135] E.g. Cyril of Scythopolis, *Life of Euthymius* Dedication [6.20].

[136] E.g. Kazhdan 1999, where the desperate need for a new literary history of Byzantium is invoked in the preface (1–5). However, Kazhdan's *History* opens with a chapter that reinforces many old prejudices about Byzantine literature: the first chapter is tellingly titled "Farewell to Historicity," suggesting that Byzantine texts can only be evaluated on the basis of their commitment (or lack thereof) to realistic description (19–35).

work of literature. There is an open-endedness about the miracle collection which belies its status as archive: the narrator recognizes that reception (and successful reception) is secondary to collection and cannot be accomplished by the archive itself. By leaving the reception of the collection open to the saint's influence and power, the text reveals a self-consciousness about its own literary form.

Thus, in the concluding passage from the same epilogue—the final passage from the work as a whole—its narrator involves his own career in the dissemination of Thekla's literary tradition:

> Along with these things, Virgin [Thekla], grant that I may been seen once again on the holy step of the holy Bema of this very church, pronouncing that which is customary [i.e. Scripture] as well as pronouncing on many other topics, on which one habitually speaks in churches: and especially concerning you, the most beautiful first-fruit of the church, after the apostles alone, or even among the apostles themselves. [Grant also] that I may be seen again to bring to harvest (κομιζομένους) that which I am accustomed to harvest, namely, the persuasion (πειθώ) of my listeners, respect (αἰδώ), the progress (προκοπήν) of the congregation, and the increase of faith and piety (τῆς εὐσεβείας). For, as you know, I was confident of the supremacy of that gift of teaching which came because of you (διὰ σέ), and that it is also because of you (διὰ σέ) that applause and acclamation has come to me, as well as having a reputation among the orators, who are as many as they are amazing (θαυμασίοις).[137]

> *Mir.* epilogue 31–41

Derek Krueger is right to see this passage in terms of the narrator's appropria-tion of Thekla's patronage for his own position in literate society; in Krueger's terms there is a "performance" of holiness going on in this passage which should be linked to the author's political outsider/insider dichotomy that he has set up elsewhere in the text, especially with regard to the bishop Basil.[138]

However, I would argue that much more integral to a literary reading of the *Miracles* is the central image of time which the narrator is constructing here, of the past expression of Thekla's deeds and the future expression of

---

[137] The repetition of διὰ σέ in this passage is perhaps reminiscent of *Life* 26, where Thekla uses the phrase διὰ σοῦ multiple times in succession during her speech to Paul at Myra. If an allusion is intended, then the author is asking for Thekla to grant something like apostolic succession (διαδοχή) on the model of her relationship with the Apostle Paul.

[138] See Krueger 2004:79–92; and p. 164 above.

them. He places this dedication between these two timeframes: as he says, he was once accustomed to "harvest" or "recover" (κομίζω) Thekla's deeds in public and he hopes to do so again. As in the passage quoted above, the literary project that he is technically at the point of completing is thus actually indeterminate. Therefore, instead of interpreting this passage via the hermeneutic of patronage, I would like to highlight the cognitive issue of reception and see this conclusive prayer as an affirmation of the literary character (and, indeed, achievement) of the *LM* as a whole. The invocation that is supposedly "performed" in this passage—in terms of Thekla as patroness—is actually much more than that. The invocation is instead an evocation which represents an attempt to take account of Thekla's entire personal history, as just recounted over two volumes of text. At the end of the *Life* Thekla descended into the earth still alive only to take on a spiritual, haunting presence that continues to work miracles and will do so forever: that moment in the text defines the transition from one volume to another and at the same time defines the transition from ancient (literary) history to the indeterminate present/future, to the reception of his own collection. The unique history that he has constructed for Thekla in this way becomes a metaphor for the text as a whole; the two parts of Thekla's actual career represent and are represented by the two separate literary forms.

# Conclusion

A READER OF THIS STUDY will note that I have only at a few points highlighted the implications of Thekla's female gender for the *LM*.[1] This is
because I do not feel that this work is a "gendered" text in the way that
word is used in scholarship on antiquity and the middle ages.[2] Thekla's status
as a woman has almost no special role at all for the author of the *LM*, especially
in comparison with the *ATh*.[3] Much research has been done by other scholars
to set the *ATh* in an original context and a reception-history of female piety,
and in the Introduction I drew attention to the recent work of Stephen Davis
in this regard.[4] Readers interested in this aspect of Thekla devotion through
the centuries would do well to read his book.

What is lacking in Davis's study, and Dagron's edition for that matter,
I have attempted to provide in the chapters above: namely, a reading of the
*LM* that would take account of its literary nature. I have emphasized from the
beginning that the *LM* is, first and foremost, an artful work of late antique

---

[1] See especially pp. 35–36, 46–48, 50, 59, 142–143, and 212 above.

[2] See, e.g. *Gendered Voices: Medieval Saints and their Interpreters*, ed. Catherine M. Mooney
(Philadelphia, 1999). While a recent treatment of saints under the salacious rubric of their
"sex lives" certainly should have a voice in scholarship on hagiography (Burrus 2004), I would
be resistant to this methodology being used on the *LM*. This is because I am convinced that
the internal logic of the text produces a more meaningful and, from a literary historical point
of view, more challenging interpretation than the anachronistic imposition of "sexuality" as a
known quantity. In other words, the dissonance between narrative saints' Lives of the fourth
and fifth centuries in terms of their literary form remains a wellspring of interpretive opportunity still untapped by scholarship focusing on the salacious (perhaps circumstantially so?)
aspects of late antique hagiography.

[3] Dagron notes that the treatment of female gender, Thekla's and others', in the *LM* appears
completely ad hoc: the author sometimes appears misogynist and other times highlights the
pro-female elements of the *ATh* (1978:37–39). Also, the miracles that Thekla works are spread
evenly among male and female recipients. Simply put, gender has very little to do with the
literary deployment of the text.

[4] Davis 2001. See also Burrus 1987 and Cooper 1996:45–67. Cf. Dunn 1993. Davis, incidentally,
includes the *LM* as part of the pro-female reception of the *ATh*. In my opinion there is little
basis for this interpretation (cf. n. 3 above).

writing in Greek. My conviction is that to appreciate it in its cultural context is to read it as such. The close readings that I provide in Chapters One and Three attempt to carry this argument to fruition. Likewise, the literary histories in Chapters Two and Four stress above all that the *LM* is not alone in its endeavor but can be read alongside vibrant literary traditions of paraphrase and collecting in the ancient and late antique worlds.

It remains, therefore, for me to say in conclusion something about the theological context of Thekla devotion in the fifth century. This plays only a minor role in the chapters above, but it is nevertheless important because the author of the *LM*, an educated reader and orator on the scriptures (*Mir.* epilogue 31–45), would doubtless have been aware of the theological landscape taking shape around him.

In particular, a natural person to compare with Thekla is the Virgin Mary herself, whose title and role in the birth of Christ was a central topic of doctrinal debate just before the *LM* was completed (c. 470). One reason, however, that Mariology and Christology play a minor role in this study is because the author of the *LM* barely cites the Virgin (or the Christological debates in which she was prominent). He only mentions her accepted title Theotokos ("God-bearer") at one point in the whole of the *LM*, and even that is in passing (*Mir.* 14.63). In a similar vein, Dagron says "le nom du Christ apparaît au total assez peu dans les *Miracles*."[5] There is a near complete absence of contemporary theological language in the *LM*. Nevertheless, this absence is noteworthy in itself and is worthy of further investigation.

When the author does use theological terminology, it comes from an earlier period, in particular, from the late fourth century. Thus, when a reader of the *Life* comes across an anachronistic doctrinal statement in the mouth of Paul or Thekla (e.g. *Life* 7.38–50), it is without fail a Trinitarian one, which reflects the concerns of earlier Ecumenical Councils, such as Nicea (325) and Constantinople (381).[6] So, first (as I note several times in Chapter One), it is significant in terms of his literary art that the author does not feel uncomfortable using fourth-century terminology when inserting a speech into the mouth of a first century apostle, but, second and more apropos to the conclusion of this study, it is striking that he does not include in these passages any definition of Christ's two natures or any formal title of Mary, except for the one instance just noted. While he may have a particular affinity for the writers involved in the Council of Constantinople (mainly Gregory of Nazianzus—see

---

[5] Dagron 1978:96.
[6] See e.g. pp. 32–35, 43, 62, 136, and 159 above.

pp. 32–35 above), there is no question that, writing as he is in the 460s, he has taken some pains to leave out more recent doctrinal formulations.

The absence of references to Mary may seem odd as well considering the level to which Thekla devotion had risen by the late fifth century. Surely these two female figures had similar trajectories over time within the cult of the saints? Surprisingly, this is not the case at all. It is precisely at the point when Thekla seems to have achieved the pinnacle of her success in Christian devotion and pilgrimage that the cult of Mary, at least in the eastern Mediterranean, is only just beginning to take off. Thus, it is not until the mid to late fifth century, after Mary's role in Christology has been acknowledged by the Council of Ephesus (431), that personal devotion to her begins to grow in a substantial, textual way. Prior to this time it appears that Thekla is by far the most revered female saint, that is, if the popularity of her foundational legend, the *ATh*, can serve as an indicator. (And, as we have seen, there is little to show that Thekla's cult continued to flourish at Seleukeia after the sixth century, at the latest.)

This is obviously not the place for a history of Marian devotion in the Christian East; however, a few high points can be mentioned for the sake of comparison with Thekla.[7] First, one of the only early apocryphal narratives to deal in any detail with Mary is the late second-century *Protoevangelium of James*, a fascinating text which describes the birth of Mary and her young life up to and including the birth of Jesus.[8] As a literary work the *Protoevangelium* clearly depends, as the *ATh* does, on certain holes in the narratives of the Gospels and Acts. These holes allowed for further elaboration: the elaboration in this case centers on Mary's parents, Anna and Joachim, who are of course not mentioned in the New Testament and appear in the *Protoevangelium* to be literary inventions based upon Old Testament models (such as Hannah, mother of Samuel, and Sarah and Abraham). While the story does not include a doctrine of Mary's "immaculate conception," her conception and birth are suitably miraculous (imitating Samuel's).[9] The *Protoevangelium* does, however, include Mary's perpetual virginity and claims that Jesus' "brothers" (e.g. Mark 3:33) were only half-brothers by a previous marriage of Joseph. For this reason the text was condemned by the western church in the so-called "Gelasian

---

[7] For this see now the elegant catalogue of the "Mother of God" exhibition held at the Benaki Museum, Athens in 2000–2001 (Vassilaki 2000) and the new volume of essays (Vassilaki 2004).

[8] See Strycker 1961 and Hennecke and Schneemelcher 1992:421–439.

[9] The Immaculate Conception was not declared official Roman Catholic doctrine until 1854 (*Ineffabilis Deus*, Pius IX). Similarly, the Assumption of the Virgin (see below) was not officially declared until 1950 (*Munificentissimus Deus*, Pius XII).

Decree" of the sixth century.[10] The *Protoevangelium* also insists, interestingly, on Mary's descent in the Davidic line, over and against the Gospel accounts that it was Joseph who descended from David (Matthew 1:16; Luke 3:23).

Following this initial outburst of devotion to the Virgin—coincident, by the way, with Justin Martyr's and Irenaeus' declarations that Mary was the "Second Eve"—there is more or less silence for a couple of centuries.[11] It will be good to reiterate here that in Methodius' *Symposium* (c. 300), it is not the Virgin Mary who is crowned chief of the virgins but Thekla. Nevertheless, in the fourth and fifth centuries some examples of Marian devotion show up, such as the few wall paintings of Mary in the catacombs of Rome and the incomparable mosaics of the Annunciation and Adoration of the Magi in Santa Maria Maggiore. It is not until the sixth century, however, that eastern devotion to her begins in earnest: in sixth-century Constantinople, for example, icons of the Virgin are produced, liturgical feasts are dedicated to her, and hymns, such as the famous "Akathistos," are written in her honor. While it is true that Mary's virginity is often cited in the fourth and fifth centuries as proof of the value of sexual renunciation (especially by Ephrem, Ambrose, and Augustine), her role in the doctrinal debates of the fifth century is, as noted above, primarily for the purpose of defining Christ's two natures, divine and human—is she to be called Theotokos ("God-bearer") or Christotokos ("Christ-bearer")? Thus the Council of Ephesus in 431 declared Nestorius anathema and Mary Theotokos in the same breath. Nestorius, in the view of Ephesus, had not allowed the divine nature of Christ its proper place; and the positive counterpart of his condemnation is to name the mother of Jesus the "the one who bore God."

From the time that Theotokos was formally defined and accepted, eastern sermons on the Virgin increase in their detail and emotional attachment to her. Thus, the important sermon by Proclus of Constantinople before the attendees of the Council of Ephesus inaugurates a new era of personal devotion which in time produces the characteristically Byzantine "Dormition" sermons of the next few centuries.[12] The first texts in the East that describe

---

[10] Hennecke and Schneemelcher 1992:38–40. The *ATh* is likewise condemned, but had been for some time due to Tertullian and Jerome. Jerome also condemns the *Protoevangelium* and says that Jesus' brothers were actually his cousins, which remains the official Roman Catholic position (Elliott 1999:50–51).

[11] For the following paragraphs I have relied primarily on Averil Cameron 2000a and Shoemaker 2002. See also these other recent studies: Peltomaa 2001; Constas 2003; and Averil Cameron 2004.

[12] See Constas 2003:56–71 and Daley 1998 and 2001.

the Virgin Mary's Dormition, or "going to sleep" (κοίμησις), date from the late fifth century. They seek to define how Mary left the earth in a special manner appropriate to her status. Common to almost all of these accounts are the following elements: Mary died in Jerusalem; some of the apostles were involved; Christ received his mother's soul; and Mary was transferred in body and/or soul into Heaven. Beyond this essential story, the variations are huge—notably on the question of whether Mary is bodily taken up to heaven (i.e. "assumed," thus the western term "Assumption"). Most important to note, however, is that the Dormition stories begin at the same time that devotion to Mary is beginning to take off in every other area of late antique Christian piety.[13] Moreover, this is the very point in time when devotion to Thekla is, from all appearances, starting its speedy decline in Asia Minor.[14]

The great irony of these differences in trajectory between Thekla and Mary is that there is very little evidence that Thekla was a real person at all, whereas Mary has numerous early witnesses in the Gospels and Acts. In this study I have left to the side the question of Thekla's historicity, partly because I am simply more interested in the *ATh*'s literary reception, but partly also because there is no evidence with which to address this problem. It goes without saying that the *ATh* is not the sort of text that you would want to base a historical study on, even though that has been attempted in the past.[15] What is so striking from a late antique point of view, however, is that the prominent romantic or nostalgic element in the *ATh*, Egeria's pilgrimage account, and especially the *LM* is not applied elsewhere to the historically grounded person of Mary until the fourth and fifth centuries (except for the rather unique *Protoevangelium of James*).[16]

One lesson to be learned from this brief comparison is that the cult of the saints is rarely simply a "bottom-up" or "top-down" social phenomenon. In reality the development of devotion to Thekla and to Mary shows both elements: text and cult mutually interacted to the point that there is no

---

[13] Shoemaker 2002:31: "The sudden appearance of these [Dormition] traditions at this moment [in the late fifth and sixth centuries] identifies this time as the era when various traditions of the end of Mary's life first became an important component of the now well-preserved 'orthodox mainstream' of ancient Christianity."

[14] There is evidence that Thekla devotion continued in Egypt into the sixth century (Davis 2001:177–194).

[15] Ramsay 1893:375–428.

[16] It is significant that the *Protoevangelium of James* mainly survives in hagiographical collections, not collections of apocryphal Acta. The earliest papyrus (Bodmer 5) probably dates from the fourth century and the earliest Syriac fragments date from the late fifth or sixth century: see Hennecke and Schneemelcher 1992:421–422.

way today to separate them without doing damage to the surviving record. Nevertheless, in Thekla's case the *ATh* is preeminent in every surviving reception of her persona: not least because there was nothing else to go on—for the ancients as much as for us. The crowning jewel of late antique devotion to Thekla, the *LM*, is in one way a "top-down" approach: it is clearly a literary text in both its paraphrase and collection forms. However, the genius of the *LM* is its reorientation of the cult: this is less a "top-down" imposition as a "bottom-up" (i.e. localized) exegesis of a mysterious, haunting, living saint.

The *ATh* provides above all the possibility of locating Thekla's home in Seleukeia. The author of the *LM* is obviously dependent on the fact that this was already established by the second century, yet it is still his genius to declare that she disappeared into the ground alive and spiritually claimed Seleukeia as her own. His is both an ex post facto argument and a felicitous conjunction of cult and text. Of course, he is not the only one to say that she disappeared: the contemporary (or later) extension of the *ATh* also knows this.[17] The writer of that other text, however, cannot see beyond the disappearance. The author of the *LM*, by contrast, has a masterful literary vision and a personal devotion that is itself a type of "bottom-up" cult. He lets us in on that vision and attempts to adorn it with all the trappings of a classical or biblical epic. While Dagron has perceptively announced that the *Life* is his *Iliad* and the *Miracles* his *Odyssey*,[18] the author himself claims the canonical Luke-Acts pair as his literary model (*Life* preface).

Thus, it is a sad conclusion to the saga of this author that, despite his extensive reworking and adornment of the received tradition, his unique reading of Thekla's local legend in the *LM* was ultimately unsuccessful in the Byzantine literary world. Among the three main Byzantine witnesses to the legend of Thekla, all three appear to know only the second-century *ATh*: Pseudo-Photius, Nicetas the Paphlagonian, and Symeon Metaphrastes all work exclusively from the earlier text.[19] Consequently, no mention of the *LM* occurs outside the twelve Byzantine manuscripts that preserve it. This is a silence which testifies more, one would hope, to the long term resonance of Thekla's association with the Apostle Paul than it does to the literary success of the *Life and Miracles* in overturning that tradition.

---

[17] See Appendix 1 below.

[18] Dagron 1978:19.

[19] Dagron 1978:50–51. Likewise, the Syriac tradition does not seem to know the *LM*, and its translations of the *ATh* are very literal—typical, perhaps, for sixth-century Syriac translation technique, but also indicating a reverence for the original legend: see Wright 1990 [1871]:2.116–145 and Burris and Van Rompay 2002 and 2003. The Armenian tradition also seems to know only the *ATh*, but its translation is based on the Syriac (Burris and Van Rompay 2003:10).

# Appendix 1
## A Variant Ending to Thekla's Apostolic Career

THE OVERALL SIGNIFICANCE of the changed ending in the *Life* can be brought into greater relief by comparing a near-contemporary version of these events, which also attempts to wrest control away from the *ATh*, though in different ways. This version is a Greek extension (and not a paraphrase) of the *ATh* and was written probably in the fifth or sixth century.[1] It betrays no direct knowledge of the *Life* but contends with the *Life*'s revision of Thekla's death/disappearance.

The extension comes from one manuscript (G) of the *Acts of Paul* and begins with Thekla already having left Iconium:

> And a cloud of light guided her. And having come into Seleukeia she went outside the city one stade. And she was afraid of them for they worshipped idols. And it guided her to the mountain called Calaman or Rhodeon, and having found there a cave she went into it. And she was there many years and underwent many and grievous trials by the devil and bore them nobly, being assisted by Christ.
>
> LB 1.271

Two elements are shared between this passage and the *Life*: she stayed outside the city on a mountain, and the inhabitants of Seleukeia were pagan worshippers. The *Life*, on the other hand, does not have her retreating to the wilderness, or living in a cave, nor does it have her being tempted by the devil in imitation of Saint Antony.[2] However, the extension does claim to know details about the region, such as her residence outside Seleukeia and the name of the mountain.

---

[1] For the text, see LB 1.271-272.
[2] On "withdrawal" (ἀναχώρησις) in Athanasius' *Life of Antony*, see Brakke 1995:106–107 and Rubenson 1995:116–119.

Additionally, this text also knows that Thekla had developed a reputation for healing, recording just below the passage quoted that, "All the city, therefore, and the country around, having learnt this, brought their sick to the mountain, and before they came near the door [of the cave?] they were speedily released of whatever disease they were afflicted with" (LB 1.271). The most important element here is that Thekla is performing miracles prior to her disappearance, while she is still alive. Like many famous holy persons from the fifth century—and also in imitation of the Gospels—townspeople brought their sick to her, and her power was so great that she did not even need to exit her cave to heal them.[3] The *Life* does not allow her to perform healings until after her disappearance, though she does "miracles which led them to faith" beforehand (*Life* 27.3–6).

The extension goes on to tell the story of some physicians who are incited by a demon to get rid of Thekla because their medical practice has disintegrated in the face of her healing ministry on the mountain. They encourage one another in this plan:

> This holy virgin has influence upon the great goddess Artemis and if she ask anything of her she hears her, being a virgin herself, and all the gods love her ... The physicians said to themselves that if they should be able to defile her neither the gods nor Artemis would listen to her in the case of the sick.
>
> LB 271

Thus, Thekla's virginity and her divine favor are also elements of her character for the writer of this text, who cleverly puts them into the mouths of her enemies as well. The physicians are unwilling to do the defiling themselves, so they bribe two drunk thugs to do the deed. The thugs proceed up the mountain, "rush on the cave like lions," and try to force themselves on her. In their grip she prays to God for help, beginning with a short recapitulation of the *ATh* which emphasizes her escape from Thamyris, Alexander, the "wild beasts," "the abyss" (?), and the "lawless men" now assaulting her.

She ends by praying, "let them not insult my virginity which for your name's sake I have preserved until now" (ibid.). In response, "a voice from heaven" replies with comforting words, "Fear not, Thekla, my true servant, for I am with you. Look and see where an opening has been made for you, for

---

[3] Healing from a distance was surely in imitation of Jesus' miracles from the Gospels (e.g. Matthew 8:5–13), but there are many contemporary uses of the topos: e.g. *Life of Daniel the Stylite* 37, 86, and 88 (by post!).

there shall be for you an everlasting house and there you shall obtain shelter" (LB, 272). Thekla looks around to see that a rock has opened up "big enough for a person to enter" and escapes from the men long enough to disappear into it, leaving behind only her dress in the hands of her attackers (cf. Genesis 39:12). The fissure in the rock reforms itself so completely that "not even a joint could be seen."

Finally, there comes a summary conclusion of the scene: "All this happened by the permission of God for the faith of those seeing the venerable place and for a blessing in the generations afterwards to those who believe in our Lord Jesus Christ out of a pure heart" (ibid.). This smacks of a pilgrim audience more than anything in the ending of the *Life*, and the emphasis on the physical materials in her extended legend—the rock and dress in particular—is also strikingly different.

The last paragraph of the extension offers salient details about Thekla's time at Seleukeia. It says she came from Iconium when she was eighteen years old. After her "journeying and travels (ὁδοιπορίας καὶ περιόδου)" (with Paul?) and her time at Seleukeia, "her retirement on the mountain" (τῆς ἀσκήσεως τῆς ἐν τῷ ὄρει), she lived seventy-two more years. "The Lord took her" when she was ninety: "and thus is her consummation (τελείωσις)." The extension closes with the note that her "commemoration" (ἡ ὁσία μνήμη) is celebrated on the twenty-fourth of September (LB 272).

The character of the extension could not be more different from the *Life*. First, the image it offers of Thekla is that of a female hermit, teaching "wellborn women" from Seleukeia about "the miracles of God." Thekla in the *Life* has no explicit contact with one people group in Seleukeia; she "catechizes" locals and "makes war" against Sarpedon and Athena in a very general manner. The way Thekla is depicted in the extension is not characteristic of the first and second centuries but belongs firmly in late antiquity. In that sense, both texts are trying to introduce contemporary concepts of holy persons and sites into an older, received text. Likewise, the ire of the physicians is a topos shared between the extension and a few miracles (as well as other collections; e.g. Saints Cyrus and John), indicating that these texts rely on a shared rhetoric for Thekla's local battles.

Nevertheless, the *Life* has thoroughly rewritten the *ATh* for the sake of reconstructing Thekla's character from the ground up, and gradually moves post-Antioch towards an explicit image of Thekla as medical healer. It includes no mention of her death, no mention of her ἄσκησις, no mention of the cave, the rock, or any piece of clothing left behind. Thekla is a spiritual being in the *LM*, who continues to haunt the area and perform miracles for the local pilgrims. She is not the female Antony she is made out to be in the extension to the *ATh*. The *Life* could represent, in turn, a significant attempt at wresting Christian biography away from the popular narrative models of the time.

Ironically, even though the author of the extension has left the *ATh* in tact, his version of her activities at Seleukeia does more violence to the narrative style of the *ATh* than the *Life* does, and is more in line with contemporary thinking about narrative representation. The *Life* is an attempt to re-write apocryphal *Acta*, not to write over them; it re vivifies an ancient, received genre and builds onto it.

It is true that these two texts are different literary endeavors with different apparent aims and different apparatus for achieving those aims, but they are also competing forms of a genre. For the author of the *Life*, his association of Thekla with the healing miracles still ongoing at her shrine in Seleukeia did not overrun the necessity of maintaining the order and essential form of his source text. On the other hand, the author of the extension was content to adjust Thekla's character to suit contemporary literary interests that were then manifesting themselves in narrative, ascetic Lives.

# Appendix 2

## The Reception of the *Acts of Paul and Thekla* in Late Antique Sermons (Pseudo-Chrysostom and Severus of Antioch)

THE CLOSE READING OF THE *LIFE* offered in Chapter One above is designed to illustrate the literary activity of one writer on one text. The *Life* is a literary paraphrase of the *ATh* that exhibits certain choices in language and technique unique to its author and setting. However, it is hoped that this analysis also has important things to say about late antique literature and religious culture more widely. With this in mind, I would like now to present and analyze briefly below two late antique sermons that receive the legend of Thekla and change it in a similar way to the *Life*. The homilists' changes to the original story reveal, along with the *Life*, the diversity of the reception of early Christian literature in late antiquity.

The first sermon comes from the large and varied corpus of writings falsely attributed to John Chrysostom. Most of these texts have been shown on manuscript evidence to originate in the fifth and sixth centuries.[1] This *Panegyric to Thekla* is on that basis assumed to come from this period, even though no firm date can be offered.[2] Despite the fact that this sermon is relatively short (a few columns in PG) its reception and re-presentation of the Thekla legend is interesting on a number of counts.

First, it begins with a brief *ekphrasis* on a visual depiction of Thekla that is ostensibly placed before the congregation. The liturgical setting appears to be the saint's feast day:

---

[1] For "Pseudo-Chrysostom" see Aldama 1965, though much unedited material still awaits scholarly attention.

[2] The text of the *Panegyric* exists in two parts: the majority of the text is printed in PG 50, cols. 745–748, but Aubineau 1975:351–352 provides the three concluding paragraphs. See *BHG* 1720 for full manuscript details. See also the translation and short analysis by MacDonald and Scrimgeour 1986.

Today it seems appropriate to reflect on that blessed maiden as she is represented on the icon of memory. On the one side it depicts the crown she won against pleasures, and on the other the crown she won against dangers. On the one side it depicts her virginity, and on the other her presentation of martyrdom to the Master of all.[3]

The binary theme of victory over pleasure and danger is then continued throughout the exposition, corresponding to the two sides or panels of this diptych. But Thekla's victory over physical pleasure is emphasized at the beginning with so much attention to female concerns that it seems reasonable the preacher is speaking to a group of women.[4] "Indeed, nature submitted to the maiden. Even though nature rules as a tyrant among other people, raging for sexual intercourse, in Thekla it adorned virginity." He goes on to cite 1 Corinthians 7:34 in this context: "The unmarried woman cares for the things of the Lord, how to be holy in body and spirit." Then a short lecture on the difficulties of child-bearing and rearing is presented with rhetorical flourish: "How will one provide their education? How should one prepare their marriage contracts? How should one clothe them?"[5]

There are very few direct references to the details of the legend as represented in the *ATh* and the *Life*.[6] Nevertheless, it is clear that the homilist knows the basic story, at least the first half of it: for example, he knows 1) Thekla's parents were ignorant of her desire to be a virgin, 2) she was seduced by Paul's words, 3) she had a suitor that "titillated her" with marriage, and 4) the judges were hesitant to condemn her. There is no mention of fire, or wild beasts, or the arena at Antioch, or her baptism, and there is no suggestion of a ministry of miracles and healing. The suitor who tempted her with marriage is presumably Thamyris, and this may refer to the mysterious "another temptation worse than the first" of *ATh* 25, but there is no indication elsewhere in the sermon that the homilist was reading the text very closely.

Finally, he adds a new story to Thekla's struggles: while pursuing Paul through "the desert," a "suitor on horseback" attacked her where she had

---

[3] Trans. MacDonald and Scrimgeour 1986:154. See also their discussion of Thekla in iconography (157–159), along with the fuller study of Nauerth and Warns 1981.

[4] MacDonald and Scrimgeour 1986:153.

[5] Trans. MacDonald and Scrimgeour 1986:155.

[6] Nauerth and Warns 1981 presents two hypotheses on the icon relating to why the sermon does not recount the story more precisely: either the diptych represents a more primitive version of the legend (49), or its actually an image of Apollo's pursuit of Daphne on horseback being reinterpreted *ex tempore* in a Christian festival setting (72–81). They suggest this sermon was delivered in Pisidian Antioch, a city known for its plethora of classical statuary, but there is little evidence to support this suggestion.

no refuge; immediately after praying to God for rescue, she was made invisible and the rider went away with only "a horse-race of licentiousness."[7] Even though the homilist elsewhere reveals little of which recension of the Thekla legend he might have known, this climactic disappearance may be referring to the extension to the *ATh* discussed above in Appendix 1. Just following her disappearance and the rider's frustration the text reads, "The bride presents herself to the Bridegroom, perhaps singing, 'Truly my help is from the God who save the upright in heart' (Psalm 7:10)."[8] The scene is written as if, when made invisible, Thekla is translated directly into heaven, becoming the (multivalent?) bride for the bridegroom Christ. This interpretation would coincide with how her disappearance was read in the extension, and also to some degree in the *Life*, in that she turns into a spiritual being with spiritual powers.[9] This narrative addition, common to all three late antique texts considered thus far, was perhaps necessary because she was never ultimately martyred in the original; the conflict between divine agency in her rescue(s) in the *ATh* and her lackluster "falling asleep" at Seleukeia precipitated revisions for the sake of a heroic finale to her legend.

In this sermon by "Pseudo-Chrysostom" Thekla's legend has been even further reified. Her virginity is highlighted in this text to such a degree that even her famous battle with the beasts at Antioch, depicted on what must originally have been hundreds of contemporary pilgrim flasks from Egypt, is completely ignored.[10] Thus, when close textual adjustments are not central, given the homiletic genre, the setting, or perhaps even the homilist's general ignorance of the legend, Thekla's virginity has become the focus—not her martyrdoms and, especially, not her miracles. Stephen Davis has shown how this kind of reification of Thekla's legend was also occurring among female monastic communities in the Egyptian desert.[11] A century or more earlier than the pseudo-Chrysostomic homily, Athanasius delivered an address to a community of virgins in which he appropriated Thekla as a model for female chastity.[12] Likewise, in the later homily, the residual memory of Thekla's two

---

[7] Trans. MacDonald and Scrimgeour 1986:156.

[8] Trans. MacDonald and Scrimgeour 1986:156–157.

[9] The new scene could thus be 1) a re-interpretation of Apollo/Daphne (n. 6 above), 2) a much-streamlined version of the attack on Thekla by the thugs in the *ATh* extension, or 3) as Aubineau suggests, "un épisode inconnu de la vie de sainte Thècle" (1975:353). Aubineau, however, unnecessarily assumes the antiquity of the episode and, like Nauerth and Warns, does not provide the comparative research on the *Life* and *ATh* that could contextualize this kind of heroic finale to the *ATh*.

[10] For the sixteen surviving, published *ampullae*, see Davis 2001:195–200.

[11] Davis 2001:87–94.

[12] See Brakke 1995:301–309 for textual information (n. 7) and a translation of the address *On*

heroic martyrdoms—"martyrdom before martyrdom"—is translated into an appeal for courage in the present, sexual battle. In both situations, Thekla's legend has already been "embraced" by the ascetic community.[13] But what is characteristic of each is the synecdochic emphasis on the part for the whole.

While the pseudo-Chrysostomic sermon focuses on one aspect of the Thekla legend, thus reifying her virginity—and in so doing corresponds to Athanasius' attention to that element in *On Virginity*—a sixth-century sermon on Thekla by Severus of Antioch attempts in grand style, like the *Life*, to take in and retell the whole of the legend, albeit in a much shorter narrative space.[14] Severus, in addition, interprets the legend metaphorically as an image of the Church and offers the most interpretatively audacious and sophisticated re-presentation of the *ATh* of all four late antique texts considered in this study (*LM*, *ATh* Greek extension, Pseudo-Chrysostom, and Severus). The sermon is in fact so complex in its intertextuality that the short analysis below will not do justice to all its facets—the sermon's reception of the Thekla legend deserves a dedicated study in its own right. Nevertheless, some important comparative material can be brought to bear on the significance of the *ATh* for late antique literature more broadly.

Severus' sermon begins with what appears to be the scripture reading set for the occasion, Psalm 45:10–17. In later eastern exegesis, this passage was employed as a proof text for Mary's Dormition.[15] Here, however, in sixth-century Syria, Severus interprets the Canaanite "queen" to be the Church. Woven into this interpretation is the story of Thekla, who "by her works produces a reading (*yahba l-meqra*) in her very self (*bah*) of these words of the prophecy."[16] In retelling Thekla's legend, Severus thus makes the *ATh* serve as the avatar of an ecclesiological reading of Psalm 45.

Further analogies between Thekla and the Church are made through examples of marital imagery elsewhere in the Bible. For instance, Severus quotes from Ephesisans 5:25–27 toward the beginning of the sermon, before he has even recounted the story of Thekla's self-baptism. "Christ loved his Church and delivered himself unto her, in order to sanctify her by purifying

---

*Virginity*. The Athanasian authorship of this work is not absolutely secure: see the Introduction above (n. 11) and Johnson 2004a, a review of Davis 2001.

[13] As Davis 2001:89 says for the Egyptian community.

[14] The sermon has been edited and translated into French by Brière (1975 = *PO* 25.121–138). While my interpretation of this sermon differs considerably from her own, I am grateful to Catherine Burris for a pre-publication copy of her forthcoming paper in *Studia Patristica*.

[15] E.g. John of Damascus *Homilies* 3.4. See Daley 1998:236 and, more generally, Mimouni 1995 and Daley 2001.

[16] Brière 1975:121.

her through the bath of water (*shata d-maya*) according to the word . . . in order that she be holy and immaculate."[17] Immediately he adds, "Do you see the agreement of these words?"; Paul and David "cry out" to one another in their mutual identification of Thekla and the Church. As might be expected, Severus also makes use of the Song of Songs, the textual site of so many patristic sermons on the Church. "She entered into the bedroom, in the manner/type of a bride (*ba-dmut kalta*), of which [scene] she spoke through the means of (*b-yad*) the Song of Songs, 'the king made me enter his chamber.'"[18] The spousal imagery in regard to Thekla's virginity appears to be particularly late antique, since the *ATh* makes no use of it, and in that broader sense this sermon falls in line with the extension to the *ATh* and the pseudo-Chrysostomic sermon. However, Severus explicitly calls Thekla the "primary/typical image" (*yuqna tapnkaya*) of the Church, which theologizes both her physical sufferings and her chastity far beyond any text considered thus far.[19]

Severus proceeds after a lengthy introduction to recount the whole story of Thekla as recorded in the *ATh*. A few details of his narration are worth mentioning. First, he pinpoints her hearing Paul's teaching for the first time at the window as the exact moment at which Thekla "fulfilled the image of the Church" (*mmalya l-yuqnah d-'idta*): as if she were an iconographer painting its image through her life. Severus includes no reflection on the writer who penned the legend; rather, Thekla accomplished it all herself.[20] Second, when she visits Paul in prison, she learns from his chains, as the Church does, "how to suffer for Christ."[21] Thekla's intellectual growth through the course of the narrative thus becomes paradigmatic for apostolic history as a whole. For instance, Severus goes on to adduce Matthew 16:18 in describing God's quenching of the flame on the pyre in Iconium:

> Do you see how the martyr resembles up to the end the maternal image (*yuqna 'emhaya*)—of the Church ('*idta*), I mean—in connection to her first elevation [to martyrdom]? "On this rock," says our Savior, "I will build my Church, and the gates of Sheol will not prevail against her." This is why the flame did not conquer the valiant [girl].[22]

---

[17] Brière 1975:122.
[18] Brière 1975:124–125; cf. Song of Songs 1:4, which John of Damascus quotes in his first Dormition homily (*Homilies* 1.11, trans. Daley 1998:196).
[19] Brière 1975:126.
[20] Brière 1975:127.
[21] Brière 1975:129–130.
[22] Brière 1975:130–131.

Severus' use of a verse typically associated with the West in this period demonstrates very well the creativity with which he is intertwining a parainetic ecclesiology and Thekla's legend. Thirdly, and finally—though there is much more of interest in his retelling—Severus addresses directly the question of Thekla's right to teach, which (he affirms) she inherited from Paul.[23] He poses some rhetorical questions:

> And how could Paul write to the Corinthians, "When it comes to the woman, I do not allow her to teach"? And how have those who govern the holy churches ordered in a canon (*qanuna*), "It is not lawful for a woman to cut her hair nor to cover herself with the clothing of a man?"[24]

Severus' answer to these questions is ultimately an appeal to her presence with Paul, but his analogy between her and the Church also saves him. "In effect, Thekla was in possession of, before the [male] appearance (*'eskima*), the force of the reality (*ḥayla da-'bada*)."[25] Thus, the intricacy of his audacious dual exposition of Psalm 45 and Thekla's legend serves the complementary purpose of rescuing Thekla's legitimacy as a virginal model.

Severus' conclusion places Thekla at Seleukeia, as in the *ATh*, but he is also clearly aware of secondary traditions. "She committed (*'ag'lat*) her body to the earth," he says, "[where] it is now hidden in a holy and glorious temple and does those things that are proper to Thekla, that is to say, healings and wonders (*'asyawata w-tedmrata*)." Severus seems to imply here something similar to the *Life*: that she went into the ground of her own volition and did not die, even though he states that her body is still present there, in contradiction to the *LM*. Nevertheless, her continuing spiritual existence at Seleukeia, well known in the *LM*, is consciously affirmed in a way that also affirms the Church's own spiritual activity at Seleukeia "in a joyous and peaceful manner" and in the whole world. He reveals at the end the location of his own sermon, that is, "the church dedicated to the name/memory of Stephen and indeed of her [Thekla]."[26] Like the author of the *Life*, Severus reminds his audience that these two form a pair because they stand as the first martyrs of the Church, male and female.[27] At this point, therefore, his analogy between Thekla and

---

[23] See Brière 1975:132: "And she was attached to a preacher of the truth, while preaching at the same time as him. And, in effect, as she was also his disciple (*mettalmada*), she was in possession of the preparation/purpose (*'utada*) of the master."

[24] Brière 1975:132–133.

[25] Brière 1975:133. This sentence is admittedly rather obscure in the Syriac.

[26] Brière 1975:137.

[27] Cf. *Life* 1.13–18.

the Church breaks down somewhat while he ponders Thekla's place in the company of martyrs (no doubt in remembrance of her feast day, 24 September). In his final exhortation he speaks specifically to the virgins, pointing to Thekla as "an image of perfection similar to the Mother of God" and "the first of the martyrs," and he encourages them "to imitate her intellectual beauty (*šupra methawnana*)."[28] Thus, even though Severus has interrupted the analogy, he returns at the end to the maternal theme he emphasized at the beginning and thereby constructs a unity of metaphor and presentation that far surpasses the pseudo-Chrysostomic sermon.

How, then, does Severus fit into the history of the reception of Thekla in late antiquity? It should be emphasized up front how audacious the conception of this compact sermon really is: in the sense that it places Thekla into a grand literary endeavor similar to, though more subtle and much shorter than, the *LM*. Whereas the extension to the *ATh* and the pseudo-Chrysostomic sermon reify Thekla's virginity—of course, already reified to some degree in the *ATh* itself—Severus' sermon actually seeks to unpack the reification and re-apply Thekla's legend, subverting the traditional picture by proposing an analogy (or even an allegory) of her and the Church. The element of surprise in Severus' sermon is unique to him—perhaps somewhat present in the *Miracles* also—and shows the high level to which the best late antique writers could take cultic and literary intertextuality. While he shares certain narrative devices with the *Life*, his presentation is not dominated by narrative, and at points the original story—which, to reiterate, he includes in toto—runs with real fluidity. This is a very different experience from reading the *Life*, with its plodding speeches and formal Greek. Severus has, in fact, improved on the *ATh* both in narrative speed and elocution: he assumes some knowledge of the legend but neverthe-less furnishes his audience with the whole story, all the while pointing to a larger, more homiletically powerful theme.

Although the *Life* and Severus' sermon represent different genres, a comparison of their use of source material proves instructive. The genre of the paraphrase, at least as it is deployed in the *Life*, seems like much more of a school exercise which the author is working through, not feeling that he has something new to contribute, even though he claims that he does. The immediacy of Severus' appropriation of Thekla is plain from the beginning, where he starts, however, with neither Thekla or the Church but with Psalm 45, and he continues to interweave this text at various points throughout the

---

[28] Brière 1975:138.

sermon. Overall, the sermon is convincing in a way that the *Life* is not. The *Life* is an important work from late antiquity in terms of its length, in terms of its genre, in terms of its reorientation of the legend towards Seleukeia, and in terms of its author's unique self-presentation. However, in terms of literary value and success, Severus' collage of Thekla, Pauline ethical texts, Psalm 45, and late antique ecclesiology is a greater achievement of creativity and authorial control.

# Appendix 3

## Early Byzantine Miracle Collections: A Select Catalogue

T HE LIST BELOW comprises a select (alphabetical) catalogue of miracle collections in Greek from early Byzantium, fifth to eighth centuries.[1] While I have included the *Miracles of Thekla* as part of this catalogue, I would at the same time seek to distinguish the *Miracles* from these other collections on the basis of three factors. First, I have attempted to show in this study that the *LM* is written as a narrative whole, and the stories in the *Miracles* correspond to a unique, authorial vision of Thekla's spiritual activities laid out at the end of the *Life*. Second, I believe that the author of the *LM* is consciously looking back to earlier, classical models for his literary endeavor and is relatively uninterested in the literary products of his own day. Third, the collections listed below mostly come from the seventh century and later and belong to what I would consider to be a different epoch in Greek writing. Nevertheless, to insist upon a complete breach between the *LM* and the early Byzantine collections would be unwise, especially since no one has yet written a literary study that takes them all into account.[2] I hope in the future to have the opportunity to perform such a study.

---

[1] See the catalogue of Efthymiadis 1999 for more comprehensive coverage, including collections up to the end of Byzantium. However, his entry for Thekla's collection includes a few minor errors: 1) a closing date for its composition before 448 (Dagron 1978:17–19 rightly assigns it to between c. 468 and c. 476); 2) the claim that there are only two MSS of the *Miracles* (four are extant according to Dagron 1978:140–147); and 3) the suggestion that the miracles belong to the distant past of the 1st century (*Mir.* preface 12–13 clearly states that the miracle stories are contemporary or near contemporary to the composition of the collection).

[2] There is still a very limited amount of scholarship on Greek miracle collections per se. However, interest is beginning to grow: see Déroche 1993, Csepregi 2002, Talbot 2002b, and especially the bibliography collected in Efthymiadis 1999.

Saint:                   Anastasios the Persian (d. 628)
Author:              Anonymous
Miraculous Content:   18 miracles (Flusin: 1.109–153)
Date of Composition:  7<sup>th</sup> century
Location of Activity:   Asia Minor and Palestine
Catalogue Entry:     *BHG* 89g–90
Edition:            Flusin, B. ed. and trans. 1992. *Saint Anastase le Perse et l'histoire de la Palestine au début du VII<sup>e</sup> siècle.* 2 vols. Paris.

Saint:                   Artemios (4<sup>th</sup> century)
Author:              Anonymous
Miraculous Content:   45 miracles (Crisafulli and Nesbitt: 76–225)
Date of Composition:  7<sup>th</sup> century
Location of Activity:   Constantinople, church of St. John the Baptist (the "Forerunner")
Catalogue Entry:     *BHG* 173
Editions:          Crisafulli, V. S. and Nesbitt, J. W., trans. 1997. *The Miracles of Saint Artemios: A Collection of Miracle Stories by an Anonymous Author of Seventh-Century Byzantium.* Medieval Mediterranean 13. Leiden.
                    Papadopoulos-Kerameus, A. I., ed. 1909. *Varia graeca sacra.* St. Petersburg.

Saints:                  Cosmas and Damian (4<sup>th</sup> century)
Author:              Anonymous
Miraculous Content:   47 miracles (Deubner: 97–208; Rupprecht: 1–82; Festugière: 83–213)
Date of Composition:  6<sup>th</sup> century (with later redactions: see Efthymiadis 1999:197–198)
Location of Activity:   Constantinople, Kosmidion shrine of the Saints; and elsewhere
Catalogue Entries:    *BHG* 385–391 (Deubner); 373b (Rupprecht)
Editions:          Deubner, L., ed. 1980 [1907]. *Kosmas und Damian: Texte und Einleitung.* Aalen.
                    Rupprecht, E., ed. 1935. *Cosmae et Damiani sanctorum medicorum vita et miracula e codice londinensi.* Neue deutsche Forschungen, Abteilung klassische Philologie 1. Berlin.

Festugière, A. J., trans. 1971. *Collections grecques de Miracles: Sainte Thècle, Saints Côme et Damien, Saints Cyr et Jean (extraits), Saint Georges—traduits et annotés.* Paris.

| | |
|---|---|
| Saints: | Cyrus and John (4th century) |
| Author: | Sophronios "the Sophist" of Jerusalem |
| Miraculous Content: | 70 miracles (Fernandez Marcos: 241–400; Festugière: 215–256) |
| Date of Composition: | Early 7th century |
| Location of Activity: | Menouthis, near Canopos in Egypt |
| Catalogue Entries: | *BHG* 477–479, *CPG* 3.7646 |
| Edition: | Fernández Marcos, N., ed. 1975. *Los thaumata de Sofronio: Contribución al estudio de la incubatio christiana.* Madrid. |
| | Festugière, A. J., trans. 1971. *Collections grecques de Miracles: Sainte Thècle, Saints Côme et Damien, Saints Cyr et Jean (extraits), Saint Georges—traduits et annotés.* Paris. [partial translation] |

| | |
|---|---|
| Saint: | Demetrios (4th century) |
| Author: | John of Thessalonica and anonymous |
| Miraculous Content: | 15 miracles by John (Lemerle: 1.47—165) |
| | 6 miracles by anonymous (Lemerle: 1.167–241) |
| Date of Composition: | 7th century |
| Location of Activity: | Thessalonica |
| Catalogue Entries: | *BHG* 499–523, *CPG* 3.7920 |
| Edition: | Lemerle, P. ed. and trans. 1979. *Les plus anciens recueils des Miracles de Saint Démétrius.* 2 vols. Paris. |

| | |
|---|---|
| Saint: | Menas (4th century) |
| Author: | Timothy of Alexandria (possibly Timothy Aelurus) |
| Miraculous Content: | 13 miracles (Detorakis: 165–179) |
| Date of Composition: | Late 5th century or later |
| Location of Activity: | Around Abu Mina, near Lake Mareotis in Egypt |
| Catalogue Entries: | *BHG* 1256–1269, *CPG* 2.2527 |
| Edition: | Detorakis, T., ed. 1995. Μηνᾶς ὁ Μεγαλομάρτυς ὁ ἅγιος τοῦ Μεγάλου Κάστρου: Ἁγιολογικά, Ὑμνολογικά, Ἱστορικά. Herakleion. |

Saint:              Nikolaos of Myra (4th century)
Author:             Anonymous
Miraculous Content: 6 miracles *ex encomio Methodii*, incl. *Tria Miracula*
                    (Anrich: 1.168–197)
                    Miracle *de navibus frumentariis* (Anrich: 1.288–299)
                    Miracle *de arbore* (Anrich: 1.333–336)
                    19 miracles (Anrich: 1.339–390)
                    [several more individual miracles and small collec-
                    tions: see *BHG*]
Date of Composition: 6th century and later
Location of Activity: Myra
Catalogue Entry:    *BHG* 1348d–1348e, 1350k, 1351–1351s, 1352–1352x,
                    1353–1360m
Edition:            Anrich, G., ed. 1913. *Hagios Nikolaos: Der heilige Nikolaos*
                    *in der griechischen Kirche.* 2 vols. Leipzig.

Saint:              Patapios the Egyptian (7th century)
Author:             Andrew of Crete
Miraculous Content: 4 miracles (PG)
Date of Composition: after 685
Location of Activity: Constantinople
Catalogue Entries:  *BHG* 1426–1427, *CPG* 3.8189
Edition:            PG 97.1221–1233

Saint:              Symeon Stylites the Younger (521–592)
Author:             Anonymous
Miraculous Content: several mini-collections within the narrative *Life* (esp.
                    §§ 14, 39–56, 73–77, 79–93, 114–122, 136–156, 166–185,
                    188–201, 212–232, 234–239, 241–254; Ven: 1–224)
Date of Composition: c. 600
Location of Activity: Monastery of the Saint at the Wondrous Mountain
                    near Antioch
Catalogue Entries:  *BHG* 1689, *CPG* 3.7369
Edition:            Ven, P. van den., ed. and trans. 1962–1970. *La Vie*
                    *ancienne de S. Syméon Stylite le Jeune (521–92).* Subsidia
                    Hagiographica 32. 2 vols. Brussels.

| | |
|---|---|
| Saint: | Thekla (1st century) |
| Author: | Anonymous |
| Miraculous Content: | 46 miracles contemporary with the collection (Dagron: 284–412) |
| Date of Composition: | c. 470 |
| Location of Activity: | Seleukeia and environs |
| Catalogue Entry: | *BHG* 1718, *CPG* 3.6675 |
| Edition: | Dagron, G., ed. and trans. 1978.*Vie et Miracles de Sainte Thècle: Texte grec, traduction, et commentaire.* Subsidia Hagiographica 62. Brussels. |

| | |
|---|---|
| Saint: | Theodore Tiro (4th century) |
| Author: | Chrysippos of Jerusalem & anonymous |
| Miraculous Content: | 12 miracles (Sigalas: 50–79) |
| | 8 miracles (Delehaye: 194–201) |
| Date of Composition: | 5th and 8th century |
| Location of Activity: | Euchaita |
| Catalogue Entry: | *BHG* 1765c, *CPG* 3.6706 (Sigalas); *BHG* 1764 (Delehaye) |
| Editions: | Sigalas, A., ed. 1921. *Des Chrysippos von Jerusalem Enkomion auf den hl. Theodoros Teron.* Byzantinisches Archiv 7. Leipzig. |
| | Delehaye, H. ed. 1909. *Les légendes grecques des Saints militaires.* Paris. |

| | |
|---|---|
| Saint: | Therapon |
| Author: | Anonymous (possibly Andrew of Crete) |
| Miraculous Content: | 15 miracles in 28 narrative sections (Deubner: 120–134) |
| Date of Composition: | c. 700 |
| Location of Activity: | Constantinople, church of the Theotokos of Elaia |
| Catalogue Entry: | *BHG* 1797–1798, *CPG* 3.8196 |
| Edition: | Deubner, L., ed. 1900. *De incubatione capita quattuor: Accedit Laudatio in miracula sancti hieromartyris Therapontis denuo edita.* Leipzig. |

# References

Accorinti, D., ed. 1996. *Nonno di Panopoli—Parafrasi del Vangelo di S. Giovanni, Canto XX: Introduzione, testo critico, traduzione e commento.* Pisa.

Achtemeier, P. 1970. "Towards the Isolation of Pre-Markan Miracle Catenae." *JBL* 89:265–291.

Adler, W. 1989. *Time Immemorial: Archaic History and its Sources in Christian Chronography from Julius Africanus to George Syncellus.* Washington, DC.

Agosti, G., ed. 2003. *Nonno di Panopoli—Parafrasi del Vangelo di San Giovanni, Canto Quinto: Introduzione, edizione critica, traduzione, e commento.* Florence.

Aland, K. 1987. "Alter und Entstehung des D-Textes im Neuen Testament: Betrachtungen zu P69 und 0171." *Miscellania Papirologica Ramon Roca-Puig* (ed. S. Janeras) 37–61. Barcelona.

Aldama, J. A. de, ed. 1965. *Repertorium Pseudochrysostomicum.* Documents, études, et répetoires 10. Paris.

Alexander, P. S. 1992. "Targum, Targumim." *ABD* 6:320–331.

Alter, R. 2004. *The Five Books of Moses: A Translation and Commentary.* New York.

———. 2000. *Canon and Creativity: Modern Writing and the Authority of Scripture.* New Haven.

Alter, R. and Kermode, F., eds. 1987. *The Literary Guide to the Bible.* Cambridge, MA.

Aly, W. 1935. "Aretalogoi." *RE Supplementary Volume* 6:13–15.

Amand, D. and Moons, M.-C., eds. 1953. "Une curieuse homélie grecque inédite sur la virginité adressée aux pères de famille." *Revue Bénédictine* 63:18–69, 211–238.

Ammassari, A., ed. 1996. *Bezae Codex Cantabrigiensis: Copia esatta del manoscritto onciale greco-latino dei quattro Vangeli e degli Atti degli Apostoli scritto all'inizio del V secolo e presentato da Theodore Beza all'Università di Cambridge nel 1581.* Vatican City.

Amsler, F., Bovon, F., and Bouvier, F., eds. 1996. *Actes de l'apôtre Philippe; Introduction, traductions, et notes.* Apocryphes 8. Turnhout.

Anrich, G., ed. 1913. *Hagios Nikolaos: Der heilige Nikolaos in der griechischen Kirche.* 2 vols. Leipzig.

Arnar, A. S., ed. 1990. *Encyclopedism from Pliny to Borges.* Chicago.

Ashbrook Harvey, S. 2002. "Why the Perfume Mattered: The Sinful Woman in Syriac Exegetical Tradition." In *Dominico Eloquio—In Lordly Eloquence: Essays on Patristic Exegesis in Honor of Robert Louis Wilken* (ed. P. M. Blowers et al.) 69–89. Grand Rapids, MI.

Athanassiadi, P., ed. 1999. *Damascius: The Philosophical History.* Athens.

Aubin, M. 1998. "Reversing Romance? The *Acts of Thekla* and the Ancient Novel." In Hock, Chance, and Perkins 1998:257–272.

Aubineau, M., ed. 1975. "Le *Panégyrique de Thècle* attribué à Jean Chrysostome (*BHG* 1720)." *AnBoll* 93:349–362.

Austin, J. L. 1975. *How to do Things with Words: The William James Lectures Delivered at Harvard University in 1955.* 2nd edition. Oxford.

Bandy, A. C. 1983. *Ioannes Lydus: On Powers, or The Magistracies of the Roman State.* Philadelphia.

Barnes, Robert. 2000. "Cloistered Bookworms in the Chicken-Coop of the Muses: The Ancient Library of Alexandria." *The Library of Alexandria* (ed. R. MacLeod) 61–77. London.

Barnes, Timothy D. 1971. *Tertullian: A Historical and Literary Study.* Oxford.

———. 1989. "The Date of the Council of Gangra." *JTS* N.S. 40:120–125.

Barthélemy, D., ed. 1963. *Les devanciers d'Aquila: première publication intégrale du texte des fragments du Dodécapropheton trouvés dans le désert de Juda, précédée d'une étude sur les traductions et recensions grecques de la Bible réalisées au premier siècle de notre ère sous l'influence du rabbinat palestinien.* Supplements to Vetus Testamentum 10. Leiden.

Beattie, D. R. G. and McNamara, M. J., eds. 1994. *The Aramaic Bible: Targums in their Historical Context.* Journal for the Study of the Old Testament Supplement Series 166. Sheffield.

Beck, R. 1996. "Mystery Religions, Aretalogy, and the Ancient Novel." In Schmeling 1996:131–150.

Bedouelle, G. 2002. "The Paraphrases of Erasmus in French." In Pabel and Vessey 2002:279–290.

Behr, C. A. 1968. *Aelius Aristides and the Sacred Tales*. Amsterdam.

———, ed. 1976. *P. Aelii Aristidis Opera Quae Exstant Omnia*. Leiden.

———. 1981. *P. Aelius Aristides: The Complete Works*. Leiden.

Berger, A. 1953. *Encyclopedic Dictionary of Roman Law*. Philadelphia.

Bernstein, M. J. 1994. "4Q252: From Rewritten Bible to Biblical Commentary." *JJS* 45:1–27.

Bethe, E., ed. 1967. *Pollucis Onomasticon*. 3 vols. Stuttgart.

Bidez, J. and Hansen, G. C., eds. 1995. *Sozomenus Kirchengeschichte*. GCS 4. Berlin.

Birdsall, J. N. 1990. Review of Livrea 1989. *CR* N.S. 40:472–473.

Bloch, M. E. F. 1998. *How we Think they Think: Anthropological Approaches to Cognition, Memory, and Literacy*. Boulder, CO.

Bloom, A. 1994. *The Western Canon: The Books and School of the Ages*. New York.

Bolton, J. D. P. 1962. *Aristeas of Proconnesus*. Oxford.

Bonwetsch, D. G. N., ed. 1917. *Methodius*. GCS 27. Leipzig.

Borges, J. L. 2002 [1970]. *The Book of Imaginary Beings*. Trans. J. L. Borges and N. T. di Giovanni. London.

Borries, J. von, ed. 1911. *Phrynichi Sophistae Praeparatio Sophistica*. Leipzig.

Bovon, F. 1988. "The Synoptic Gospels and the Non-canonical Acts of the Apostles." *HTR* 81:19–36.

———. 1999a. "Byzantine Witnesses for the Apocryphal Acts of the Apostles." In Bovon, Brock, and Matthews 1999:87–98.

———. 1999b. "Editing the Apocryphal Acts of the Apostles." In Bovon, Brock, and Matthews 1999:2–35.

———. 2001. "Facing the Scriptures: Mimesis and Intertextuality in the Acts of Philip." In MacDonald 2001:138–153.

———. 2002. *Luke 1: A Commentary on the Gospel of Luke 1:1–9:50*. Hermeneia. Minneapolis.

Bovon, F., Bouvier, B., and Amsler, F., eds. 1999. *Acta Philippi: Textus*. CCSA 11. Turnhout.

Bovon, F., Brock, A. G., and Matthews, C. R., eds. 1999. *The Apocryphal Acts of the Apostles: Harvard Divinity School Studies*. Religions of the World. Cambridge, MA.

Bowersock, G. W. 1994. *Fiction as History: Nero to Julian*. Sather Classical Lectures 58. Berkeley and Los Angeles.

———. 1995. *Martyrdom and Rome*. Wiles Lectures. Cambridge.

Bowersock, G. W., Brown, P., and Grabar, O., eds. 1999. *Late Antiquity: A Guide to the Postclassical World*. Cambridge, MA.

Boyarin, D. 1990. *Intertextuality and the Reading of Midrash*. Bloomington, IN.

Brakke, D. 1998 [1995]. *Athanasius and Asceticism*. Baltimore.

Braund, D. and Wilkins, J., eds. 2000. *Athenaeus and his World: Reading Greek Culture in the Roman Empire*. Exeter.

Brière, M., ed. 1975. "Les *Homiliae Cathedrales* de Sévère d'Antioche: Homélies CIV à CXII." *PO* 25:121–138. Paris.

Brock, S. P. 1990. *Hymns on Paradise: Saint Ephrem*. Crestwood, NY.

———. 1992a. *The Luminous Eye: The Spiritual World Vision of Saint Ephrem the Syrian*. Kalamazoo, MI.

———. 1992b. "To Revise or not to Revise: Attitudes to Biblical Translation." In Brooke and Lindars 1992:301–338.

Brooke, G. J. and Lindars, B., eds. 1992. *Septuagint, Scrolls, and Cognate Writings: Papers Presented to the International Symposium on the Septuagint and Its Relations to the Dead Sea Scrolls and Other Writings*. Atlanta.

Brown, P. 1973. "A Dark Age Crisis: Aspects of the Iconoclastic Controversy." *English Historical Review* 88:1–34. [Reprinted in Brown 1982:251–301.]

———. 1981. *The Cult of the Saints: Its Rise and Function in Latin Christianity*. Haskell Lectures on the History of Religions (New Series) 2. Chicago.

———. 1982. *Society and the Holy in Late Antiquity*. Berkeley and Los Angeles.

———. 1988. *The Body and Society: Men, Women, and Sexual Renunciation in Early Christianity*. Lectures on the History of Religions. New York.

———. 2002. *Poverty and Leadership in the Later Roman Empire*. Menahem Stern Jerusalem Lectures. Hanover, NH.

Browning, R. 2000. "Education in the Roman Empire." In Averil Cameron, Ward-Perkins, and Michael Whitby 2000:855–883.

Budge, E. A. W., ed. 2002. *The Book of Medicines: Ancient Syrian Anatomy, Pathology, and Therapeutics*. London.

Burgess, R. W. 1999. *Studies in Eusebian and Post-Eusebian Chronography*. Historia Einzelschriften 135. Stuttgart.

Burridge, R. A. 1992. *What are the Gospels? A Comparison with Greco-Roman Biography*. Cambridge.

Burris, C. forthcoming. "Imagining Thecla: Rhetorical Strategies in Severus of Antioch's 97th Cathedral Homily," *Studia Patristica: Papers Presented at the Fourteenth International Conference on Patristic Studies.*

Burris, C. and Van Rompay, L. 2002. "Thekla in Syriac Christianity: Preliminary Observations." *Hugoye: Journal of Syriac Studies* [http://syrcom.cua.edu/hugoye] 5.2.

———. 2003. "Some Further Notes on Thekla in Syriac Christianity." *Hugoye: Journal of Syriac Studies* [http://syrcom.cua.edu/hugoye] 6.2.

Burrus, V. 1987. *Chastity as Autonomy: Women in the Stories of Apocryphal Acts.* Studies in Women and Religion 23. Lewiston, NY.

———. 2004. *Sex Lives of Saints: An Erotics of Ancient Hagiography.* Divinations. Philadelphia.

Cadbury, H. J. 1966. "Four Features of Lucan Style." *Studies in Luke-Acts* (ed. L. E. Keck and J. L. Martyn) 87–102. London.

Callahan, A. D. 1996. "Again: The Origin of the Codex Bezae." In Parker and Amphoux 1996:56–64.

Cameron, Alan D. E. 1965. "Wandering Poets: A Literary Movement in Byzantine Egypt." *Historia* 14:470–509.

———. 1982. "The Empress and the Poet: Paganism and Politics at the Court of Theodosius II." *YClS* 27:217–289.

———. 2004. "Poetry and Literary Culture in Late Antiquity." *Approaching Late Antiquity* (ed. M. Edwards and S. Swain) 327–354. Oxford.

Cameron, Averil M. 1990. "Models of the Past in the Late Sixth Century: The Life of the Patriarch Eutychius." *Reading the Past in Late Antiquity* (ed. B. Croke, A. E. Nobbs, and R. Mortley) 205–223. Rushcutters Bay, Australia. [Reprinted in Averil Cameron 1996, II]

———. 1991. *Christianity and the Rhetoric of Empire: The Development of Christian Discourse.* Sather Classical Lectures 55. Berkeley and Los Angeles.

———. 1992. "New Themes and Styles in Greek Literature." *The Byzantine and Early Islamic Near East* (ed. Averil Cameron and L. I. Conrad) 81–105. Princeton.

———. 1996. *Changing Cultures in Byzantium.* Variorum Reprints. Aldershot.

———. 1998. "Education and Literary Culture." In Averil Cameron and Garnsey 1998:665–707.

———. 1999. "Remaking the Past." In Bowersock, Brown, and Grabar 1999:2–20.

——. 2000a. "The Early Cult of the Virgin." In Vassilaki 2000:3–15.

——. 2000b. "Form and Meaning: The *Vita Constantini* and the *Vita Antonii*." In Hägg and Rousseau 2000:72–88.

——. 2003a. "How to Read Heresiology." *Journal of Medieval and Early Modern Studies* 33:471–492.

——. 2003b. "Jews and Heretics—A Category Error?" *The Ways that Never Parted* (ed. A. H. Becker and A. Y. Reed) 345–360. Tübingen.

——. 2004. "The Cult of the Virgin in Late Antiquity: Religious Development and Myth-Making." *The Church and Mary* (ed. R. N. Swanson) 1–21. Woodbridge.

Cameron, Averil M. and Garnsey, P., eds. 1998. *The Cambridge Ancient History: The Late Empire AD 337–425*. Cambridge.

Cameron, Averil M. and Hall, S. G. 1999. *Eusebius: Life of Constantine*. Clarendon Ancient History Series. Oxford.

Cameron, Averil M. and Herrin, J., eds. 1984. *Constantinople in the Early Eighth Century: The Parastaseis Syntomoi Chronikai—Introduction, Translation, and Commentary*. Columbia Studies in the Classical Tradition 10. Leiden.

Cameron, Averil M., Ward-Perkins, B., and Whitby, Michael, eds. 2000. *The Cambridge Ancient History: Late Antiquity, Empire and Successors AD 425–600*. Cambridge.

Caner, D. 2002. *Wandering, Begging Monks: Spiritual Authority and the Promotion of Monasticism in Late Antiquity*. Transformation of the Classical Heritage 33. Berkeley and Los Angeles.

Canivet, P., ed. 1977–1979. *Histoire des moines de Syrie: Histoire Philothée*. 2 vols. SC 234, 257. Paris.

——, ed. 2000–2001. *Théodoret de Cyr: Thérapeutique des maladies helléniques*. Revised edition. 2 vols. SC 57. Paris.

Carey, S. 2003. *Pliny's Catalogue of Culture: Art and Empire in the Natural History*. Oxford.

Carruthers, M. 1997. *The Craft of Thought: Meditation, Rhetoric, and the Making of Images, 400–1200*. Cambridge.

Ceresa-Gastaldo, A. 1988. *Gerolamo: Gli Uomini Illustri*. Florence.

Chabot, J.-B., ed. 1902. *Synodicon Orientale ou Recueil de synodes nestoriens*. Paris.

Chaniotis, A. 1988. *Historie und Historiker in den griechischen Inschriften: Epigraphische Beiträge zur griechischen Historiographie*. Stuttgart.

Charlesworth, J. H., ed. 1985. *The Old Testament Pseudepigrapha.* 2 vols. New York.

Chartier, R. 1997. *On the Edge of the Cliff: History, Language, and Practices.* Trans. L. G. Cochrane. Baltimore.

Clark, E. A. 1992. *The Origenist Controversy: The Cultural Construction of an Early Christian Debate.* Princeton.

———. 2004. *History, Theory, Text: Historians and the Linguistic Turn.* Cambridge, MA.

Cohen, G. M. 1995. *The Hellenistic Settlements in Europe, the Islands, and Asia Minor.* Berkeley and Los Angeles.

Coleman, J. 1992. *Ancient and Medieval Memories: Studies in the Reconstruction of the Past.* Cambridge.

Collins, A. Y. 1992. *The Beginning of the Gospel: Probings of Mark in Context.* Minneapolis.

Constas, N., ed. 2003. *Proclus of Constantinople and the Cult of the Virgin in Late Antiquity: Homilies 1-5, Texts and Translations.* Supplements to Vigilliae Christianae 66. Leiden.

Conzelmann, H. 1987. *Acts of the Apostles: A Commentary.* Edition by E. J. Epp and C. R. Matthews. Trans. J. Limburg et al. Hermeneia. Philadelphia.

Cooper, K. 1995. "A Saint in Exile: The Early Medieval Thekla at Rome and Meriamlik." *Hagiographica* 2:1–23.

———. 1996. *The Virgin and the Bride: Idealized Womanhood in Late Antiquity.* Cambridge, MA.

Copeland, Kirsti. 2000. "Mapping the Apocalypse of Paul: Geography, Genre, and History." Ph.D. dissertation, Princeton University.

Copeland, Rita. 1991. *Rhetoric, Hermeneutics, and Translation in the Middle Ages: Academic Traditions and Vernacular Texts.* Cambridge Studies in Medieval Literature 11. Cambridge.

Coulie, B. and Sherry, L. F. 1995. *Thesaurus Pseudo-Nonni Quondam Panopolitani: Paraphrasis Evangelii S. Ioannis.* Thesaurus Patrum Graecorum. Turnhout.

Cox Miller, P. 1983. *Biography in Late Antiquity: A Quest for the Holy Man.* Transformation of the Classical Heritage 5. Berkeley and Los Angeles.

———. 1994. *Dreams in Late Antiquity: Studies in the Imagination of a Culture.* Princeton.

Craig, J. 2002. "Forming a Protestant Consciousness? Erasmus' Paraphrases in English Parishes, 1547–1666." In Pabel and Vessey 2002:313–359.

Crisafulli, V. S. and Nesbitt, J. W. 1997. *The Miracles of Saint Artemios: A Collection of Miracle Stories by an Anonymous Author of Seventh-Century Byzantium.* Medieval Mediterranean 13. Leiden.

Croke, B. 1982. "The Originality of Eusebius' *Chronicle.*" *AJP* 103:195–200.

———. 1990a. "City Chronicles of Late Antiquity." *Reading the Past in Late Antiquity* (ed. B. Croke, A. E. Nobbs, and R. Mortley) 165–203. Rushcutters Bay, Australia.

———. 1990b. "The Early Development of Byzantine Chronicles." *Studies in John Malalas* (ed. E. A. Jeffreys) 27–38. Sydney.

———. 2001. *Count Marcellinus and his Chronicle.* Oxford.

Crouzel, H. 1969. *Grégoire le Thaumaturge: Remerciement à Origène suivi de la letter d'Origène à Grégoire—texte grec, introduction, traduction, et notes.* SC 148. Paris.

Csepregi, I. 2002. "The Miracles of Saints Cosmas and Damian: Characteristics of Dream Healing." *Annual of Medieval Studies at the Central European University* 8:89–121.

Culler, J. 1979. "Jacques Derrida." *Structuralism and Since: From Lévi-Strauss to Derrida* (ed. J. Sturrock) 154–180. Oxford.

Culpepper, R. A. 1994. *John, the Son of Zebedee: The Life and Legend.* Columbia, SC.

Dagron, G. 1974. "L'auteur des 'actes' et des 'miracles' de Sainte Thècle." *AnBoll* 92:5–11.

———, ed. 1978. *Vie et Miracles de Sainte Thècle: Texte grec, traduction, et commentaire.* Subsidia Hagiographica 62. Brussels.

———. 1984. *Constantinople Imaginaire: Études sur le recueil des Patria.* Bibliothèque Byzantine 8. Paris.

Dain, A. 1954. *Le Philétaeros, attribué à Hérodien.* Paris.

Daley, B. E. 1998. *On the Dormition of Mary: Early Patristic Homilies.* Crestwood, NY.

———. 2001. " 'At the Hour of Our Death': Mary's Dormition and Christian Dying in Late Patristic and Early Byzantine Literature." *DOP* 55:71–89.

Daniélou, J. 1955. *Origen.* Trans. W. Mitchell. New York.

Davis, S. J. 2000. "A 'Pauline' Defense of Women's Right to Baptize? Intertextuality and Apostolic Authority in the *Acts of Paul.*" *JECS* 8:453–459.

——. 2001. *The Cult of St Thecla: A Tradition of Women's Piety in Late Antiquity*. Oxford Early Christian Studies. Oxford.

Dean, J. E., ed. 1935, *Epiphanius' Treatise on Weights and Measures: The Syriac Version*. Studies in Ancient Oriental Civilization 11. Chicago.

Denniston, J. D. 1954. *The Greek Particles*. 2nd edition. Oxford.

Déroche, V. 1993. "Pourquoi écrivait-on des recueils de miracles? L'exemple des Miracles de saint Artémios." *Les saints et leur sanctuaires à Byzance: textes, images et monuments* (ed. C. Jolivet-Lévy et al.) 95–116. Paris.

Derrida, J. 1974. *Of Grammatology*. Trans. G. Spivak. Baltimore.

——. 1996. *Archive Fever: A Fruedian Impression*. Trans. E. Prenowitz. Chicago.

Detorakis, T., ed. 1995. *Μηνᾶς ὁ Μεγαλομάρτυς ὁ ἅγιος τοῦ Μεγάλου Κάστρου: Ἁγιολογικά, Ὑμνολογικά, Ἱστορικά*. Herakleion.

De Stephani, C., ed. 2002. *Nonno di Panopoli-Parafrasi del Vangelo di S. Giovanni, Canto 1; Introduzione, testo critco, traduzione e commento*. Eikasmos 6. Bologna.

Deubner, L. 1900., ed. *De incubatione capita quattuor: Accedit Laudatio in miracula sancti hieromartyris Therapontis denuo edita*. Leipzig.

——, ed. 1980 [1907]. *Kosmas und Damian: Texte und Einleitung*. Aalen.

Dewald, C. 1987. "Narrative Surface and Authorial Voice in Herodotus' *Histories*." *Arethusa* 20:147–170.

——. 2002. " 'I didn't give my own genealogy': Herodotus and the Authorial Persona." *Brill's Companion to Herodotus* (ed. E. J. Bakker, I. J. F. de Jong, and H. van Wees) 267–289. Leiden.

Díez Merino, L. 1994. "Targum Manuscripts and Critical Editions." In Beattie and McNamara 1994:51–91.

Diller, A. 1938. "The Tradition of Stephanus Byzantinus." *TAPA* 69:333–348.

Dilts, M. R., ed. 1974. *Claudii Aeliani Varia historia*. Leipzig.

Dinzelbacher, P. 1991. "La *Visio S. Pauli*: Circulation et influence d'un apocryphe eschatologique." *Apocrypha* 2:165–180.

Doctorow, M., Wittock, M. C., and Marks, C. 1978. "Generative Processes in Reading Comprehension." *Journal of Educational Psychology* 70:109–118.

Dodds, E. R. 1951. *The Greeks and the Irrational*. Sather Classical Lectures 25. Berkeley and Los Angeles.

Dombart, B. and Kalb, A., eds. 1981. *Augustinus de civitate dei*. 5th edition. 2 vols. Stuttgart.

Dorandi, T., ed. 1999. *Antigone de Caryste: Fragments.* Paris.

Dorati, M. and Guidorizzi, G. 1996. "La letteratura incubatoria." *La letteratura di consumo nel mondo greco-latino* (ed. O. Pecere and A. Stramaglia) 345–372. Cassino.

Dunn, P. W. 1993. "Women's Liberation, the *Acts of Paul*, and Other Apocryphal Acts of the Apostles: A Review of Some Recent Interpreters." *Apocrypha* 4:245–261.

Edelstein, E. J. and Edelstein, L. 1998 [1945]. *Asclepius: Collection and Interpretation of the Testimonies.* Baltimore.

Edelstein, L. 1968. *Ancient Medicine: Selected Papers of Ludwig Edelstein.* Edited by O. Temkin and C. L. Temkin. Baltimore.

Edwards, M. J. 1997. "Simon Magus, the Bad Samaritan." In Edwards and Swain 1997:69–91.

Edwards, M. J. and Swain, S., eds. 1997. *Portraits: Biographical Representation in the Greek and Latin Literature of the Roman Empire.* Oxford.

Efthymiadis, S. 1999. "Greek Byzantine Collections of Miracles: A Chronological and Bibliographical Survey." *Symbolae Osloenses* 74:195–218.

Ehrman, B. D. 1993. *The Orthodox Corruption of Scripture: The Effect of Early Christological Controversies on the Text of the New Testament.* Oxford.

———. 1994. "Heracleon and the 'Western' Textual Tradition." *NTS* 40:161–179.

———. 1995. "The Text as Window: New Testament Manuscripts and the Social History of Early Christianity." *The Text of the New Testament in Contemporary Research: Essays on the Status Quaestionis* (ed. B. D. Ehrman and M. W. Holmes) 361–379. Grand Rapids, MI.

———. 1996. "The Text of the Gospels at the End of the Second Century." In Parker and Amphoux 1996:95–122.

Eisenstein, E. L. 1980. *The Printing Press as an Agent of Change: Communications and Cultural Transformations in Early-Modern Europe.* 2 vols. Cambridge.

Elliot, J. K. 1996. "Codex Bezae and the Earliest Greek Papyri." In Parker and Amphoux 1996:161–182.

———. 1999. *The Apocryphal New Testament: A Collection of Apocryphal Christian Literature in an English Translation Based on M. R. James.* Revised edition. Oxford.

Elsner, J. 1997. "The Origins of the Icon: Pilgrimage, Religion, and Visual

Culture in the Roman East as 'Resistance' to the Centre." *The Early Roman Empire in the East* (ed. S. E. Alcock) 178–199. Oxford.

———. 2000. "The *Itinerarium Burdigalense*: Politics and Salvation in the Geography of Constantine's Empire." *JRS* 90:181–195.

Emmett, L. A. H. 2001. "The Divine Rhetor: A Study of Clement of Alexandria." D.Phil. thesis, University of Oxford.

Epp, E. J. 1966. *The Theological Tendency of Codex Bezae Cantabrigiensis in Acts.* Cambridge.

Ettlinger, G. H., ed. 1975. *Theodoret of Cyrus, Eranistes: Critical Text and Prolegomena.* Oxford.

———. 2003. *Theodoret of Cyrus: Eranistes.* Fathers of the Church. Washington, DC.

Feldman, L. H. 1998a. *Josephus' Interpretation of the Bible.* Berkeley and Los Angeles.

———. 1998b. *Studies in Josephus' Rewritten Bible.* Supplements to the Journal for the Study of Judaism 58. Leiden.

Ferguson, J. 1991. *Clement of Alexandria: Stromateis, Books One to Three.* Fathers of the Church. Washington, DC.

Fernández Marcos, N., ed. 1975. *Los Thaumata de Sofronio: Contribución al estudio de la incubatio christiana.* Madrid.

Festugière, A. J. 1944–1954. *La révélation d'Hermès Trismégiste.* 4 vols. Paris.

———, ed. 1970. *Vie de Théodore de Sykéon.* 2 vols. Subsidia Hagiographica 48. Brussels.

———. 1971. *Collections grecques de Miracles: Sainte Thècle, Saints Côme et Damien, Saints Cyr et Jean (extraits), Saint Georges—traduits et annotés.* Paris.

Fischer, E., ed. 1974. *Die Ekloge des Phrynichus.* Sammlung griechischer und lateinischer Grammatiker 1. Berlin.

Flesher, P. V. M. 1995. "The Targumim." *Judaism in Late Antiquity: Part One, The Literary and Archaeological Sources* (ed. J. Neusner) 40–63. Leiden.

Flusin, B., ed. 1992. *Saint Anastase le Perse et l'histoire de la Palestine au début du VII<sup>e</sup> siècle.* 2 vols. Paris.

Foucault, M. 1983. *This is Not a Pipe.* Trans. J. Harkness. Berkeley and Los Angeles.

———. 1989 [1970]. *The Order of Things: An Archaeology of the Human Sciences.* London.

Frank, G. 2000. *The Memory of the Eyes: Pilgrims to Living Saints in Christian Late Antiquity*. Transformation of the Classical Heritage 30. Berkeley and Los Angeles.

Gabba, E. 1981. "True History and False History in Classical Antiquity." *JRS* 71:50–62.

——. 1983. "Literature." *Sources for Ancient History* (ed. M. Crawford) 1–79. Cambridge.

Gebhardt, O. von, ed. 1902. *Passio S. Theclae Virginis: Die lateinishecn Übersetzungen der Acta Pauli et Theklae nebst Fragmenten, Auszügen, und Beilagen*. TU 22.2. Leipzig.

Gelzer, H. 1880–1898. *Sextus Julius Africanus und die byzantinische Chronographie*. 3 vols. in 2 parts. Leipzig.

Gessler, J. 1946. "Notes sur l'incubation et ses suvivances." *Le Muséon* 59:661–670.

Giannini, A. 1963. "Studi sulla paradossografia greca, I; Da Omero a Callimaco: motivi e forme del meraviglioso." *RIL* 97:247–266.

——. 1964. "Studi sulla paradossografia greca, II; Da Callimaco all'età imperiale: la letturatura paradossographia." *Acme* 17:99–140.

——, ed. 1966. *Paradoxographorum Graecorum Reliquae*. Milan.

Gill, C. and Wiseman, T. P., eds. 1993. *Lies and Fiction in the Ancient World*. Exeter.

Girone, M., ed. 1998. Ἰάματα: *Guarigioni miracolose di Asclepio in testi epigrafici*. With a contribution by M. Totti-Gemünd. Bari.

Goldhill, S. 2001. *Being Greek Under Rome: Cultural Identity, the Second Sophistic, and the Development of Empire*. Cambridge.

——. 2002. *Who Needs Greek? Contests in the Cultural History of Hellenism*. Cambridge.

Golega, J. 1930. *Studien über die Evangeliendichtung des Nonnus von Panopolis*. Breslauer Studien zur historischen Theologie 15. Breslau.

——. 1960. *Die Homerische Psalter: Studien über die dem Apolinarios von Laodikeia zugeschriebene Psalmenparaphrase*. Studia Patristica et Byzantina 6. Ettal.

Gollancz, H., ed. 1912. *The Book of Protection: Being a Collection of Charms*. London.

Goody, J. 1977. *The Domestication of the Savage Mind*. Cambridge.

——. 1986. *The Logic of Writing and the Organization of Society*. Cambridge.

——. 1987. *The Interface between the Written and the Oral*. Cambridge.

———. 2000. *The Power of the Written Tradition*. Smithsonian Series in Ethnographic Inquiry. Washington, DC.

Grafton, A. and Williams, M. forthcoming. *Scholars, Books, and Readers in Late Antiquity: From Origen to Eusebius.*

Green, W. M. et al., eds. 1957–1972. *Augustine: The City of God Against the Pagans.* 7 vols. LCL. Cambridge, MA.

Gribomont, J. 1957. "Le monachisme au IV$^e$ s. en Asie Mineure: de Gangres au Messalianisme." *Studia Patristica II* (ed. K. Aland and F. Cross) TU 64:400–415.

———. 1980. "Saint Basil et le monachisme enthousiaste." *Irenikon* 53:123–144.

Grosdidier de Matons, J. 1977. *Romanos le Mélode et les origines de la poésie religieuse à Byzance.* Paris.

Gruen, E. S. 1998. *Heritage and Hellenism: The Reinvention of Jewish Tradition.* Hellenistic Culture and Society 30. Berkeley and Los Angeles.

———. 2002. *Diaspora: Jews amidst Greeks and Romans.* Cambridge, MA.

Guarducci, M. 1977. "La Statua di 'Sant' Ippolito'." In *Ricerche su Ippolito* 17–30. Rome.

Gulick, C. B., ed. 1927–1941. *Athenaeus, The Deipnosophists.* 7 vols. LCL. London and Cambridge, MA.

Haar Romeny, R. B. ter. 1997. *A Syrian in Greek Dress.* Louvain.

Hägg, T. 1983. *The Novel in Antiquity.* Berkeley and Los Angeles.

Hägg, T. and Rousseau, P., eds. 2000. *Greek Biography and Panegyric in Late Antiquity.* Transformation of the Classical Heritage 31. Berkeley and Los Angeles.

Haines-Eitzen, K. 2000. *Guardians of Letters: Literacy, Power, and the Transmitters of Early Christian Literature.* Oxford.

Haldon, J. 1992. "The Works of Anastasius of Sinai: A Key Source for the History of Seventh-Century East Mediterranean Society and Belief." *The Byzantine and Early Islamic Near East* (ed. Averil Cameron and L. I. Conrad) 107–147. Princeton.

Halleux, R. and Schamp, J., eds. 1985. *Les lapidaires grecs.* Paris.

Hamilton, M. 1906. *Incubation or The Cure of Disease in Pagan Temples and Christian Churches.* St Andrews.

Hansen, Dirk U., ed. 1998. *Das attizistische Lexicon des Moeris: Quellenkritische Untersuchung und Edition.* Sammlung griechischer und lateinischer Grammatiker 9. Berlin.

Hansen, Günther C., ed. 1995. *Sokrates Kirchengeschichte*. GCS 1. Berlin.

Hansen, William. 1996. *Phlegon of Tralles' Book of Marvels*. Exeter.

——, ed. 1998. *Anthology of Ancient Greek Popular Literature*. Bloomington, IN.

Harl, M. and de Lange, N., eds. 1983. *Origène, Philocalie 1-20: Sur les écritures; et La lettre à Africanus sur l'histoire de Suzanne*. SC 302. Paris.

Hays, G. 2002. "Tales Out of School: Grammatical Culture in Fulgentius the Mythographer." In Lanham 2002:22–47.

Heil, G., ed. 1990. "De vita Gregorii Thaumaturgi." *Gregorii Nysseni Sermones, Pars II* (ed. G. Heil, J. P. Cavarnos, and O. Lendle) 10.1:lxxxix–cxxxiii, 1–57. Leiden.

Helm, R. and Treu, U., eds. 1984. *Eusebius Werke: Die Chronik des Hieronymus (Hieronymi Chronicon)*. 3rd edition. GCS 17. Berlin.

Hennecke, E. and Schneemelcher, W., eds. 1992. *New Testament Apocrypha*. Trans. R. M. Wilson. 2 vols. Revised edition. Louisville, KY.

Hennig, J. 1964. "Quelques notes sur la mention de Sainte Thècle dans la *Commendatio animae*." *Nuovo Didaskaleion* 14:21–27.

Henry, R., ed. 1959–1977. *Photius: Bibliothèque*. 8 vols. Paris.

Hercher, R., ed. 1864. *Claudii Aeliani de natura animalium libri xvii, Varia historia, epistolae, fragmenta*. 2 vols. Leipzig.

Herzfeld, E. and Guyer, S. 1930. *Meriamlik und Korykos: Zwei christliche Ruinenstätten des rauhen Kilikiens*. Monumenta Asiae Minoris Antiqua 2. Manchester.

Herzog, R. 1931. *Die Wunderheilungen von Epidauros: Ein Beitrag zur Geschichte der Medizin und der Religion*. Philologus Supplementband 22.3. Leipzig.

Hild, F. et al. 1984. "Kommagene, Kilikien, Isaurien." *Realexikon zur byzantinishen Kunst* (ed. K. Wessel and M. Restle) 4:182–356. Stuttgart.

Hild, F. and Hellenkemper, H. 1990. *Kilikien und Isaurien*. 2 vols. Tabula Imperii Byzantini 5. Vienna.

Hill, S. 1996. *The Early Byzantine Churches of Cilicia and Isauria*. Birmingham Byzantine and Ottoman Monographs 1. Aldershot.

Hock, R. F., Chance, J. B., and Perkins, J., eds. 1998. *Ancient Fiction and Early Christian Narrative*. Society of Biblical Literature Symposium Series 6. Atlanta.

Høgel, C. 2002. *Symeon Metaphrastes: Rewriting and Canonization*. Copenhagen.

Holford-Strevens, L. 2003. *Aulus Gellius: An Antonine Scholar and his Achievement*. Revised edition. Oxford.

Holladay, C. R., ed. 1983–1996. *Fragments from Hellenistic Jewish Authors.* 4 vols. Atlanta.

Hollis, A. 1994. "Nonnus and Hellenistic Poetry." In Hopkinson 1994:43–62.

———. forthcoming. "The Hellenistic Epyllion and its Descendents." *Greek Literature in Late Antiquity* (ed. J. George and S. F. Johnson). Aldershot.

Honigmann, A. 1929. "Stephanos Byzantios." *RE* 2.3:2369–2399.

Hopkinson, N.. ed. 1994. *Studies in the Dionysiaca of Nonnus.* Cambridge Philological Society Supplementary Volumes 17. Cambridge.

Hornblower, S. 1987. *Thucydides.* London.

Inglebert, H. 2001a. "L'histoire des hérésies chez les hérésiologues." *L'historiographie de l'église des premiers siècles* (ed. B. Pouderon and Y.-M. Duval) 105–125. Paris.

———. 2001b. *Interpretatio Christiana: Les mutations des savoirs (cosmographie, géographie, ethnographie, histoire) dans l'Antiquité chrétienne.* Collection des Études Augustiniennes Série Antiquité 166. Paris.

Jacob, C. 1983. "De l'art de compiler à la fabrication du merveilleux: Sur la paradoxographie grecque." *Lalies* 2:121–140.

Jacob, C. and Polignac, F. de, eds. 2000. *Alexandria, Third Century BC: The Knowledge of the World in a Single City.* Trans. C. Clement. Alexandria, Egypt.

Janson, T. 1964. *Latin Prose Prefaces: Studies in Literary Conventions.* Stockholm.

Japhet, S. 1997. *The Ideology of the Book of Chronicles and its Place in the History of Biblical Thought.* 2nd revised edition. Beiträge zur Erforschung des alten Testaments und des antiken Judentums 9. Frankfurt-am-Main.

Jarick, J. 1990. *Gregory Thaumaturgos' Paraphrase of Ecclesiastes.* Septuagint and Cognate Studies 29. Atlanta.

Jeffreys, E. A. 1990. "Malalas' Sources." *Studies in John Malalas* (ed. E. A. Jeffreys) 167–216. Sydney.

Joannou, P.-P. 1962–1963. *Discipline Générale Antique.* 3 vols. "Fonti": Pontificia Commissione per la Redazione del Codice di Diritto Canonico Orientale 9. Rome.

Johns, A. 1998. *The Nature of the Book: Print and Knowledge in the Making.* Chicago.

Johnson, S. F. 2002a. "Cult and Competition: Textual Appropriation in the Fifth-Century *Life and Miracles of Thecla.*" Unpublished paper delivered at the Byzantine Studies Conference (Columbus, Ohio) October 2002.

———. 2002b. "The Sinful Woman: A *memra* by Jacob of Serugh." *Sobornost/ Eastern Churches Review* 24:58–90.

———. 2003. "Classical Sources for Early Christian Miracle Collections." Unpublished communication delivered at the Fourteenth International Conference on Patristic Studies (Oxford) August 2003.

———. 2004a. Review of Davis 2001. *Heythrop Journal* 45:80–82.

———. 2004b. Review of Hägg and Rousseau 2000. *JRS* 94:274–275.

———. 2005. Review of Agosti 2003. *CR* 55:474–476.

———. forthcoming. "Late Antique Narrative Fiction: Apocryphal Acta and the Greek Novel in the Fifth-Century *Life and Miracles of Thekla*." In *Greek Literature in Late Antiquity* (ed. S.F. Johnson) 189–207. Aldershot.

Jones, A. H. M. 1964. *The Later Roman Empire: A Social, Economic, and Administrative Survey*. 3 vols. Oxford.

Kaibel, G., ed. 1887–1890. *Athenaei Naucratitae Dipnosophistarum libri XV*. Leipzig.

Karst, J., ed. 1911. *Eusebius Werke: Die Chronik aus dem armenishen Übersetzt mit textkritischem Commentar*. GCS 20. Leipzig.

Kaster, R. A. 1988. *Guardians of Language: The Grammarian and Society in Late Antiquity*. Transformation of the Classical Heritage 11. Berkeley and Los Angeles.

———, ed. 1995. *C. Suetonius Tranquillus: De Grammaticis et Rhetoribus*. Oxford.

Kazhdan, A. 1999. *A History of Byzantine Literature (650–850)*. In collaboration with L. F. Sherry and C. Angelidi. Athens.

Keaney, J. J. 1973. "Alphabetization in Harpocration's Lexicon." *GRBS* 14:415–423.

Kee, H. C. 1980. *Miracle in the Early Christian World: A Study in Sociohistorical Method*. New Haven.

Keil, B., ed. 1898. *Aelii Aristidis Smyrnaei quae supersunt omnia*. 2 vols. Berlin.

Keydell, R. 1978. "Zu Stephanos von Byzanz." *Studi in onore di Anthos Ardizzoni* 1:477–81. Rome.

Klostermann, E., ed. 1902. *Eusebius Schrift: ΠΕΡΙ ΤΩΝ ΤΟΠΙΚΩΝ ΟΝΟΜΑΤΩΝ ΤΩΝ ΕΝ ΤΗ ΘΕΙΑ ΓΡΑΦΗ*. TU 23 N.F. 8.2b. Leipzig.

Krueger, D. 2004. *Writing and Holiness: The Practice of Authorship in the Early Christian East*. Divinations. Philadelphia.

Kugel, J. L. 1990. *In Potiphar's House: The Interpretive Life of Biblical Texts*. Cambridge, MA.

——. 1998. *Traditions of the Bible: A Guide to the Bible as it was at the Start of the Common Era.* Cambridge, MA.

——. 2001. "Ancient Biblical Interpretation and the Biblical Sage." *Studies in Ancient Midrash* (ed. J. L. Kugel) 1–26. Cambridge, MA.

Lanham, C. D., ed. 2002. *Latin Grammar and Rhetoric: From Classical Theory to Medieval Practice.* London.

Lateiner, D. 1989. *The Historical Method of Herodotus.* Toronto.

Legge, F., ed. 1921. *Philosophumena, or the Refutation of All Heresies, formerly Attributed to Origen, but now to Hippolytus, Bishop and Martyr, who Flourished about 220 AD.* 2 vols. London.

Lemerle, P. ed. 1979. *Les plus anciens recueils des Miracles de Saint Démétrius.* 2 vols. Paris.

——. 1986. *Byzantine Humanism, the First Phase: Notes and Remarks on Education and Culture in Byzantium from its Origins to the 10th Century.* Byzantina Australiensia 3. Canberra.

Lenski, N. 1999. "Assimilation and Revolt in the Territory of Isauria: From the 1st Century BC to the 6th Century AD." *JESHO* 42:413–465.

Lentz, A., ed. 1965 [1883–1901]. *Herodiani Technici reliquiae.* Grammatici Graeci 4. Hildesheim.

Leone, P. A. M., ed. 1968. *Ioannis Tzetzae Historiae.* Pubblicazioni dell'Instituto di Filologia Classica 1. Naples.

Lewy, H. 1978 [1960]. *Chaldean Oracles and Theurgy: Mysticism, Magic, and Platonism in the Later Roman Empire.* Edited by M. Tardieu. Paris.

LiDonnici, L. R., ed. 1995. *The Epidaurian Miracle Inscriptions: Text, Translation, and Commentary.* Texts and Translations 36. Atlanta.

Lightfoot, J. L., ed. 1999. *Parthenius of Nicea: The Poetical Fragments and the Ἐρωτικά παθήματα.* Oxford.

Lindars, B. 1992. "Introduction." In Brooke and Lindars 1992:1–7.

Lipsius, R. A. and Bonnet, M., eds. 1891 [1972]. *Acta Apostolorum Apocrypha.* 3 vols. Hildesheim.

Livrea, E., ed. 1989. *Nonno di Panopoli—Parafrasi del Vangelo di S. Giovanni, Canto XVIII: Introduzione, testo critico, traduzione, e commentario.* Naples.

——, ed. 2000. *Nonno di Panopoli: Parafrasi del Vangelo di San Giovanni, Canto B.* Biblioteca Patristica 36. Bologna.

Loi, V. 1977. "La problematica storico-letteraria su Ippolito di Roma." *Ricerche su Ippolito* 9–16. Rome.

Lord, A. B. 2000. *The Singer of Tales*. Edited by S. Mitchell and G. Nagy. 2nd edition. Harvard Studies in Comparative Literature 24. Cambridge, MA.

Lyman, J. R. 2000. "Ascetics and Bishops: Epiphanius on Orthodoxy." *Orthodoxie, Christianisme, Histoire* (ed. S. Elm, É. Rebillard, and A. Romano) 149–161. Rome.

Maas, M. 1990. *John Lydus and the Roman Past: Antiquarianism and Politics in the Age of Justinian*. London.

MacDonald, D. R. 1983. *The Legend and the Apostle: The Battle for Paul in Story and Canon*. Philadelphia.

——. 2000. *The Homeric Epics and the Gospel of Mark*. New Haven.

——, ed. 2001. *Mimesis and Intertextuality in Antiquity and Christianity*. Studies in Antiquity and Christianity. Harrisburg, PA.

MacDonald, D. R. and Scrimgeour, A. D. 1986. "Pseudo-Chrysostom's Panegyric to Thecla: The Heroine of the Acts of Paul in Homily and Art." *Semeia* 38:151–159.

MacKay, T. W. 1986. "Response to Stevan L. Davies." *Semeia* 38:145–149.

Maraval, P., ed. 1971. *Grégoire de Nysse: Vie de Sainte Macrine*. SC 178. Paris.

——. 1985. *Lieux saints et pèlerinages d'Orient: Histoire et géographie des origines á la conquête arabe*. Paris.

——, ed. 2002. *Journal de voyage, itinéraire: Egérie*. Revised edition. SC 296. Paris.

Marcovich, M., ed. 1986. *Hippolytus: Refutatio omnium haeresium*. Patristische Texte und Studien 25. Berlin.

Marincola, J. 1987. "Herodotean Narrative and the Narrator's Presence." *Arethusa* 20:121–137.

——. 1997. *Authority and Tradition in Ancient Historiography*. Cambridge.

Marshall, P. K., ed. 1990 [1968]. *A. Gellii Noctes Atticae*. Revised edition. 2 vols. OCT. Oxford.

McKenzie, D. F. 1999 [1986]. *Bibliography and the Sociology of Texts*. Panizzi Lectures 1985. Cambridge.

McLuhan, M. 1962. *The Gutenberg Galaxy: The Making of Typographic Man*. London.

Merkelbach, R. 1994. "Novel and Aretalogy." *The Search for the Ancient Novel* (ed. J. Tatum) 283–295. Baltimore.

Meineke, A., ed. 1849. *Stephani Byzantini ethnicorum quae supersunt.* Berlin.

Mimouni, S. C. 1995. *Dormition et assomption de Marie: histoire des traditions anciennes.* Paris.

Momigliano, A. 1975. *Alien Wisdom: The Limits of Hellenization.* Cambridge.

——. 1987. "Ancient Biography and the Study of Religion." *On Pagans, Jews, and Christians* 159–177. Middletown, CT.

——. 1993 [1971]. *The Development of Greek Biography.* Revised edition. Cambridge, MA.

Morgan, J. R. 1993. "Make-believe and Make Believe: The Fictionality of the Greek Novels." In Gill and Wiseman 1993:175–229.

Morgan, J. R. and Stoneman, R., eds. 1994. *Greek Fiction: The Greek Novel in Context.* London.

Morgan, T. 1998. *Literate Education in the Hellenistic and Roman Worlds.* Cambridge Classical Studies. Cambridge.

Mosshammer, A. A. 1979. *The Chronicle of Eusebius and the Greek Chronographic Tradition.* Cranbury, NJ.

——, ed. 1984. *Georgius Syncellus: Ecloga Chronographica.* Leipzig.

Murphy, T. 2004. *Pliny the Elder's Natural History: The Empire in the Encyclopedia.* Oxford.

Musso, O., ed. 1985. *[Antigonus Carystius] Rerum mirabilium collectio.* Hellenica et byzantina neapolitana 12. Naples.

Musurillo, H. 1958. *Saint Methodius: The Symposium, A Treatise on Chastity.* ACW 27. New York.

Myres, J. L. 1953. *Herodotus: Father of History.* Oxford.

Nagy, G. 1987. "Herodotus the *Logios*." *Arethusa* 20:175–184.

——. 1990. *Greek Mythology and Poetics.* Ithaca, NY.

——. 1996. *Poetry as Performance: Homer and Beyond.* New York.

Nauerth, C. and Warns, R. 1981. *Thekla: Ihre Bilder in der frühchristlichen Kunst.* Studien zur spätantiken und frühchristlichen Kunst 2.3. Wiesbaden.

Nautin, P. 1977. *Origène: Sa vie et son oeuvre.* Paris.

O'Donnell, J. J. 1998. *Avatars of the Word: From Papyrus to Cyberspace.* Cambridge, MA.

Olson, D. R. 1994. *The World on Paper: The Conceptual and Cognitive Implications of Writing and Reading.* Cambridge.

Ong, W. J. 2002 [1982]. *Orality and Literacy: The Technologizing of the Word*. London.

Pabel, H. M. and Vessey, M., eds. 2002. *Holy Scripture Speaks: The Production and Reception of Erasmus' Paraphrases on the New Testament*. Toronto.

Panella, R. J. 1990. *Greek Philosophers and Sophists in the Fourth Century AD*. Leeds.

Papadopoulos-Kerameus, A. I., ed. 1909. *Varia graeca sacra*. St. Petersburg.

Parker, D. C. 1992. *Codex Bezae: An Early Christian Manuscript and its Text*. Cambridge.

Parker, D. C. and Amphoux, C.-B., eds. 1996. *Codex Bezae: Studies from the Lunel Colloquium, June 1994*. Leiden.

Parsons, M. C. and Pervo, R. I., eds. 1993. *Rethinking the Unity of Luke-Acts*. Minneapolis.

Peltomaa, L. M. 2001. *The Image of the Virgin Mary in the Akathistos Hymn*. Medieval Mediterranean 35. Leiden.

Peppink, S. P., ed. 1936–1939. *Athenaei Deipnosophistae*. Leiden.

Pervo, R. I. 1987. *Profit with Delight: The Literary Genre of the Acts of the Apostles*. Philadelphia.

———. 1996. "The Ancient Novel Becomes Christian." In Schmeling 1996:685–711.

Petsalis-Diomidis, A. I. 2001. " 'Truly Beyond Miracles': The Body and Healing Pilgrimage in the Eastern Roman Empire in the Second Century AD." Ph.D. dissertation, The Courtauld Institute of Art.

Phillips, J. E. 2002. "*Sub evangelistae persona*: The Speaking Voice in Erasmus' Paraphrase on Luke." In Pabel and Vessey 2002:127–150.

Piédagnel, A., ed. 1982. *Jean Chrysostome: Panégyriques de S. Paul*. SC 300. Paris.

Price, R. M. 1985. *A History of the Monks of Syria by Theodoret of Cyrrhus*. Kalamazoo, MI.

Price, S. R. F. 1986. "The Future of Dreams: From Freud to Artemidorus." *Past and Present* 113:3–37.

Pucci, J. 1998. *The Full-Knowing Reader: Allusion and the Power of the Reader in the Western Literary Tradition*. New Haven.

Ralfs, A., ed. 1979 [1935]. *Septuaginta: Id est Vetus Testamentum graece iuxta lxx interpres*. Stuttgart.

Ramsay, W. M. 1890. *The Historical Geography of Asia Minor*. Royal Geographical Society's Supplementary Papers 4. London.

———. 1893. *The Church in the Roman Empire before AD 170*. London.

Rapp, C. 1995. "Byzantine Hagiographers as Antiquarians, Seventh to Tenth Centuries." *Byzantinische Forschungen* 31:31–44.

———. 1998a. "Comparison, Paradigm, and the Case of Moses in Panegyric and Hagiography." In Mary Whitby 1998b:277–298.

———. 1998b. "Storytelling as Spiritual Communication in Early Greek Hagiography: The Use of *Diegesis*." *JECS* 6:431–448.

Reardon, B. P. 1991. *The Form of Greek Romance*. Princeton.

Refoulé, R. P. and Drouzy, M., eds. 2002. *Tertullien: Traité du Baptême*. SC 35. Paris.

Reitzenstein, R. 1906. *Hellenistische Wundererzählungen*. Leipzig.

Rey, A.-L., ed. 1998. *Patricius, Eudocie, Optimus Côme de Jérusalem: Centons Homériques (Homerocentra)—introduction, texte critique, traduction, notes et index*. SC 437. Paris.

Richardson, E. C., ed. 1896. *Hieronymus, Liber de Viris Inlustribus; Gennadius, Liber de Viris Inlustribus*. TU 14.1. Leipzig.

Roberts, M. 1985. *Biblical Epic and Rhetorical Paraphrase in Late Antiquity*. Liverpool.

Rolfe, J. C., ed. 1946–1952. *The Attic Nights of Aulus Gellius*. Revised edition. 3 vols. LCL. London.

Rousseau, A. and Doutreleau, L., eds. 1965–1982. *Contre les hérésies: Irénée de Lyon*. 9 vols. SC 100, 152, 153, 210, 211, 263, 264, 293, 294. Paris.

Rousseau, P. 2002. *The Early Christian Centuries*. London.

Roussel, B. 2002. "Exegetical Fictions? Biblical Paraphrases of the Sixteenth and Seventeenth Centuries." In Pabel and Vessey 2002:59–83.

Rubenson, S. 1990. *The Letters of Saint Antony: Monasticism and the Making of a Saint*. Studies in Antiquity and Christianity. Minneapolis.

Rummel, E. 2002. "Why Noël Béda Did Not Like Erasmus' Paraphrases." In Pabel and Vessey 2002:265–278.

Rupprecht, E., ed. 1935. *Cosmae et Damiani sanctorum medicorum vita et miracula e codice londinensi*. Neue deutsche Forschungen, Abteilung klassische Philologie 1. Berlin.

Russell, D. A. and Winterbottom, M., eds. 1972. *Ancient Literary Criticism: The Principal Texts in New Translation*. Oxford.

Schama, S. 1995. *Landscape and Memory*. London.

Scheindler, A., ed. 1881. *Nonni Panopolitani Paraphrasis S. Evangelii Ioannei.* Leipzig.

Schembra, R. 1995. "Analisi Comparativa delle Redazioni Lunghe degli Homerocentones." *Sileno* 21:113–137.

Schepens, G. and Delcroix, K. 1996. "Ancient Paradoxography: Origin, Evolution, Production, and Reception." *La letturatura di consumo nel mondo greco-latino* (ed. O. Pecere and A. Stramaglia) 375–460. Cassino.

Schmeling, G., ed. 1996. *The Novel in the Ancient World.* Memnosyne 159. Leiden.

Schmidt, C., ed. 1936. *Acta Pauli nach dem papyrus der Hamburger staats- und universitäts-bibliothek unter mitarbeit von Wilhelm Schubart.* Glückstadt and Hamburg.

Schmidt, P. L. 1968. *Julius Obsequens und das Problem der Livius-Epitome: Ein Betrag zur Geschichte der lateinischen Prodigienliteratur.* Akademie der Wissenschaften und Literatur, Abhandlungen der geistes- und sozialwissenschaftlichen Klasse (Jahrgang 1968) 5. Wiesbaden.

———. 1991. "Suetons 'Pratum' seit Wessner (1917)." *ANRW* 2.33.5:3794–3825.

Scholfield, A., ed. 1958–1959. *Aelian: On the Characteristics of Animals.* 3 vols. LCL. Cambridge, MA.

Schulte, R. and Biguenet, J., eds. 1992. *Theories of Translation: An Anthology of Essays from Dryden to Derrida.* Chicago.

Ševčenko, I. and Ševčenko, N. P., eds. 1984. *The Life of Nicholas of Sion.* Brookline, MA.

Shaw, B. D. 1990. "Bandit Highlands and Lowland Peace: The Mountains of Isauria-Cilicia." *JESHO* 33:199–270.

Sherry, L. F. 1991. "The Hexameter Paraphrase of St. John Attributed to Nonnus of Panopolis: Prolegomenon and Translation." Ph.D. dissertation, Columbia University.

———. 1996. "The Paraphrase of St. John Attributed to Nonnus." *Byzantion* 66:409–430.

Shils, E. 1981. *Tradition.* London.

Shoemaker, S. 2002. *Ancient Traditions of the Virgin Mary's Dormition and Assumption.* Oxford.

Sigalas, A., ed. 1921. *Des Chrysippos von Jerusalem Enkomion auf den hl. Theodoros Teron.* Byzantinisches Archiv 7. Leipzig.

Sillet, H. 2000. "Orthodoxy and Heresy in Theodoret of Cyrus' *Compendium of*

*Heresies." Orthodoxie, Christianisme, Histoire* (ed. S. Elm, É. Rebillard, and A. Romano) 261–273. Rome.

Sivan, H. 1988a. "Holy Land Pilgrimage and Western Audiences: Some Reflections on Egeria and Her Circle." *CQ* N.S. 38:528–535.

——. 1988b. "Who was Egeria? Piety and Pilgrimage in the Age of Gratian." *HTR* 81:59–72.

Slater, C. 1986. *Trail of Miracles: Stories from a Pilgrimage in Northeast Brazil.* Berkeley and Los Angeles.

Smith, Jonathan Z. 1978. *Map is Not Territory: Studies in the History of Religions.* Leiden.

Smith, Morton. 1971. "Prolegomena to a Discussion of Aretalogies, Divine Men, the Gospels, and Jesus." *JBL* 90:174–199.

Smyth, H. W. 1956. *Greek Grammar.* Revised by G. Messing. Cambridge, MA.

Söder, R. 1932. *Die apokryphen Apostelgeschichten und die romanhafte Literatur der Antike.* Würzburger Studien zur Altertumswissenschaft 3. Stuttgart.

Spiegel, G. M. 1997. *The Past as Text: The Theory and Practice of Medieval Historiography.* Baltimore.

Speyer, W. 1971. *Die literarische Fälschung im heidnishen und christlichen Altertum.* Munich.

Stein, P. 1909. "ΤΕΡΑΣ." Ph.D. dissertation, University of Marburg.

Stock, B. 1990. *Listening for the Text: On the Uses of the Past.* Philadelphia.

Stoneman, R. 1991. *The Greek Alexander Romance.* Harmondsworth.

——. 1994. "The Alexander Romance: From History to Fiction." In Morgan and Stoneman 1994:117–129.

Strycker, E. de, ed. 1961. *La forme la plus ancienne du Protoévangile de Jacques: Recherches sur le Papyrus Bodmer 5 avec une édition critique du texte et une traduction annotée.* Subsidia Hagiographica 33. Brussels.

Swete, H. B. 1900. *An Introduction to the Old Testament in Greek.* Cambridge.

Talbert, C. H. 1978. "Biographies of Philosophers and Rulers as Instruments of Religious Propaganda in Mediterranean Antiquity." *ANRW—Principat* 16.2:1619–1651.

Talbot, A.-M. 1991. "Old Wine in New Bottles: The Rewriting of Saints' Lives in the Palaeologan Period." *Twilight of Byzantium: Aspects of Cultural and Religious History in the Late Byzantine Empire* (ed. S. Ćurčić and D. Mouriki) 15–26. Princeton.

———. 2002a. "Female Pilgrimage in Late Antiquity and the Byzantine Era." *ABzF* N.S. 1:73–88.

———. 2002b. "Pilgrimage to Healing Shrines: The Evidence of Miracle Accounts." *DOP* 56:153–173.

Telfer, H. 1936. "The Cultus of St. Gregory Thaumaturgus." *HTR* 29:225–344.

Thee, F. C. R. 1984. *Julius Africanus and the Christian View of Magic.* Tübingen.

Thomas, Christine M. 2003. *The Acts of Peter, Gospel Literature, and the Ancient Novel: Rewriting the Past.* Oxford.

Thomas, Rosalind. 2000. *Herodotus in Context: Ethnography, Science, and the Art of Persuasion.* Cambridge.

Thurn, J., ed. 2000. *Ioannis Malalae Chronographia.* CFHB 35. Berlin.

Tolbert, M. A. 1989. *Sowing the Gospel: Mark's World in Literary Historical Perspective.* Minneapolis.

Tov, E. 1992. "The Contribution of the Qumran Scrolls to the Understanding of the LXX." In Brooke and Lindars 1992:11–47.

Trombley, F. R. 1993–1994. *Hellenic Religion and Christianization, c. 370–529.* 2 vols. Leiden.

Ulrich, E. C. 1978. *The Qumran Text of Samuel and Josephus.* Harvard Semitic Monographs 19. Missoula, MT.

Urbainczyk, T. 1997. *Socrates of Constantinople: Historian of Church and State.* Ann Arbor.

Usher, M. D. 1997. "Prolegomenon to the Homeric Centos." *AJP* 118:305–321.

———. 1998. *Homeric Stitchings: The Homeric Centos of the Empress Eudocia.* Lanham, MD.

———, ed. 1999. *Homerocentones Eudociae Augustae.* Stuttgart and Leipzig.

Van Dam, R. 1982. "Hagiography and History: The Life of Gregory Thaumaturgus." *Classical Antiquity* 1:272–308.

Vassilaki, M. 2000. *Mother of God: Representations of the Virgin in Byzantine Art.* Athens and Milan.

———, ed. 2004. *Images of the Mother of God: Perceptions of the Theotokos in Byzantium.* Aldershot.

Ven, P. van den, ed. 1962–1970. *La Vie ancienne de S. Syméon Stylite le Jeune (521–92).* Subsidia Hagiographica 32. 2 vols. Brussels.

Vermes, G. 1975. *Post-Biblical Jewish Studies*. Studies in Judaism in Late Antiquity 8. Leiden.

———, ed. 1998. *The Complete Dead Sea Scrolls in English*. Harmondsworth.

Vessey, M. 2002a. "Introduction." In Pabel and Vessey 2002:3–25.

———. 2002b. "The Tongue and the Book: Erasmus' Paraphrases on the New Testament and the Arts of Scripture." In Pabel and Vessey 2002:29–58.

Veyne, P. 1988. *Did the Greeks Believe in their Myths?* Trans. P. Wissing. Chicago.

Vieillefond, J.-R., ed. 1970. *Les "Cestes" de Julius Africanus: Étude sur l'ensemble des fragments avec édition, traduction, et commentaires*. Paris.

Vinel, F. 1987. "La Metaphrasis in Ecclesiasten de Grégoire le Thaumaturge: entre traduction et interprétation, une explication de texte. *Cahiers de Biblia Patristica* 1:191–216.

Wachsmuth, C., ed. 1897. *Ioannis Laurentii Lydi Liber de Ostentis et Calendaria Graeca Omnia*. Leipzig.

Wachsmuth, C. and Hense, O., eds. 1884–1912. *Ioannis Stobaei Anthologii*. 5 vols. Berlin.

Wallace-Hadrill, A. 1995. *Suetonius*. 2nd edition. London.

Walsh, P. G. 1975. *The Poems of Saint Paulinus of Nola*. ACW 40. New York.

Weinreich, O. 1909. *Antike Heilungswunder: Untersuchungen zum Wunderglauben der Griechen und Römer*. Giessen.

Weiss, C. G. 1998. "Literary Turns: The Representation of Conversion in Aelius Aristides' *Hieroi Logoi* and Apuleius' *Metamorphoses*." Ph.D. dissertation, Yale University.

Wellesz, E. 1961. *A History of Byzantine Music and Hymnography*. 2nd edition. Oxford.

Wendland, P., ed. 1916. *Hippolytus Werke: Refutatio Omnium Haeresium*. GCS 26. Leipzig.

Whitby, Mary. 1998a. "Defender of the Cross: George of Pisidia on the Emperor Heraclius and his Deputies." In Mary Whitby 1998b:247–273.

———. 1998b. *The Propoganda of Power: The Role of Panegyric in Late Antiquity*. Memnosyne 183. Leiden.

———. 1998c. Review of Accorinti 1996. *CR* N.S. 48:17–18.

———. 2000. Review of Usher 1998. *CR* N.S. 50:275–276.

——. 2001b. Review of Usher 1999. *CR* N.S. 51:385–386.

——. 2004. Review of De Stefani 2002. *CR* N.S. 54:358–360.

——. forthcoming. "The Bible Hellenized." *Texts and Culture in Late Antiquity: Inheritance, Authority, and Change* (ed. D. Scourfield). Classical Press of Wales.

Whitby, Michael. 2000. *The Ecclesiastical History of Evagrius Scholasticus.* Translated Texts for Historians. Liverpool.

Whitehead, D. 1994. "Site-Classification and Reliability in Stephanus of Byzantium." *Historia Einzelschriften* 87:99–124.

Wilkinson, J. 1999. *Egeria's Travels.* 3rd edition. Warminster.

Willamovitz-Moellendorff, U. von. 1881. *Antigonos von Karystos.* Philologische Untersuchungen 5. Berlin.

Williamson, G. A. 1989 [1965]. *Eusebius: The History of the Church from Christ to Constantine.* Edited by A. Louth. Harmondsworth.

Wills, L. M. 1995. *The Jewish Novel in the Ancient World.* Ithaca, NY.

——. 1997. *The Quest of the Historical Gospel: Mark, John, and the Origins of the Gospel Genre.* London.

——, ed. 2002. *Ancient Jewish Novels: An Anthology.* Oxford.

Wilson, N. G., ed. 1997. *Aelian: Historical Miscellany.* LCL. Cambridge, MA.

Winkler, J. J. 1985. *Auctor and Actor: A Narratological Reading of Apuleius' Golden Ass.* Berkeley and Los Angeles.

Witherington, B. 1984. "The Anti-Feminist Tendencies of the 'Western' Text in Acts." *JBL* 103:82–84.

Woodman, A. J. 1988. *Rhetoric in Classical Historiography: Four Studies.* London.

Wright, W. 1870–1872. *Catalogue of Syriac Manuscripts in the British Museum Acquired Since the Year 1838.* 3 vols. London.

——, ed. 1990 [1871]. *Apocryphal Acts of the Apostles* [in Syriac]. 2 vols. Hildesheim.

Wünsch, R., ed. 1898. *Ioannis Laurentii Lydi Liber de mensibus.* Leipzig.

Yates, F. A. 1966. *The Art of Memory.* London.

Zahn, T., ed. 1975 [1880]. *Acta Joannis.* Hildesheim.

Zeitlin, F. I. 2001. "Visions and Revisions of Homer." In Goldhill 2001:195–266.

Ziegler, K. 1949. "Paradoxographoi." *RE* 18:1138–1166.

# Index of Greek Words

σταυρόω, 41
στήλη/στήλαι, 199
στίγμα, 55
Στρωματεῖς, 180, 183–184, 188
συγγενής, 48, 117
συγκαθεύδω, 145
σύγκοιτος, 145
συκοφαντία, 137
συλλέγω, 119
συλλογή, xvii, 13, 118–119, 171
σύμβολον, 163, 167
συμπάθεια, 53
συναγωγή, 176, 179
συναξάρια, 108
συνθήκη, 19, 47
σύνταγμα, 20, 126, 192
σφραγίς, 22, 43–44
σωτήρ, 43
σωτηρία, 148
σωφροσύνη, 50, 53

τάξις, 19, 34, 46, 133
ταρχύω, 124
τάσσω, 129
τάχος, 154
τελείωσις, 229
τέρας/τέρατα, 196–200, 203
τερατολογέω/τερατολογία/τερατα-
    λόγος, 197–198
τεκμήριον, 33
τέτρας, 13, 119, 168

τεχνή, 161, 186–187
τόλμη, 30, 134
τράπεζα, 7, 65
Τριάς, 33–34, 43, 62
τρόφιμος, 135
τρυφή, 51, 53
τύπος, 41, 101
τύραννος, 31, 128, 133

ὕπαρ, 158
ὑποδραμέω, 145
ὑπομνήματα, 182–183, 190–191
ὑπόταξις, 115

φάρμακον/φαρμακεία, 35, 148,
    161–162
φιλοτιμία, 203
φύσις, 33, 41, 179
φώριον, 122

χασμάομαι, 119
χοιράδες, 149
χοροστασία, 166
χρησμολογέω, 203
χρησμός, 203
χριστιανός, 160
χρίω, 147
χῶρος, 147

ψυχαγωγία, 57
ψυχή, 53, 94, 179, 197
ψυχόω, 59–60

# Index

This book was designed and composed by Ivy Livingston
and manufactured by Victor Graphics, Baltimore, MD

The typeface is Gentium, designed by Victor Gaultney
and distributed by SIL International

---

THE CENTER FOR HELLENIC STUDIES
3100 Whitehaven Street, N.W., Washington, D.C. 20008
chs.harvard.edu

CPSIA information can be obtained at www.ICGtesting.com
Printed in the USA
BVOW021929230512

290590BV00006B/3/P